Debt, Financial Fragility, and Systemic Risk

Debt, Financial Fragility, and Systemic Risk

E. P. DAVIS

CLARENDON PRESS · OXFORD
1992

Oxford University Press, Walton Street, Oxford OX2 6DP
Oxford New York Toronto
Delhi Bombay Calcutta Madras Karachi
Petaling Jaya Singapore Hong Kong Tokyo
Nairobi Dar es Salaam Cape Town
Melbourne Auckland
and associated companies in
Berlin Ibadan

Oxford is a trade mark of Oxford University Press

Published in the United States
by Oxford University Press, New York

British Library Cataloguing in Publication Data
Data available

Library of Congress Cataloging in Publication Data
Davis, E. P.
Debt, financial fragility, and systemic risk / E. P. Davis.
p. cm.
Includes bibliographical references and index.
1. Corporate debt—Great Britain. 2. Finance—Great Britain.
3. Finance—European Economic Community countries. 4. Finance—United States. I. Title.
HG4028.D3D39 1992 332'.094—dc20 92—24780
ISBN 0–19–828752–6

Typeset by Pentacor PLC, High Wycombe, Bucks.
Printed and bound in
Great Britain by Biddles Ltd.,
Guildford and King's Lynn

Contents

Acknowledgements

The book was prepared during the author's own time, but while he was employed by the Bank of England. He is grateful to senior management in the Economics Division for granting permission to proceed with the project. While the content was naturally influenced by the author's background as a Central Banker as well as an economist, the views expressed are very much his own, and none should in any way be attributed to a Bank view, if indeed such a stable entity could be held to exist.

The author is also grateful to colleagues in the Bank of England, the Bank for International Settlements, and the economics profession for helpful advice and suggestions during the preparation of the material for the book, notably P. Andersen, P. Artus, T. R. G. Bingham, J. Bisignano, F. Breedon, C. B. Briault, A. S. Courakis, N. Dimsdale, P. Doyle, J. J. M. Exeter, J. S. Flemming, E. Hansen, S. G. B. Henry, J. G. S. Jeanneau, T. Johnsen, M. A. King, A. R. Latter, Miss F. C. Mann, J. Marquardt, C. P. Mayer, J. Metais, D. K. Miles, L. D. D. Price, I. D. Saville, B. Scott-Quinn, A. Smith, C. T. Taylor, and Miss S. A. Wilson; also participants in seminars at the Bank of England, Brasenose College, Oxford, the Industrial Economics Study Group (meeting in Cambridge), LSE, University of Paris-Dauphine, University of Bergen, Caisse des Depots et Consignations, and Southampton University; C. Giraldi (Italy), C. Bismut (France), C. Luckett and R. Rosenblatt (US), K. Clinton and E. Sussman (Canada) and J. Veale (Australia), for assistance with data; S. Friend and M. Scudder for typing; and R. Pryor, C. Smith, A. Whiteside, and K. Woodfine for research assistance.

E. P. D.

List of Charts and Figures

Charts

Figures

List of Tables

Introduction

For an observer of the behaviour of financial markets, a remarkable feature of the period since 1970 has been the patterns of rapid and turbulent change in financing behaviour and financial structure in many advanced countries. These patterns have in turn often been marked by rising indebtedness, volatile asset prices, and periods of financial stress, whether in the non-financial sector, the financial sector, or both. At the same time, the economics profession has seen a notable advance in the scope and depth of the theory of finance, particularly as it relates to the nature and behaviour of financial institutions and markets. This book seeks to confront these developments.

More precisely, the objective of the book is to explore, in both theoretical and empirical terms, the nature of the relationships in advanced industrial economies between levels and changes in borrowing (debt), vulnerability to default in the non-financial sector (financial fragility), and widespread instability in the financial sector (systemic risk). Can theory help us to understand these developments? Have such linkages become more common in recent years? If so, can underlying factors be discerned? Are there differences between the various national and international markets? And what should be the policy response?

The work seeks to provide a survey and critical assessment of current economic theory relating to debt and financial instability, to offer empirical evidence casting light on the validity of the theories, and it suggests a number of policy implications and lines of further research. Unlike most extant texts on these matters, which generally relate to one country's experience (usually the USA), the book focuses on the way similar patterns are observable in several countries—but not in others—as well as in the international capital markets themselves. In addition, it seeks to provide a balanced approach to the various theoretical analyses of these issues, rather than narrowly focusing on a single preferred line. Third, unlike much recent work, theory is confronted with evidence and judgements drawn from the results. Finally, particular attention is paid to the importance of the nature and evolution of financial structure to the genesis of instability. Whereas a structural approach is common in analysis of comparative behaviour of financial systems—notably in corporate finance—its application to instability is relatively rare.

The book comprises eight chapters, each of which includes a summary or interim conclusions and assessment of implications. The first chapter provides essential background by outlining the economics of the debt contract and features of credit supply—in particular the nature of credit rationing, factors that lead to intermediated as opposed to market supply of debt, and 'stylized facts' regarding different national and international markets. The information in this chapter is taken as read in the rest of the book.

The second chapter offers an analysis of financial fragility in the corporate sector, where 'fragility' is defined as a state of balance sheets offering heightened vulnerability to default in a wide variety of circumstances. Factors underlying levels and changes in indebtedness, and their relationship to default, are probed both in theory and using evidence from six major OECD countries (the USA, UK, Germany, Japan, Canada and France). In particular, an attempt is made to assess reasons for the parallel growth of debt and default in recent years that has been a feature of a number of these countries. The third chapter provides a similar analysis of the household sector.

However, implications of financial fragility are not limited to highly geared companies and households. Ch. 4 draws out the broader economic implications of fragility, and suggests it may have a marked impact on overall economic performance. A brief case study is made of experience in the UK over 1990–1 to illustrate the mechanisms identified.

The fifth, sixth, seventh, and eighth chapters address the problem of 'systemic risk', defined as the danger that disturbances in financial markets will generalize across the financial system so as to disrupt the provision of payments services and the allocation of capital. Why are financial institutions and markets sometimes subject to illiquidity or insolvency, which may threaten to spread across the entire financial sector? How do such problems link to financial fragility in the non-financial sectors?

The fifth chapter offers a survey of the theoretical literature, including an assessment of the rationale for financial regulation in the light of systemic risk, while the sixth offers empirical evidence based on an examination of six recent periods of financial instability in the light of these extant theories of financial crisis. It is concluded, first, that no individual theory is sufficient in itself to explain all the features of instability, instead a synthesis is required. Second, the distinction between risk and uncertainty is a crucial one. Third, it is suggested that extant approaches, while extremely fruitful, still omit some of the crucial common features of systemic risk. This lacuna is addressed in the seventh chapter, which seeks to offer a distinctive view of the development of financial fragility and systemic risk based on an industrial-organization approach to financial market structure and dynamics, which complements the existing approaches. The eighth chapter outlines ten further financial crises to clarify the generality of these various mechanisms for a wide variety of countries, and to provide further insight into the various types of instability to which financial markets are subject.

In the conclusion a number of general themes relating to the theory of finance, financial structure and regulation are addressed, in particular the role of financial liberalization, innovation and competition in the genesis of financial instability. A summary of policy issues, suggestions for further research, and an assessment of prospects are also provided.

1

Debt

This section offers essential background for the analysis of the rest of the book. It outlines the nature of the debt contract; aspects of the economics of debt; theories of credit rationing and intermediation; key differences between financial systems interpreted in the light of these concepts; and (in an appendix) stylised facts of the overall development of finance. To motivate this chapter, it suffices to note that the book suggests that the influence of credit rationing, the nature and locus of intermediation, and the type of financial system, all have a key influence on the genesis of financial fragility and systemic risk; and that these features in turn relate directly to the underlying nature of the debt contract itself. Note that there are three main types of debt: that owed by end-users to investors (direct finance), by end-users to intermediaries (generally loans), and by intermediaries to investors (generally deposits). Focus is mainly on the first two here and in Chs. 2–4; the third comes to the fore in the second part of the book, relating to financial instability.

(1) The Nature of the Debt Contract

Popular misconceptions regarding debt and credit often stem from the assumption that debt is a commodity and borrowing is like purchase of any other good or service, where prices alone equilibrate supply and demand. In fact, unlike most market transactions, which can largely be summarized in terms of prices and quantities, debt is a highly complex contract. This is because debt entails a *promise* to repay principal and interest on a loan or advance—a promise whose fulfilment is by its nature uncertain and will differ among borrowers. Key features of such a promise include the following:

- quantity advanced;
- specification of interest, whether fixed or variable in relation to a benchmark rate;[1]
- specification of maturity, i.e. when the loan must be repaid;

[1] Generally, to enable debt to qualify for tax deductability, payment must be 'sum certain', i.e. a specified payment except in case of distress. In other words, obligations cannot be state contingent (e.g. falling in a recession) in the way dividends are (Gertler and Hubbard 1991). As discussed below, such flexibility is the main advantage of equity as an alternative to debt. But equity also suffers a number of adverse incentive problems.

- collateral that the borrower must provide as security for the lender, if any;
- specification of the circumstances in which the loan is in default, thus giving the lender the right to seize the borrower's assets. In the simplest case this will be failure to pay interest or principal; in other cases it will entail breach of any covenants (indentures) that the lender may specify in order to control the borrower's behaviour;
- specification of the law under which default is to be adjudicated;
- specification of the seniority of the claim, i.e. where the lender stands in relation to other creditors in the case of default;
- pledges in relation to further borrowing, for example the lender can insist no further debt be incurred, or no further debt senior to it;
- any further commitments by the lender, e.g. to renew the loan when its term is complete;
- provisions for transferability. Can the debt be freely passed on to other holders, or must it remain with the initial lender?;
- whether or not the contract is standardized in terms of provisions or denomination (to facilitate securitization);
- any tax exemption features;
- call provisions (whether debt can be repaid early).

(2) Aspects of the Economics of Debt

Many of the additional features indicated above can be understood as means of overcoming uncertainty, transaction costs, and incomplete contracts.[2] Recent developments in the theory of finance, outlined in this and the following two sections, advance considerably our understanding of the nature and role of debt. Although most of the theory is set out in terms of corporate finance, it is also directly applicable to financial institutions and households.

The key difficulty is raised by the uncertain possibility that the borrower will default, given costs of bankruptcy, asymmetric information, and incomplete contracts. If there were no costs of bankruptcy, default risk would be of no concern to the lender; assets to pay off the loan would pass smoothly to him in the case of default. In practice, resolution of default takes time and effort, the lender may find that assets seized from the borrower have depreciated in value, and/or he may find that second-hand markets for such assets are weak or non-existent. But even given costs of bankruptcy, if there were no asymmetries of information or if the lender were able to specify and verify the borrower's behaviour in every eventuality, then issue of debt would be a relatively straightforward

[2] Complete contracts would specify the behaviour of the borrower under every possible contingency.

transaction (as well as being 'irrelevant' to real activity), because probability of default could be known or controlled precisely, and charged or collateralized accordingly.

Since in practice neither of these conditions hold, the lender faces a problem of *screening* potential borrowers before making an advance, and *monitoring* the behaviour of the borrower after the loan is made, both of which impose costs on the lender. We outline the issues relating to screening and monitoring in turn.

First, the lender needs to choose borrowers of high credit quality *before* the loan is granted, to minimize his losses due to default, when due to asymmetric information it may be impossible to distinguish good and bad risks. This is the problem of *adverse selection*. The classic example of adverse selection is the 'lemons problem' which Akerlof (1970) applied to the used-car market.[3] As applied to debt, the problem arises because, with asymmetric information, the lender does not know whether the borrower is a good risk (a good investment project at low risk) or a bad risk (high-risk, low-quality investment project). If the lender cannot distinguish the latter (the lemons), he will charge an interest rate reflecting the average quality of good and bad borrowers. Hence high-quality borrowers pay more than they should, and low rather less. Some high-quality borrowers will drop out of the market, thus worsening the mix. Higher interest rates will only make the problem worse; the mix worsens further as only low-quality borrowers with a low probability of repayment are willing to pay such rates. Suitable collateral[4] may be one way to protect the lender from adverse selection, as it provides compensation even if the borrower turns out to be low-quality, and defaults.

Second, the lender must monitor the borrower *after* the loan is granted, to ensure that the borrower is not acting contrary to his interests during the period that the loan is outstanding. For example, the borrower might use the funds to engage in high-risk activities that entail only a low probability that the loan will be repaid; the problem of *moral hazard*. Moral hazard (and expenditures incurred to overcome it) are a form of agency cost—i.e. costs arising from separation of principal (lender) and agent (borrower). It arises generally from the inconsistent incentives arising in a contract specifying a fixed value payment between debtor and creditor, particularly given limited liability.[5] (It also arises in the case of mispriced deposit insurance, as discussed in Ch. 5.) The debtor prefers the course of action which maximizes his wealth, the creditor prefers

[3] The basic point is that, given uncertainty as to whether a second-hand car is a 'lemon', buyers assume all cars are lemons, prices fall, and the assumption is self-fulfilling, because only owners of lemons seek to sell at low prices. Ultimately no trade may take place.

[4] Subject to the difficulties of resale and recovery outlined above.

[5] The importance of limited liability in this context is that the shareholder in the borrowing company benefits from the returns from a successful outcome, but cannot be forced to share in the losses—the value of equity cannot go below zero.

actions which maximize the expected value of his obligation from the debtor. Given the importance of this concept and generality of its application (for example, bank-borrower, bond holder-issuer, depositor-bank and deposit insurer-bank), we offer a numerical example, drawn from Fama and Miller (1972).

A firm has two alternative production plans, which require investment in period 1 for payoff in period 2. The firm has \$5 of debt in its capital structure as well as equity. There are two possible states of the world in period 2. The price of a claim in period 1 to a dollar in period 2 for either

Production plan	Pay off in period 2		Market values in period 1		
	State 1	State 2	Total	Debt	Equity
a	7	7	7	5	2
b	1	10	5.5	3	2.5

state is \$0.5. If the firm chooses plan a, the period 1 market value of debt is $D(1) = 5(0.5) + 5(0.5) = 5$, and the value of equity is $E(1) = 2(0.5) + 2(0.5) = 2$. But if the firm chooses plan b it cannot deliver on its debt if state 1 occurs; the period 1 market value of debt, $D(1) = 1(0.5) + 5(0.5) = 3$, and the value of shares is $E(1) = 0(0.5) + 5(0.5) = 2.5$. The value of debt is higher with plan a, the value of shares with the riskier plan b, and there is a *conflict of interest* between debtor and creditor.[6] The likelihood of such a conflict is greater, the larger the proportion of debt in the balance sheet. Moreover, the stimulus to seek risk is greater, the higher the interest rate charged, as borrowers seek projects with higher expected returns and higher risk to compensate.

Four main ways have been outlined in the literature to reduce these problems—although the need for screening and monitoring are never wholly absent. They are: reputation, net worth (net assets), control, and commitment. For those borrowers with a *reputation* for repaying debt, it stands as a capital asset (as it facilitates borrowing at low cost), which would depreciate in the case of non-repayment. This offers some protection to the lender against moral hazard, as well as reducing the need for screening. Meanwhile, a low *net worth* (capital, equity) means that, given limited liability, the borrower has little to lose by engaging in moral hazard, and has no collateral to pledge, either to reduce difficulties of screening, or to offset the risks in the transaction.

Control theories highlight the key feature of debt contracts which help reduce moral hazard, namely that the borrower controls the assets except in the case of default, when such control passes to the lender. In effect, the lender takes over from the owner or shareholders as the claimant on residual income of the firm. Debt implicitly changes to equity. Such

[6] Note that moral hazard can also arise from embezzlement, slacking etc.; the value of the example is to show that it arises from straightforward wealth maximization.

control prevents the borrower, for example, from threatening to repudiate the debt in order to reduce the interest rate—although the costs to the lender mean the sanction is retained as a last resort. Such control may be extended to the borrower's behaviour in non-default circumstances by aspects of the debt contract, such as covenants, collateral, and short maturity. The need for such further control instruments, which themselves impose costs on the borrower, will vary with the risk that is presented by the transaction; it is partly related to the reputation or net worth of the borrower.

Commitment is seen as an alternative means to minimise the risks in the debt contract, which can be developed when lenders and borrowers share information not available to other lenders. The lender undertakes to provide finance to the borrower even during times of financial difficulty, in return for the borrower remaining with the lender (and paying a premium) during normal times. In general, such relationships cannot be specified contractually, and tend to be informal customary features of certain financial systems and not of others (see Sect. 5). They are vulnerable both to willingness of lenders to exploit their monopoly power (given superior information) and to tendencies for borrowers to shift to cheaper sources of finance once a 'rescue' is complete.

The market failures outlined above do not arise only for debt. Information asymmetries (given limited liability) may cause even greater difficulties for *equity markets*, despite the superiority of equity over debt as a means of risk-sharing[7] (Myers and Majluf 1984; Greenwald and Stiglitz 1991). For example, insiders (owner-managers) know more about the firm than outsiders (providers of equity finance) and may therefore seek to sell shares in the firm when the market overvalues them. This leads the market to see issuance as an adverse signal about quality, which in turn deters the firm from issuance.[8] Second, the equity contract leaves it at managers' discretion to pay dividends, allowing scope for diversion of funds to the preferred uses of controlling shareholders, and to managers. The latter may include expenditures that seek to entrench managers in their current positions. This is a second form of agency cost—in this case arising from separation of ownership (shareholders) from control (managers).[9] Third, as managers only obtain a fraction of returns to their

[7] This is because, unlike debt, returns to suppliers of equity finance can vary with economic conditions for the firm. Note that there is also a social benefit, as firms are less obliged to cut investment in a recession.

[8] This effect may cause the firm to cancel investment projects that have a positive net present value, in which case it entails a social cost.

[9] As noted by Smith (1776), 'The directors of such (joint-stock) companies, however, being the managers of other peoples' money rather than of their own, it cannot well be expected that they should watch over it with the same anxious vigilance with which the partners in a private copartnery frequently watch over their own. Like the stewards of a rich man, they are apt to consider attention to small matters as not for their master's honour, and very easily give themselves a dispensation from having it. Negligence and profusion, therefore, must always prevail, more or less, in the management of such a company.'

managerial efforts, or even a purely fixed salary, incentives are attenuated. Fourth, with widely held shares (and bonds), any effort by an individual shareholder to improve the quality of management benefits all shareholders, thus reducing the incentive to make such efforts.

Meanwhile, reputation may be a weaker discipline on insiders than for debt; original owners may not wish the firm to reaccess the market, for fear of dilution of equity claims, as well as it being an adverse signal. Takeovers, which usually entail replacement of existing management, are effectively the substitute for 'control' in the case of equity. But they are not always effective in disciplining managers, especially since takeover waves are sporadic and targets often only particularly bad performers (Corbett and Mayer 1991). Greenwald and Stiglitz (1991) suggest that equity markets would not exist at all without the legal features of limited liability and prosecution of fraud, as well as technical and economic advances, e.g. in accountancy and auditing (which minimize falsification of information), and the development of secondary trading. And experience shows that, probably owing to the difficulties outlined above, they are highly unreliable as a source of funds, being subject to cyclical 'feasts and famines'.

An important point which underlies the problems with equity, even more than for debt, is that it may be more difficult to maintain appropriate incentives in the equity contract without continuous and costly monitoring of performance. Debt entails a superior form of 'incentive compatibility', enabling lenders to reduce monitoring costs (Gale and Hellwig 1985). This is due to the form of the contract, allowing the debtor to retain all the residual income from the project, while imposing penalties in the case of default, which ensures incentives for the borrower both to make the project succeed and to repay the debt.

From these basic considerations we now go on to derive theories of credit rationing and of intermediation, and also adduce various features of financial systems, all of which are relevant to study of financial instability.

(3) Theories of Credit Rationing

Availability of credit to an individual borrower is not unlimited, and the way in which its availability is rationed reflects aspects of the debt contract, as well as the nature of the borrower. Changes in the stringency and nature of such rationing are a key element in the thesis of the book regarding the genesis of financial fragility and systemic risk, as outlined in Chs. 2–8. Hence the theory in this section is crucial background.[10]

Financial institutions or direct lenders may respond to credit demand in various ways. This section outlines three paradigms of credit rationing:

[10] For recent empirical evidence on credit rationing see Berger and Udell 1990*a*; Martin 1988.

price rationing, where risk of default is compensated by the spread of the interest rate charged on a loan over a risk-free rate; disequilibrium quantity rationing, which results from direct government controls on credit or slow adjustment of rates to supply and demand for credit; and equilibrium quantity rationing, which results from severe asymmetries of information between borrowers and lenders.

(a) Price rationing

Price rationing of credit implies that the interest rate on loans is set to equilibrate supply and demand for credit, though use of instruments such as collateral to offer further protection to the lender is not ruled out. In general, the paradigm assumes away many of the information problems outlined above. It may thus only be applicable in a subset of cases.

Debt must be held by another agent as an asset. Portfolio theory[11] suggests that the return demanded by that agent will depend on the risk and the expected return on the asset. For example, an unsecured consumer loan will command a higher rate of interest than a Treasury bill of the same maturity, owing to its relative risk characteristics. A consumer may default on interest and principal, while the government can keep its promises via its power to tax and print money.[12] These considerations may be formalized into a theory of the structure of interest rates (as summarized in Robinson and Wrightsman 1980). The 'credit quality' spread between the yield on a private issue of debt and risk-free debt in the same national market depends on seven factors: the risk of default, as discussed above, and associated costs to the lender; the call risk that bonds (or loans) may be liquidated early at a possibly inconvenient time for the lender; tax exemption status; the term or period to maturity; any screening or monitoring costs; security or collateral; and market liquidity.

Default risk refers to the possibility of not collecting interest and principal as promised in the debt contract. This is an obvious difficulty if loans are unsecured but, as noted, returns may also be difficult to obtain even if a loan is collateralized.[13] The lender is likely to demand a higher expected return to compensate for the extra risk. An indicator of the market's assessment of default risk for fixed-rate debt is the differential between the yield on a private bond and public bond of the same

[11] The original reference is Tobin 1958. See also L. Fisher 1959.

[12] Government debt issued in a country's own currency is of course subject to the risk of monetization via inflation, and, for foreign holders, of the additional risk of exchange-rate changes. Hence a risk premium may be charged for conventional as opposed to indexed debt, and between governments seen as more or less likely to monetize or devalue. Meanwhile, government debt in foreign currency is subject to normal default risk (see the discussion of the ldc debt crisis in Ch. 6).

[13] One may distinguish illiquidity risk—that the collateral may cover the value of the loan, but be hard to sell—and insolvency risk—that owing to changing relative prices the collateral no longer covers the value of the principal.

maturity, callability, tax features, etc. It is important to distinguish the three returns concepts introduced here, namely the interest rate (coupon), the expected return, and the yield. The coupon may differ from the yield due to changes in the level of interest rates (or market expectations of associated capital gains and losses) from the time when the bond was issued. Such a deviation may occur for public or private debt. For private debt, the yield will also differ from the expected return, because the latter must be deflated to allow for expected default risk. For a given expected return, the yield must be higher to allow for a higher expectation of default risk (the excess allows reserves to be built up against risk of default). In practice, the lender would probably also demand a higher expected return in this case. Meanwhile, for floating-rate debt the default premium is reflected in the spread of risky over risk-free short-term debt.

The overall default risk on an individual debt instrument varies with the risk position of the borrower and the economic environment. The risk position of the borrower is obviously conditioned by the ability to generate enough cash flow to cover interest and principal (the coverage ratio, or its inverse, income-gearing), the variability of cash flow, and the availability of liquidity or other assets to repay the debt. There may also be changes in the incentive to default, which may arise from changes in the bankruptcy law.

Traditional theory suggests that, for an individual agent, default risk may be broken down into three elements.[14] While in the literature this is generally applied to companies, counterparts for households can generally be found. First, the risk position varies 'internally' with the state of the balance sheet, which may be indicated for companies by ratios such as the debt/equity or debt/assets ratio, and for households with the ratio of debt to income or unencumbered wealth. These ratios are choice variables arising from the budget constraint. Secondly, 'business risk' is defined to depend largely on the type of business or employment the agent is in and is thus partly beyond his control. Thirdly, default risk for all borrowers depends on the state of the economic cycle and other macro-economic variables such as interest rates, unemployment, and factor prices; most defaults occur during or immediately after recessions.

So far the discussion has only assessed one borrower and transaction in isolation; in practice the lender can diversify to reduce risk, and this has an important influence on the pricing of debt claims. In the sense of modern portfolio theory,[15] the first two types of risk noted above may be characterized as *diversifiable* by the holder (unsystematic risk), as they can in principle be minimized by holding a diversified portfolio of bonds or loans. In the case of 'pure' price-rationing, as for large firms in the bond

[14] Note that these categories gloss over the problems of adverse selection and moral hazard arising from asymmetric information.

[15] See Malkiel (1985) for a non-technical discussion, also the survey in Ross (1990).

market, these types of risk should be reflected in the mark-up of the rate on an individual issue of debt in relation to the market return on a diversified portfolio of such private bonds and loans, to an extent dependent on the covariance of such risks with corresponding risks for other borrowers. In practice for small firms and individual households they may well be catered for by forms of equilibrium quantity rationing (Sect. (*c*) below). On the other hand, risks that affect the aggregate economy and hence the entire company or personal sector are *non-diversifiable* by the holder (systematic risk)[16] and should be reflected in the spread of debt yields over the risk-free yield offered by government bonds (for fixed-rate debt) or Treasury bills (for floating-rate debt).

Looking ahead, it has often been observed that default premiums may fall, for example, during periods of intense competition between financial markets and institutions, when lenders offer ever-finer terms on loans in order to gain market share (Davis (1989, 1990*a*)). Risk premiums may fall below those sustainable in competitive equilibrium (i.e. where losses due to realized defaults are adequately covered). Inflation may aggravate mispricing (Ch. 5, Sect. 4). If mispricing is anything more than a temporary phenomenon, and it is not accompanied by a significant fall in realized defaults, this process may lead to increased vulnerability of financial institutions (Chs. 5–8), as well as potentially increasing risks for the borrowers themselves (Chs. 2–4), although fragility in the non-financial sectors does not *require* lenders to underprice risk, merely that borrowers be excessively optimistic about their own prospects. A further factor may be 'socialization' of risks. If it is assumed that the Central Bank or government will rescue certain debtors, the perceived risk of lending may decline.

Relating the price-rationing paradigm to the economics of debt discussed above, price-rationing presupposes either that there are no information asymmetries, or that problems relating to adverse selection and moral hazard can be overcome, whether by means of adequate screening and monitoring, reputation, net worth, control, or commitment. As discussed below, presence of these market failures could in principle lead to a form of quantity rationing. Disregard of these problems, i.e. price rationing potentially low-quality borrowers in the presence of significant asymmetric information—as may have occurred at times in the 1980s—may lead to severe adverse selection.

(b) Disequilibrium quantity rationing

In some cases, the normal market equilibrium of supply equalling demand at a market-clearing price may not operate. There may be rationing of credit at a non-market-clearing price with excess demand (or supply) of

[16] This abstracts from international diversification; where this is possible, the relevant risks are those that cannot be avoided by holding the global portfolio.

loanable funds, in the sense that among loan applicants who appear to be identical some receive a loan and others do not.

Most authors have characterized credit rationing as a disequilibrium phenomenon (i.e. a situation in which lenders are artificially prevented from offering the price for loans that will clear the market), resulting from government regulations imposed on credit markets. Such regulations typically aim to enable monetary control to be exerted without raising interest rates, and/or to 'improve' the allocation of credit to preferred sectors. Credit rationing clearly arises in the case of interest-rate controls and with sectoral direction of credit. Stiglitz and Weiss (1986) suggest that government controls on banks' balance-sheet growth can also lead to such credit rationing. However, this depends on whether banks choose to set a high market-clearing interest rate, in which case there is no rationing, or, perhaps to avoid political difficulties, they keep rates low and ration credit.

Behaviour endogenous to the market could also result in a form of disequilibrium rationing. Institutions may be slow in adjusting rates for fear of external criticism, so delay till change is clearly inevitable. There may be transactions costs, for example the cost of writing to all borrowers to inform them of changes. Disequilibrium credit rationing might also arise from the desire of banks to share interest-rate risks with customers, especially with a system of short-term or variable-rate loans which imply a continuing relation in the future between lenders and borrowers (Fried and Howitt 1980). This could lead banks and their borrowing customers to enter into informal agreements or 'implicit contracts' to guarantee stable loan rates, which allow the bank to deny credit to a predetermined fraction of (newer) customers when market interest rates are high. This can be related to the 'commitment' paradigm discussed above.[17] Alternatively, banks might wish to charge a uniform rate to ensure equitable treatment between broad classes of heterogeneous borrowers, fully accommodating the demand of the most preferred borrowers in each class but rationing credit to the least preferred members (Jaffee and Modigliani 1969, Cukierman 1978). Finally, administered interest rates may reduce search costs for borrowers; infrequent and publicly announced changes reassure uninformed borrowers that well-informed banks are not taking advantage of their relative ignorance (Goodhart 1989).

(c) Equilibrium quantity rationing

Stiglitz and Weiss (1981) have shown that credit rationing can still arise in equilibrium (i.e. a situation in which lenders are unwilling to change the conditions under which loans are offered). Thus rationing is not

[17] Note that implicit contracts may have an adverse effect on depositors, if the slack is not taken up by the bank's profits—also they may only be sustainable in an oligopoly or cartel.

necessarily a consequence of market disequilibrium resulting from sticky prices or government regulation, though obviously these may also lead to rationing. Such equilibrium rationing is a possible outcome when the problems of the debt contract set out in Sect. 2 apply particularly strongly, i.e. there is imperfect and *asymmetric information* (the borrower knows more about his characteristics than the lender) and there are *incomplete contracts* (i.e. lenders cannot control all aspects of the borrower's behaviour). Stiglitz and Weiss's analysis entails some imperfect substitution, borrowers have access only to banks and not to the bond market—perhaps because they lack reputation, or are too small to pay fixed costs of securities issuance. It is thus particularly applicable to small businesses and households, and not normally to large firms or governments.[18]

As foreshadowed in Sect. 2, the key is that the interest rate offered to borrowers influences the riskiness of loans in two main ways.[19] First, borrowers willing to pay high interest rates may, on average, be worse risks. They may be willing to borrow at high rates because the probability that they will repay is lower than average. This is the problem of *adverse selection* i.e. a reduction in the average quality of the mix of applicants for loans due to the increased price. Second, as the interest rate increases, borrowers who were previously 'good risks' may undertake projects with lower probabilities of success but higher returns when successful—the problem of *moral hazard*, that the incentives of higher interest rates lead borrowers to undertake riskier actions.

These considerations suggest that under the conditions outlined, there may exist an optimal interest rate on loans, beyond which the return to the bank falls despite excess demand for loans at that rate.[20] This is because, at a higher interest rate, increased defaults more than offset any increase in profits. The bank maximizes profit by denying loans to individuals who are observationally equivalent to those receiving them. They may be unable to obtain loans at any interest rate at a given supply of credit.[21] Or alternatively, and perhaps more common in the household

[18] The boundary between price and quantity rationing may shift in a financial crisis; see Ch. 5, Sect. 7.

[19] This view is not entirely new. As noted in Smith (1776); allocation of credit by higher interest rates could lead to a situation whereby 'the greater part of the money which was to be lent will go to prodigals and projectors, who alone would be willing to give this high interest. Sober people, who will give for the use of the money no more than a part of what they are likely to make by the use of it, would not venture into the competition. A great part of the capital of the country would thus be kept out of the hands most likely to make a profitable and advantageous use of it, and thrown into those most likely to waste and destroy it'. See also Jaffee and Russell (1976), Keeton (1979).

[20] Implicitly the bank is using the interest rate as a screening device, to help identify 'good' borrowers.

[21] This is distinct from the question as to why an individual faces an upward-sloping interest-rate schedule—primarily because the default probability rises as the amount borrowed increases.

sector, banks provide smaller loans than the borrowers demand. Note that the analysis implies that an increase in interest rates arising from tighter monetary policy may lead to a collapse of quantity-rationed credit markets (Mankiw 1986), as adverse selection and moral hazard make it unprofitable to make any advances.

The assumption above is that the bank can only control the price and quantity of credit. Bester (1985) suggested that banks can use collateral to distinguish high- and low-risk borrowers, because 'safe' borrowers will be more willing to offer higher collateral in return for a lower interest rate than will risky borrowers. Stiglitz and Weiss (1986), in response, argue—perhaps less convincingly—that increasing collateral requirements (or reducing the debt/equity ratio) may *reduce* bank profits. This is because wealthier individuals may be less averse to risk than poorer individuals[22] and so those who can put up most capital would be willing to take the greatest risk with the lowest probability of repayment. Hence varying collateral may not eliminate equilibrium rationing. In practice, fear of loss of reputation would presumably prevent rich people acting in the manner suggested. A more serious objection to Bester is that many 'safe' borrowers may lack collateral.

Note the contrast between this analysis of collateral as a means of screening across types of borrower, and the more common view in banking circles, alluded to in Sects. 2 and 3*a*, that collateral is needed to offset risk, especially when borrowers are known to be of low quality. Berger and Udell (1990*b*) characterize these respectively as 'sorting by private information' and 'sorting by observed risk'. They offer evidence that suggests that the latter is somewhat better supported by the data (i.e. high collateral is correlated with higher risk).

Returning to the nature of equilibrium quantity rationing, at a theoretical level, the analysis can be generalized to any number of control instruments: rationing is possible so long as contracts remain incomplete, i.e. the bank cannot directly control the choice of project under very possible contingency (see Stiglitz and Weiss 1986; Hart 1986). The analysis also applies in the case of several observationally distinguishable groups; a group may be excluded although there is excess demand for credit, and its expected return on investment is highest.

In terms of the economics of debt (Sect. 2), the Stiglitz and Weiss result arises directly from the inability of lenders to overcome market failures arising from asymmetric information and incomplete contracts. This may occur when screening and monitoring are costly or impossible, borrowers

[22] 'Wealthy individuals may be those who, in the past, have succeeded in risky endeavours. In this case they are likely to be less risk averse than the more conservative individuals who have in the past invested in relatively safe securities, and are consequently less able to furnish large amounts of collateral.' (Stiglitz and Weiss 1986: 402.) Obviously, collateral also has positive incentive effects.

lack a reputation or have low net worth, where suitably detailed contracts (control) cannot be prepared, and long-term relationships are hard to establish or one-off transactions predominate.[23]

(4) Theories of Intermediation

An understanding of why certain types of transaction may occur only in banking markets, while others may arise either via banks or securities markets, is essential background to comprehending the locus of financial fragility and systemic risk, as well as being important to understanding differences between financial systems. Davis and Mayer (1991) distinguished four main theories of intermediation, several of which derive from the general economic features of the debt contract as outlined above. These are, respectively, theories of economies of scale, information, control, and commitment. A key suggestion in this book is that reliance on control may lead to instability more readily than commitment.

All of the theories rely on a degree of market imperfection, such as asymmetric information or economies of scale—in the absence of market imperfections, banks' deposit-creation and asset-management services play no independent role in the economy (Fama 1980). This is because, given perfect[24] capital markets, no information costs, or transactions costs, banks and other financial intermediaries are just passive holders of portfolios; depositors can offset any actions of banks via private portfolio decisions. This theorem applies even if individuals' access to capital markets is limited, as long as access is costless for banks and competitive conditions prevail, for banks would then offset each others' portfolio shifts. (Compare the Modigliani–Miller theory of corporate finance outlined in Ch. 2.)

(a) Economies of scale

The traditional theory of intermediation relies on the presence of economies of scale, which benefit specialized intermediaries (Gurley and Shaw 1960). Economies of scale arise from indivisibilities and non-convexities in transaction technologies which restrict diversification and risk-sharing under direct financing via securities markets. Banks can pool risk and diversify portfolios more cheaply than individual investors, given fixed costs of acquiring investments. On the liabilities side, they can be seen as providing a form of insurance to risk-averse depositors

[23] In another paper (Stiglitz and Weiss 1983) the authors note that in a multiperiod context, the threat of future credit rationing may reduce moral hazard.

[24] i.e. markets where individuals can freely borrow against human and non-human wealth.

against liquidity risk (i.e. their need for cash in the future), if it is assumed these individuals are 'small' and risks cancel over the population.[25] There are also economies of scale in the provision of payments services. On the assets side, banks can lend more easily than individuals, owing to their ability to manage investments at lower cost. (As a corollary, any reductions in fixed costs of direct financing will increase markets' comparative advantage.)

However, this theory does not distinguish banks from other financial intermediaries such as mutual funds (unit trusts), which may also benefit from economies of scale[26]—and which may themselves be part of the payments mechanism.[27] It also does not address the issues of information asymmetry, incomplete contracts, and monitoring, which it is suggested above are central to the nature of debt.

(b) Information asymmetries: screening, monitoring, and reputation

A second set of theories confronts these issues directly. As discussed in Sect. 2, information asymmetries in the absence of complete contracts give rise to a need for lenders to *screen* the quality of entrepreneurs and firms and to *monitor* their performance to avoid adverse selection and moral hazard.[28] But Sect. 2 also showed these to be general features of the debt contract. Why should banks have a specific advantage?

First, there are links to scale economies; for example, expertise and fixed technology costs in screening by banks may give rise to economies of scale for depositors financing large-scale projects (Chan 1983). There may also be economies of scale in monitoring, making delegation of monitoring to banks desirable, and economies of scope linking screening and monitoring.

As regards sources of these advantages, banks may have informational advantages arising from ongoing credit relationships, from access to the

[25] Insurance is one aspect of the Diamond and Dybvig (1983) model of banking. The suggestion is that banks can provide a liquidity service even when insurance companies cannot, i.e. when depositors' need for liquidity is private information. The model is discussed in more detail in Ch. 5, Sect. 1, where the focus is on its predictions regarding bank runs. Note that markets also provide a form of insurance via their liquidity.

[26] Note that the economies of scale arise from existing technology rather than any unique feature of banks. (Goodhart 1989).

[27] Presence of money-market mutual funds in the payments system shows that confidence of customers and third parties in payments intermediaries can be established either via owners' capital (banks) or stable-valued assets (mutual funds). This suggests dominance of the payments system is *not* the distinguishing feature of banks.

[28] See Leland and Pyle 1977; Diamond 1984. Diamond (1991) cautions that for very low quality borrowers, monitoring does not eliminate incentives to moral hazard. This is because such borrowers have both less to lose by defaulting, and also less to lose by revealing bad news about themselves by being caught indulging in moral hazard. So monitoring in this case only screens out certain borrowers caught taking high-risk actions. If the cost of monitoring is sufficiently high, they may be excluded from credit.

borrower's deposit history (Fama 1985), and from use of transaction services (Lewis 1991). The intangible nature of this information makes it difficult to transmit to markets or other lenders, hence loans are typically *non-marketable*; as a corollary, many borrowers from banks are unable to access finance from securities markets. Moreover, even if transfer were possible, given economies of scale it might be uneconomic for small borrowers to generate information themselves and transfer it to the market, rather than have it collected by a bank.

A consequence of non-marketability, which buttresses banks' positions, is that such investments are by definition held on the banks' own books. This will avoid free rider problems typical of securities markets, where an individual investor in marketable securities can costlessly take advantage of information on borrowers produced by other investors, thus reducing the incentive to gather it. Even abstracting from such problems, it also reduces the costly duplication of information collection that should otherwise be reflected in loan pricing.

An indicator of the importance of banks' roles as monitors is that even when firms can access securities markets, a continuing supply of bank debt may reduce the cost of market funds to the borrower (Fama 1985; James 1987). This is because markets may regard bank loan renewals as a positive signal, given banks' superior information; and this reduces the costs of monitoring for external debt and equity holders. Where this is the case, there is thus a positive externality from banks.

The key theoretical work in this area has been produced by Diamond (1984), who shows why it may be efficient for investors to delegate monitoring to banks, given information asymmetries between borrowers and lenders. In Diamond's model, banks offer standard debt contracts to borrowers, which pay a fixed return in non-default states and impose penalties in the event of default, thus ensuring adequate incentives.

There is of course also a problem of screening and monitoring banks by depositors, given information asymmetry about banks' activities. Diamond suggests that the costs of this are reduced by portfolio diversification by banks, which also allows standard debt contracts to be offered to depositors.[29] The holding of bank assets in the form of debt ensures compatibility between the interests of the bank owner and depositor. This is because, unlike equity, efforts by the intermediary to increase the probability of the highest return, by ensuring borrowers do not default, also increase the probability that depositors' claims will be met. Chant (1987) suggests an additional mechanism is bank owners' equity. This gives depositors grounds for confidence in banks, as owners suffer initially from any losses. A further back-up is of course regulation, whereby supervisors assume the burden of monitoring banks (Ch. 5, Sect. 2).

[29] The corollary is that inadequate diversification may leave banks vulnerable to changes of opinion by depositors as to the risk-free nature of bank deposit contracts.

Reputations are important in a multiperiod context (Diamond 1989, 1991). As noted, reputations of borrowers may be adequate to avoid excessively high-risk investments and other moral hazard problems associated with imperfect information. In the absence of reputations, firms may be dependent on bank finance owing to moral hazard and adverse selection.[30] Only when a reputation has been established and has itself become a capital asset, by facilitating future access to cheaper sources of funds, are adverse selection and associated agency problems reduced, and firms can be relied on to select safe rather than risky projects. At that stage firms are able to access the bond or commercial paper markets and avoid the costs of bank finance.[31] Rating agencies may have an important role to play in this process, by offering monitoring services for investors in bond markets.

(c) Control

In the absence of complete contracts, specifying the actions of the borrower in every eventuality, lenders of long-term debt are vulnerable to exploitation by borrowers. This may, for example, take the form of forced refinancing to avoid threats of repudiation (Hellwig 1977). Where possible, creditors will seek protection from such threats by retaining rights to control assets in the event of default—often called 'enforcement'. These rights may, for example, allow creditors to engage in liquidations that are costly to debtors (Hart and Moore 1988). Conversely, borrowers are vulnerable to exploitation by lenders during the period of gestation of the investment project when costs have already been sunk. These offsetting factors suggest that funding of long-term investment needs a balance of control between borrowers and lenders.

A debt contract may provide such a balance, by allowing entrepreneurs to remain in control as long as they are not in default (Aghion and Bolton 1992). If there is a default, control transfers to lenders (albeit at a cost, e.g. in terms of low prices for second-hand assets, that the lender will hesitate to incur). Banks may be better suited to exercise control than bondholders—they may have lower 'enforcement costs'—if there are free rider problems to the involvement of the latter in corporate restructurings. (In other words, if one lender takes action to increase his return, all others who may not contribute will benefit equally, thus reducing the incentive to the active lender (Stiglitz 1985; Bolton 1990).) Control may be reinforced by features of the debt contract such as

[30] However, Chant (1987) suggests that an underwriter may be able to substitute his reputation for the borrower's in some cases (such as junk bonds, as discussed in Chs. 2 and 8).

[31] Particularly the costs of screening and monitoring, and the higher rates that banks may need to charge to offset residual adverse selection and moral hazard.

short maturities, collateral, and covenants.[32] Focus on control in banking is often dubbed 'transactions banking', i.e. where borrowers and lenders seek to maximise returns from each individual transaction.

(d) Commitment

Authors such as Mayer (1988) and Hellwig (1991a) suggest that an alternative to control is commitment or 'relationship banking'. For example, banks may only rescue firms that are in financial difficulties if they anticipate being able to participate in the returns from such rescues. Superior information on the part of banks may tie borrowers to their original lenders, and thereby allow creditors to capture the required benefits. Conversely, firms will only be willing to commit themselves to particular creditors if they believe that their creditors will not exploit their dominant position. Reputations of financial institutions may be adequate to ensure that this condition holds (see also Sharpe 1990), although they may be buttressed by equity participations of banks, which also reinforce banks' influence over the firm in non-default states. Participants in bond markets may be unable to commit themselves in the way outlined.

It has been suggested that the bank-oriented systems of Germany and Japan may be better suited to commitment than the market-oriented Anglo-Saxon systems and the euromarkets. Competition between financial institutions (and limitations on bank equity holdings) in the latter may make commitment on the part of large borrowers difficult (see Sect. 5 for more detail), although small and medium-sized borrowers tend to rely on banking relationships in all countries. Note that commitment is a form of 'implicit contract'—the nature of the agreement to provide credit (by the lender) and to remain a customer (by the borrower) cannot be specified formally.

Furthermore, the theory as outlined only focuses on interactions after the loan is made (i.e. superior monitoring). But relationships based on implicit contracts may also arise from the costs of pre-loan evaluation of firm risk (or more general relationship-specific capital investment), where borrowers and lenders form an implicit contract to share benefits (Wachter and Williamson 1978).

These four theories need not be exclusive. For example, monitoring theories of intermediation rely on economies of scale in monitoring. Control and commitment models require incomplete contracts, which might result from imperfect observability or verifiability of outcomes. But

[32] However, recent experience of bondholders in the US, where losses due to 'event risk' following takeovers and restructurings have been sizeable, show the weakness of covenants—or their inability to cover all outcomes—in the case of long-term debt.

control models suggest actions on the part of lenders that do not feature in monitoring models, and commitment models involve intertemporal relations that are not present elsewhere.

(e) Applications

The versatility of these concepts—applied in the theoretical section above to a rather stylized version of traditional 'retail' banking—can be seen in their applicability to two of the recent developments in financial markets, namely *securitization* and *wholesale banking*.

(i) Securitization

Securitization may be defined (Cumming 1987) as 'matching up of borrowers and savers wholly or partly by way of the financial markets'. It thus covers both direct intermediation via bonds and commercial paper, and repackaging of loans such as mortgages, where financial intermediaries originate loans but securities markets are used to seek investors.

As regards stimuli to this process, first, it is suggested that *relationships* or 'implicit contracts' between banks and borrowers weakened in countries such as the US in the 1980s. On the one hand, *volatile* interest rates rendered highly unprofitable the options implicit in such facilities as credit lines and lending commitments. On the other hand, the high *level* of interest rates would often make the costs of reserve requirements and of capital exceed the benefit of holding the loan on the balance sheet, even if the borrower chose to exercise his right to borrow. In addition, increased competition in finance has reduced the market power of banks and the cost of severing ties with them.

As banking relationships ceased to offer continuous access to funds in a manner distinct from securities markets, price differences came to the fore. Here, the *economies of scale* offered by banks may have weakened, as increased capital requirements and the high level of interest rates raised the minimum spread acceptable to banks, and thus made the fixed costs of securities issuance acceptable to a wider range of borrowers. In addition, improved issuance techniques such as shelf registration,[33] as well as competition among underwriters (Ch. 7 Appendix), were acting to reduce these fixed costs[34] Banks themselves have found it attractive to sell assets in this context, thus economizing on capital, as well as reducing

[33] An amendment to rules in US securities markets which allowed blanket registration of bond or equity issues over two years, rather than having to register each issue individually, and which thus increased the flexibility of US domestic securities markets.

[34] Berger and Udell (1992) suggest there were also improvements in monitoring technology in securities markets which reduced costs of issuance, although these could be partly offset by improvements in *banks*' monitoring technology.

duration[35] of assets relative to liabilities, while taking advantage of lower costs of packaging loans. The collateral on such loans (e.g. mortgage deeds) substitutes for bank capital as a 'buffer' from the investors' point of view. The institutionalization of saving—itself partly a response to changes in relative transactions costs—has increased demand for securities over deposits, and hence reduced relative costs of securities market financing.

Also by use of packaging (for household loans), guarantees and letters of credit (for corporate loans), and sometimes both packaging and guarantees (securitization with recourse)[36] banks could use their continuing comparative advantage in *monitoring* certain types of customer unable to access securities markets direct, while using up little capital.

Turning to *control* aspects, the more complete the debt contract, the easier it is to securitize. The new financial instruments noted above have increased the potential for this. However, apart from the use of junk bonds in the US, in most countries—and in the euromarkets—banks' advantage in exerting control has prevented securitization of high-risk transactions such as takeover credits or project credits (Allen 1990). Moreover, there are clear limits to packaging; it has not been a feature for small-business loans. This may be due to features such as the importance of personal confidential information about idiosyncratic borrowers, the fact that loans may be unsecured or the security difficult to sell, and all such loans may be vulnerable in a downturn (i.e. the risk is largely non-diversifiable).

(ii) Wholesale banking

Lewis (1991) suggests that certain wholesale banking activities such as syndicated lending and interbank borrowing can also be explained by theories of intermediation. For example, as regards *economies of scale*, risk-pooling of liabilities via interbank markets occurs outside the bank via market transactions, instead of within the bank as with traditional deposits. Similarly, a diversified portfolio of loans can be obtained either by a bank itself making many small loans or participating in many large loans made by other banks. Again, in syndicated lending, the banks taking participations can be seen as delegating the *screening* and *monitoring* of the borrower to the lead bank, which in turn has incentives to perform its function based on its reputation and on the credit risk it absorbs (but see the discussion of the debt crisis in Ch. 6).

On the other hand, it is less clear that interbank lending entails *relationships*, with implicit contracts guaranteeing support to correspondents

[35] Duration is the average time to an asset's discounted cash flow, which relates to the vulnerability of its price to interest rate changes. It differs from maturity by distinguishing fixed and floating rate instruments of the same maturity; a floating rate asset has a lower duration.

[36] See Benveniste and Berger (1987), 38.

(Ch. 6, Sect. 1). Although there has to be a basis of trust in such markets, a reaction to stress is often the cutting of interbank credit lines. The dispersion of creditors to any one bank may make this a likely outcome. Even in terms of *control*, groups of banks may find it more difficult to reorganize non-financial firms in difficulty than a single bank (i.e. they face similar free rider problems to bond-market investors). The difficulty of co-ordination of a large group of banks has been the basis of public intervention in countries such as the UK.

(5) Aspects of the Structure and Development of Financial Systems

(a) Long-term structural aspects

There are systemic contrasts between the behaviour of financial institutions and markets in the major OECD countries, and hence in the nature of debt, an outline of which provides a further introductory section of the book. The general division is between the 'Anglo-Saxon' systems of the UK, US, and Canada, together with the international capital markets (or 'euromarkets'), on the one hand, and the systems in Continental Europe and Japan (CEJ). At a superficial level the contrasts in terms of *financial structure* include the following:

- The banks have a much more dominant role in corporate finance in the CEJ countries, traditionally, Anglo-Saxon banks have only lent short term for working capital.
- Reflecting this, the securities markets and institutional investors in CEJ are relatively underdeveloped, with a low level of reliance by firms on market finance; bond and equity markets are larger in the Anglo-Saxon countries (although use of new equity issues to finance investment is rare); as a corollary, there is also a greater belief in the efficiency of market allocations in Anglo-Saxon countries.
- In CEJ, there is a wider involvement of the public sector in lending (and also ownership of banks).
- In CEJ countries the banking relationships for medium and large companies are closer, often cemented by formal links, e.g. bank representatives on company boards, as well as bank holdings of equity; in contrast, banks and bondholders in Anglo-Saxon countries are discouraged from seeking control of corporate affairs.

Other key features of CEJ countries in this context include the following:

- In terms of *banks' balance sheets*, banks in CEJ countries are able to hold equity stakes, a feature absent in Anglo-Saxon countries.
- There are much higher levels of indebtedness for companies, almost exclusively bank rather than bond financed.

- Traditionally, there is a greater unwillingness to extend credit to the personal sector (primacy of corporate customers).
- In terms of *financial market behaviour*, there are lower levels of financial innovation and (particularly) securitization of loans.
- Levels of competition are lower in banking, as well as between banks and other financial institutions and markets, often entailing extensive cross-subsidization of loan rates by deposit rates, or between types of borrower, and high levels of co-operation between banks.[37]
- There is a virtual absence of hostile corporate takeovers.
- *Features of corporate finance* include extensive corporate cross-holdings of equity[38] and more generally greater concentration of securities holdings.
- There are tendencies to industrial cartelization, which effectively protect banks' holdings of equity or equity-like loans.
- Financing conflicts are resolved by consensus and not litigation.
- Banks are more willing to rescue companies, often using their own staff to aid or replace management.
- There are more closely held companies.
- There is a lower level of information disclosure by companies direct to the public, offset by private disclosure to relationship banks, and via institutions such as central risk offices run by the public sector, through which banks share information on large business borrowers.

A number of authors (such as Cable 1985; Cable and Turner 1985; Mayer 1988) suggest these differences can be understood as means of overcoming the problems of the debt contract outlined in Sect. 2. In particular, the information advantage offered to banks in CEJ by features such as their having representatives on boards and close sharing of information, as well as the reduction in conflicts of interest occasioned by equity holdings by banks and reduced free rider problems arising from concentration of debt holdings, may make 'commitment' a more likely outcome. This in turn may be superior to 'control' in terms of risk-sharing; for example, avoiding unnecessary liquidations arising from illiquidity (inability to pay interest owing to lack of cashflow) rather than insolvency (liabilities exceeding assets), as well as helping to stabilize company profits and promote long-term investment. It should be noted that such 'commitment' is absent in many of the cases of financial fragility and systemic risk outlined in the rest of the book.

However, commentators also note that the structures have developed over a long period on the basis of country-specific conditions, and hence could not easily be reproduced elsewhere. Second, although risk is

[37] e.g. as noted by Aoki (1988) and Hoshi *et al.* (1990), Japanese firms typically borrow from many banks, but have only one main bank. The latter will take the lead in rescues and incur most of the costs, on the basis that (i) its reputation for monitoring is at stake, and (ii) other banks will reciprocate for their own firms when it is a creditor but not the main bank.

[38] The influence of banks in Germany is increased by their ability to vote on behalf of investors for whom they hold shares in custody.

reduced for non-financial borrowers, it may be increased for the lender if it holds both debt and equity in the same firm (or if it holds debt in a non-corporate firm that has equity characteristics). Low inflation and stable interest rates may have helped prevent realization of such risks. Moreover, also offsetting the advantages may be serious problems of inefficiency, monopoly, and conflict-of-interest dilemmas for banks.

Bisignano (1991) points out that many of the features of CEJ arose from deliberate public policy and not historical accident. In particular, he argues that stability of financial and non-financial industries was sought by limiting public disclosure of business information; promoting close business ties between industry, financial institutions, and government; providing domestic industries with equity/debt structures and financial/government links that shielded them from foreign competition and takeover; and limiting competition in strategic industries, notably banking and finance, by promotion of cartels and/or restraint on activities that could lead to excessive competition.

However, before moving on, it is appropriate to note that recent studies of corporate finance for some of the major 'bank dominated' countries cast doubt on uncritical acceptance of the sharp distinction between Anglo-Saxon and CEJ systems as outlined above. Edwards and Fischer (1991*a*, 1991*b*), for example, show that in Germany bank lending only predominates as a source of finance for small firms, that do not have supervisory boards on which banks are represented. This suggests that such boards are not an important channel for reducing information asymmetries and permitting more bank-loan finance to be made available. Second, it is not clear that supervisory boards have enough information to evaluate performance of the management board closely. Third, the large banks, given their control via proxy votes of their own shareholders' meetings, may have little incentive to act either in their own shareholders' interests or those of companies they monitor via supervisory boards. Finally, most firms have many banks rather than just one, and some large firms claim not to have a 'house bank'.

In addition, Hoshi *et al.* (1990) show that, despite evidence that Japanese banking relationships reduce information problems and relax liquidity constraints, many companies have sought to weaken bank ties, following liberalization of financial markets.[39] Four possible costs of banking relationships were identified: direct monitoring costs; imposition of reserve requirements (and capital requirements)[40] on banks, leading them to require a higher rate of return on their loan assets than individual investors would on securities; lower liquidity of loans than bonds, giving rise to costs of portfolio adjustment for banks that are passed on to

[39] Increased generation of internal funds may have facilitated these reductions in bank ties.

[40] To the extent that they enforce levels of capitalization above that desired by banks.

borrowers; and imposition of an excessively conservative investment policy on firms, to protect banks' debt claims.

Moreover, the groups described above are not homogeneous; there are also cross-cutting differences. For example, in the US, Japan, and (until 1984) in France, there was a degree of regulatory compartmentalization to financial institutions absent elsewhere, in particular a separation of commercial from investment banking.[41] This was intended to provide stability by avoiding contagion—albeit at a possible cost in terms of concentration of risk. Despite this, there is now a widespread tendency in all advanced countries towards the formation of 'universal banks' and other links between types of financial institutions.

In addition, France and (to a lesser extent) Japan show some convergence with the Anglo-Saxon pattern (e.g. developing capital markets and some weakening of bank relationships), while the use of securities markets as opposed to banks in Anglo-Saxon countries has intensified (the process of securitization and institutionalization), as has development of wholesale banking. Although partly autonomous, these changes also relate to financial deregulation, a brief outline of which is given below.

(b) Deregulation

In a number of countries, both among the Anglo-Saxon group and the CEJ countries, recent years have seen a degree of financial liberalization. Generally, these policies have tended to shift financial systems towards Anglo-Saxon behaviour patterns as outlined above. Several major types of deregulation can be discerned:

- abolition of interest-rate controls, or cartels that fixed rates;
- abolition of direct controls on credit expansion;
- removal of exchange controls;
- removal of regulations restricting establishment of foreign institutions;
- development and improvement of money, bond, and equity markets;
- removal of regulations segmenting financial markets;
- deregulation of fees and commissions in financial services;
- and, partly to offset these, tightening of prudential supervision, particularly in relation to capital adequacy, and often harmonized internationally. This point shows that liberalization is not a removal of all regulation but a shift in its locus from *structural* to *prudential* regulation (see Ch. 5, Sect. 2).

The main motivations of the authorities have been:

- to increase competition (and hence to reduce costs of financial services);

[41] Japan also segments short- and long-term business, and banking and trust business.

- improved access to credit for the private sector;
- to improve efficiency in determining financial prices and allocating funds;
- pressures from competition authorities to remove cartels;
- desire to maintain competitiveness of domestic markets and institutions;
- increased flexibility, responsiveness to customers, and innovation;
- securing a ready market for increasing sales of government bonds, and
- desire to secure stability of such a system against excessive risk-taking.

However, it would be wrong to see deregulation purely as a proactive shift by the authorities. In many cases, as is emphasised in the text, it was necessitated by structural and technological shifts which had already made existing regulations redundant. A particular stimulus was the challenge to domestic markets provided by the development of the euromarkets (Davis 1992*b*), as well as the growing preponderence of institutional investors such as life-insurance companies and pension funds (Davis 1988*a*; 1991*b*). Moreover, once the process of liberalization began, one measure quickly led to others, due to desire to maintain a level playing-field (within countries) and competitive equality (between countries).

Second, the suggestion that deregulation entails a shift towards markets and away from relationship banking is not universal. The Germans removed direct controls on credit and exchange controls in the 1960s, but have retained the distinctive features of their financial system.[42]

The consequences of deregulation are among the key themes of the book. But it is relevant to note that many of the benefits have clearly been realized. These include extension of the scope of financial services; greater flexibility for households and companies to smooth shocks in income or expenditure; greater resilience of economies to short run financial price volatility; improvements in efficiency of financial markets and reduced cost of services; and improvements in resource allocation owing to reduced credit rationing. The consensus is that there has been an overall welfare improvement.

However, as pointed out by the OECD (Blundell-Wignall and Browne 1991), liberalized financial markets have been associated with certain undesirable outcomes, which may partly offset the benefits. Among those highlighted by the OECD are:

- increased use of credit to purchase assets and finance consumption, resulting in sharp and perhaps unsustainable increases in personal-sector debt, and concomitant lower saving;
- asset price inflation and volatility, with asset price occasionally deviating sharply from 'fundamentals';

[42] The crucial development that was not pursued, and which may help explain this pattern, is that money markets were until recently not allowed to develop. This would limit scope for companies and investors to disintermediate via commercial paper etc.

- inflation and balance of payments difficulties, arising from the slow adjustment of goods markets compared with financial markets;
- changes in the effectiveness of monetary policy;
- financial fragility and systemic risk.

Summary

In the context of the book, this chapter is largely offered as background for the discussion of financial fragility and systemic risk, although the theories outlined are of interest in themselves and have a wider applicability to analysis of finance. Among the insights into the nature of debt are the following:

- the complexity of the debt contract;
- the importance of monitoring and screening to debt transactions, given uncertainty, costs of default, asymmetric information, and incomplete contracts;
- the way in which credit is rationed is likely to depend on the nature of the borrower and the information available to the lender, though government controls may also impinge;
- banks' uniqueness is best defined in terms of their non-marketable assets;
- access to the bond market is probably only possible for large, reputable borrowers;
- two principal types of financial system can be discerned; while the most obvious difference relates to the role of banks, at a deeper level the difference is in terms of the way in which the problems of information and incomplete contracts are overcome.

However, it should be noted that much of the theory outlined is 'equilibrium' or steady state—it does not describe how debt markets behave when states change, or in the transition between them. As shown in the following chapters, analysis of fragility and instability generally requires the theories to be extended to cover dynamics, in particular the reactions of borrowers and lenders to unfamiliar market conditions in the presence of intense competition.

Appendix: The Development of Financial Systems—A Long View

In order to give perspective to the analysis of the book, which focuses on developments over the past twenty five years, we briefly note the main features of the development of finance over a longer period, as outlined by Goldsmith (1985). His analysis shows the place of recent financial changes in the broader context of financial development as societies industrialize.

Goldsmith, in his magisterial analysis of national balance sheets over 1688–1978, presented data for a number of indicators of the role of the financial sector in an economy. He suggested that the broadest measure that can be drawn from balance sheets is the *financial interrelations ratio*, that is, the ratio of financial claims of the principal macroeconomic[43] sectors to tangible assets, which measures the relative size of an economy's financial superstructure. Goldsmith's data for the countries studied and a selection of others are reproduced in Table 1.1. Goldsmith's conclusion is that the interrelations ratio tends to rise during economic development (see Mexico and India in the table), after which it tends to be constant (implying constant ratios of financial to real assets). As regards the countries studied in this book, the UK and Canada were the highest in 1978, at 111 per cent, above Japan (102 per cent), the USA (99 per cent), France (83 per cent), and Germany (89 per cent).

Table 1.1. Financial interrelations ratio, 1850–1978 %

	1850	1875	1895	1913	1929	1939	1950	1966	1973	1978
Canada	—	—	—	—	—	—	119	118	129	113
France	25	56	—	98	81	—	55	124	92	83
Germany	20	38	72	76	39	56	40	92	85	89
Great Britain	68	93	196	196	245	270	177	150	129	111
India	64	47	40	34	30	38	45	54	57	54
Italy	21	39	45	47	68	73	42	85	116	104
Japan	—	30	34	64	123	142	55	81	92	102
Mexico	—	—	—	—	36	64	74	68	75	71
Russia	—	—	—	40	9	28	32	22	22	29
USA	47	64	71	83	129	132	117	128	111	99

Source: Goldsmith (1985).

A second ratio highlighted in Goldsmith's book is the *financial intermediation ratio*, the ratio of the assets of financial institutions (including institutional investors) to all domestic and foreign financial assets, which measures the importance of financial intermediaries in terms of resources within the financial superstructure. Data are presented in Table 1.2 for 1850–1978. In most countries the ratio is flat or declining in recent years, reflecting development of direct intermediation. However, a strong rise in the UK ratio commenced in 1929, reaching a level of 41 per cent in 1978—which appears to be average for most developed countries, though some way above the USA (27 per cent) and Japan (30 per cent). It is of interest that levels of this ratio do not correspond to the

[43] Persons, companies, public sector, banks, other financial institutions, foreign sector.

divide between Anglo-Saxon and bank-dominated financial systems; the UK is closer to Germany than the USA, Canada, Japan, and France. In addition, Goldsmith presents further evidence that the share of banks in this ratio tends to fall.[44] This reflects the growth of non-bank financial intermediaries—themselves often dependent on development of securities markets—as financial development proceeds. Relating this to theories of intermediation (Sect. 4), more enterprises in a developed economy have sufficient reputation to convey information credibly direct to potential lenders, although development of market infrastructure, legal framework, etc. is clearly also crucial to the development of securities markets (see Stiglitz 1991; Greenwald and Stiglitz 1991).

Table 1.2. Financial intermediation ratio, 1850–1978 %

	1850	1875	1895	1913	1929	1939	1950	1965	1973	1978
Canada	—	—	—	—	—	—	25	27	31	32
France	4	10	—	17	27	—	27	26	32	33
Germany	20	22	26	30	37	40	33	33	41	39
Great Britain	15	20	15	17	18	21	31	33	38	41
India	1	2	4	8	12	14	19	21	22	24
Italy	8	16	22	33	34	34	33	41	51	55
Japan	—	26	31	33	41	39	32	31	29	20
Mexico	—	—	—	8	19	24	27	32	38	33
Russia/USSR	—	—	—	32	22	34	30	53	53	54
USA	13	14	20	21	16	29	29	24	26	27

Source: Goldsmith (1985).

An update was performed for the more recent period for the countries studied in Chs. 2 and 3, namely the UK, the USA, Germany, Japan, Canada, and France (Table 1.3). Due to problems of data definition the

Table 1.3. Intercountry comparison of financial ratios %

	Financial Intermediation			Financial Interrelations		
	1978	1978	% change	1978	1978	% change
UK	40	45	12.5	134	194	45
USA	32	36	12.5	132	174	31
Germany	45	45	0	89	98	10
Japan	31	35	13	107	113	6
France	46	44	−4	100	152	52
Canada	38	37	−2	107	149	40

Source: National flow-of-funds data.

series do not exactly match Goldsmith's. As regards financial intermediation there has been common growth of around 13 per cent in the ratio over

[44] This is not to deny that regulation etc. may induce periods of 'disequilibrium' disintermediation and reintermediation.

1978–87 for the UK, USA, and Japan. All three financial sectors have experienced some degree of deregulation and structural change over this period. Note that the rise in intermediation appears contrary to securitization and the reduced role of banks—it partly reflects more than offsetting increases in holdings of securities by institutional investors. In contrast, the German, Canadian, and French ratios were completely unchanged over the same period, suggesting a relatively stable financial system as regards the preponderence of intermediation.[45] Meanwhile, the financial interrelations ratio has grown strongly in the USA, the UK, France, and Canada (by 31, 45, 52 and 40 per cent) while the ratios in Germany and Japan are both far lower and have seen relatively little growth over the decade. Shifts in gearing and asset valuation, themselves driven by the changing financial structure, may be responsible. A comparison with Goldsmith's Table 1.1 shows that the current UK, US, French, and Canadian interrelations ratios far exceed current or past experience for any country, with the exception of the UK itself over 1895–1939 and Switzerland in 1978. Comparison with Goldsmith's Table 1.2 shows that the intermediation ratio for these countries remains average. Hence growth over the last decade has not led intermediation (as defined here) to levels far exceeding other countries.

To summarize: comparison of recent patterns with longer term developments suggests that, despite securitization, growth in share prices, etc., there has been little change in the overall level of financial intermediation, albeit more in its locus. The intermediation ratios are clearly not far out of line with historical trends. In contrast, the overall value of financial claims relative to tangible assets, which historically has been rather constant once development reached a certain stage, has risen sharply in a number of countries. And as shown in Ch. 2, these are the same countries that have seen sharply increased default rates in the corporate sector. The suspicion is that these increases represent disequilibrium shifts that could be reversed. The process of reversal itself could entail fragility and systemic risk; a more comforting conclusion could be that developing technology and financial liberalization have made higher interrelations ratios sustainable.

[45] In practice, the French and Canadian systems underwent much more change than the German.

2

Financial Fragility in the Corporate Sector

Introduction

This chapter assesses the causes and implications of recent trends in debt and default in the corporate sectors of the major OECD countries, namely the USA, UK, Canada, Germany, Japan, and France. Essential background is provided by the discussion in Ch. 1, in particular that relating to credit rationing, which is taken as read. The data show a sharp rise in defaults in the Anglo-Saxon countries and France over the 1980s, which is echoed only partially in Germany and in Japan. These patterns in turn can be related to changes in corporate indebtedness, modified by the nature of financial systems; the main reasons for such shifts are examined.

The chapter is structured as follows; the first section presents balance-sheet data for the corporate sector in the six countries. The second offers an outline of theories of corporate debt and balance-sheet structure as presented in the literature, in particular as they relate to default. The third probes the nature of default, its costs and implications. The analysis of this section has broader applications to both households and financial institutions. The fourth and fifth sections interpret empirical patterns (levels and changes in leverage) in the light of theory, while the sixth seeks to estimate the empirical relationship between debt and default. Interim conclusions are drawn, and some policy implications suggested, in the final section.

(1) Recent Trends in Corporate Sector Indebtedness[1]

A comparison of corporate debt/equity ratios over the past two decades, as shown in Chart 2.1, shows a clear distinction between corporate sectors

[1] Trade credit and overseas direct investment are excluded. The data are drawn from national flow of funds statistics and feature a number of conceptual and definitional differences (see Davis 1986); in particular, the company sector for Germany includes unincorporated enterprises and public-sector firms. More attention should hence be devoted to changes than levels. Owing to reunification, German data were not available for the end of 1990; a change in the basis of calculation for French data has meant they too stop in 1989. Finally, it should be noted that the distinctions between instruments have become

with low gearing (UK, USA, and Canada) and those with high gearing (France, Japan, and Germany). This corresponds to the capital market/ bank divide outlined in Ch. 1. Despite a degree of convergence in recent years, due largely to rising equity values in the latter countries, the differences remain substantial. The differences for capital gearing or leverage[2] (i.e. gross debt/total assets, with fixed assets valued at replacement cost) is less marked but still apparent. Unsurprisingly, this ratio is more stable than debt/equity; however, some sizeable changes in gearing are apparent, notably in the USA in 1982–9, in Canada over 1979–81, and (to a lesser extent) in the UK and France since 1985. As shown below, these shifts are often correlated with changes in default (the implication of this observation, together with the contrast with Chart 2.1, is that equity markets may have overestimated earnings potential). It is notable that this measure of gearing is relatively flat or declining in Germany and Japan.[3]

Charts 2.3 and 2.4 deflate corporate debt by measures of income, respectively GNP[4] and profits.[5] In each case, the UK and USA generally show a lower level of indebtedness than the other countries, though the measure for Canada is comparable with Germany and France. Japanese gearing on these measures is extremely high and rising.[6] Chart 2.5 proxies income gearing (interest payments as a proportion of profits), by multiplying debt/profits by bank lending rates and bond yields, weighted by portfolio shares. There is a remarkable peak for Canada in 1981 and again in 1990. The UK and USA show rapid growth in the second half of the 1980s, although generally they have had among the lowest levels of income gearing. Nevertheless, the dispersion between countries is less than for debt/profits, illustrating the lower interest rates in the CEJ countries.

These data of course only show patterns for the corporate sector as a whole. However, work on micro data by Bernanke and Campbell (1988, 1990) and Bernanke, Campbell and Whited (1990) suggests that in the US at least, the patterns are mirrored by the experience of individual firms, while Bank of Japan (1991a) shows that in Japan aggregate patterns are borne out at sectoral level.

more blurred in recent years due to financial innovation; junk bonds, while ostensibly debt, have equity characteristics given low seniority and vulnerability of interest and principal to declines in company earnings. Offsetting use of options and futures can also change instruments' characteristics.

[2] The USA and UK terms leverage and gearing are used interchangeably in the text.

[3] Some have suggested the difference arises purely from omission of intangible assets from Chart 2.2—but if so, the correlation with default shown in Sect. 6. would not occur.

[4] Data for Italy (not shown) give a debt/GNP ratio of 0.6–0.7, between France and Japan on the chart.

[5] Profits are defined simply as GNP less labour income—a measure that includes depreciation.

[6] The contrast with leverage suggests a sharply rising capital/output ratio.

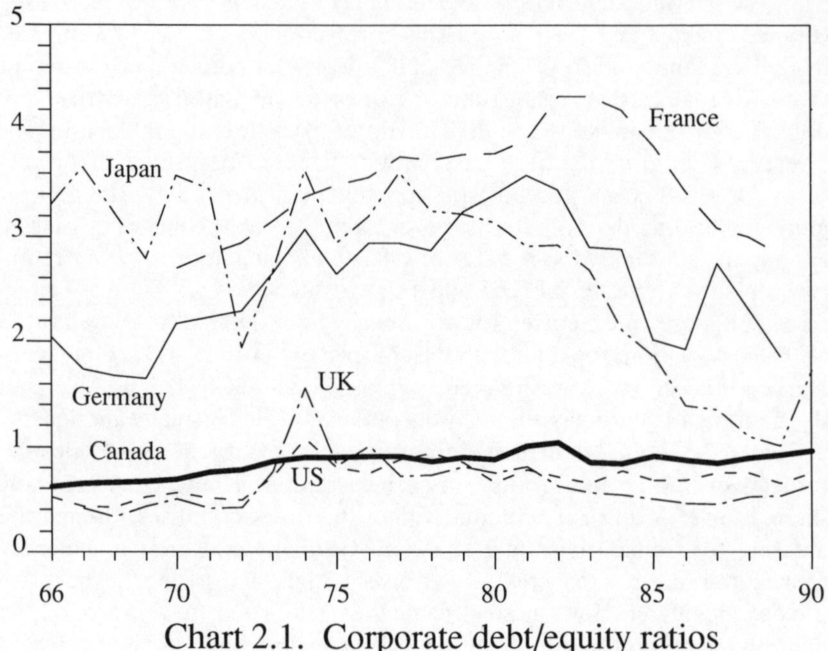

Chart 2.1. Corporate debt/equity ratios

0.6
0.5
0.4
0.3
0.2
0.1
0.0
Japan
Canada
Germany
France
US
UK
66
70
75
80
85
90

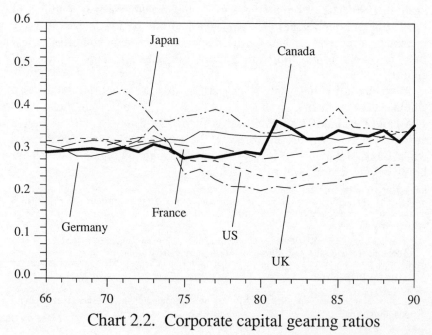

Chart 2.2. Corporate capital gearing ratios

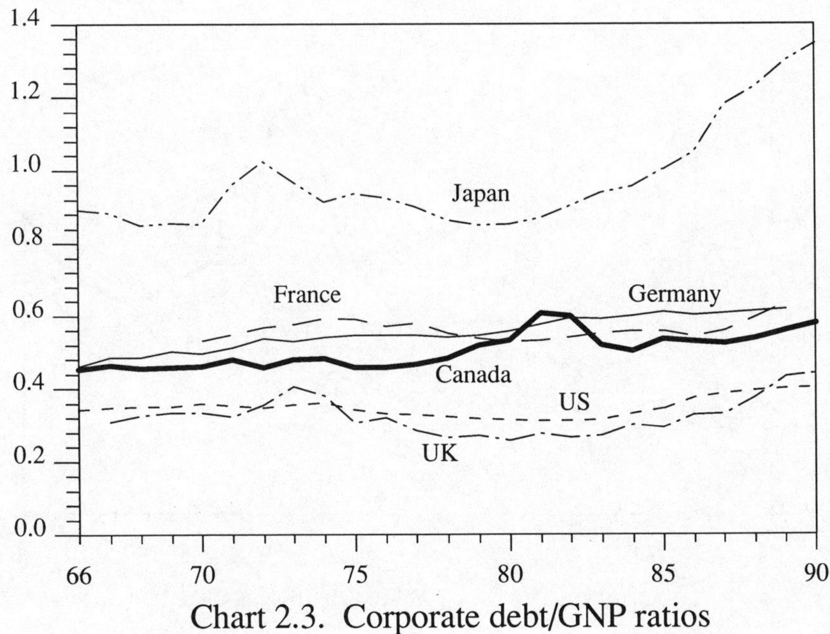

Chart 2.3. Corporate debt/GNP ratios

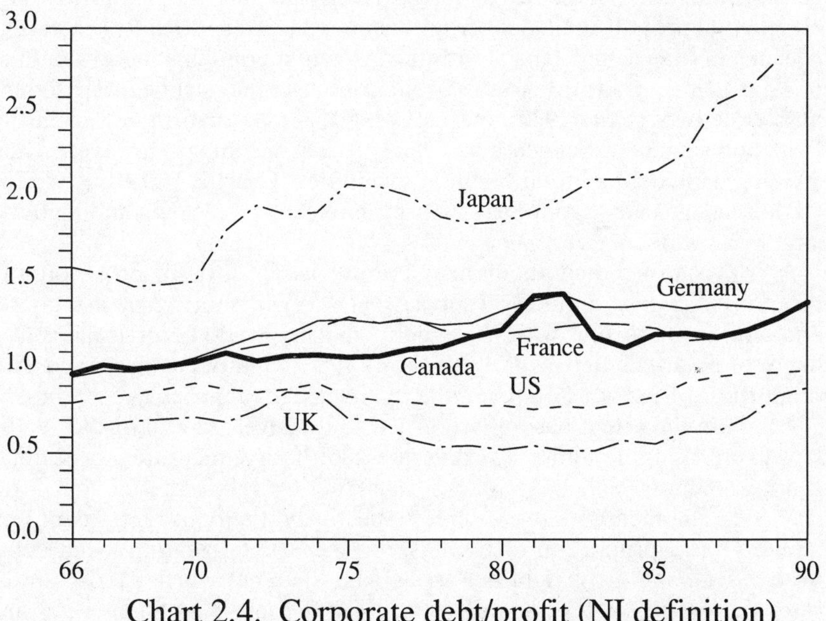

Chart 2.4. Corporate debt/profit (NI definition)

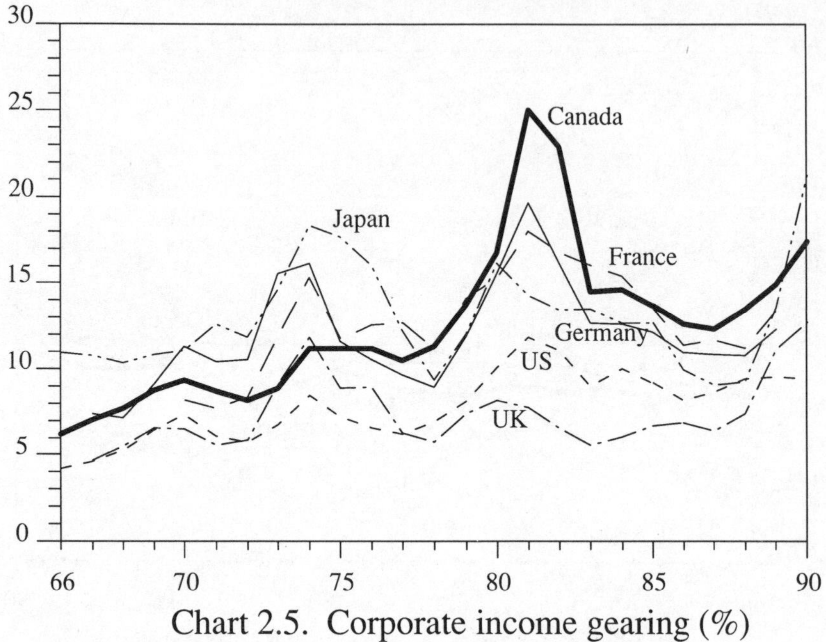

Chart 2.5. Corporate income gearing (%)

Charts 2.6 and 2.7 explore the nature of corporate debt, by respectively showing ratios of bank debt to total debt and total liabilities. As shown in 2.6, companies in Japan,[7] Germany, and France historically obtained almost all their debt from commercial banks—subject to recent declines in France and Japan, with the growth in bond financing—and the UK has made a transition to this group following the decline of UK bond-market activity in the 1970s and early 1980s. Bank-financing ratios in the USA and Canada are much lower, and latterly declining. However, when dividing bank debt by total corporate liabilities (Chart 2.7) the UK rejoins the market-financed group, as UK firms have few bonds outstanding but a large volume of equity.

A criticism of the charts discussed above is that little or no account is taken of company liquidity (deposits and other short-term assets). If liquidity grows in line with gross debt, the implications for fragility are likely to be attenuated. Chart 2.8 shows that liquidity has increased as a proportion of gross assets over the 1980s in all countries except Japan, although in the UK it has only returned to the levels typical of the 1960s. However, using liquidity to generate alternative measures of capital gearing (Charts 2.9–2.11) shows that the overall patterns are little changed. The measures shown are, respectively, net debt (gross debt less liquidity) as a proportion of total assets ('net capital gearing'), net debt/fixed assets, and gross debt/net assets (the 'debt/net worth ratio'). In all cases the rise in US leverage over the 1980s is sharply highlighted, as are

[7] Bank debt for Japan in the chart includes private and public loans.

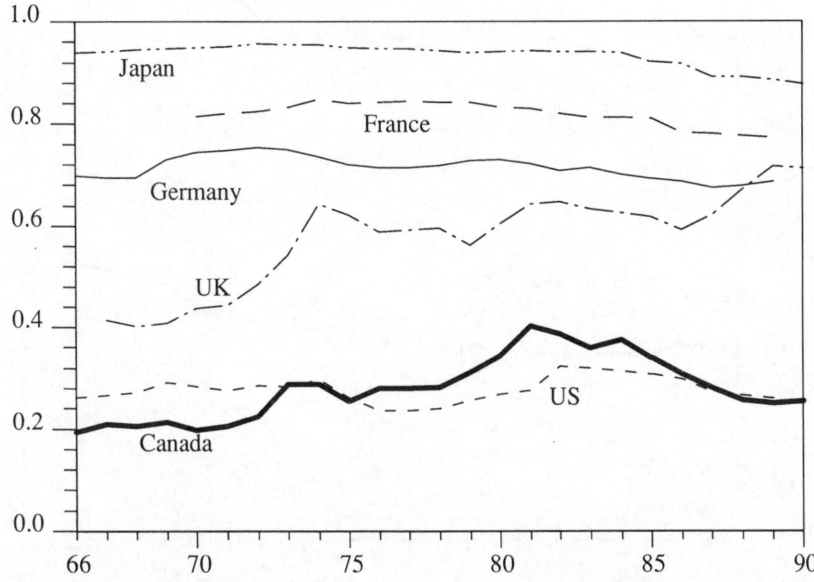

Chart 2.6. Bank lending/corporate debt ratios

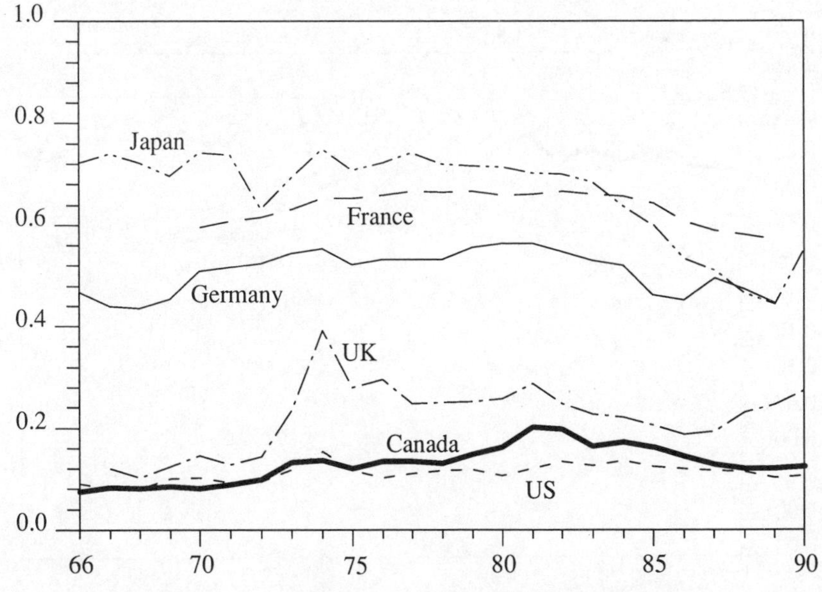

Chart 2.7. Bank lending/corporate liabilities

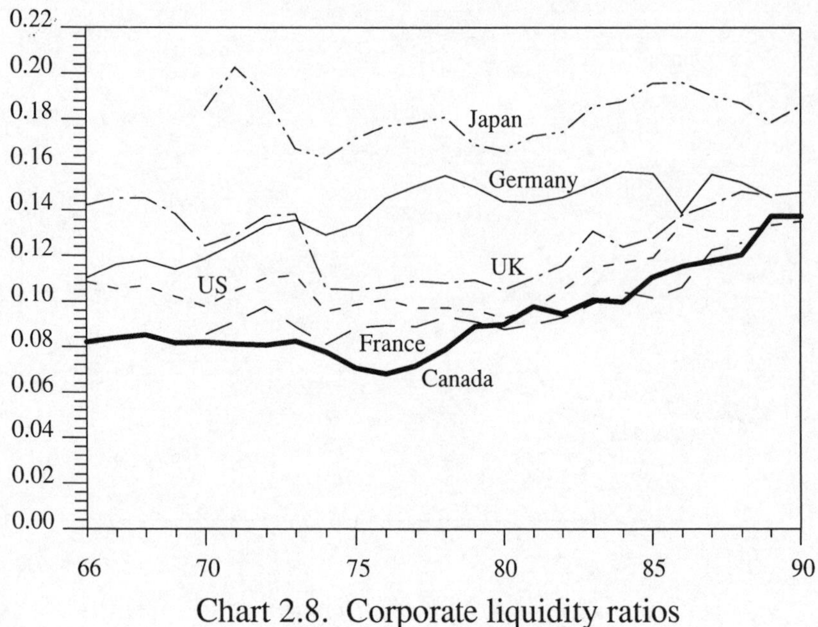

Chart 2.8. Corporate liquidity ratios

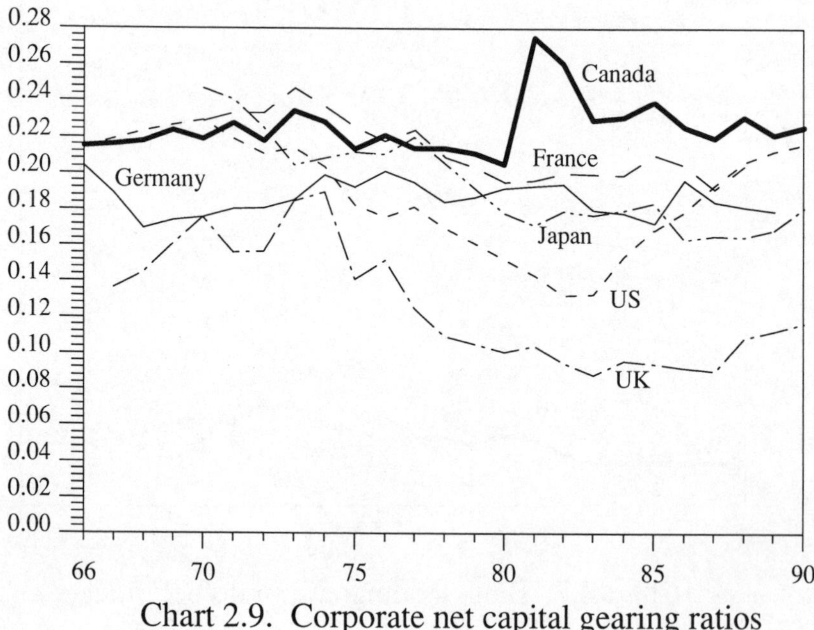

Chart 2.9. Corporate net capital gearing ratios

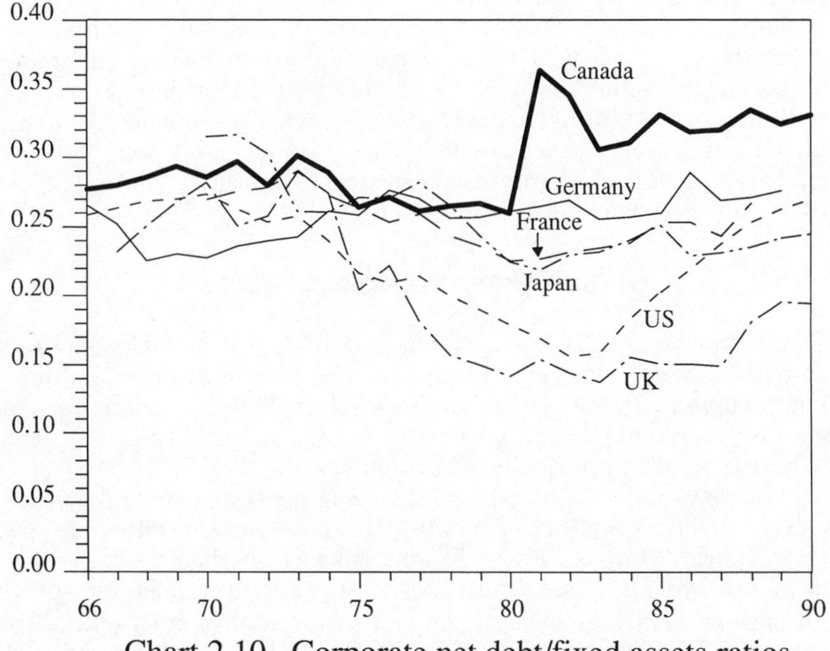

Chart 2.10. Corporate net debt/fixed assets ratios

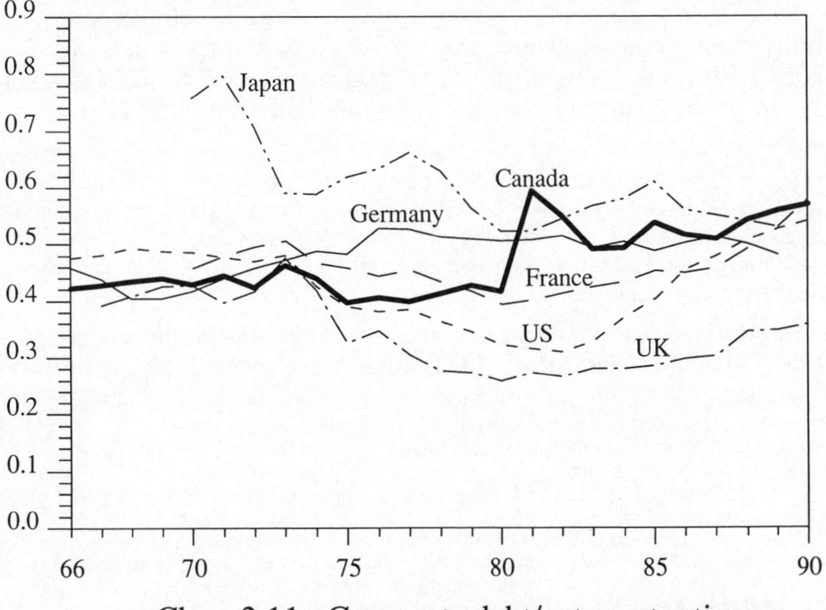

Chart 2.11. Corporate debt/net asset ratios

the steep rises in Canada in the early 1980s, and the smaller rises in the UK and France over the 1980s. Ratios for Germany and Japan remain flat or declining.

Finally, it is important to note that this section focuses on balance sheets and not sources of funds (as the former are thought most relevant to the issue at hand). In fact, as shown by Mayer (1990), in a broad range of countries, very little external finance comes from securities, particularly equities; most external finance is from banks—and retentions dwarf external finance as a whole.[8]

(2) Theories of Corporate Debt

This section examines the traditional and Modigliani–Miller views of corporate finance, together with recent extensions, for insights regarding the relationship between debt and financial fragility. It is concluded that increased corporate debt in relation to equity, assets or cash flow is likely to lead to a greater probability of bankruptcy.

Firms have a choice of external financing methods between debt and equity. Equity is more risky to stockholders because creditors are paid first.[9] Hence equity is costlier, as well as being discriminated against by most tax systems[10] (see Tanzi 1984 and King and Fullerton 1984). Meanwhile, debt may increase the risk to the firm of bankruptcy. The analysis of the nature of debt in Ch. 1 included some discussion of corporate bankruptcy and debt issue, which suggested that rising debt increases financial risks, and hence the cost or availability of finance offered by the market, particularly when adverse conditions arise. The conventional view of these potential adversities, which affect the components of firms' budget constraints, was summarized by Robinson and Wrightsman (1980), who concluded (authors' italics):

> The surest way for a firm to avoid bankruptcy is, of course, to keep its financial house in order. The main lessons learned by the survivors of the 1970s bankruptcy wave are (1) to go easy on debt financing when operating *earnings* are unstable, (2) to go easy on short-term borrowing when operating assets are *illiquid*, and (3) to pay much more attention to expected *cash flow* and *bank balances* than to reported earnings and assets.

A strand of economic theory appears to contradict these assertions. Modigliani and Miller (MM) (1958) proved that under certain rather strict conditions the debt/equity ratio, is *irrelevant* to the cost of capital, and,

[8] Mayer also suggests that flow data tend to be more directly comparable than stocks, especially at the level of individual firms' balance sheets, given inconsistencies in accounting conventions for revaluation of assets.

[9] Also dividends are not fixed (distribution is optional), thus exposing shareholders to agency costs, as outlined in Ch. 1, Sect. 2.

[10] Brealey and Myers (1988) discuss the effects of tax on corporate financial decisions. See also Miller (1977), who emphasised the importance of personal as well as corporate tax in determining the net tax gain from borrowing. Recently, attempts have been made in countries such as the UK and France to increase neutrality.

implicitly, to the lenders' assessment of risk. Irrelevance occurs when financing decisions cannot affect investment/consumption opportunities, and hence perceived pay-offs to claimants on the firm. In order for this to be the case, it is necessary for the firm to be unable to alter the income stream produced, and also to be unable to repackage the stream by changing the nature of claims held against it. The first is ensured by the independence of real decisions, whereby perceptions of investment decisions and the resulting stream of income are given independent of financing. Second, the firm is unable to repackage the stream of income if monopoly power over it is ruled out. This is ensured by the ability of individuals to offset changes introduced by the firm by means of shifts in their own portfolios.

An example clarifies this concept (see Hay and Morris 1979). Suppose there is uncertainty, but two firms have the same mean and variance of return. One is geared (levered), the other is not, and initially the value of equity is the same in each firm; the geared firm has a higher total value (debt plus equity). Then (given the lower legal priority of the claims of shareholders than those of bondholders to the income of the geared firm) there is an incentive for shareholders in the geared firm to increase their income by selling their shares or borrowing at a given interest rate, and buying shares in the ungeared firm. The process depresses share prices in the geared firm and raises them in the ungeared until returns to the shareholders in each firm, net of interest payments, are equal. At this point the valuation of the firms is the same and so, therefore, is the cost of capital (expected profit divided by valuation), which is equal to that of an equity-financed firm of the same risk class. The equity yield of the geared firm is of course higher, reflecting the larger proportion of debt in the capital structure. 'Home-made gearing' thus offers a shareholder the advantages that the geared firm seeks, and the cost of capital is the same for all firms with the same mean and variance of return. Figure 2.1 contrasts this with the traditional view as summarized above; (D/M)* is the 'equilibrium' ratio in the traditional view.

Several comments can be made. First, the analysis concerns firms in the same risk class. MM allow firms in different risk classes to have different costs of capital. Hence, even if the theorem applied, increased debt might raise the cost of capital should the distribution of debt issue shift to riskier firms. However, the main problems with the theorem are that MM's analysis excludes *taxation* and the possibility of costly *bankruptcy*, and assumes *perfect capital markets* and *symmetry of information*, and/or *complete contracts*, between borrowers and lenders.

If costly bankruptcy is admitted, the story changes. Market interest rates will rise with gearing because of the higher risk of default, as the traditional theory suggests. In fact, there is an incentive with costly

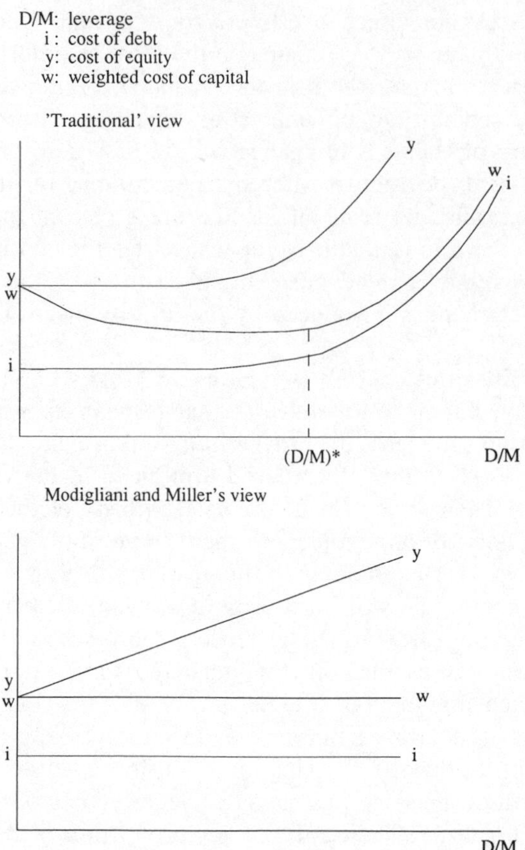

Fig.2.1 Debt/equity ratios and the cost of capital

bankruptcy to issue only equity. (A detailed discussion of bankruptcy costs follows this section.) This is offset by tax deductibility of interest payments, which, as noted above, gives a spur to debt issue, since it means higher leverage entails a reduction in the cost of capital.[11] Gordon and Malkiel (1981) concluded that observed corporate financial structures comprising both debt and equity arise from a balance between these offsetting forces. Gertler and Hubbard (1989) make the further distinction between individual and business–cycle (or unsystematic and systematic) risk[12] and suggest that tax deductibility induces firms to absorb

[11] Although this is partly offset by loss of non-interest tax shields such as depreciation allowances as a result of tax exhaustion.

[12] In terms of the discussion in Ch. 1, Sect. 3, individual risk includes internal and business risk, while business-cycle risks are non-diversifiable risks affecting the aggregate economy.

more of the latter than they otherwise would, thus increasing default risk. This arises from the tax subsidy noted here, as well as the restrictions on indexation of interest payments to the cycle. It also results from costs of renegotiation (see the discussion below), that ensure that debt cannot take on the equity features needed to respond to business-cycle risk.

Further objections to MM relate to imperfections or asymmetries in capital markets. For example, investors may not be able to borrow at the same interest rate as firms, either because their credit rating is lower than firms, owing to differences in perceived default risk, or, as discussed in Ch. 1, because of disequilibrium credit rationing they may not be able to borrow at all. There may be legal limits on the distribution of their portfolios (e.g. life insurers, which in some countries are unable to hold significant amounts of equity).[13] In these cases home-made gearing may not be possible. In addition, transactions costs are likely to prevent fully offsetting financial moves by investors.

Finally, there may be problems arising from asymmetric information between lenders and borrowers (MM assume information acquisition is costless). Only observable actions may be specified in contracts; other unverifiable actions may be undertaken by borrowers to the detriment of the lenders—or at least the lenders may be unable to verify the quality of borrowers. This brings in the basic problems of the debt contract as outlined in Ch. 1: the ability of borrowers to commit themselves credibly to remunerating lenders—and the ability of lenders to screen and monitor borrowers—sets a limit to feasible transfers of funds.

Such phenomena are thought to give rise to a number of features of corporate finance, such as distribution of dividends despite tax disadvantages,[14] dependence of firms on retained earnings for investment, and also preference for debt rather than equity as a source of external finance.[15] However, the key result in the present context is that, given asymmetric and costly information, the choice of project is not independent of finance; a more highly geared firm may choose riskier investments—a problem of 'agency costs', in this case costs arising from the conflict of interest between a firm's owners and creditors (see Jensen and Meckling 1976, Myers 1977, and the example given in Ch. 1, Sect. 2).

In the context of corporate finance, Auerbach (1985) explains this phenomenon succinctly as follows:

> In dynamic models, managers may have the incentive to choose socially inefficient investment plans, because they do not internalize the effects of such plans on the

[13] See Davis (1990*b*; 1991*a*).

[14] According to signalling models (Bhattacharya 1979), dividends tend to reduce asymmetries of information between managers and investors by conveying information about firms' prospects and quality.

[15] The intuition is that equity issues are particularly prone to exploitation of mispricing by well-informed insiders (Myers and Majluf 1984). See the discussion in Ch. 1, Sect. 2.

value of outstanding long-term debt. For example, firms with high levels of outstanding long-term debt can choose to undertake very risky projects that have a high expected return but also increase the probability of bankruptcy. Under limited corporate liability, this transfers resources from debt holders to equity holders, and may do so to a sufficient extent that risky projects with low total pay-offs will dominate (from the equity holders' viewpoint) safer projects. Or they may choose not to make the effort required to avoid bankruptcy, accelerate dividend payments prior to default or issue more senior claims to stave off default. The inefficiency induced by this moral hazard is a social cost that, presumably, must be borne by the firm and its owners ex-ante in the form of higher interest payments to holders of debt.[16] It would clearly be in the stockholders' interest to constrain the firm's behaviour in order to avoid such costs. While mechanisms to achieve this do exist (e.g. bond covenants restricting future borrowing), it would be costly if not impossible to use them to replicate the desired outcome.

The scope for such conflicts is clearly related to the ratio of debt to equity in the capital structure, although (as discussed in Sect. 4 below) the conflict may be reduced in some countries by structural features of corporate/financial relations. In addition, it is important to note that some authors argue that the conflicts of interest are exaggerated—indeed, higher debt may have net benefits because of the incentives it offers to effective management (Sect. 5).

Abstracting from this last point, the suggested modifications of the MM model together imply a U-shaped cost-of-capital curve, increased debt leading to higher risk, which is reflected in the spread of corporate over risk-free debt yields. Of course, with imperfect capital markets the problems of high leverage may go further; indebted firms may face limits on borrowing and have to miss opportunities for profit. This may be the case particularly if highly leveraged firms in Anglo-Saxon financial systems are dependent on banks for funds and lack reputation, in which case equilibrium quantity rationing of credit may apply.

(3) Costs of Bankruptcy

Broadly speaking, default occurs when a borrower does not pay interest or repay principal due to its creditors (or breaks covenants). This may lead to bankruptcy (a court-supervised process of breaking and rewriting contracts), liquidation (sale of firm's assets and distribution to claimants), or private renegotiation of contracts ('workouts'). It may arise because the market is unwilling to advance more credit, i.e. because it feels that the present value of returns on such a loan is negative, and profit is maximised by realizing the assets of the debtor. Default may also occur when shareholders declare themselves unable to pay their debts, even if

[16] This assumes adequate foresight by bondholders.

further credit is available, leaving the creditors to recover such assets as they may (Bulow and Shoven 1979). A key distinction is between default caused by illiquidity (inability to pay debts owing to lack of realisable assets or income) and insolvency (negative net worth, liabilities exceed assets); the former can in principle be resolved short of bankruptcy. Important additional determinants of default—and in turn the level of debt regarded as acceptable by borrowers —are the costs imposed by bankruptcy on owners and providers of finance to the firm, which are specified in bankruptcy law, and which may differ between countries and over time (see KPMG 1988; some details are given in Sect. 6).

The nature and consequences of bankruptcy are important to the concept of financial fragility, because the underlying assumption that widespread default on debt will have adverse economic consequences requires that bankruptcy be costly rather than a smooth and costless shift of ownership. One argument against this is the common observation that a rapid turnover of small businesses is often a feature of a dynamic economy. Some economists, for example Warner (1977), would go further and argue on the basis of empirical evidence that, even for large firms (bankrupt US railroads), the *direct* legal and administrative costs of default are in fact so low as to be trivial; hence even if increased debt leads to bankruptcy, the only effect is distributional, debt claims being effectively changed to equity. Weiss (1990) offers more recent evidence, again showing low direct costs of around 3 per cent of assets.

On the other hand, other economists have suggested that the direct legal and administrative costs of bankruptcy are significant and form a sizeable deadweight loss. This in turn should affect pricing of debt and equity. Gordon and Malkiel (1981) estimated direct corporate bankruptcy costs as a proportion of market value of the firm to be between 2½ and 9 per cent, but felt that these estimates were biased downwards, while Baxter (1967) estimated costs as 20 per cent of assets in the case of households. Altman (1984) again suggested direct corporate bankruptcy costs were high, obtaining a result of 6 per cent of assets just before bankruptcy, as well as five years prior to it, for a sample of large US retailers and industrial companies. A survey by M. J. White (1989) gave a range of 3–21 per cent. It is clear that these costs arise partly from conflicts of interest between claimholders (notably managers, equityholders, and senior and junior debtholders). For example, secured creditors have an incentive to liquidate the firm rapidly at a low price; junior creditors and equity holders wish to delay in order to obtain a higher price, to maximize the value of their claim. Managers wish to continue in operation, with their own position maintained.

Informal workouts, which require such conflicts either not to exist or to be resolved, may be cheaper; Wruck (1990) suggested direct costs are ten times less in the case of private restructuring of debt (see also Gilson *et al.* 1990). As noted in Sect. 4 below, workouts are more common in CEJ countries; and when bankruptcy *is* declared, auctions are often used in Germany to resolve conflicts over the valuation of assets of bankrupt firms (Easterbrook (1990), however, suggests the costs of such auctions may exceed those of judicial valuations). Again, consistent with the importance of conflicts of interest, Asquith *et al.* (1991) suggest that restructuring is easier when companies have simple debt structures (e.g. bank debt only), which is more common in CEJ (and the UK) than the USA.

It can also be argued that an approach focusing purely on direct costs ignores certain other costs, which arise for the lender and firm in question. In other words there are significant *indirect costs*, even abstracting from general macroeconomic effects of financial fragility. In particular, imminent bankruptcy may change the firm's stream of cash flow, owing to various factors, such as inability to obtain trade credit; inability to retain key employees; declining faith among customers in the product, owing to uncertainty over future availability of servicing or spare parts; diversion of management's energies, resulting in lost sales and profits; increases in costs of debt finance owing to default risk, which may foreclose investment opportunities—and even if finance is available, firms may be unwilling to invest if benefits accrue to bondholders (a form of agency cost). Altman (1984) estimated such costs to be an extra 6 per cent three years before bankruptcy, and 10 per cent at bankruptcy.[17] In contrast, Wruck (1990), while acknowledging the existence of such costs, suggested there may also be benefits, particularly as imminent bankruptcy ('financial distress') gives creditors the right to demand restructuring because their contract with the firm has been breached. She suggests high leverage is advantageous, when financial distress is caused by poor management,[18] in ensuring that restructuring occurs at an early stage in the deterioration in the firm's performance.

Wider costs of bankruptcy may include distributional shifts, which may be socially undesirable and involve costs of portfolio readjustment; there may also be social costs from breaking up unique bundles of assets, where synergies mean they are more productive together than apart; workers and managers who have skills specific to the firm in question may find it hard to obtain alternative employment if bankruptcy entails closure; managers and directors, even with general skills, may suffer 'loss of reputation' (Gilson 1990; Kaplan and Reishus 1990); debt issuers which default may face difficulties in issuing debt later (again due to 'loss of

[17] However, Hoshi *et al.* (1990) point out that Altman's indirect costs may be hard to distinguish from the more general consequences of poor performance of the firm, which would arise even if bankruptcy costs were negligible.

[18] She acknowledges that the case for leverage does not apply if financial distress is due to exogenous shocks, such as recessions, changes in regulations, or falls in commodity prices.

reputation'); banks may face problems of illiquidity or declining valuation in disposing of collateral; and when creditors are dispersed, they may foreclose on firms that are illiquid and not insolvent, instead of renegotiating the debt contract, owing to free rider problems.

Moreover, especially when default is widespread and involves households and large businesses as well as small businesses, all of these analyses may be guilty of taking a partial view (of an agent or firm in isolation), because there may be significant *externalities* to widespread loan default. The failure of a company is likely to impact on other companies and could cast their solvency into doubt, for example if it defaults on loans due, or if it is costly for firms to switch suppliers or markets. Unemployed workers may default on their own debts. For a discussion of public policy and capital structure in the context of such spillovers see Bernanke and Gertler (1990). The wider economic implications of financial fragility are discussed in more detail in Ch. 4.

Such fragility may link in turn to systemic risk. If defaults in the non-financial sector affect banks, perhaps because risk premiums were too low to allow for the actual level of default, these effects may include declining confidence in the financial system, bank failures, and in extreme cases a disruption of credit intermediation and significant macroeconomic effects on aggregate consumption and investment (see Bernanke (1983) for an analysis of the 1930s depression based on similar arguments). Such externalities may amplify themselves, because in a world of imperfect information the failure of one institution in the financial sector may raise doubts about the liquidity and solvency of others[19]—the so-called problem of contagion. This is the main subject of Chs. 5–8. Even if instability does not result, the need for provisioning and heightened caution on the part of banks may restrain credit and hence economic growth (Ch. 4).

Suffice to add at this point that the relationship between individual default and wider economic instability is unlikely to be linear. Rather, there is likely to be a threshold level of defaults, beyond which fragility or instability increase sharply. The height of the threshold will depend on risk premiums on debt and indebtedness of other non-financial agents, as well as such factors as capital ratios of financial institutions, and the extent to which their sources of income are diversified. The degree to which these externalities arise for individual financial institutions is likely to depend also on the relative size of the lenders and borrowers and the precise nature of the debt contract.

[19] The interdependence of agents may be greater in the case of some financial innovations which, for example, 'unbundle' risk (see Bank for International Settlements 1986*a*: 204).

(4) Explaining Relative Levels of Corporate Indebtedness

It was shown in Sect. 1 that there are marked differences between average levels of gearing in the Anglo-Saxon countries (the USA, the UK, and Canada) and Continental Europe and Japan (CEJ). In the present context, it is suggested that such differences in *levels* should be distinguished from *changes* in levels that have occurred in recent years, and which are analysed in the following section. The hypothesis is that relative levels of gearing are structural phenomena that are consistent with low levels of financial fragility; fragility tends to occur when the structural patterns shift or break down.[20] But it is necessary to assess structural patterns in order to evaluate departures.

As assessment of causes of relative levels of gearing is provided in Borio (1990a), who considers four aspects: tax, institutional features, asymmetric information, and government policy.

In terms of *tax*, equilibrium leverage may differ between countries, if the after-tax income stream received by investors differs on the basis of the form of distribution (capital gains, dividends, or interest payments). However, an analysis in the light of Alworth (1988) suggests that in all countries there is the same ranking in terms of sources of funding, namely that borrowing is superior to equity, while retained earnings are superior to new issues. Germany is the exception, as financial investors should on the face of it be indifferent between borrowing and new issues, with retentions less favoured. It is hence suggested that tax provisions were unable to explain differences in gearing.

A second suggestion is that institutional *impediments to equity issue* may explain intercountry differences in leverage. Marked contrasts are apparent in terms of market capitalization, turnover of equity, and number of listed companies (relative to the size of the country). Possible impediments in CEJ include the relatively small size of institutional investor sectors (see Davis 1991*b*, 1992*c*); higher issuing costs (given absence of competition in underwriting); the dominant position of the banks, which may discourage equity issue to bolster their own positions; and weaker disclosure standards and insider trading rules which reduce investor confidence. But on the other hand, the data suggest that, even in the Anglo-Saxon countries, the proportion of investment financed by new equity issues has been small (Mayer 1990).[21] And firms may be dissuaded from listing by dislike of information disclosure and fear of loss of control rather than low liquidity of markets and high flotation costs.

[20] In terms of Goldsmith's ratios (Ch. 1, Appendix) we are distinguishing levels and changes in the financial interrelations ratio, assuming constant levels of equity.

[21] Indeed, in the US, the scale of buybacks in the 1980s often made the ratio negative.

Asymmetric information issues, following the analysis of Ch. 1, Sect. 5, were felt to be the most promising factor for explaining differences in gearing. First, limited reliance on securities relative to loans may give rise to a greater concentration of debt. Supporting this hypothesis, banks themselves are permitted to have larger exposures to individual firms in CEJ. It is suggested that such concentration favours high leverage, as it minimises free riding (benefiting from resolution of a crisis without incurring part of the cost). In terms of the analysis in Ch. 1, Sect. 4, it tends to favour commitment between firm and bank, and hence long-term relationships. Such relationships are bolstered by equity holdings of banks (and, as in Germany, exercise of voting rights on behalf of custodial holdings). Such holdings help form the basis of close control of companies by banks, e.g. representatives on boards, or at least close involvement in management. All of these factors tend to improve information and reduce asymmetries. In turn, this tends to make equilibrium quantity rationing of credit less likely (Cable 1985). They also reduce the scope for conflict of interest between equity and debtholders outlined above, particularly during times of financial difficulty, when relationship banks will often play a leading role in organizing corporate rescues. Parallel corporate cross-holding of equity and heavy use of trade credit induce similar risk-sharing between corporates, reinforcing and supporting that between corporates and banks. Note that small firms may not always benefit from these various links and hence are more subject to distress (Hoshi *et al.* 1989). Moreover, even if the firm is rescued, existing management may not always be.

A final factor is *government policy*. In several of the CEJ countries, the public sector owns a proportion of the financial sector, and the institutions concerned have historically been used to channel medium- or long-term lending to companies, with various forms of subsidy (such as low-interest or government guarantees). Second, the governments have often taken parts of the corporate sector into public ownership, facilitating write-off of losses and implicitly protecting banks. Third, there have been policies discouraging use of securitized debt, which the 'commitment' analysis suggests may have increased debt capacity by restricting firms to bank finance. Examples include restrictions on financing in international markets or discriminatory taxation, motivated by aims such as restricting capital flows for balance of payments reasons or reserving the bond market for government debt issues.[22]

Fourth, in developing *bankruptcy law*, legislators and courts in countries such as Japan and Germany have ensured that informal

[22] e.g. Hoshi *et al.* (1989) note that in Japan prior to deregulation, corporate bonds had to be secured while bank loans did not; permission, which was rarely forthcoming, had to be sought to issue foreign currency bonds (that could be unsecured); and there were interest-rate ceilings on corporate debt that made bonds uncompetitive (banks could compensate by requiring borrowers to hold low-interest balances with them).

workouts are more common than formal bankruptcy proceedings,[23] with banks often given a lead role; in contrast, in the UK and USA, close relationships are discouraged by provisions that seek to ensure equity between creditors of failing firms and prevent banks becoming involved in management. Banks involving themselves too closely with firms may have the seniority of their claims reduced by bankruptcy courts (Frankel and Montgomery 1991). Such rules can be seen conceptually as limiting risk-sharing between banks and firms. Finally, and more generally, macro-economic policy that has achieved price stability and hence avoided marked economic instability—as in Germany—may encourage borrowers and lenders to engage in long-term debt contracts, even if they entail high leverage.

(5) Explaining Divergences from Structural Patterns of Gearing

The charts shown in Sect. 1, as well as illustrating the main contrasts in gearing, show a number of deviations from historical levels. The best-known is the rise in corporate leverage in the USA during the 1980s,[24] however, the charts also show a marked growth in the debt of UK firms in the mid–late 1980s;[25] similar growth in debt for Canada in the late 1970s and early 1980s, in France in the late 1980s, and most recently in Japan on certain measures. (Similar patterns occurred in countries such as Australia[26] and New Zealand.) These trends have been most apparent in capital gearing, income gearing, and debt/profits; the debt/equity ratio has been flat or declining for much of these episodes, suggesting the equity market has valued the assets more highly than book or replacement costs would suggest.[27]

In this section, we discuss causes of heightened leverage, including cyclical patterns, takeover waves, property lending, balance-sheet management of non-financial firms, and loans to small business. We then probe the reasons why there has been an increased availability of credit for such purposes.

[23] e.g. in Germany bankruptcy proceedings are to some extent reserved for cases where workouts prove impossible, there is evidence of a fraudulent act by the main bank, or of desire to harm interests of other creditors in the firm. In Japan, formal bankruptcy is seen as a punitive 'last resort' when informal restructuring fails; it involves severe sanctions on managers and owners, such as revocation of professional licences, prohibition from serving as a director in future, and assignment of personal responsibility for certain debts.

[24] See e.g. Crabbe *et al.* (1990). Commentators are not unanimous in seeing this as historically atypical, some point out that at least up to the mid-1980s, US gearing was comparable to the 1960s (cf. Chart 2.2)

[25] See Wilson 1991.

[26] McFarlane 1990; Reserve Bank of Australia 1991.

[27] The rise in the financial interrelations ratio (Ch. 1, Appendix) illustrates the same phenomenon.

During recent *cyclical* upturns, notably in the Anglo-Saxon countries, investment-financing needs have outstripped available retentions, thus leading to an increase in external financing requirements, entailing rising debt. Loose monetary policy and inflation often made the real cost of such borrowing relatively low. Increased reliance on credit by firms led to a deterioration in balance-sheet strength, with higher capital gearing, as well as shorter maturity of debt and declining liquidity. When, at the cyclical peak, profits began to fall also, companies were left with a backlog of committed investment, which further increased demand for credit. Such a pattern would be reversed by the normal adjustments of expenditure (on capital and labour) that occur in a recession, as well as by increased credit rationing in terms of prices (higher risk premiums) and quantities, although occasionally also by direct closure of credit markets arising from financial instability, as discussed in Chs. 5–8.

As an example of such cyclical patterns, evidence for Canada (Tetlow 1986) suggests that there was a sharp rise in external financing leading to the cyclical peak in 1981, which was due mainly to rising expenditures on fixed capital, notably in the mining and extraction sector. In addition, the National Energy Programme encouraged takeovers of foreign-owned oil and gas companies, and deductability of nominal interest payments cushioned the rise in rates which followed inflation. But eventually high real and nominal interest rates eroded profitability, leading first to a sharp rise in external financing, and then to a collapse along with investment as the recession began and profits declined further. Defaults rose sharply (Chart 2.12). Reflecting balance-sheet weakness of firms and households, recovery from the recession was sluggish.

Takeover waves can have both cyclical and secular influences on debt. As detailed in King (1988), such waves have tended to occur at irregular intervals longer than the cycle. They often take a particular form (conglomerates, breakups) and may be triggered by policy shifts, e.g. in antitrust policy or tax provisions (Schleifer and Vishny 1991). Availability of finance is obviously also crucial, as discussed below. While there may be other explanations for mergers, such as desire to transfer corporate control to new management or to transfer wealth from existing bondholders or workers to shareholders, it is less clear that these vary in a cyclical manner.

As noted, hostile takeovers tend to be features of Anglo-Saxon countries—the main focus here is on recent experience in the USA and UK—although recently they have spread to countries such as France, and EC guide-lines may spread them more generally in Continental Europe (Smith and Walter 1990; Mayer and Franks 1991). Such takeovers may of course be financed by equity issues or internal funds as well as debt; whereas the wave of the 1960s and early 1970s tended to be financed by equity, more recently debt has predominated.

The secular element in indebtedness arising from takeovers may come from changes in financial markets that facilitate provision of debt for such purposes.[28] In particular, the USA has seen financial innovations such as development of the junk-bond market, as well as the various innovations directly associated with leveraged takeovers and buyouts (LBOs), such as bridge loans (high-risk short-term loans to cover periods while financing is arranged) and strip financing (combinations of equity and debt, discussed below). Interest-rate risk can be reduced through the use of innovations such as swaps and interest-rate caps, as well as by hedging with futures and options (see Bank for International Settlements 1986*a*).

Some of these financing techniques have spread to other countries such as the UK and France, where leveraged takeovers and buyouts, often financed in the euromarkets,[29] have also played a major part in growth of corporate debt. However, the principal innovative means of finance has tended to be short-term, high-risk (mezzanine) debt provided by banks and not bond issuance.

Further insights from agency theory are an important intellectual background to use of debt in this context (see Jensen 1988). Besides the shareholder–creditor conflict outlined in Sect. 2 and Ch. 1, the divorce of ownership (shareholders) from control (managers) in the modern corporation may also give rise to agency costs, given the latter have firm-specific human capital, and are typically unable to diversify sources of income to reduce risk. In addition, the incentives of managers to maximize firm value are limited by their (small) share of equity and the lack of correlation between their income and profits. In particular, they may waste cash flow in excess of that required to fund profitable investment (what Jensen (1986) calls 'free cash flow'), rather than distributing it to shareholders in the form of dividends. Such problems may have worsened in the 1980s with the increasing number of maturing industries and conglomerates, as well as the rise in real interest rates that reduced the scope for profitable fixed investment (Blair and Litan 1990).

In Anglo-Saxon countries, the takeover sanction generally is an important means to avoid agency costs, as it forces managers to act in shareholders' interests. But takeovers financed by debt may be particularly effective, in that replacement of equity by debt forces distribution of free cash flow[30] and requires managers to concentrate on generating sufficient cash flow to service the debt.[31] Also, managers may

[28] Gertler and Hubbard (1989) note that these amount also to means of using more efficiently the tax incentive to debt finance.

[29] See Allen 1990.

[30] The tax subsidy to debt ensures the dominance of this approach over theoretical alternatives such as fixed dividend equity.

[31] However, it can be argued that in the UK, similar incentives have been established without leverage via institutional pressure to maintain or increase dividends, even in straitened circumstances.

have better incentives if they hold much of the equity—as their reward is closely tied to performance—and high leverage may entail closer monitoring by creditors. Such results can ensue independent of takeovers if firms gear up and/or buy back equity as part of a management buy-out (MBO), or merely to avoid the threat of takeover (in the USA this often occurred via share repurchases). Note that in each of these cases capital gearing and income gearing rises—debt is incurred to restructure the balance sheet, not to purchase productive assets which generate earnings.

Of course, such an increase in debt entails rising agency costs, in terms of potential conflict of interest between debt and equity holders, especially in the case of default. But proponents suggest these can be minimized by strip financing (whereby creditors hold a combination of equity, junior, and senior debt); by the ability of dominant underwriters in junk bonds to facilitate costless renegotiation[32] of terms rather than costly bankruptcy; by the incentives for investors to seek reorganization, given their potential losses in the case of liquidation; as well as the choice of firms that are in profitable mature industries, where cash flow is sizeable and risk of default is low.

However, although evidence suggests US takeovers and LBOs were initially concentrated in mature, non-cyclical firms, later the practice spread to inappropriate cyclical industries (Ryding 1990*b*). This has also been the case in the UK, where cyclical industries such as furniture retailing were subjected to buyouts. And although strips do help to reduce agency costs, dispersed holdings via securities markets or large syndicates of banks suggest sizeable agency costs are likely to remain—as difficulties of resolution of some cases have shown. Moreover, they do not compensate existing bondholders for losses made owing to downgrading of credit quality as leverage was increased.[33] As outlined above, in the CEJ countries, close monitoring by banks and the concentration in banks of external finance (both debt and equity) are felt to minimize agency costs; this enables them to limit hostile takeovers and renders takeovers otiose as a control mechanism.

A separate source of growing corporate debt, notably in the USA, UK, and Japan (but also in countries such as Sweden, Norway, and Australia (Ch. 8)), has been *property and construction lending*. For UK banks, such loans grew from 7 to 12 per cent of the balance sheet between 1986 and 1990. Similar patterns were evident in the USA and Japan. There are some parallels with takeovers: such lending tends to be risky, given the volatility of demand for property and hence construction relative to the

[32] Warschawsky (1991) notes that the suggestion that strip and junk-bond financing makes renegotiations costless is inconsistent with the original free cash-flow/efficiency argument, which assumes costs of default, as a means of changing existing managers, are high.

[33] Losses due to such 'event risk' may have been as much as $14 bn in the USA over 1984–8 (Crabbe *et al.* 1990).

cycle, the frequently long lead times before cash flow becomes positive, and the fact property begun at a time of shortage may only be ready at a time of surplus; it often entails large exposures; and property booms tend to occur at fairly long intervals similar to takeover waves. Fiscal changes (e.g. in the USA and Australia) may help stimulate property booms. Moreover, to the extent that property values are distorted by overshooting in asset markets, there may be particular risks for loans secured on such collateral. Realization of such collateral may be needed if declines in rental income—earmarked to repay interest—accompany falling capital values, if the building is never occupied due to a fall in demand for space, or if the constructors go bankrupt while the building is incomplete. Given uncertainty over the duration and amplitude of the property cycle, pricing of the lending risk is extremely difficult.

Fourth, there has been a form of *balance-sheet management* by companies, notably in the UK in the mid-1980s and in France later in the decade, where both debt and liquid assets were built up simultaneously. It seems clear that companies have sought to boost both their financial assets and liabilities because greater competition in the financial sector reduced the spread between borrowing and lending rates, thus reducing the cost of the operational flexibility provided by such behaviour. In France a form of fiscal arbitrage also played a part. Such balance-sheet management clearly does not have major implications for financial fragility, as long as the maturity and liquidity of assets and liabilities are similar. On the other hand, if funds are used for speculation, spectacular losses can ensue (this was the case for certain firms in Japan involved in such 'Zaitech' in the mid-1980s).

Finally, there has been an increase in credits to *small companies*. Competition between banks for high-risk, high-yield business has been a factor underlying this. But also, following the logic of Ch. 1, Sect. 4, such business may be one of the few areas where banks retain a comparative advantage over securities markets, given that securitization of small-business loans has not proved viable.

These analyses, however, leave open the reason why an increased *supply* of debt has been forthcoming, notably for takeovers and property lending. In the *banking* sector, banks in a number of countries—but not Germany—had lost much of their highly rated corporate business, as they could not offer funds to such borrowers as cheaply as highly rated companies could raise it themselves (via bonds or commercial paper). This can be attributed partly to the ldc debt crisis, both for its direct effects on banks' credit ratings, and on the need to widen spreads to generate reserves to cover losses. In addition, however, a number of factors weakened banks' low-cost deposit bases. These included deregulation of deposit rates in countries such as the USA and, currently, Japan; also in some countries there was disintermediation by non-bank financial institutions,[34] offering liquid saving or payments services at attractive interest rates.

On the asset side, there has also been increased competition from securities markets themselves, given technological advances and institu tionalization. Particularly in the cases of France and Japan, the deregulation of corporate access to bond markets was also important (Melitz 1990; Hoshi *et al.* 1989).[35] For example, in Japan, bank borrowing was 84 per cent of external corporate financing in 1971–5 and 57 per cent in 1981–5. The issue of international dollar bonds with equity warrants attached enabled Japanese firms to raise debt at yen interest rates, after a swap, of around zero. It remains unclear whether these trends entail a breakdown of Japanese relationship banking. In all countries, technical advance often made it viable for large firms to undertake many 'banking' functions themselves. Finally, as noted in the analysis of securitization (Ch. 1, Sect. 4), particularly in the Anglo-Saxon countries, banks, under pressure from low profitability and high and volatile interest rates, often undertook policies such as cutting credit lines and increasing prepayment penalties, which reduced the value of banking relationships to companies.

These factors led to a willingness on the part of banks to finance riskier activities such as leveraged takeovers in order to maintain balance-sheet growth and profitability (Borio 1990*b*). Entry of foreign banks such as the Japanese to the USA and UK markets heightened competition for such financings, as did intense competition in the euromarkets. In addition to relatively wide spreads on leveraged transactions, banks were also attracted by fees gained on LBO transactions from provision of investment banking services.[36]

Institutional investors, notably in the USA, proved willing to hold high-yield bonds to improve performance, given intense competition for underlying products (such as life-insurance contracts). Additional factors stimulating demand by institutions were that investment bankers prom ised to make markets, thus offering confidence that liquidity would be maintained, and investors counted on ability to diversify so as to minimize risk[37] (especially life insurers who are forced to hold large

[34] In the USA, the key sector in this regard was the money-market mutual funds, in the UK, building societies, and in France, 'SICAVs monetaires' (which though often owned by banks, did raise the cost of funds by investing in wholesale instruments). However, the shift to long-run institutional saving may also have reduced demand for deposits in some countries, such as Switzerland (Hepp 1991).

[35] Although French firms reportedly reverted to bank loans after 1987.

[36] This can be seen as part of a more general shift by banks away from traditional banking, which with the focus on such corporate finance activities has entailed increased trading/market making, distribution of securities and other financial services (Stigum 1990). All of these functions economise on bank capital—which is at a premium, given the impact of the debt crisis and the other developments outlined above.

[37] They may have miscalculated the extent of systematic (non-diversifiable) as opposed to unsystematic risk.

proportions of bonds). The development of money-market mutual funds in countries such as the USA provided a ready market for short-term securitized debt such as commercial paper. Securitization of loans more generally enabled finer spreads to be offered on loans—and possibly entailed weaker monitoring. Holders perhaps believed that they could sell before a decrease in credit quality was perceived by the market. Credit enhancement techniques provided with securitization such as credit guarantees and insurance may blur credit risk. Meanwhile securities, being more widely held than loans, increase the difficulty of renegotiating debt in case of financial difficulty.

Institutions such as pension funds also contributed indirectly to the rise in leverage via their willingness to take profits from takeovers, rather than maintaining 'relationships', under pressure from increased monitoring of performance by trustees (Davis 1988*a*). Their indirect effects on the banks were also important, as noted above.

Certain *US savings and loan* associations in the 1980s proved willing holders of junk bonds, with losses often ensuing (see the description in Ch. 6). And the development of junk bonds themselves was stimulated by competition between *investment banks*, where profits on existing products were typically at a low level. In this context, the junk bond can be seen as an attempt to innovate by certain investment banks and thus gain excess profitability. This would result initially by means of a monopoly on the product, and later by means of reputation in the market (see Davis (1988*b*) and the appendix to Ch. 7).

More general factors underlying the willingness of financial markets to extend credit may include increased 'socialization of risk'—if it was felt that monetary policy would seek to prevent a recession and/or save financial firms in difficulty, lenders would be readier to provide funds, and borrowers to accept them (Friedman 1990). A number of commentators have also suggested that the prolonged expansion in the 1980s led to an underestimate by lenders of default risk on junk bonds and bank lending, as well as overconfidence by borrowers in their ability to repay (mispricing by lenders, at least ex-ante, is not essential to the development of fragility, however). Debt claims may also have been mispriced if lenders failed to understand the implications of legal changes, such as the US Bankruptcy Act, which includes provisions for 'subordination adjustment' whereby senior creditors forego some of their claim to make reorganization plans acceptable to junior creditors; or unsecured creditors may be denied priority over equity holders (Webb 1989; Weiss 1990). Fourth, belief in the efficacy of leverage as a means of increasing profitability (as outlined above) might give lenders confidence that debt burdens would be rapidly reduced. Asset sales would also be important in this context. However, even if this were true, there may be a 'time inconsistency' problem if illiquidity problems arise before efficiency gains are realized (see Bernanke and Campbell 1990). Finally, companies (but presumably not their creditors) may have been willing to incur debt in anticipation of inflation, rising asset prices, and low real rates, as occurred in the 1970s (see Chart 6.6). Easing of monetary policy in the wake of the 1987 crash may have reinforced these expectations.

Interpreting these shifts in terms of the paradigms of credit rationing (Ch. 1), it is suggested that most companies above a certain size historically tended not to be subject to disequilibrium quantity rationing, even during periods of credit control. (The largest companies could in any case access bond and euromarkets.) Credit controls have tended instead to impinge on the household sector (historically the residual recipient of credit), as discussed in the following chapter. This asymmetry is clear from the way household debt increased immediately once liberalization occurred, while growth in corporate debt has been less strongly correlated with liberalization. What has been observed is rather a shift in the degree of equilibrium quantity rationing, and in the strength of price rationing. As evidence of the former, one could cite the development of markets such as junk bonds and commercial paper (equilibrium quantity rationing can only apply to borrowers who have no alternative to banks), also the willingness of banks to finance high-risk transactions and provide larger amounts of credit for small firms. Evidence of the latter includes the declining spreads on syndicated credits to large companies (see Chart 6.3).

In terms of the theory of intermediation, the pattern implies an intensification of the prior tendency of Anglo-Saxon financial systems to 'control' and not 'commitment'—and a marked shift in the same direction for France and even Japan.[38] The linkage of 'control' to rising indebtedness suggests it may have a strong link to financial fragility, especially given that the logic of 'control', in excluding long-run relationships, is for firms to be cut off from credit or liquidated rather than rescued in adverse conditions, the lenders having protected themselves via provisions of the debt contract. Note also that, in line with 'control' theories, the shift towards bond finance or syndicated bank credit that this has entailed for large firms increases the co-ordination difficulties likely to be encountered by lenders when a firm needs financial reorganization or restructuring (even if this is desired by the lenders), and may make liquidation a more likely outcome of financial difficulties.

This analysis suggests that the debt buildup by companies was not associated with financial liberalization in the same direct way as for persons (discussed in Ch. 3). Nevertheless, heightened competition arising from such liberalization may have been a key contributory factor to some of the forces described above, while the opening of new markets

[38] See the discussion of Hoshi *et al.* (1990) in Ch. 1, Sect. 5.

and removal of controls on foreign entry have also been spurs to increased corporate debt in some countries.

(6) Company Sector Debt and Default

Given the conclusion that a link exists in theory between debt and default (Sect. 2), the acid test of whether patterns of indebtedness discussed in Sects. 4 and 5 have in fact led to financial fragility is default experience over the cycle and in the longer term. However, the debt–default relation cannot be studied in isolation but in the context of other factors that may lead to default (arising from illiquidity or insolvency) and changes to costs of default.

The patterns to be explained are shown in Charts 2.12 and 2.13, which show business failure rates (failures as a proportion of active companies). Comprehensive data for total liabilities of failed firms, which would indicate whether failure rates are for firms of comparable size, are not available. However, data for the US, Germany, and Japan for 1985 suggest that, for these countries at least, there is broad comparability (the average Japanese failure had liabilities of \$1.0 mn, US \$0.7 mn, German \$0.8 mn).

Chart 2.12 shows that in the Anglo-Saxon countries there is a marked contrast between the earlier and later parts of the 1966–90 sample. Default rates were relatively stable over 1966–78, despite experience of the worst recession since the war in 1974–5. The UK was clearly worst affected. Since 1978 there has been a significant rise in the average level of failures, and although some declines were apparent after 1985, it did not fall back to earlier levels after the recession of the early 1980s.[39] The hypothesis to be tested is that rising debt underlies these patterns. It should be noted, however, that certain changes to the bankruptcy law may also have impinged. The US Bankruptcy Code of 1978 may have reduced costs of bankruptcy via a more favourable treatment of debtors (Webb 1989)—though an offset should be an increased cost of debt. Changes have also occurred in the UK (1986) and Canada. The birth rate of new firms may also influence bankruptcy rates (new firms are most likely to fail).[40] These additional hypotheses are also tested below.[41]

Chart 2.13 shows outturns for Japan, Germany, and France. There is a marked contrast between Japan, where failures are flat or declining over

[39] Partly this is a consequence of regional economic problems such as those in farming and oil production in the USA, which are difficult to capture in an aggregate analysis.

[40] However, Friedman (1990) notes that, in the USA, the rate of new business formation was low in the 1980s.

[41] Note that if bankruptcy law is unchanged, its influence should be captured in the constant of the equation.

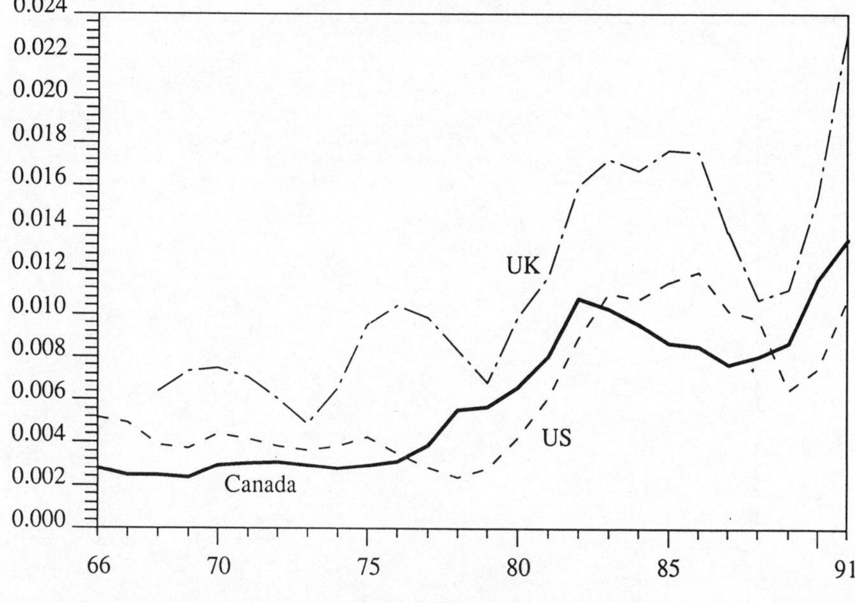

Chart 2.12. Business failure rates

the entire period, Germany, which shows a slight uptrend, and France, which has shown a clear long-term rise in failures, similar to the Anglo-Saxon countries[42] and consistent with a partial breakdown of traditional corporate/financial links, as noted above. In contrast, changes in failures in Germany and Japan appear mainly cyclical, with marked peaks in the mid-1970s and (in Germany) the early 1980s.

Note that failure rates are likely to differ between countries according to bankruptcy law,[43] the definition of failure, and of the corporate sector, and hence caution is needed in making direct comparisons of levels. To illustrate the types of differences involved, there follows a brief comparison of bankruptcy law.

An international comparison does reveal major differences in insolvency procedures, which in turn may affect their usage, incidence, and cost. Note, however, that these differences should not influence the *trends* and determinants of failure, which are the main focus in the current analysis, and even differences in the level of failure rates are not particularly marked. There is usually a menu of alternative procedures, ranging from outright liquidation, through 'stays of execution' to enable prospects for survival to be explored, to informal reorganizations. Key differences include the fact that the *priority of secured creditors* over

[42] See Bordes and Melitz (1989) for an empirical investigation of business failures in France.

[43] See KPMG (1988).

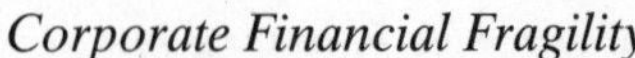

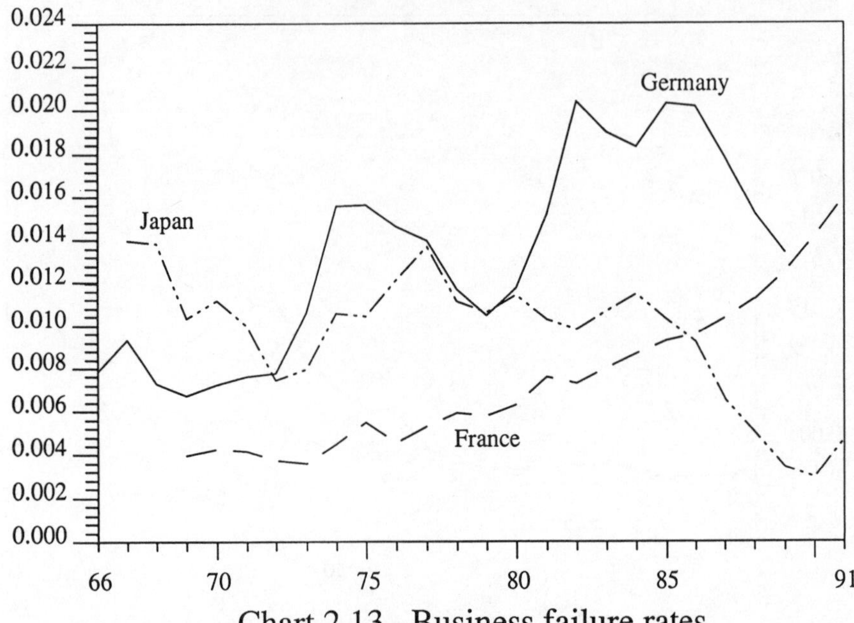

Chart 2.13. Business failure rates

unsecured can in some cases be reduced in the USA and Japan, but not in the UK and Germany. The Crown may have priority in Canada over secured creditors, and employees in France. *Managers and directors* may in some circumstances temporarily continue to operate the company in the USA and France, once insolvency procedures have begun. This appears to be ruled out in most cases in Japan and Germany. In Canada it requires creditors' approval. *Continuation of the business* occurs in Germany only if it improves the situation for creditors, whereas in France priority is also given to continuation of employment. *Auctions* of bankrupt businesses, to realize the best market value, may occur in Germany and as a last resort in France, but are not a feature of the other countries. More generally, as noted in Sect. 4, there are differences in the degree to which bankruptcy proceedings are regarded as *normal* (Anglo-Saxon countries) rather than *a last resort* (CEJ), which are supported by legal provisions.

One general point that can be made about levels of default rates is that long-term levels of gearing do not appear to entail comparable differences in average failure rates between countries,[44] consistent with the hypothesis of Sect. 3 that differences in structural patterns of leverage are explicable in terms of the nature of the financial system (commitment/relationship banking) rather than implying differing levels of default risk.

[44] The failure rate in Germany (for AGs and GMBHs) is none the less quite high at times. Some authors have suggested an explanation for this, namely that there are gradations in the benefits offered by banking relationships, and that small firms are allowed to go bankrupt with relative equanimity on the part of banks. That said, it was noted above that the *average size* of failures in Germany is similar to Japan and the USA.

An alternative, ex-ante measure of risk to the business failure rate is provided by corporate bond spreads, to the extent the company sector is subject to price rationing of credit, and bond markets are active and efficient.[45] These are shown in Charts 2.14 and 2.15. In most countries, spreads have tended to be counter-cyclical, similar to defaults, although declines in spreads in the Anglo-Saxon countries in the 1980s have not always coincided with lower defaults.

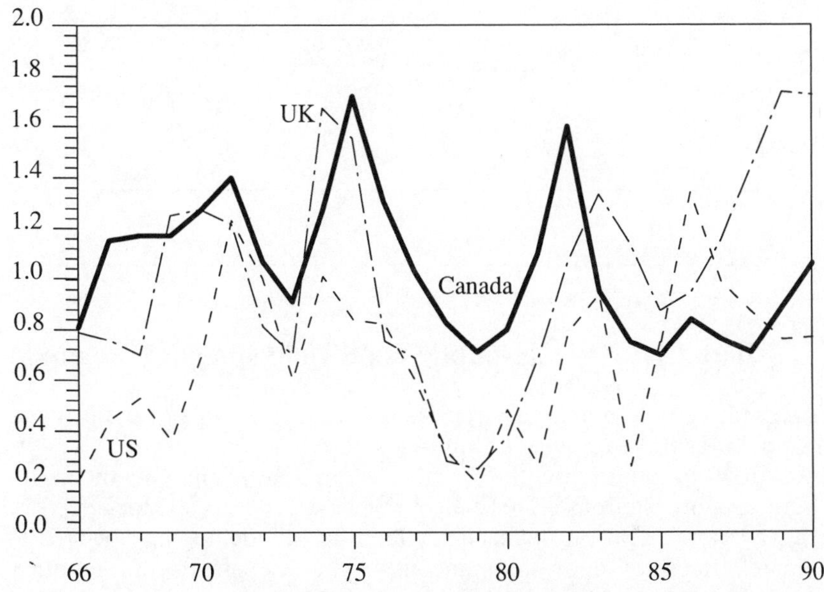

Chart 2.14. Private-public bond yield spreads (% points)

Various explanations for such patterns in Anglo-Saxon countries can be suggested. On the one hand, the high level of defaults noted above may involve small firms unable to access the bond market. On the other hand, markets may have underpriced risk.[46] Default rates on junk bonds in 1989 and 1990 of 5.6 and 8.8 per cent (1991 estimate: 11.5 per cent) were the highest on record. Experience in this period, during which 'many ill-conceived LBOs came apart' (Moody's 1991*a*) suggests to some observers that risk was indeed underpriced.

A third measure of risk is average bond ratings, although their availability outside the US is restricted. As pointed out by Kaufman (1986*b*), the 1980s saw a sharp decline in AAA ratings for US companies, which relates to increasing leverage. Warschawsky (1991) showed that the

[45] See Ch. 1, Sect. 3(a).

[46] This is a highly controversial issue; for contrary views see Fons (1986), Miller (1991), who argue that spreads were sufficient to cover default risk.

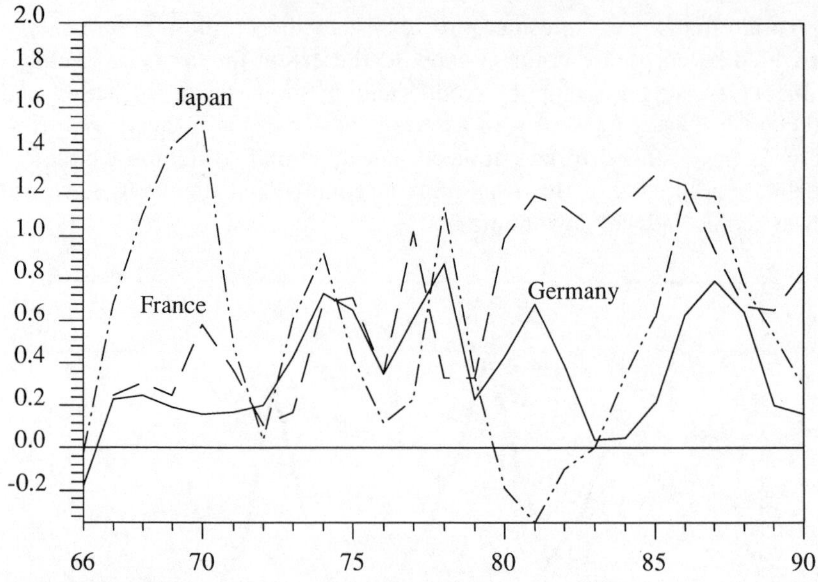

Chart 2.15. Private-public bond yield spreads (% points)

median rating of a sample of US firms fell from A in 1978 to BB in 1988, while the weighted average fell from AA+ to A.

We now go on to use the insights offered by economic theory to develop a more rigorous empirical approach, in order to test for effects of company sector debt on financial fragility. The modelling approach is to estimate effects of debt simultaneously with the effects of the other determinants of default risk. It should be noted at the outset that important factors such as taxation and the distinction between fixed and variable rate debt are largely omitted from the analysis. None the less, we would still argue that the results show that company sector debt has had a significant and measurable effect on insolvency rates and market default premiums. Those wishing to avoid the technicalities of modelling and econometrics—and take the result on trust—should move to the summary following Table 2.5 at the end of this section.

The aim was to test for a significant effect of a suitably scaled measure of corporate debt on default rates and spreads, given the other determining variables. The model uses a specification similar to that used by Wadhwani (1986) to investigate the effects of inflation on liquidation rates and default premia. (For an alternative, see Cuthbertson and Hudson 1990.) His technique is to model the behaviour of an individual firm, and then to test the resulting specification using macroeconomic data.[47] Thus, his model combines the objective function of a firm in perfect competition, a borrowing constraint, and the budget constraint, to

[47] For micro evidence on determinants of bankruptcy see Altman (1968).

derive an equation in which the probability of bankruptcy (μ), measured as the proportion of all firms that go bankrupt in the year in question, depends on wages (W), real interest rates (q), debt (D), the firm's market value (MV), and the mean (ρ) of the output price.

We suppose that in a world of perfect competition and zero inflation a firm chooses the level of employment (L) to maximise expected profits (Π), net of expected bankruptcy costs to the firm (C), where

$$E(\Pi) = E(\rho)\,F(L) - WL - C\mu(.) \tag{2.1}$$

where E is the expectations operator, ρ is the uncertain output price, W the money wage, F(L) is a twice-differentiable production function with $F_{LL}<0$ (capital being given in the short run), C is the cost of bankruptcy, and μ (.) is the probability of bankruptcy.

We also assume that the firm owes debt of D with real rate of interest q, and that if the firm cannot meet its current commitments from cash flow, it can raise up to $S = MV - D$ to finance its losses, where MV is the present value of expected earnings and S is the value of shares.

These assumptions regarding the availability of credit mean that the firm goes bankrupt when

$$\rho F(L) - WL - qD + S < 0 \tag{2.2}$$

Then, combining (2.1) and (2.2), employment is given by

$$L = L(W, q, D, MV, \rho, \sigma) \tag{2.3}$$

where ρ and σ are the mean and variance of the output price. Using (2.2) and (2.3), the probability of bankruptcy is a similar function

$$\mu(.) = \mu(W, q, D, MV, \rho, \sigma) \tag{2.4}$$

In practice, the variance of the output price was never significant.

In the perhaps more likely case of imperfect competition, where a firm chooses the output and price to maximize profits net of expected bankruptcy costs, taking other firms' outputs and prices as given, the bankruptcy function will include a measure of aggregate demand (AD).

Wadhwani augmented this basic specification in three ways, all of which are adopted for the current analysis. First, allowance was made for the effects of inflation on the probability of bankruptcy. Given limits to borrowing, a firm which is in 'financial distress' because its debt exceeds its borrowing limit will have increasingly to survive on its cash flow. But with non-indexed and variable rate debt, inflation hurts cash flow, because, for any positive real interest rate, a given rise in inflation leads to a greater proportionate increase in the nominal interest rate (conceptually, part of interest is capital repayment). Such an effect can be tested by including a nominal (r) as well as the real interest rate in the estimating equation. Secondly, he extended the production function to include raw materials, which implies that their price (PM) enters the bankruptcy function along with W (the price of labour). Thirdly, the mean of the output price was replaced by the actual output price (GNP deflator, denoted p).

The default premium on corporate bonds (ϵ) is a function of the market's ex-ante view of the probability of bankruptcy, as discussed above. It can thus be shown that the default premium rises with the probability of bankruptcy and therefore should be related to the same variables. If it is not, the market may be mispricing risk, whether due to uncertain events that could not be anticipated (ex-post mispricing), or, more controversially, through not taking into account all information available at the time of issue (ex-ante mispricing). Strictly, the inference regarding mispricing only relates to defaults by bond issuers, not all firms as in the current analysis.

Assume the investor recovers a proportion R of his original investment in the case of bankruptcy. Then a risk-neutral lender equates expected returns to corporate lending with those to risk-free lending G (to the government). The real interest rate on corporate lending B must include an allowance for the risk $[1-\mu(.)]$ and cost k of bankruptcy;

$$(1+qG)=(1+qB)[1-\mu(.)]+k\mu(.) \tag{2.5}$$

giving the default premium ϵ

$$\epsilon = Qb - qG = \frac{(\mu(.)\,[(1-R)+qG]}{[1-\mu(.)]}$$

where

$$\frac{\delta\epsilon}{\delta\mu(.)} > 0 \tag{2.6}$$

i.e., the default premium rises with the probability of bankruptcy. This means that the default premium may be related to the same variables as affect the probability of bankruptcy:

$$\mu(.) = \mu\,(W, PM, q, r, D, MV, \rho, \sigma, AD) \tag{2.7}$$

$$\epsilon = \epsilon\,(W, PM, q, r, D, MV, \rho, \sigma, AD) \tag{2.8}$$

$$Bo(L)\left[{\mu \atop \epsilon}\right] = B_1(L)\ln(W/p)_t + B_2(L)\ln(PM/p)_t + B_3(L)(D/MV)_t + B_4(L)\,qt + B_5(L)\,r_t + B_6(L)\ln(AD/p)_t + \text{const} \tag{2.9}$$

where (L) is the lag operator. Wadwhani showed, using this model for the United Kingdom, that price inflation had a significant effect on bankruptcy and default premiums, independent of real interest rates, though he found the structure of default premiums and bankruptcy equations rather different (as noted above, market perceptions ex-ante may not be good predictors of ex-post bankruptcies; also there are other influences on the spread besides default risk).

We commenced with a version of the general equation (2.9), and tested directly for effects of debt ratios on bankruptcy and market default premiums in the major economies. Wadwhani's model seemed useful for this, as it sets the problem of debt within a well-structured specification drawn from the firm's production function, objective function, borrowing limit, and budget constraint. However, given our focus, some changes were made to his specification. First, in the basic equations, the net debt to market value ratio was replaced by gross debt to GNP. This assumes that GNP is an adequate proxy for expected profits and that gross debt is relevant independent of corporate liquidity. (Variants on this using net debt and asset values are reported below). Secondly, aggregate demand was proxied by the first difference of the log of real GNP. All other variables are rates or ratios and hence are in principle non-trended.[48] Apart from the interest rates, which were entered as a percentage, the equations were specified in logs, thus facilitating analysis of elasticities.

First, separate equations were run for each country. Due to the shortage of observations with annual data (denoted N in the tables), a simple partial adjustment approach was adopted, with levels of the independent variables and a lagged dependent variable. (Hendry *et al.* (1983) discuss the shortcomings of this method.) Second, a pooled cross-section/time-series model was estimated, stacking individual countries' data (technically, this used Least Squared with Dummy Variables: Maddala 1977). Given the number of observations this could use the Granger–Engle two step method. Since the Durbin Watson statistic is biased in the presence of a lagged dependent variable, we report the Lagrange Multiplier (LM) test, distributed χ^2 where $\chi^2(1) = 4.5$. (See Breusch and Pagan 1980.)

Results are given in Tables 2.1–2.5. The most noteworthy feature of the estimates by country of default functions in Table 2.1 was that a higher level of debt tends to coincide with a higher failure rate, except for Japan, where the relationship was strongly negative, and Germany, where the coefficient was positive but insignificant. The significant positive coefficients were also similar in magnitude. In the Anglo-Saxon countries and France, the result suggests strongly that growth in debt underlay growth in default. For Germany and Japan, this result implies that, in the latter, companies are largely protected from the consequences of gearing, while in the former, effects of gearing are much weaker than in the Anglo-Saxon countries and France.

[48] In technical terms, one would expect them to be integrated at I(0).

Among the other results were that nominal interest rates (or inflation, implicit in a negative sign on real rates) tended to be positively related to default in the UK, USA, and Germany but real rates came to the fore in Canada and France. Only in Japan was no interest-rate effect found. There were strong cyclical effects on the default rate in all countries except Japan. However, effects of real factor prices only arose in some countries, although they had a generally positive effect on business failures. The US Bankruptcy Act of 1978 had a significant effect on the level of business failures while the UK Act of 1986 did not. Finally, all the equations had a strong autoregressive element, i.e. high levels of default in one year tend to predict high levels the next year. The statistical tests show a reasonable fit and absense of autocorrelation.

Moving on to the spreads equations (Table 2.2), these are quite similar for the USA, UK, and Canada. There is a smaller degree of autoregression, a strong cyclical effect, and a negative effect of interest rates. No significant coefficients could be obtained for debt/GNP ratios. The spreads equations in the other countries are poorly determined, consistent with a moribund bond market. In Japan spreads appear to be procyclical, suggesting a portfolio balance rather than a price-rationing effect.

As regards the variants on the default equations (Table 2.3), the first test was for different leverage variables. Net debt/GNP and net debt/capital stock gave similar results to those in the main case. The main contrast was in the German results, where both the capital gearing measures were highly significant. The contrast with the main case of debt/GNP may relate to a focus on the part of German banks on collateralized lending—and hence on assets (at replacement cost) rather than ongoing valuations or cash flow (proxied by GNP), as is more common in some Anglo-Saxon countries. It is also consistent with a 'commitment' approach which would rescue illiquid firms but not insolvent ones. Equity in the denominator gave poor results for most countries. Moreover, neither extra coefficients in the share of bank lending in corporate debt (to proxy banks' advantages in rescues) nor the birth rate of firms added significantly to the results. This may imply that it is appropriate to focus on gross rather than net (of new formations) business failures.

Table 2.4 sets out the pooled estimates, which show the average effect across countries. However, given the somewhat different results noted above for individual countries, rather less credence should be given to these results, which in effect impose similar coefficients.[49] As regards long-term effects, the cointegrating vector for business failures suggests a strong positive effect of debt ratios on default on average across the countries, as well as a positive effect of nominal and real interest rates.

[49] Consistent with this, the statistical properties are often rather poor, especially in the dynamic equations.

Table 2.1. Equations for business failure ratio (dependent variable: log of business failure rate)

	USA[a]	UK[b]	Canada[c]	France[d]	Germany[e]	Japan[f]
Constant	0.48 (1.7)	−0.81 (1.5)	−3.0 (3.8)	6.4 (2.2)	0.01 (0.1)	1.45 (1.8)
Lagged dependent	0.97 (19.2)	0.94 (13.2)	0.55 (6.6)	0.4 (2.1)	0.98 (8.2)	0.8 (7.8)
Log debt/GNP	0.85 (3.0)	0.63 (2.1)	1.1 (2.0)	1.1 (2.8)	1.1 (1.4)	−0.75 (2.1)
Log difference of GNP	−3.3 (4.4)	−7.2 (5.1)	−3.3 (3.7)	−5.6 (3.3)	−3.5 (4.1)	
Log wages/GNP deflator				0.6 (1.8)	−0.5 (2.1)	
Log raw materials price/GNP deflator			1.1 (5.1)	−0.4 (1.5)	—	
Nominal short-term interest rate	0.035 (2.5)	0.07 (7.3)	−0.04 (2.8)		0.05 (4.8)	
Real short-term interest rate		−0.06 (5.5)	0.05 (5.2)	0.028 (2.5)	—	−0.025 (4.1)
Dummy (US bankruptcy law)	0.2 (3.1)					
$\bar{R}^2$	0.98	0.94	0.94	0.97	0.96	0.94
se	0.06	0.09	0.07	0.07	0.08	0.1
LM(1)	6.0	0.5	2.1	4.9	0.6	9.1
N	17	22	24	19	23	23

a 1967–83
b 1969–90
c 1967–90
d 1971–89
e 1967–89
f 1968–90
g ‘t’ ratios in parentheses

Table 2.2. Equations for spreads (dependent variable: spread of corporate over government bonds yields)

	USA[a]	UK[b]	Canada[c]	France[d]	Germany[e]	Japan[f]
Constant	14.9 (2.2)[g]	1.8 (3.6)	0.3 (2.1)	1.2 (9.8)	0.53 (6.5)	6.36 (2.3)
Lagged dependent	0.36 (2.2)	0.49 (2.9)	0.46 (4.6)			0.55 (3.8)
Log debt/GNP						−1.7 (2.1)
Log difference of GNP	−9.1 (3.8)	−12.0 (3.1)	−7.6 (4.4)	−3.4 (1.4)	19.5 (5.1)	9.4 (2.0)
Log wages/GNP deflator	5.1 (2.0)		− 1.3 (4.3)		0.2 (1.0)	0.6 (1.1)
Log raw materials price/GNP deflator		1.3 (1.9)				
Nominal short-term interest rate	−0.07 (3.1)					−0.15 (2.4)
Real short-term interest rate		− 0.07 (2.5)		0.05 (3.0)		−0.094 (3.3)
$\bar{R}^2$	0.5	0.6	0.63	0.64	0.1	0.55
se	0.23	0.28	0.16	0.23	0.24	0.35
LM(1)	0.1	1.8	1.1	0.1	3.9	7.0
N	24	22	25	19	23	25

a 1967–90
b 1969–90
c 1966–88
d 1971–89
e 1967–89
f 1966–90
g ‘t’ ratios in parentheses

Table 2.3. Variants on the basic equations

	Gross debt/ gross assets[a]	Gross debt/ equity[a]	Net debt/ GNP[a]	Net debt/ capital stock[a]	Net debt/ equity[a]	Bank lending rate[b]	Firm birth rate[b]
USA	0.62 (2.8)[c]	−0.15 (1.3)	0.79 (2.5)	0.3 (2.5)	−0.2 (1.1)	−0.4 (1.0)	−0.2 (0.2)
UK	0.1 (0.2)	−0.02 (0.2)	0.2 (1.3)	0.2 (1.3)	0.06 (0.3)	0.14 (0.5)	−0.1 (0.4)
Canada	0.3 (0.6)	0.3 (1.8)	0.7 (1.7)	0.1 (0.3)	0.4 (1.7)	0.1 (0.6)	0.3 (0.1)
France	1.1 (1.8)	−0.8 (3.2)	1.3 (2.5)	0.8 (1.9)	−2.3 (3.3)	−1.1 (0.4)	−0.1 (0.1)
Germany	1.4 (2.5)	0.1 (0.1)	0.7 (1.2)	1.3 (3.0)	0.1 (0.1)	0.8 (0.6)	0.2 (1.3)
Japan	−0.1 (0.3)	0.14 (1.4)	−0.1 (0.2)	−0.1 (0.5)	0.1 (0.8)	−0.5 (0.1)	0.1 (0.2)

a In place of gross debt/GNP
b Extra variable
c 't' ratios in parentheses

Meanwhile, the dynamic equation is dominated by the cyclical variable; rising debt ratios tend to dampen default in the short run (possibly because rising as opposed to high debt implies continuing provision of credit, or alternatively because defaults entail a writing off of debt).

Table 2.4 Pooled cross-section and time series equations for business failure rate (BFR) ('t' ratios in parenthesis)

(1) Cointegrating vector

$$\ln BFR = -6.6 + 1.03\ln(D/GNP) + 0.8\ln GNP - 1.02\ln(W/P)$$
$$(1.4)\ (2.7)\qquad (2.2)\qquad (2.3)$$

$$-0.04\ln(PM/P) + 0.028\,r + 0.033\,q + \text{dummies}$$
$$(0.2)\qquad (2.0)\qquad (3.1)$$

$\bar{R}^2 = 0.99$ CRDW $= 0.7$ DF $= -4.9$

(2) Dynamic equation

$$\Delta\ln BFR = 0.07 - 0.4\,\Delta\ln(D/GNP) - 1.51\,\Delta\ln GNP + 0.13\,\Delta\ln(W/P)$$
$$(3.1)\ (2.9)\qquad (3.1)\qquad (0.2)$$

$$+\,0.12\,\Delta\ln(PM/P) - 0.01\Delta r + 0.001\,\Delta q - 0.16\,RES_{t-1} + \text{dummies}$$
$$((0.8)\qquad 1.0)\qquad (0.1)\qquad (2.7)$$

$\bar{R}^2 = 0.96$ se $= 0.16$ DW $= 1.0$ LM(1) $= 44.0$

(3) Separate debt ratios (levels) in cointegrating vector

US:	2.5 (2.5)	UK:	0.43 (0.8)	Canada:	4.8 (3.4)
Germany:	−0.5 (0.4)	Japan:	1.3 (1.3)	France:	−1.6 (0.7)

(4) Separate debt ratios (differences) in dynamic equation

US:	1.2 (1.3)	UK:	0.2 (0.4)	Canada:	1.8 (2.1)
Germany:	−0.2 (0.2)	Japan:	−0.8 (1.7)	France:	0.77 (0.6)

As a further experiment, separate estimates were made within the pooled estimates of the national coefficients on debt ratios, while retaining the other coefficients in common. These show a broad difference between Anglo-Saxon countries, where levels and differences of leverage are always positive and generally significant, and the other countries where effects are negative or insignificant. This may reflect the superiority of relationship banking systems in dealing with financial distress, as outlined above. Broadly similar patterns arise in the pooled estimates for spreads (Table 2.5), though the equations are less well determined.

Table 2.5 Pooled cross-section and time series equations for spreads (SPR) ('t' ratios in parentheses)

(1) Cointegrating vector

$$SPR = \underset{(3.1)}{15.2} + \underset{(1.7)}{0.66}\ \ln(D/GNP) - \underset{(2.1)}{0.79}\ \ln GNP - \underset{(2.2)}{1.0}\ \ln(W/P) - \underset{(4.1)}{0.93}\ \ln(PM/P)$$

$$+ \underset{(0.9)}{0.013}\ r - \underset{(1.3)}{0.013}\ q + \text{dummies}$$

$\bar{R}^2 = 0.36$ CRDW = 1.1 DF = −5.1

(2) Dynamic equation

$$\Delta SPR = \underset{(0.7)}{0.03} - \underset{(1.7)}{0.45}\ \Delta\ln(D/GNP) - \underset{(1.7)}{1.45}\ \Delta\ln GNP + \underset{(1.2)}{1.45}\ \Delta\ln(W/P)$$

$$- \underset{(2.4)}{0.69}\ \Delta\ln(PM/P) - \underset{(3.0)}{0.029}\Delta q - \underset{(5.9)}{0.49}\ RES_{t-1}$$

$\bar{R}^2 = 0.36$ se = 0.3 DW = 1.7 LM(1) = 8.6

(3) Separate debt ratios (levels) in cointegrating vector

US:	1.6 (1.6)	UK:	1.7 (3.1)	Canada:	0.001 (0.1)
Germany:	3.1 (2.4)	Japan:	−3.2 (3.3)	France:	−1.5 (0.7)

(4) Separate debt ratios (differences) in dynamic equation

US:	0.6 (0.4)	UK:	1.1 (1.2)	Canada:	1.4 (0.9)
Germany:	−1.9 (0.9)	Japan:	−2.7 (2.8)	France:	2.2 (0.9)

To summarize this section, the econometric results suggest a strong correlation between leverage and default in all countries except Japan and (to a lesser extent) Germany. Results were similar for various measures of indebtedness. Interest rates, the cycle, and factor prices also had an impact on business failure rates. No significant relationship was detected between leverage and default premiums on corporate bonds, even in the USA. The results are consistent with the hypotheses that rising debt in Anglo-Saxon countries and France has entailed increased financial fragility and (more tentatively) that lenders may have under-priced associated risk, at least ex-post. They also imply that business failures are less strongly related to leverage in countries characterized by 'relationship banking'. This may be because of superior risk-sharing, lower information asymmetries, and lower agency costs, as outlined in Sect. 4 and Ch. 1, Sect. 5.

Of course, in drawing these inferences a number of caveats need to be borne in mind. First, comprehensive data are not available to show whether failures relate to comparable sizes of firms, although observations for the US, Germany, and Japan suggest they are broadly similar. Second, it was noted above that bankruptcy procedures, and the relative costs to different parties, differ. This implies that the broader economic implications of a given failure rate may differ between countries (although in the econometrics, intercountry differences in law and procedures should be captured in the constant). Third, more precision in estimation would be obtained from use of quarterly data. Fourth, no explicit role has been given to falling property prices, although these have often been associated with default (interest rates and equity prices may capture this effect).

Conclusions

Three main conclusions can be drawn from the analysis of this chapter.

1. There are sharp long-term distinctions between levels of gearing in major OECD countries, which do not appear associated with levels of risk, but rather with structural differences in financial systems.

2. In certain countries, there have also been shifts over time in indebtedness, associated largely with changes in equilibrium credit rationing, which do appear to have led to higher risk.

3. Underlying factors include heightened competition, innovation, and other structural changes in financial markets, some of which are associated with financial liberalization and globalization.

The welfare implications of increased default in the corporate sector depend on a number of factors. An a priori view is that higher rates of corporate default owing to leverage are undesirable, given the costs and externalities of default as outlined in Sect. 3. This conclusion is strengthened if default arises from the cyclical context rather than poor management. However, the following qualifications can be made. First, bankruptcies of a certain number of small firms in the context of rapid formation of new businesses may be a sign of a healthy growing economy. Second, loss of firms due to insolvency may be less damaging than unnecessary losses of productive firms due to illiquidity, though the distinction is difficult to make in the aggregate data. Third, costs of reorganization of assets in case of default will depend on the precise provisions of bankruptcy law. Fourth, to the extent that costly default results from excessive levels of leverage, this must be offset against any benefits that such levels may cause, e.g. in increasing flexibility to finance investment; or in reducing agency costs between managers and security holders, with greater ensuing efficiency (to the extent that this is proven); or (at the level of the firm) taking advantage of tax concessions. Finally, it is important to assess whether risks are known and correctly priced, in which case default is an unlucky but calculated event (though externalities may still justify intervention).

The following policy issues are raised by the analysis. Note that most are means of prevention of fragility, but that some, particularly the last four, are also means to avoid its most deleterious consequences.

Given the ability of relationship banking/commitment to reduce financial distress to borrowers for a given level of debt, moves towards this would seem to be justified on some grounds although other factors (efficiency, competition, conflicts of interest, risk to lenders) may argue against it. Note that this is against much of the thrust of financial liberalization to date, including EC Single Market proposals. The other suggestions largely relate to potential improvements to an 'Anglo-Saxon' system of corporate finance.

Tax advantages to debt and, correspondingly, double taxation of equity, may give an unnecessary extra stimulus to fragility, and should be eliminated. This is particularly relevant to the extent fragility entails externalities that are not taken into account by borrowers (discussed in Ch. 4). A consumption tax (Summers 1986) would be one way of resolving these difficulties. Alternatives are integration of corporate and individual tax systems, or institution of a corporate cash-flow tax (Gertler and Hubbard 1989).

Similarly, moves to reduce costs of equity finance (including issuance) could help stem tendencies to excessive indebtedness.

Promotion of means of exerting corporate control other than takeovers (e.g. non-executive directors, or direct involvement of institutional investors in changes of management) may reduce average levels of leverage, as well as promoting continuity in management and (possibly) long-term investment.

To the extent that there is underpricing of risk, creditors need to be made more aware of risks involved, in particular of the potential correlations between risks believed to be independent (such as junk-bond market collapse (Ch. 8); or effects of a recession), and changes to the security of their claims arising from bankruptcy law.

Sharing of information on corporate debt exposures may help reduce overlending; such 'Central Risk Offices', often run by the public sector, are more common in the CEJ than Anglo-Saxon countries (they face problems, however, in capturing international lending and off-balance-sheet exposures).

Capital adequacy of financial intermediaries must be maintained, both to reduce incentives to risk-taking ex-ante and to ensure corporate default does not lead to wider financial instability.

Macroeconomic policymakers should resist undue pressure to avoid a recession solely in order to prevent financial distress in a financially fragile economy. Otherwise, moral hazard is created which will aggravate risk-taking and indebtedness.

Fiscal policy may have implications for corporate sector fragility that should be borne in mind, especially if it causes crowding out of private sector borrowers. Defaults may also result from high real interest rates caused by lax fiscal policy, and sectoral difficulties may arise from exchange-rate shifts caused by the stance of fiscal policy. (See also Ch. 4, Appendix.)

There may be a case for the central bank or other public agency to act as a referee in cases where co-ordination of a large group of banks is required to prevent unnecessary failure of solvent companies facing liquidity problems (Leigh-Pemberton 1990).

3

Financial Fragility in the Personal Sector

Complementing the previous chapter, this chapter seeks to assess the causes and implications of recent developments in personal-sector indebtedness and default in the major economies. A number of common features can be discerned for several of the countries: rising levels of debt/income and (to a lesser extent) debt/asset ratios; apparent declines in credit rationing; rising levels of default, particularly, but not exclusively, during recessions; and frequently also declining saving. It is suggested that these features can partly be related to financial deregulation and liberalization.

The chapter is structured as follows; first, data are presented relating to personal-sector indebtedness; then a theoretical approach to the house hold sector's demand for credit is outlined. These provide background for the analysis of the third section, where an interpretation is made of empirical trends based on the theory; and the fourth, where an econometric analysis is made relating debt to default. In a further section, patterns of indebtedness are related to changes in saving ratios and asset prices. The results, *inter alia*, enable an assessment to be made in the conclusions of the net benefits of financial liberalization as they relate to the personal sector, and lead on to certain policy implications.

(1) Recent Trends in Personal-Sector Indebtedness

Charts 3.1–3.6 illustrate the behaviour of personal-sector indebtedness in six major economies over the period 1966–90, namely the UK, USA, Germany, Japan, France, and Canada.[1] Chart 3.1 shows that debt has grown as a proportion of personal disposable[2] income over this period in

[1] The data are drawn from national sources and differ conceptually, hence greater focus should be put on trends than on levels in the charts. Data for the USA and France cover the household sector; the UK, Canada, and Japan cover the personal sector (including non-corporate business); and data for Germany cover the household and housing sectors, which includes financial transactions relating to dwellings, construction and ownership of rented accommodation. For a detailed discussion see the appendix to Davis (1986).

[2] Note that income is not adjusted for the degree to which interest payments compensate inflation losses on net liquid assets (floating-rate assets less floating-rate debt), which boost measured income during inflationary periods for sectors with positive net liquidity (Taylor and Threadgold 1979). Such a pattern is typical of all the sectors concerned, except the UK in the late 1980s, where the personal sector held negative net liquid assets.

all the countries studied, albeit extremely rapidly in the UK since 1980 and in Japan since 1985. Complementing this, Chart 3.2 indicates that mortgage debt[3] accounts for the bulk of the increase, while Chart 3.3 shows a similar pattern to Chart 3.1 when normalized[4] by GNP.

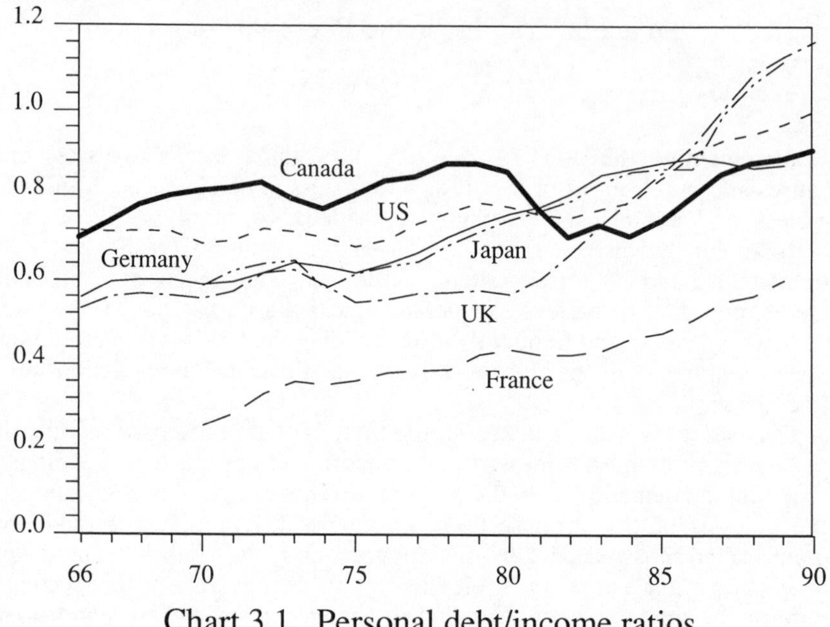

Chart 3.1. Personal debt/income ratios

In contrast, Chart 3.4 shows that the debt/assets ratio has been much more stable, suggesting that the market value of wealth has kept pace with debt, even if income has not.[5] On the other hand, the charts of course cannot show the distribution of debt, wealth, and income; it could be that a part of the population is highly indebted, while another part holds unencumbered wealth. Moreover, a large proportion of gross assets may be highly illiquid and hence of little use in financial distress, such as pension rights, consumer durables, and some forms of property. Third, to the extent that market values rise beyond the ability of marginal purchasers to pay for assets such as housing and/or beyond replacement costs[6] (abstracting from land) they may be vulnerable to sharp declines.

[3] The German data include certain corporate debts (property and construction companies) so the ratio may be overestimated.

[4] Data for Italy show an exceptionally low (and constant) ratio of debt/ GNP of 0.1.

[5] Friedman (1990) notes a similar pattern of asset accumulation to households for the US unincorporated business sector (this sector is not separately identified for the other countries).

[6] In this case, there are parallels with the debt-equity ratio of firms *vis-à-vis* capital gearing.

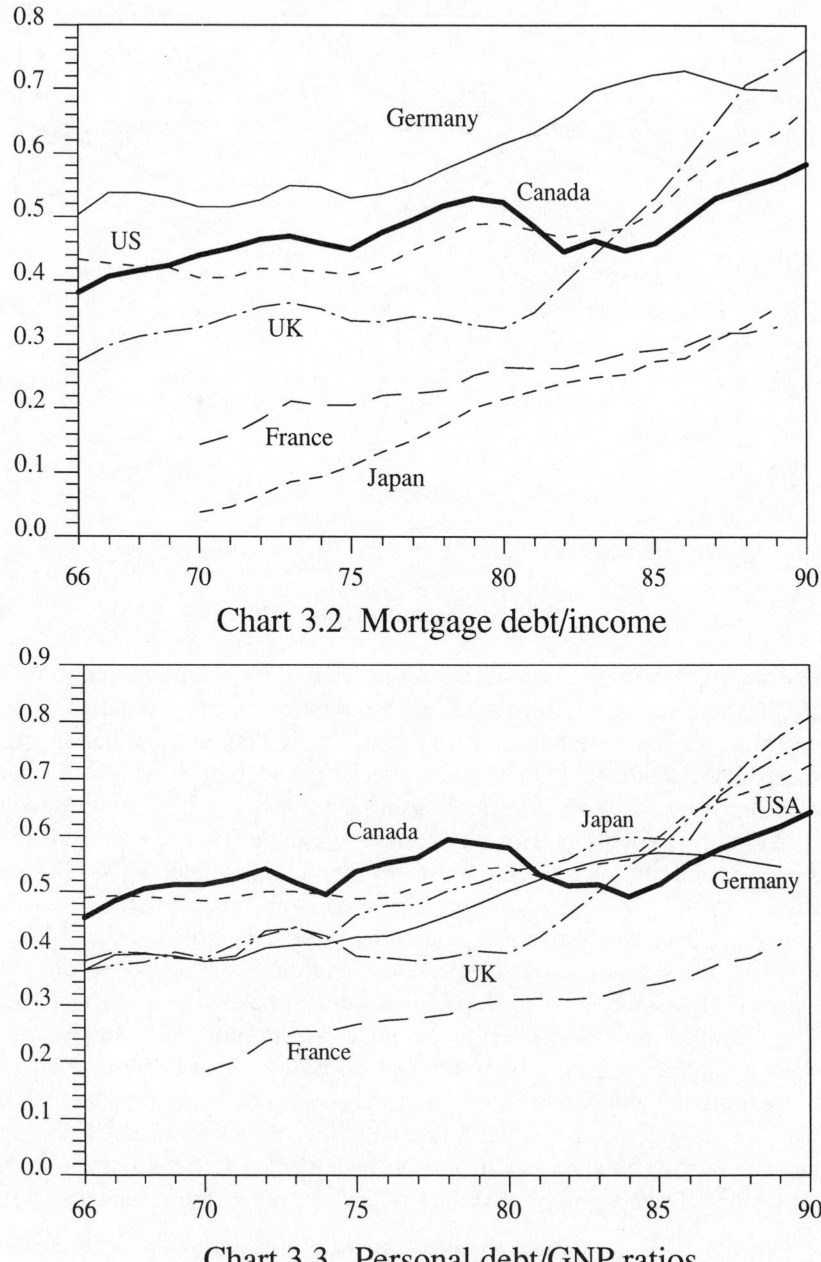

Chart 3.2 Mortgage debt/income

Chart 3.3. Personal debt/GNP ratios

Chart 3.5 shows a similar stability for capital gearing in the housing market (mortgages/value of housing), although marked growth in this case has occurred for the US in the 1980s. However, this partly relates to the

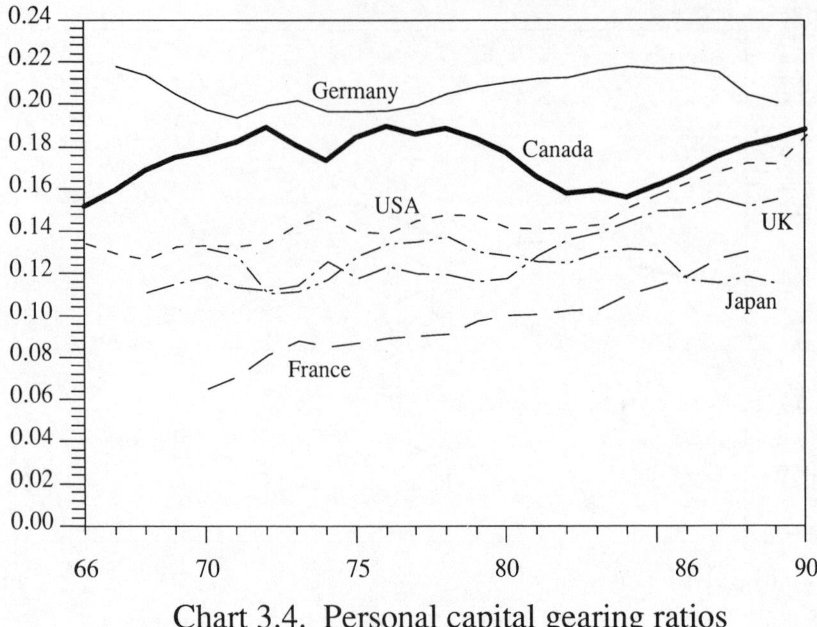

Chart 3.4. Personal capital gearing ratios

US tax reform of 1986, which abolished tax concessions for consumer credit and stimulated borrowing against housing equity.[7] Note that the levels in this chart are more directly comparable than in the other charts, since the definitions match more precisely; a contrast is observable between levels of gearing in the housing market in the USA and Canada with the other countries. Housing-market gearing in Japan has historically been particularly low, reflecting the extremely high value of the housing stock.[8] In the UK low gearing has resulted from rapid growth of house prices (see Sect. 5), despite sharp increases in debt (Chart 3.1).

Chart 3.6 shows estimates of income gearing, i.e. the proportion of personal disposable income devoted to interest payments on gross debt. The estimates assume payments are made at the mortgage interest rate (hence underestimating the effect of consumer credit, but probably overestimating that of fixed-rate mortgages, which predominate in the USA, Canada, Germany, and France).[9] In most countries, a rise in income gearing is apparent in the early 1980s, in line with the rise in inflation and tightening of monetary policy; however, reflecting growth in

[7] Some have also argued that this relates to an exceptional number of young (high-debt) people in the population in the 1980s.

[8] Falls in land prices in 1991 boosted gearing.

[9] As shown by Goodman (1991), the actual US long rate on mortgages *on offer* over the 1970s and 1980s of 7½–15% contrasts with averages on mortgages *held* of 6–10½%, owning to prepayment as interest rates fell.

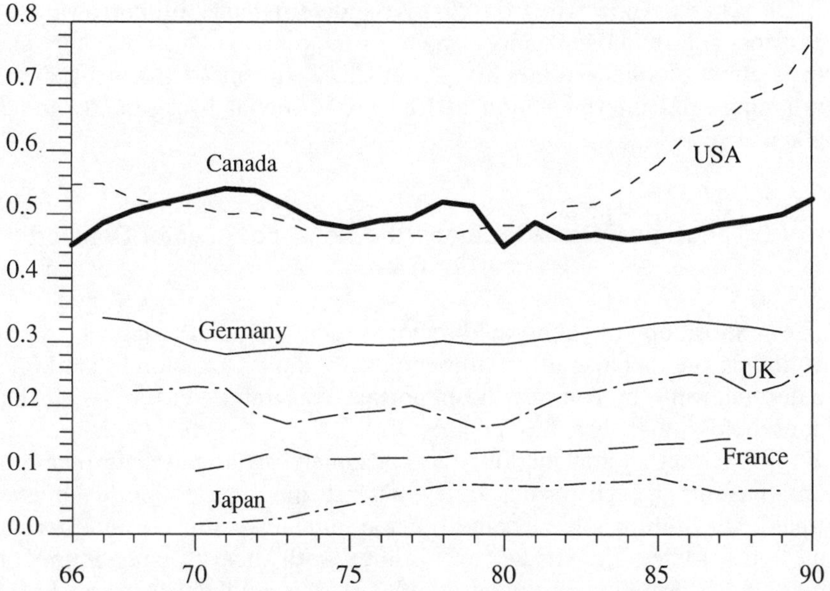

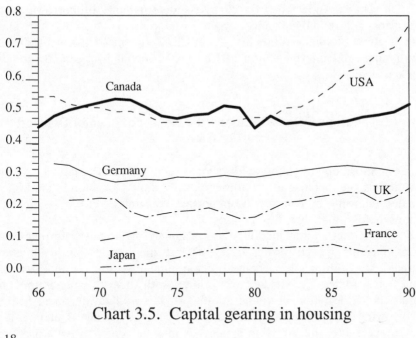

Chart 3.5. Capital gearing in housing

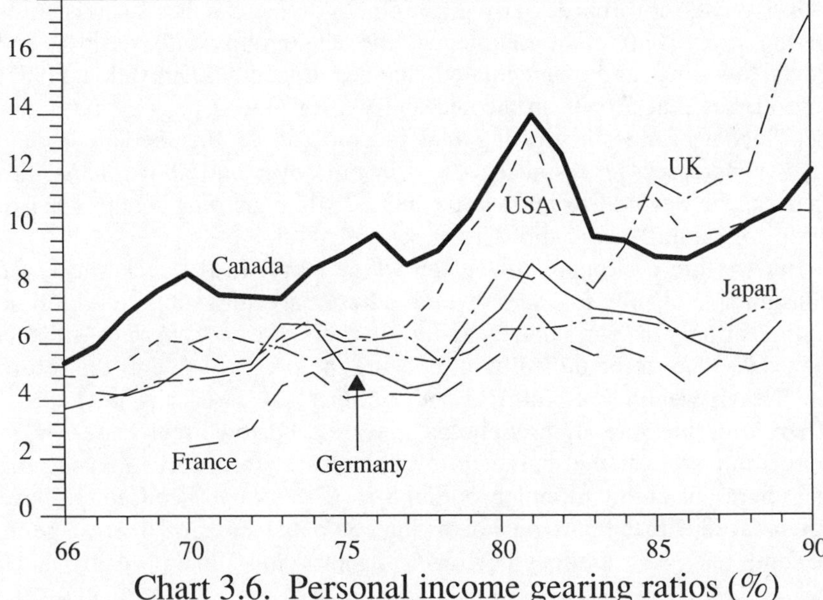

Chart 3.6. Personal income gearing ratios (%)

debt, this ratio has not tended to decline in the later 1980s. As is the case for capital gearing, the distribution of this interest burden is likely to be particularly skewed, with high burdens for young first-time house buyers.

The chapter now goes on to assess determinants of borrowing by persons, before making an assessment of the patterns illustrated here and their effect on financial fragility. As in Ch. 2, the analysis of debt, credit rationing, and intermediation in Ch. 1 is essential background, and is taken as read.

(2) Theoretical Considerations: the Household-Sector Demand for Credit

The exposition of household-sector credit demand commences by outlining the behaviour of households in a perfect capital market,[10] before showing by contrast the important constraints on borrowing that households are likely to face in practice.

In a perfect capital market, the consumer carries out 'intertemporal optimization' by borrowing freely against the security of his human wealth (i.e. future wage income) or non-human wealth. Given a normal income profile, i.e. rising over time, with heavy expenditure on household formation in young adulthood, this is likely to mean heavy borrowing early in the life cycle and corresponding repayments later.

In aggregate, the life-cycle hypothesis may be consistent with a rising debt/income ratio, particularly given demographic changes such as shifts in the proportion of households in the age groups with positive and negative saving, and unanticipated changes in income. Christelow (1987) also argues that growth in income and wealth more generally may raise debt/income ratios; a growing real income (up to the median income range) increases the residual part of income over and above necessities that can be devoted to interest payments, while growing wealth (due to saving or capital appreciation) increases collateral.

But the life cycle may not be the whole story. In the real world, the consumer is likely to face several additional constraints on lifetime optimization. In particular, capital markets are not perfect—this is especially due to the difficulty of pledging the present value of the return on human wealth (i.e. future wage earnings) as a security on loans.[11] Therefore, in general, households may not borrow freely and on an unsecured basis at the market rate of interest. Moreover, following the paradigms of credit rationing outlined in Ch. 1, many consumers have often faced direct limits on borrowing, or penal rates of interest going beyond this, e.g. limiting borrowing against non-human wealth. Such

[10] A theoretical construct entailing a full set of markets covering every possible contingency, and freedom to borrow against wealth (including future wage income—returns to 'human wealth'). See Lancaster 1966, 1971; Deaton and Muellbauer 1980.

[11] We concentrate initially on unsecured consumer borrowing, i.e. we assume the loan is not used to purchase an asset which itself forms adequate collateral.

consumers are *liquidity constrained*[12] and their consumption will be closely tied to receipts of income, though current non-human wealth (especially that which is most liquid) will also be available to decumulate for consumption. In many cases, liquidity constraints imply that consumers cannot consume at the level defined by their lifetime consumption plan, at the points where heavy borrowing would be required early in the life span.

The contrast between liquidity constraints and the life-cycle pattern is illustrated in Figure 3.1, from Davis (1984*b*). The common life-cycle earnings path of the constrained and unconstrained is Y. The unconstrained (denoted u) are able to borrow, making their net assets Au negative early in the life cycle and hence their consumption Cu can be above their income. After Cu=Y the borrowing is paid back and net assets are built up to maintain consumption after retirement at R. The constrained (denoted c) are forced to consume Cc at a level equal to their income, until the point at which income exceeds their modified optimal consumption path, after which they enjoy more consumption than the unconstrained later in the life cycle. To this point, net assets Ac are 0, i.e. greater than Au. After this point, saving is required, such as to give a higher level of net assets at retirement than the unconstrained, in order to continue the higher desired level of consumption. This analysis assumes no bequests and zero interest rates.

Liquidity constraints imply that welfare losses are incurred by constrained consumers, even though consumption can be made up later in the life cycle, owing to forced intertemporal rearrangement of consumption; hence the release of liquidity constraints offers welfare gains. Constraints may apply even to consumers with substantial assets if these are illiquid, i.e. either costly to encash or unacceptable as collateral for short-term loans. Pension rights, used consumer durables, houses, equities, and bonds fall, or have historically fallen, into at least one of these categories in many countries. This has a major implication for the indebtedness of consumers. To the extent that liquidity constraints bind—and there is strong evidence for this[13]—then a loosening of these constraints will be marked by a sharply rising debt/income and (to a lesser degree) debt/wealth ratio, and falling saving (see Sect. 5).

A second implication of liquidity constraints is that the constrained's marginal propensity to consume will be higher than that of unconstrained consumers. Those able to borrow less than they wish will spend any increase in their resources in order to move towards their optimal

[12] See Tobin 1972; Flemming 1973; Pissarides 1978; Hayashi 1985.

[13] If liquidity constraints were not operative, there would not be a strong relationship between disposable income and consumption. Most studies of the consumption function have found such a relationship (see, e.g. Davis 1984*a*).

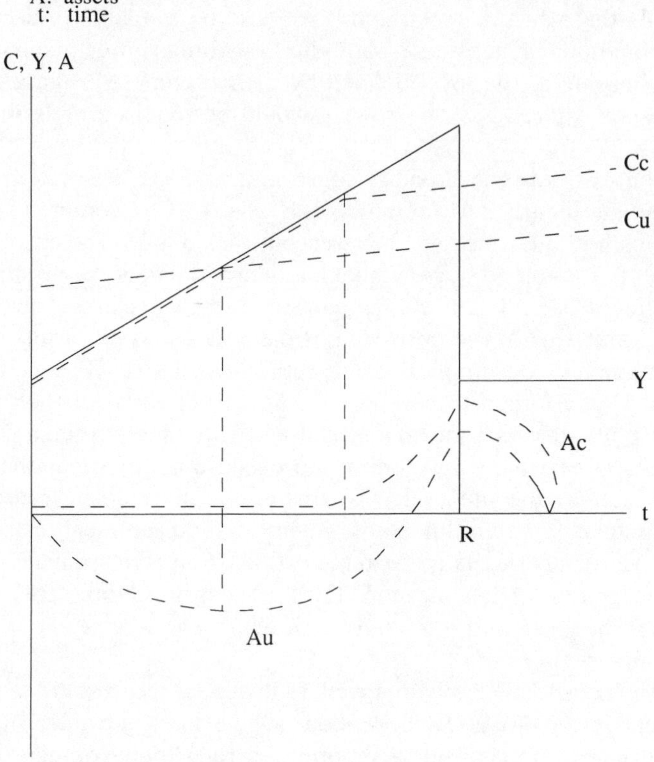

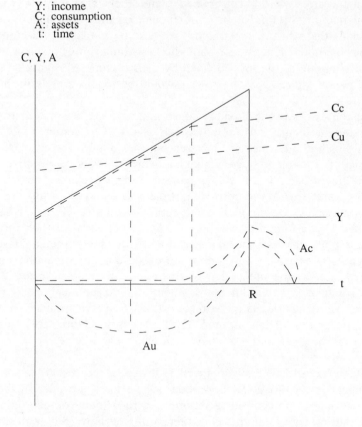

Fig.3.1. The life cycle and liquidity constraints

consumption path, while those already on this path will save a proportion of the increase, distributing the resulting increase in consumption over the life cycle (see Deaton and Muellbauer 1980). This suggests that a loosening of liquidity constraints should be indicated by a falling marginal propensity to consume.[14]

Thirdly, the life-cycle model, together with the existence of liquidity constraints, suggests that one should view the household sector as containing different groups. While some households are relatively unconstrained, others will be liquidity-constrained, and households will differ in age, and hence borrowing needs, as well as income and assets. Changes in the weights of these groups will affect sectoral debt. We return to this subject below when we summarize the relationship between debt and default. First, the implications of secured lending to households are analysed.

[14] Consistent with such a loosening, Blundell-Wignall *et al.* (1990) show that consumption's sensitivity to transitory income declined in the 1980s in the USA, Canada, and Japan.

The discussion so far relates largely to consumer credit, because it has been assumed that no suitable collateral is available other than human wealth. Whether these arguments apply as strongly to credits for personal-sector investment, i.e. house purchase, is less clear. Collateral for house purchase is immediately available in the form of the title-deeds to the property—and, as noted in Ch. 1, collateral tends to reduce the credit-market problems arising from information asymmetry and incomplete contracts. Additionally, loans are generally tax subsidized, and in many countries only housing loans are thus deductible (hence income gearing net of the subsidy may be relatively low).[15] In some countries, such as the UK, the social welfare system will pay interest during periods of unemployment. Compared with consumer credit, the risk to the lender relates to the risk that, owing to regional or national depression, the value of the collateral will have fallen below the outstanding principal of the loan, in which case the borrower may have an incentive to default.[16] There are obviously also transactions costs to foreclosure. However, despite this lower level of risk, it is argued in Sect. 3 below that certain non-price constraints on such lending have often been operative, and thus the earlier insights regarding liquidity constraints are not invalidated.

Note that the housing market itself may impose dynamics on the pattern of demand for borrowing. In particular, researchers such as Hendry (1984) and Muellbauer and Murphy (1991) have found evidence of 'frenzies' where rising house prices enter a spiral with demand for mortgages, partly driven by fear on the part of first-time buyers of being left behind. In other words, the rate of return tends increasingly to dominate transactions costs. This implies that housing markets may be subject to 'positive feedback trading' whereby rising prices induce purchases purely intended for profit by resale (Cutler *et al.* 1989). The counterpart may be sharp reductions in prices following such frenzies.

Abstracting from this last point, the same arguments as for house purchase apply in principle to lending to buy securities; collateral is immediately available. The valuation risks to the lender may be large, however, and in most countries it is difficult to borrow in order to buy bonds or equities (owing, for example, to margin requirements).

[15] Tanzi (1984) gives a discussion of tax deductibility on debt interest payments in the various economies. At present, interest is deductible for corporate debt in all the countries studied, but mortgage interest is not deductible in Canada and France, and interest on consumer credit is not deductible in any of the countries (the USA abolished deductibility for consumer credit in 1987). There are generally also limits on deductibility of mortgage interest; and in Germany housing equity is taxed, although saving for house purchase is tax subsidized.

[16] As long as the collateral exceeds principal ('positive equity'), the borrower can always sell the property to cover any arrears of interest. Of course, for fixed-rate loans, the lender may face risks independent of borrower default, relating to its own maturity mismatch (see the discussion of USA thrifts in Ch. 6).

(3) An Interpretation of Patterns of Indebtedness

We now turn to an assessment of the patterns of indebtedness in the light of the theory of the demand for credit outlined above, and the paradigms of credit rationing described in Ch. 1, Sect. 3. It is conceivable that part of increased debt results purely from an increase in credit demand in equilibrium—i.e. a pure 'free market' story can be told. It was suggested in Sect. 2 that the life-cycle hypothesis is consistent with rising debt/income ratios, particularly in the case of unanticipated changes in income or increases in expectations of income growth. And it is clear that such expectations have played a major part in growth of debt in countries such as the UK (Sargent 1990). Another explanation could be shifting demographics—although this would be expected to be gradual. Moreover, a more rapid shift in indebtedness could be stimulated by tax changes. But, as shown in Table 3.4 below, such fiscal stimuli were generally established long before the recent lending boom.

It seems likely, however, that a key factor permitting the recent growth in lending in a number of countries has also been a loosening of rationing constraints on the supply side which were previously binding (a shift from a situation of disequilibrium[17] quantity rationing of credit to one where it is either rationed by price or by equilibrium quantity rationing). Indicative evidence on these hypotheses is provided in Tables 3.1–3.3 It is suggested that disequilibrium quantity rationing would entail no strong relationship between the lending rate and the risk-free or funding rate, as the lender varies (or is forced to vary) rates beyond those consistent with profitably funding loan demand. Second, price rationing should be marked by a close relation between changes in spreads over the reference rate and default risk. Third, equilibrium quantity rationing should be marked by evidence of binding constraints on loan-to-value or loan-to-income ratios and a rather weak relation between defaults and spreads.

Table 3.1 shows a marked rise in the correlation of mortgage rates to reference rates[18] in the UK, France, and Japan in the 1980s, and a smaller

[17] However an explanation of *mortgage* rationing prior to liberalization based solely on government controls, e.g. of loan rates, is not completely satisfactory. Although market sources of disequilibrium rationing, such as 'risk-sharing' and 'equitable treatment', could be the correct explanations for mortgage rationing, one can equally put forward an 'optimal loan rate' explanation partly based on the Stiglitz and Weiss (1981) analysis. Firstly, a higher rate (especially with variable-rate loans) may lead to defaults by borrowers sufficient to lower profits, perhaps because borrowers already have debt not declared to the lenders, or highly variable incomes. Secondly, even if such defaults are not sufficient to lower profits, the social opprobrium of some foreclosures may lead to fewer deposits, government action to lower tax benefits, or increased profits taxes. Thirdly, if the loan rate had been increased, the institutions concerned may have feared the disintermediation of loan supply.

[18] In the UK and Japan, the correlation shown is between the rate on (floating-rate) mortgages and money-market short-term rates; in Germany, the USA, France, and Canada the correlation is between fixed-rate mortgages and yields on government bonds.

one in Germany. In contrast, the relationships have been flat in the USA and Canada These are consistent with a shift away from disequilibrium quantity rationing in the loan market for the personal sector in the UK, France, and Japan.

Table 3.1. Correlation between changes in mortgage rate and reference rate

	1966–1990	1966–1979	1980–1990
UK	0.74	0.62	0.91
USA	0.77	0.81	0.76
Germany	0.89	0.87	0.96
Japan	0.8	0.56	0.96
Canada	0.93	0.92	0.93
France	0.81	0.7	0.84

Table 3.2 shows an increase in the correlation of mortgage spreads over reference rates to defaults in the UK, Germany, and Canada in the 1980s, suggesting a shift to price rationing. However, consistent with a degree of equilibrium quantity rationing, the correlations are still often less than for companies.[19] Table 3.3 provides further evidence of equilibrium quantity rationing, given widespread limits of lending in relation to income or assets. However, there is also a marked contrast between the Anglo-Saxon countries and the others, as lending ratios are much higher and maturities longer in the former.[20] Such a relaxation is partly a recent phenomenon. UK ratios of loan to value for first-time buyers *on average* were 0.72 in 1980 and 0.83 in 1990. Wojnilower (1985) reports similar results for the USA. Such a high permitted level of gearing is of course very attractive to borrowers, given the potential capital gains on a low

Table 3.2. Correlation of change in spreads to change in defaults

	1966–1990	1966–1979	1980–1990	Companies (1980–1990)
UK	0.256	0.228	0.375	0.19
USA	0.191	0.351	0.196	0.40
Germany	0.299	0.229	0.638	0.14
Japan	0.205	0.269	−0.284	0.25
Canada	0.278	−0.015	0.54	0.70

[19] French data for household defaults were not available.

[20] The suggestion that households are subject to quantity rationing in CEJ countries contrasts with the view, expressed in Ch. 2, that low agency costs make such rationing less likely for companies there. Households and many small companies undoubtedly fall outside the circle of close relationships and are treated at arm's length. Indeed, given the favourable comparative treatment of companies it is intuitively likely that households would be more heavily rationed than in the Anglo-Saxon countries. In Italy, where household debt/income ratios are exceptionally low, Jappelli (1991) suggests additional factors are poor information on consumers' indebtedness (lack of credit reference agencies) and costs of enforcement (legal protection for debtors and slow court procedures).

downpayment (Muellbauer 1991). Another indicator of the tightness of quantity rationing is availability of home equity loans—a common phenomenon in the Anglo-Saxon countries but relatively unknown elsewhere.[21]

What are the key factors which underlie this loosening of rationing constraints? The survey of credit-rationing paradigms in Ch. 1 implies several channels which could lead to such a loosening of rationing. Among the factors are reduced risk of lending, better information, a reduction in the degree to which markets are segmented and/or uncompetitive, and changing government regulations. Risk aversion of lenders will clearly also be important.

It seems unlikely that the ex-post risk of lending has fallen (see Charts 3.7 and 3.8 below) although lenders' ex-ante perceptions of risk were probably affected by the rise in collateral values which accompanied growing debt (see Sect. 5). As noted, collateral reduces agency problems, and means there may be less incentive to screen—but if the trend in collateral values goes into reverse, agency problems, and hence screening, may be sharply increased. In some cases information may have improved, for example credit scoring to improve screening, or new and more restrictive contracts or covenants may have been introduced, but generally the contrary appears to hold: lenders appear to require less information and perform less monitoring than was traditionally the case. As shown in Table 3.4, there does, however, appear to have been increased entry into lending to the relevant sector, either in the form of new institutions lending directly, or development of new sources of funds via securitization, thus reducing segmentation. This is particularly true of mortgage lending (Lomax 1991). Ch. 7 assesses the broader implications of such new entry for financial fragility and instability.

Furthermore, the removal of quantitative controls on the growth of banks' balance sheets was an important factor in elimination of disequilibrium quantity rationing in several countries such as the UK and France. The deregulation of deposit rates (as in the USA), meant the loan rate (for example on mortgages) had to be increased relative to free market rates in order for lenders to remain profitable. This again led to replacement of quantity-rationing of credit by market equilibrium. Evidence about the effects of deregulation on growth in debt was sought by estimation of the effects of known measures of liberalization (see Table 3.4) in an equation for equilibrium debt growth based on wealth and income growth (not reported in detail). A dummy variable was set to one in the five years following liberalization and zero elsewhere. In fact

[21] Demand for such loans could also be lower elsewhere if there are lower owner-occupation rates and hence housing is a smaller proportion of personal-sector wealth, and also if house prices are sluggish, thus generating little excess equity.

Table 3.3. Indicators of credit rationing in the mortgage market

	UK	USA	Germany	Japan	Canada	France	Italy
Maximum loan to value ratio (%)	100	95	60–80[a]	60	90	80[b]	50
Maximum loan to income ratio	3½×	3×	—	3½×	Repayments to be 32% of family income	Repayments to be 30–5% of cash flow[c]	—
Maturity (years)	25	28	12–30	25–30	25	15	10–15

a Mortgage bond funded loans cannot exceed 60%. Top-up loans to 80% can usually be obtained.
b To be eligible for refinancing in secondary market.
c Equivalent to 2–2½× salary at 10% interest rate and flat repayment.
Source: Lomax (1991).

only in the UK and Germany was such a dummy significant, suggesting the relationship between liberalization and debt growth was a more diffuse process in the other countries.

Finally, it appears that in many cases banks and other financial institutions have become more tolerant of risk (while not necessarily underpricing it). Several underlying factors can be suggested, many of which parallel those for companies given in Ch. 2. Risk tolerance by lending institutions might have increased because, for example, they can pass on the debt in securitized form to other institutions (which may also mean there may be less incentive to monitor the debt).[22] This has been particularly common for residential mortgages in countries such as the USA. Alternatively, the implicit government guarantee on their assets may have become stronger (if social security pays mortgage interest, or the government insures loans). There could be greater risk-sharing with insurance companies (which, as in the UK, might insure the lender against losses on a proportion of the loan). Most crucially, competition arising from new entry and deregulation may have either stimulated competition for market share at the expense of margins, or reduced margins so much that profitability could only be maintained by rapid growth. (See Ch. 7 and Davis 1990*a*). This effect has been compounded by the loss of much profitable corporate business owing to the debt crisis (which, as discussed in Ch. 2, raised banks' costs of funds above some companies') and deregulation of securities markets.

Institutional investors, too, appear to be more ready to hold asset-backed securities. One reason is the high levels of collateralization (e.g. by mortgages), and in some countries government insurance. Also (particularly for non-mortgages), it was important that the market-making investment bank stood ready to supply a ready market, thus ensuring liquidity, while the risk associated with individual securities can be reduced by appropriate portfolio diversification. Use of such securities can provide large quantities of credit at prices that banks could not match, owing to the cost disadvantages of banks in the 1980s (see Ch. 2). However, on the other hand, this process of securitization may also mean that market liquidity in these instruments is vulnerable to failure of the market-maker or the desire of certain holders to disinvest.

The tendencies outlined in this section differ in importance between countries, but generally they help to explain a shift from disequilibrium quantity-rationing to market equilibrium in the credit market.

In the context of these changes, the nature of the relationship between borrowers and lenders has changed in several countries. Whereas

[22] The bank in this case puts its reputation at risk by failing to monitor, rather than its balance sheet. Rating agencies will help to offset the risk of underpricing of securitized debt.

Table 3.4. Key policy and structural stimuli to personal sector indebtedness

	UK	USA	Germany	Japan	Canada	France
Tax changes	Mortgage relief limits introduced 1974, tightened 1988	Act of 1986 removed tax concessions to consumer credit, stimulated mortgage borrowing	Tax concessions to mortgages 1970, abolished 1987	Mortgages tax deductible 1967	—	—
Financial liberalization	Abolition of quantitative controls on banks' balance sheets 1980	Deposit rate deregulation 1980–2	End of interest-rate ceilings on loans 1967	—	End of interest-rate controls 1967	Abolition of credit ceilings 1985
Institutional changes	New entrants to mortgage market 1980–1, banks and centralized lenders	Securitization beginning 1960s, expansion of mortgage banks in 1980s	Entry of banks to mortgage market after 1967	Housing Loan Corporation established 1970, new consumer credit houses mid-1960s	Growth of securitization in 1970s and 1980s	—

formerly mortgage lending occurred in the context of a long-term relationship, where compulsory saving often was needed prior to lending, now competition means this can no longer be enforced. Borrowers and lenders may thus be now seen as less committed to each other; and the lender may be more ready to foreclose in case of difficulty (relying on 'control'). Such tendencies may be heightened by narrow margins, which leave less scope for flexibility of terms or restructuring of debt. The chapter now goes on to assess the implications of personal-sector indebtedness for financial fragility and for saving.

(4) Personal-Sector Debt and Default

Besides offering explanations of the causes of the recent growth of debt, the theoretical analysis of Sect. 2, together with the credit-rationing paradigms (Ch. 1, Sect. 3), offer insights into the relation between debt and financial fragility. In particular, they imply that default risk is dependent not merely on debt or income but also on the other assets in the balance sheet of the borrowers, and macroeconomic variables such as interest rates and the trade cycle. It has also been noted in Sect. 2 that the household sector consists of groups with differences in age, assets, income, and liquidity constraints.

Various a priori suggestions can be made; for example, if debt increases following demographic shifts or increases in income or asset values which are sustainable, i.e. remaining at the life-cycle optimum, there should be no widespread increase in default risk, as individual agents are not overextended in this case. If liquidity constraints ease, the situation is harder to judge. Individuals are then able to attain their life-cycle optima and hence welfare gains are realized. However, to the extent that liquidity constraints were based on analyses of risk, as suggested above, their relaxation may increase the default risk faced by financial institutions. Finally, an increase in the desired level of debt by an individual, with no change in income, appears unambiguously to increase the risk to that individual, especially if his assets do not increase, i.e. the loan merely funds consumption. Income gearing and capital gearing both increase in this case and the consumer is henceforth more vulnerable to changes in income or interest rates. In all of these cases, the analysis also suggests that the risk of a default leading to a loss for a lending institution is greater, the greater the proportion of a household's debt that is constituted by unsecured consumer lending. (In practice, greater quant itative losses have been made on mortgage credit, perhaps because the lower default rate makes lenders complacent about absolute risks to balance sheets arising from market risk in real estate.)

The charts show patterns of personal-sector financial fragility in recent decades. Chart 3.7 shows the number of bankruptcies (affecting both consumers and unincorporated businesses) and Chart 3.8, the rate of mortgage foreclosure. A marked pattern of increasing default is apparent for some countries in the 1980s (the UK, the USA, Canada, and to a lesser extent Germany) but not for others (Japan).[23] This section seeks to relate these patterns to balance-sheet and income/expenditure developments. Those wishing to miss the details of the modelling and econometric exercise—and take the result on trust—should pass to the summary which begins at the bottom of p.94.

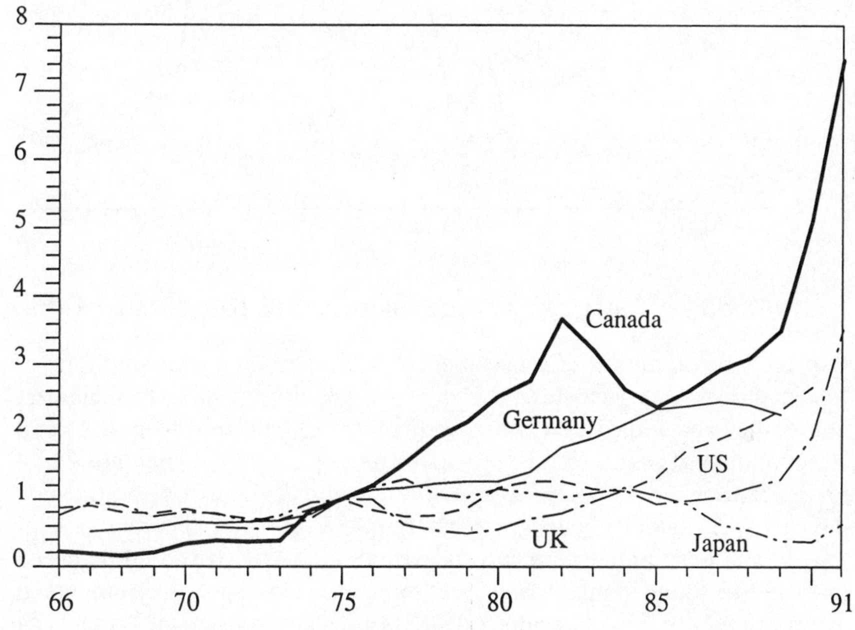

Chart 3.7. Personal bankruptcies (1975=1)

A specification was derived, in the spirit of the Wadhwani (1986) model outlined in Ch. 2, within which effects of debt ratios on loan default may be analysed (note, however, that the equation cannot capture the varying reasons for changes in debt outlined above). For households, we have in real terms the objective function set in terms of expected consumption:[24]

$$E(C) = E(qA + WL - qD) - K\mu H(.) + \Delta(D - A) \tag{3.1}$$

[23] Data are not available for France, but anecdotal evidence suggests that a similar pattern to the UK obtains.

[24] Obviously this ignores the disutility of labour, but in practice labour hours are not likely to be flexible for many households.

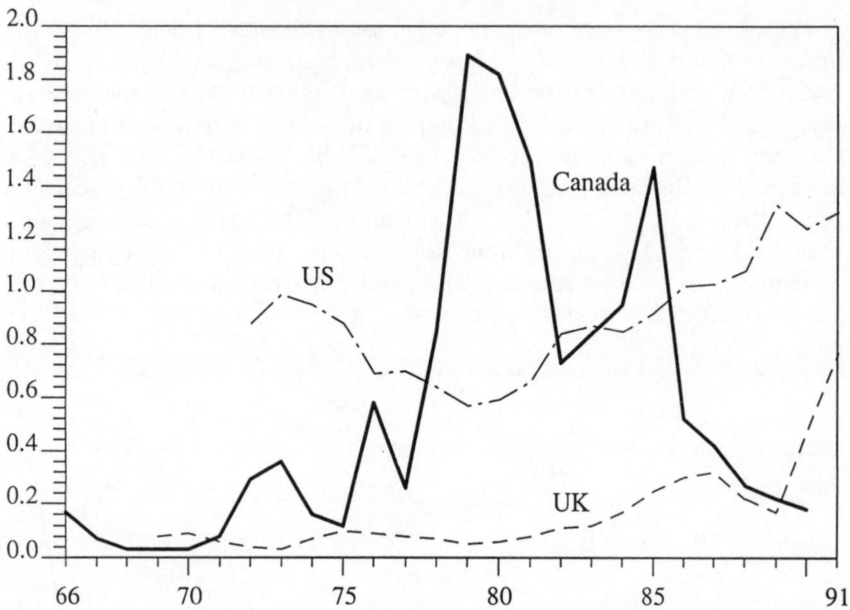

Chart 3.8. Mortgage repossessions and foreclosures (%)

Expected consumption (C) in a period is maximised by expenditure of expected disposable income and changes in net debt, subject to minimization of the expected cost (K) of the probability of bankruptcy ($\mu H(.)$) and accumulation of assets (A), to provide future income and expenditure and for precautionary purposes. Disposable income derives from real labour income WL, income from gross assets qA where q is the real rate of return, and net of real interest to be paid on debt qD. It should be noted that all debt and some assets are monetary; for such instruments q incorporates a nominal receipt (r) offset by some erosion of purchasing power (p). Other assets (housing, equities, pensions) are real, and provide real returns via capital appreciation as well as dividends/services. Given the absence of indexed debt, nominal interest payments on floating-rate debt during periods of high interest rates may pre-empt a large proportion of cash flow, even if real rates are constant. Conceptually, lenders are obtaining early repayment of capital via interest payments. Thus nominal rates offer an independent determinant of default risk.

The theory discussed above suggests that future income alone may not be legally pledged against increased debt, while some assets such as pensions may not be used as collateral.[25] Some households lacking assets may not be able to borrow at all. This suggests a borrowing constraint (S).

[25] However, in the case of unincorporated businesses some 'equity' may be taken into account (Hudson and Cuthbertson 1990).

$$S \leqslant A - D \tag{3.2}$$

where borrowing may not exceed the value of net assets (proxied here by total assets). (Implicitly we ignore the possibility of sizeable unsecured loans.) Obviously, this equation also shows that funds may be raised by liquidating assets, to the extent that this is possible in a given period. Falling asset prices, independent of associated income, have a clear implication for financial distress in this condition. Finally, the bankruptcy condition for households is as follows:

$$PDI - C + S < 0 \tag{3.3}$$

where PDI, personal disposable income, equals (WL + qA − qD). Clearly there are different groups in the household sector; *rentiers* rely on income from assets, while *employees* rely on their income from employment. Moreover, financial institutions will take into account the costs to them of putting borrowers into bankruptcy (legal fees, loss of reputation).

Using these considerations, we derive the following bankruptcy function from the last three equations.

$$\mu H = \mu H(PDI, q, r, D, A, U) \tag{3.4}$$

Personal disposable income (PDI) shows the basic effect of income. Unemployment (U) and the interest rates q and r show the vulnerability of employees and asset holders to bankruptcy. Interest rates obviously also affect both groups via interest payments on debt. Debt outstanding is an indicator of income gearing and of the likelihood of the binding of the borrowing constraint. Real gross wealth (A) shows the possibility of running down assets during periods of financial difficulty, as well as offering collateral for borrowing, and indicating effects of falling asset prices. Both debt and assets were entered as a ratio to personal disposable income. Note there will also be other unobserved qualitative variables relating to costs of bankruptcy to debtors such as the degree to which assets are sheltered, social security provisions, degree of social stigma to default, and legal costs. These have changed quite considerably in some countries (see, for example, Luckett (1988) on the USA).

Two sets of tests were conducted, one relating defaults to the above determinants for each country, the other stacking the data and conducting pooled cross-section/time-series estimation with country dummies. Tables 3.5 and 3.6 show the results by country. Given shortage of observations, a simple partial-adjustment specification was chosen: its econometric shortcomings (Hendry *et al.* 1983) should be borne in mind. Since the Durbin–Watson statistic is biased in the presence of a lagged dependent variable, we report the Lagrange-Multiplier (LM) test[26] for residual autocorrelation, distributed χ^2, where $\chi^2(1) = 4.5$.

[26] See Breusch and Pagan 1980.

The results are broadly consistent across countries, but highlight different components of the default function. In the bankruptcy functions (Table 3.5) debt/income ratios come to the fore in the UK and USA, latterly the most liberalized credit markets, suggesting overindebtedness is a common problem there. A 1 per cent rise in debt/income ratios raises bankruptcy by 2.5 per cent in the UK and 1.3 per cent in the USA in the short run, and 3.6 per cent in the UK and 13 per cent in the USA in the long run. In the other countries, levels of debt are not significant determinants of default, perhaps because liquidity constraints have prevented levels of gearing being high enough to impinge on bankruptcy probabilities across the economy as a whole. Declining wealth (which may entail falling asset prices) is an indicator of bankruptcy in the UK, Germany, and Japan, unemployment in Germany and Japan, and nominal interest rates in all countries but the UK. Real rates had a negative effect on defaults in the UK and Germany—this may be consistent with a positive effect of inflation, leading to higher nominal rates which pre-empt a large proportion of cashflow.

In the mortgage repossessions/foreclosures equations (Table 3.6) the UK results are similar to those for bankruptcies, with a positive effect of debt and negative effect of wealth and real rates. In contrast, indebtedness does not feature in the US or Canadian functions. The statistical properties of both sets of estimates are reasonable.

A second test was performed using the 'least squared with dummy variables' technique (Maddala 1977), which stacked the data for the separate countries into one vector for each variable, giving 108 observations (see Table 3.7). Conceptually, the equations can be seen as giving average coefficients for all countries. An error-correction specification, distinguishing difference (short-term) and lagged levels (long-term) effects, was adopted. The equation (1) in Table 3.7 indicates a strong long-run effect of indebtedness on bankruptcy, although there is no short-run effect. Counterintuitively, unemployment has a negative sign. When country-specific coefficients are estimated for the lagged debt/income ratios, a marked contrast is apparent between the UK and USA, where debt has a sizeable effect on bankruptcy; Canada and Germany, where the effect is smaller; and Japan, where the effect is zero. Such a result, which supports the country-specific equations in Table 3.5, is consistent with a greater willingness of lenders in the UK and USA to enable borrowers to go into debt beyond their means; in other words, there has been less credit rationing there than in other countries, as is also suggested in Table 3.3.

Although the results should be seen as tentative, given the small number of observations, the specifications for household default do offer insights into

Table 3.5. Equations for personal sector bankruptcy

	UK[a] Log bankruptcies	USA[b] Log bankruptcy rate	Canada[c] Log bankruptcies	Germany[d] Log bankruptcies	Japan[e] Log suspension of transactions with banks
Constant	10.8 (3.7)[f]	− 7.1 (3.7)	1.0 (2.1)	1.1 (1.6)	3.9 (1.4)
Lagged dependent	0.29 (1.6)	0.9 (11.3)	0.92 (12.6)	0.91 (6.3)	0.71 (3.2)
Log debt/disposable income	2.5 (3.9)	1.3 (3.7)	—	—	—
Log wealth/disposable income	− 2.4 (2.9)	—	—	− 0.8 (1.7)	− 0.68 (2.0)
Log first difference disposable income	—	− 3.5 (3.7)	—	1.4 (2.4)	—
Unemployment rate	—	—	—	0.06 (5.9)	0.25 (1.8)
Nominal interest rate	—	0.01 (1.5)	0.038 (1.9)	0.035 (3.8)	0.06 (2.7)
Real interest rate	− 0.027 (2.7)	—	—	− 0.026 (3.4)	—
$\bar{R}^2$	0.79	0.96	0.96	0.99	0.90
SE	0.14	0.08	0.22	0.44	0.09
LM(1)	1.4	3.0	1.7	0.4	2.6
N	18	24	22	23	20

a 1972–89
b 1967–90
c 1966–88
d 1967–89
e 1970–89
f 't' ratios in parentheses

Table 3.6. Equations for personal sector mortgage repossessions

	UK[a] Log mortgage repossession rate	Canada[b] Log claims on mortgage insurance/sum insured	USA[c] Log mortgage foreclosure rate
Constant	13.5 (6.5)[d]	− 2.0 (2.3)	− 0.7 (1.4)
Lagged dependent	0.48 (4.4)	0.54 (3.4)	0.91 (7.7)
Log debt/disposable income	5.2 (9.1)	—	—
Log wealth/disposable income	− 6.5 (7.9)	—	—
Log first difference disposable income	—	—	—
Unemployment rate	—	0.28 (2.5)	—
Nominal interest rate	—	—	—
Real interest rate	− 0.023 (2.1)	− 0.13 (1.9)	0.015 (2.1)
$\bar{R}^2$	0.94	0.75	0.80
se	0.17	0.68	0.11
LM(1)	2.6	0.1	0.1
N	21	22	18

a 1969–90
b 1966–88
c 1972–90
d 't' ratios in parentheses

Table 3.7. Pooled cross-section and time series equations for bankruptcy ('t' ratios in parentheses)

(1) Common coefficients

Δ log bankruptcy = -0.4 $-0.81\ \Delta$ log wealth/income
(0.8) (2.1)

$-0.007\ \Delta$ real interest rate	-0.1 log bankruptcy$_{t-1}$
(1.5)	(2.7)
$+0.48$ log debt/income$_{t-1}$	-0.73 log wealth/income$_{t-1}$
(4.4)	(4.0)
$+0.1$ log real income$_{t-1}$	-0.024 unemployment$_{t-1}$
(2.9)	(2.4)
$+0.013$ nominal interest rate$_{t-1}$ + dummies	
(2.0)	

$\bar{R}^2 = 0.86$, se = 0.14, LM(1) = 2.5, LM(4) = 7.0, N = 108

(2) Country specific coefficients for log debt/income$_{t-1}$

UK:	0.76	US:	0.83	Canada:	0.39
	(3.0)		(1.7)		(1.3)
Germany:	0.36	Japan:	-0.09	[log bankruptcy$_{t-1}$:	-0.1]
	(2.2)		(0.1)		(2.2)

the determinants of financial distress, and the importance of debt therein. They suggest that a high level of debt for households in relation to income, in the context of liberalized financial markets, may lead to financial problems. These may be particularly severe should there be concomitant high nominal interest rates, high inflation, declining real gross wealth, perhaps due to falling asset prices, and high unemployment.

(5) Personal Debt, Saving, and Asset Prices

Apart from its direct effect on financial fragility—the main focus of this chapter—an effect of adjustment in personal-sector debt on saving and asset prices can also be discerned. As well as being relevant to macroeconomic policy, this may also have indirect implications for fragility. Table 3.8 shows that in the countries which have experienced financial liberalization (notably the UK) there has been a strong correlation between growth of debt and declining saving. This feature is absent in some of the other countries, as shown by simple correlations between borrowing and saving as a proportion of personal disposable income over this period. These are: UK -0.99, USA -0.57, Canada -0.91, Germany $+0.05$, France $+0.3$, Japan -0.5. To the extent that other domestic sectors do not adjust their saving in an offsetting manner, such a pattern may have an adverse impact on the balance of payments (Miles 1992). Rising debt may also affect asset prices, thus compounding the effect on saving (although reverse causality could also be envisaged, whereby rising wealth offers collateral for increased debt). Correlations of changes in borrowing to changes in house prices are: UK 0.52, USA 0.69, Canada 0.53, Germany −0.16, Japan 0.68. Hence only in Germany is the relation not present. Note that if a decline in borrowing—or a response of monetary policy to general inflation—causes asset prices to fall, existing borrowers, particularly those purchasing property at the peak of the boom, may face difficulties. Moreover, a fall in asset prices may entail a further decline in borrowing, a rise in the saving ratio, and a reduction in consumption. These links are discussed further in Ch. 4.

Conclusions

Debt growth in the personal sector has been rapid in many advanced OECD countries in recent years, although the rise is more marked in relation to income than wealth. In several cases, this can be attributed to the liberalization of financial markets, which has led to a reduction of disequilibrium quantity rationing of credit. Growth in debt has been accompanied by rising defaults. However, results suggest the debt/default relation is closest in countries where liberalization has gone furthest and credit rationing is weakest. Finally, growth in debt has also accompanied a decline in saving and rising asset prices.

It remains to assess welfare and policy implications. Rising default is undesirable a priori, given the welfare costs to individuals, the quite sizeable transactions costs to bankruptcy (Ch. 2, Sect. 3), and any unanticipated losses incurred by financial intermediaries. Given the need for capital adequacy, the requirement for provisions against such losses and/or tighter credit rationing may have a wider macroeconomic significance, if it restrains the further growth in credit (Ch. 4) or indeed if it leads to financial instability (Chs. 5–8). These costs must be set against the benefits of access to finance *per se* in enabling expenditures to be shifted over time independent of income, and for small businesses to develop. These suggest that, rather than returning to rationing, there is a need to offset deleterious effects of liberalized credit markets. For example, it appears that default risks seem greatest when individuals are unaware of potential risk and when financial institutions relax rationing to an excessive extent. Potential policy implications are as listed below. As for companies, most are means of prevention of fragility, though others, such as maintenance of capital adequacy, and renegotiation, seek to offset its consequences.

The results suggest efforts should be made to educate the personal sector about the risks of indebtedness, in particular the potential variation in interest payments on variable-rate debt when monetary policy is tightened. Costs of default—loss of assets, inability to raise credit in the

Table 3.8. Household saving and borrowing as % of disposable income

	1979	1980	1981	1982	1983	1984	1985	1986	1987	1988	1989	1990
USA												
saving	7.0	7.3	7.7	7.0	5.5	6.3	4.5	4.3	3.0	4.3	4.7	—
borrowing	10.1	6.8	5.8	3.7	7.4	8.6	10.6	10.3	8.5	9.2	8.5	8.6
housing yield[a]	14.3	5.1	8.1	2.1	10.8	8.7	7.1	6.8	7.7	6.4	5.2	—
Japan												
saving	18.2	17.9	18.3	16.5	16.3	16.0	16.0	16.4	15.1	14.8	15.3	—
borrowing	7.3	8.3	6.6	5.6	7.5	6.5	5.1	3.6	15.3	12.0	11.3	—
housing yield[a]	6.7	8.7	13.9	13.4	10.2	7.8	4.3	4.2	13.5	7.6	10.7	16.9
Germany												
saving	12.6	12.7	13.5	12.7	10.8	11.4	11.4	12.2	12.3	12.6	12.3	—
borrowing	8.7	7.5	6.0	5.3	6.6	5.5	4.3	4.5	2.3	2.5	4.1	—
housing yield[a]	9.2	11.2	13.7	8.6	5.5	4.5	3.6	4.1	4.9	4.5	6.4	8.9
Canada												
saving	13.2	13.6	15.4	18.2	14.8	15.0	13.3	10.7	9.4	10.0	11.0	—
borrowing	9.8	8.4	4.7	0.2	4.7	5.3	5.3	8.3	10.7	10.8	8.7	5.7
housing yield[a]	15.0	5.7	8.8	3.0	11.6	9.5	7.8	11.3	16.4	13.1	17.8	4.3
UK												
saving	11.7	13.1	12.5	11.4	9.8	10.5	9.7	8.1	6.5	5.2	6.5	8.5
borrowing	9.9	7.9	9.2	10.8	11.6	11.4	12.0	13.5	15.3	18.0	15.1	12.1
housing yield[a]	30.5	23.6	8.2	5.4	13.7	12.0	10.7	16.4	18.9	29.4	21.1	0.8
France												
saving	18.8	17.6	18.0	17.3	15.9	14.5	14.0	12.9	11.1	12.1	12.3	—
borrowing	7.5	6.2	4.9	5.4	4.4	5.8	4.6	5.5	6.0	5.0		—

a Nominal increase in house prices plus estimate of rental yield future—should be clearly spelt out in loan documentation and in pre-loan counselling.

Tax incentives to borrowing such as mortgage relief should be re-examined (abstracting from their effect on asset prices). Indeed, some commentators such as Llewellyn and Holmes (1991) would suggest that mortgage interest should actually be taxed. Of course, such policies would initially increase the burden on existing debtors.

Growth of mortgage debt could be limited by restrictions on the lender's right to sue for recovery to a fixed proportion of the initial value of the property.

Financial institutions should consider sharing information on the indebtedness of consumers, in order to keep track of overall indebtedness, perhaps by means of a credit reference agency. (See also Pagano and Jappelli (1991), who note that in contrast to corporate information sharing, sharing is more common for persons in the Anglo-Saxon countries than in Continental Europe).

Limits on interest rates charged could limit high-risk lending, at a cost of excluding some members of the personal sector from credit.

Limitations on the degree to which interest rates on variable-rate loans could be changed in a given period may be helpful—although this would impinge on the overall cost of credit.

A return to direct controls on credit expansion is a superficially attractive means to limit growth in debt. But such controls would be likely to be ineffective in a liberalized financial system, especially one lacking exchange controls.

Maintenance of capital adequacy of financial intermediaries is as vital to protect against losses on personal debt as on corporate debt. But even if capital adequacy is maintained, it is arguable that defaults would be fewer if financial intermediaries were more restrained in their pursuit of market share (especially since such episodes often culminate in an overtightening of credit standards in reaction). Even if lenders adequately cover their risks during such episodes, the risk to households and the macroeconomy could justify restraint. Such restraint could be encouraged by more detailed prudential oversight of risk premiums and changes in equilibrium quantity rationing (such as loan to value ratios), or limitations on tax write-offs against specific provisions.

The public sector (as in France) could seek to renegotiate loans for overindebted households, although cost and effects of potential moral hazard on borrowers and on the lending policies of banks might argue against this.

4

Economic Effects of Financial Fragility

Chs. 2 and 3 focused largely on the direct costs of financial fragility, namely increased business failures, household bankruptcies, and mortgage foreclosures. It was noted (Ch. 2, Sect. 3) that the key assumption required for such defaults to be of economic relevance is that there should be positive costs of bankruptcy, i.e. that default does not merely involve a smooth transfer of assets from debtor to creditor. Such costs might include not merely legal costs but also difficulties of firms in keeping personnel, obtaining inventory, costs of portfolio reallocation, costs of disposing of collateral, etc. But it was also noted that financial fragility may have broader economic effects. In the extreme, fragility may lead to systemic risk in the financial system; this relationship, as well as other causes and consequences of systemic risk, is explored in Chs. 5–8. Here we assess some of the wider implications of overindebtedness and default for economic performance, short of the generation of financial instability. In general, these are spillover or externality effects that are not taken into account by companies or households when selecting their level of gearing in the light of their assets and income, nor by lenders choosing their interest rates on loans. They thus constitute possible grounds for policy intervention. (For useful related surveys, see Driscoll 1991, Gertler 1988).

(1) Effects on Other Companies

When companies go into default, this may have direct effects on other companies that are suppliers and customers. Immediate problems may arise that threaten their liquidity; if stock has been received but not paid for, then the supplier may not be repaid in full and/or be paid very slowly. In other words, there is heightened counterparty risk. Such potential problems, even if not realized, may in turn make counterparties of customers or suppliers of the defaulting firm unwilling to extend credit. In other words, there may be a form of contagion, spreading from the defaulter to others closely associated with it, that may lead them to fail too, even if they are financially sound. Such effects are more likely, the smaller the counterparty is in relation to the defaulting firm, the less diversified it is, and the more adverse the state of its own balance sheet; in practice, it is vulnerable small firms which tend to grant rather than receive trade credit (lack of bargaining power may be relevant). Indeed, the severity of this problem for small firms in the UK has prompted official action to press for payment within a reasonable time, announced in the 1992 Budget.

Clearly, if all firms have heightened leverage, the risk of contagion arising via counterparty risk becomes greater. An economy with a larger proportion of trade credit as opposed to intersectoral finance may be more susceptible to these problems. Meanwhile, even assuming firms survive these initial problems, they will have to find other customers or suppliers for their services, which is likely to involve sizeable costs of adjustment, and when these are sufficiently large the firms may go into default themselves. Finally, even if default does not occur, the syndrome is likely to lead to sharp declines in expenditure, as creditors absorb their losses (see also Sect. 4).

Of course, effects such as those noted above are not the only consequences of default. Failures of other companies in sectors such as property may significantly worsen prospects for those remaining, if defaults lead to sale of assets at 'distress prices' which depresses asset prices generally. In other sectors, removal of excess capacity may be a relief to remaining firms.

(2) Effects on Public Expenditure

An impact on public expenditure, necessitating increases in current or future[1] taxation, may arise in the case of failures of banks, households, or companies. If deposit insurance is publicly funded, or the lender of last resort function is employed in the case of banks that prove to be insolvent, bank failures may impose direct costs on the state. The case of a household losing its residence due to mortgage foreclosure may impose costs on society via the need to rehouse them at public expense. Similarly, the closure of a company following business failure is likely to lead to job losses. Assuming that workers cannot find new jobs immediately, as is likely when there is regional or national recession, and/or their human capital is highly specific to the failed firm, then costs arise for the public sector in paying for unemployment benefit and (in some countries) for mortgage interest. Of course, an alternative way of regarding such expenditures is that they are automatic stabilizers that help protect against the macroeconomic consequences of financial fragility (Summers 1991).

[1] To repay borrowing.

(3) Effects of Economic Policy

In general, higher leverage, especially with floating-rate debt, may increase the effectiveness of monetary policy, as a given rise in interest rates has a greater effect on disposable income of net debtors.[2] Nevertheless, lags may still be long if credit availability is unchanged, while agents initially compare higher interest rates with expectations of inflation and still rapidly-increasing asset prices. Experience suggests that these patterns may take some time to be reversed. Note that, given information asymmetries, if lenders continue to price-ration credit in the presence of higher interest rates, there may be a severe deterioration in the mix of borrowers (see Ch. 1, Sect. 3).

However, the authorities may fear that a tightening of monetary policy will lead to widespread default, due to the state of balance sheets, and that this in turn will precipitate a deep recession via multiplier effects on income arising from demand and employment (and/or systemic failures in the financial sector). This may in turn lead to an unwillingness to counteract inflation by higher interest rates in a way that might cause a recession (Friedman 1990). Such an effect would entail both the adverse effects of inflation itself and severe moral-hazard problems arising from the validation of excessive levels of leverage. Agents would feel justified in increasing further the riskiness of their balance sheets, because they assume they will be 'saved'.[3]

At a micro level, too, similar effects on moral hazard may arise if local authorities or industrial companies in financial difficulties are bailed out in the way traditionally reserved for financial institutions (when there is systemic risk to the financial system). Wojnilower (1980) and Schwartz (1986) suggest that rescues such as Chrysler and New York City in the 1970s were particularly harmful in this respect. Such rescues have traditionally been common in Continental Europe and Japan.

[2] See Easton (1990) for the UK, Ryding (1990*a*) for the USA, Shigehara (1990; 1991) for Japan, and Blundell-Wignall and Browne (1991) for a review of international experience. The effect depends on an asymmetric response by net creditors, who may save rather than spending the increase in income, while net debtors cut expenditure.

[3] In this context, Melitz and Bordes (1991) suggest that a monetary policy which allows higher inflation, higher interest rates, and smoothing of interest-rate volatility may be *optimal* to reduce bank failures in the wake of financial liberalization. (Higher inflation is assumed to boost bank profitability, given continuing oligopoly in banking, while lower volatility protects against interest-rate risk.) But their argument relies on the assumption that interest-rate risk is more important to banks than credit risk, which is questionable, especially given a growing preponderence (even in France) of floating-rate debt. And incresed competition, leading to payment of interest on a wider range of deposits, reduces the benefit to banks from inflation.

(4) Cyclical Effects on Saving and Investment

Financial fragility may increase the volatility of personal and corporate saving, and hence the amplitude of the economic cycle. In a recession or period of monetary tightening—or more generally in the case of an unanticipated shock such as an oil crisis—weakness of balance sheets may require a sharp adjustment in expenditure. Households may cut consumption as they seek to cover interest obligations, as income falls and/or interest payments rise. They may also seek to adjust balance sheets as a precaution against the risk of unemployment (e.g. running down consumer debt). Heavily indebted companies will similarly seek sharp adjustments in expenditure (i.e. employment and investment)[4] in order to cover interest obligations as profits fall. (Cantor (1990) offers US evidence; Young (1992) discusses the UK situation.)

Both sectors will sharply reduce their demand for borrowing. Such a mechanism will be accelerated if there are restrictions on availability of further credit to make up for income shortfalls, whether due to lenders' perceptions of insolvency risk or for reasons endogenous to the financial sector (see the following section). But they can occur solely as a demand-side phenomenon. These effects may be particularly strong during the first recession after financial liberalization, because the personal saving ratio may be low and the corporate deficit high in the preceding expansion, owing to the growth in debt as balance sheets adjust (see Ch. 3, Sect. 5). They may also be greater in a system based on 'control' rather than on 'commitment', as borrowers assume they will not be rescued by their lenders from financing difficulties and hence adjust more decisively to avoid them.

These effects in turn may cause 'multiplier' effects on the economy, as 'demand externalities' arising from these adjustments impinge on other sectors (Cooper and John 1988). Difficulties for macroeconomic policy-makers are increased by the fact that forecasting models estimated over periods prior to liberalization cannot easily predict behaviour in the first recession after it.

(5) Effects Operating via the Financial System

An unanticipated increase in defaults associated with the realization of financial fragility has direct effects on the profitability of creditors, when interest on loans ceases to be paid and principal may not be recoverable.

[4] In principle, corporate dividends should also be reducible in such a situation, but this appears to depend on investor expectations. In the UK it appears that investors often find cuts in nominal dividends unacceptable almost regardless of the risk to solvency, hence firms hold out against cuts for fear of loss of reputation (such as afflicted ICI in the 1980s). In other countries this appears to be more acceptable.

As discussed in Chs. 5–8, in some conditions this may lead to systemic risk for the financial system, including contagious bank failures and collapse of liquidity in securities markets.

But even short of this, banks may find that provisioning to cover non-performing loans causes problems relating to their capital adequacy. (Such a pattern may imply risk on loans was mispriced, as otherwise reserves would have been built up against default.) Weakness in capital adequacy may also arise from stock market declines if, as in Japan, unrealized gains on banks' securities holdings count towards bank capital. In the case that the authorities set minimum capital ratios—or given prudent management—such patterns may require balance-sheet expan sion to be slowed or even reversed in order for capital ratios to be maintained (C. Johnson 1991).[5] Even the anticipation of a capital constraint may lead banks to reduce balance-sheet growth, if they prefer to retain a cushion against uncertain future losses.

The effect of the capital constraint is that credit availability from banks is reduced regardless of borrowers' credit quality or the interest rate (i.e. the loan-supply curve shifts to the left). Note that capital constraints will have this effect even if the banking system operates via relationships rather than transactions banking. But the locus of restriction may differ: banks in the former will presumably strive to sustain its established customers, the latter those currently most profitable/viable. In addition, since risk weights do not perfectly capture relative credit risks, there will be incentives to arbitrage by switching assets into lower weighted categories,[6] restricting supply of credit to certain borrowers.

Such a pattern requires that securitization of bank assets be difficult or impossible. Also, the equity market must be closed to banks—as is possible in a recession when markets are unwilling to accept rights issues in general, and may take a particularly jaundiced view of prospects for banks, as well as for the more structural reasons outlined in Ch. 1, Sect. 2.

Balance-sheet problems may be accompanied by an increase in risk aversion among bank lending officers, who have seen their earlier lending decisions fail (Budd 1990). Local managers in branch banks may feel it in their own interests to overtighten credit criteria, to avoid any bad loans. An additional factor may be increases in flat-rate deposit insurance premiums—an implicit tax on (safe) banks' profits, to the extent it is not passed on to borrowers.

[5] Note this does not imply capital adequacy is an effective monetary policy instrument, even if a mixture of prudential and monetary control were desirable (it is not, because any variation in prudential rules for monetary policy purposes is contrary to the stability and predictability required of prudential supervision). In an upturn banks would find it easier to raise equity, as well as generating retentions, thus rendering control ineffective.

[6] Since the Basle risk weights (Ch. 5, Sect. 2) apply 100% to corporate loans and 50% to residential mortgages, users of the former might be penalized at the expense of the latter.

The situation overall can lead to a reduction in credit supply, operating both via increases in spreads (price rationing) and more pervasive equilibrium quantity rationing.[7] In each of these cases, the impact of credit constraints will be concentrated on borrowers unable to access securities markets (either directly or via packaged loans). Small- and medium-sized firms are the obvious examples.[8] In addition, capital constraints should bite harder on the economy for a given level of bad debts and bank profitability, the less developed the securities markets are.

Unanticipated losses on bonds may have similar effects on other debt markets, thus giving rise to the familiar pattern of higher bond spreads/price rationing in a recession (see Davis 1992*a*). In addition, if there are externalities from bank lending to market finance, due to banks' informational advantages a reduction in bank credit may lead to a lower availability of funds overall. Note that if defaults arising from high leverage are *anticipated*, this should entail a general increase in the cost of capital, thus affecting investment and economic performance.

Greenwald and Stiglitz (1986*a*, *b*; 1987) have developed a version of the monetary transmission mechanism which operates via credit rationing. In essence, it is suggested that the factors underlying the observations, first, that tightening of the monetary stance reduces economic activity,[9] and second, that real interest rates vary little[10] in such circumstances, can be explained by appeal to credit rationing. It is assumed that borrowers face credit constraints (by price or quantity). Further, the monetary authorities can control, via banks' reserves, the 'working capital' of the banks, and hence their willingness to lend. Because of specific information concerning borrowers that banks have acquired, the cost to borrowers of raising funds from other sources (such as the equity market) will in general be higher than that of obtaining bank loans. Restricting bank credit may thus increase the marginal cost of funds to previously price-rationed borrowers, even if the bank does not sharply increase the interest rate it charges. Meanwhile, previously quantity-rationed borrowers will find their constraints tightened. This pattern may (in a trade-cycle context) reduce aggregate investment, while in financially fragile states it could help lead to heightened default.

Expanding this approach, and connecting it with the previous section on volatility of saving and investment, Bernanke and Gertler (1989) suggest that the state of balance sheets (net worth) has an impact on both the upturn and downturn. This results from a relation between the agency

[7] Some observers call this situation a 'credit crunch', but following Wojnilower (1980) we prefer to use the phrase to refer to disequilibrium credit-rationing caused by interest-rate ceilings.

[8] As noted in Sect. 1, they are also likely to be worst hit by problems with trade credit.

[9] The 'monetarist black box'.

[10] The 'Keynesian' transmission mechanism.

costs of financing investment via debt and net worth, which arises from mechanisms similar to those for equilibrium quantity rationing of credit (Ch. 1, Sect. 3). High net worth in the upturn hence boosts investment; low net worth in the downturn amplifies supply-side financing constraints, by raising the cost of external funds relative to scarce internal funds, thus enforcing cuts in investment or employment (compare the discussion in Sect. 6 below and in Ch. 5, Sects. 7 and 8). Indeed, exogenous shocks that influence net worth, such as falls in equity prices, may actually precipitate the downturn in Bernanke and Gertler's framework.

(6) Financial Fragility and Long Term Economic Performance

Recent work in the USA has also suggested that the high levels of gearing may impact on long term levels of investment. The suggestion (Bernanke and Gertler 1990) is that financially fragile states (i.e. with low levels of borrower net worth) lead to high agency costs and poor performance in the economy as a whole. Such a situation might arise when entrepreneurs, who must borrow to finance projects, know more about the success probabilities of projects they evaluate (at a cost) than do potential lenders. This leads to agency costs in that the entrepreneur has an incentive to be insufficiently selective in evaluating projects (as outlined above) which are more severe the lower borrower net worth is, and which raise the cost of finance. This in turn affects the willingness of entrepreneurs to evaluate projects in the first place. Hence the quantity of investment spending and its quality (expected return) may both be sensitive to net worth. Note that such a problem can in principle be reduced by closer monitoring, particularly in the context of relationship banking (commitment). An additional point may be that to the extent that banks are enfeebled by financial fragility, their key clients, small and medium firms, will face expensive or volatile credit. If, as is commonly believed, such firms are crucial to growth, this may impact on long-term performance.

(7) Volatility of Asset Prices

As noted in Ch. 3, Sect. 5, high levels of credit expansion to the personal sector have tended to coincide with rapid increases in house prices, while a slowdown in such lending often leaves prices vulnerable to decline, thus heightening fragility. Indeed, sharp falls in asset prices, which drive nominal asset values below the nominal quantity of outstanding loans, increase the incentive to default on interest and principal, leaving the lenders to dispose of the security. In turn, disposal of defaulting borrowers' security by lenders (such as repossessed houses) can aggravate a downward spiral in asset prices; or if lenders retain the security, an 'overhang' of such properties may weaken the market. The difficulties feed back on to the lenders, who will need to increase provisions against losses on such assets, and may tighten loan standards (compare Sect. 5 above, and the discussion in R. Johnson (1991), who calls this phenomenon a 'credit crumble').

Such arguments regarding asset prices can be made more generally, particularly for prices of commercial property, where supply is relatively inelastic in the short run, and corporate bankruptcies, leaving further unoccupied space, may aggravate excess supply arising from earlier overbuilding. It applies to a lesser extent for equities; but there is a contrast. With financial assets such as equities, price declines may occur relatively rapidly. Given the tendency of sellers of property to hold out for unrealistic prices, thus drying up liquidity, adjustment in such markets can take a protracted period. The general point remains, however, that an economy subject to high 'disequilibrium' gearing may be subject to increased volatility in asset prices. As well as causing fragility, this may discourage investment, given the implied increase in risk (e.g. for construction).

(8) Bank Insolvency

It is both relevant and appropriate to continue with a brief discussion of individual bank failure, as it provides a further implication of fragility as well as a link between the main sections of the book. Individual banks may get into difficulties due to financial fragility in the non-financial sector, without necessarily leading to the contagious runs and systemic risk discussed in Chs. 5–8. The USA has had the most experience of such failures, with over 1,000 banks failing over 1981–9, although this must be seen in the context of a banking structure with 12,500 institutions in 1990. Such failures have been most marked in the South-West and North-East that suffered economic downturns following booms (featuring extensive property development) in the 1980s. (See Tannenwald (1991) for an evaluation of the New England crisis.) Effects on banks were probably aggravated by restrictions on interstate banking, which tend to impede US banks from geographical diversification. High costs of funds, as banks faced disintermediation by money-market mutual funds, and loss of credit quality after the debt crisis, as well as increased regulatory 'insurance' (a higher threshold for deposit insurance) also accompanied these difficulties.

Nevertheless, as noted by Pantalone and Platt (1987), bad management, resulting in excessive risk-taking (as indicated by patterns of leverage or risk concentration), inadequate systems, and poor performance remain the best predictors of bank failures. Competition appeared to have changed the level but not the pattern of failure; banks with poor management that in the past would get by 'can no longer maintain an adequate return, and turn to risky alternatives or are embroiled in embezzlement and fraud, that does rapid damage with today's narrower profit margins' (ibid.: 45). In contrast, measures of a region's economic performance were not good predictors of failure in 1–2 years, because many of the loans going into default following regional depressions were made during periods of prosperity, featuring excessive speculation and inadequate diversification. Most banks survive downturns; the ones failing have often already taken excessive risks that made them vulnerable to adverse conditions. The US Comptroller of the Currency (1988), in a study that generated similar results, suggested the implication was that traditional bank examination, focusing on 'Camel' (capital, assets, management, earnings, and liquidity), was the best way to prevent failure. Only in 7 per cent of a sample of 171 failed banks were economic factors the sole determinants.[11]

As noted, the US experience of bank failure is not shared by the other countries studied. But if, as suggested by Frankel and Montgomery (1991), the principal reason for this is the geographical diversification, as well as size, of banks in other countries (reducing exposure to local risk), then the losses made due to bad loans may still be sizeable, but offset by good loans elsewhere in the same bank. This suggests that only if the costs of bank failure are high is 'national' banking preferable.[12] However, the discussion in Ch. 2 of costs of bankruptcy, as well as theories of intermediation in Ch. 1, suggest they *will* be high, especially where private and idiosyncratic information and close long-term banking relationships are important (e.g. for small- and medium-sized firms). Only if there is little private information and largely 'transactions based' banking (e.g. for domestic mortgages) could such losses be minor. One indicator of this difference is the ability to securitize such claims.

It is important to add that the 'Camel' list noted above emphasises the broader classification of potential difficulties for banks than the *credit risk* focused on in this section. In particular, most banking texts also emphasise *liquidity risk* (inability to obtain funding for current obligations) and *interest-rate* risk (risk of loss from changes in the value of assets or liabilities of different maturities or durations, associated with changes in the overall level of interest rates).[13] For investment banks, and for

[11] However, as noted by Brumbaugh *et al.* (1989), the fact that in recent years many large US banks had low capital/asset ratios (and were most active in LBOs) gives little cause for comfort.

[12] Such an argument abstracts from the possibility that regulatory/monitoring costs may be much higher for a large number of local banks.

[13] The macroeconomic impact of interest-rate risk relies on an asymmetric response of borrowers and investors. In contrast, credit risk harms the creditor with no offset for the debtor.

commercial banks allowed to trade securities, there may also be *market risk*, i.e. that the value of marketable securities will change while the investor is holding a position in them. Note that most of these risks are systematic, or non-diversifiable to the bank (although some can be *hedged*). These other risks are emphasized in some of the episodes of systemic risk discussed in Chs. 5–8.

(9) Financial Fragility: A Case-study

A number of the episodes discussed in the remainder of the book are examples of the syndromes outlined above, albeit linked to instability in the financial sector more generally; Norway and Australia in recent years are good examples (Ch. 8). However, there have also been a number of instances of fragility that have not had these broader consequences. As discussed in Ch. 2, the Canadian recession of 1981–2 had severe consequences for the wider economy, aggravated by overextended balance sheets, but was not accompanied by systemic risk (though the failure of the Western banks in 1985 (Ch. 8) can be traced back to it). The USA in 1989–91 showed signs of financial fragility, as foreshadowed in the analyses of Chs. 2 and 3 (see e.g. Bernanke and Lown 1991; R. Johnson 1991); the caution of the authorities in not provoking a recession via tight macro-economic policy was publicly admitted to relate partly to fear of the consequences of fragility. There were also increased defaults in Japan during 1990–1, despite continuing economic growth, largely due to falling land and share prices after monetary policy was tightened. Problems for banks of non-performing loans were aggravated by pressure on interest margins due to deregulation and capital adequacy problems arising from stock market declines (Sect. 5).

The example which we explore at greater length, however, is the UK in 1990/1.[14] The analysis uses publicly available data only, and draws particularly on the information set out in Joyce and Lomax (1991; see also Sargent 1990). During the late 1980s, the UK economy grew rapidly, with both inflation and imports increasing sharply. The boom was accompanied by rising gearing in both the household and company sectors, as shown in Chs. 2 and 3, and strongly rising asset prices, notably in residential and commercial property. The authorities raised interest rates sharply over 1988–9 to cool the boom and bear down on inflation, as well as to protect the exchange rate. The economy responded slowly to the tightening; real GDP did not decline until the third quarter of 1990, while house prices continued to increase until the third quarter of 1989, company-sector borrowing remained high until the end of 1990, and the personal sector continued to borrow heavily until mid-1990.

[14] Note that since the recession is not over at the time of writing (Spring 1992), further effects of financial fragility may yet emerge.

Although some of the consequences of the recession which ensued, such as increased loan defaults, business failures, and rising unemployment, are common to any downturn, some aspects of behaviour were particularly reminiscent of the mechanisms described above. This is apparent in comparing the 1990–1 recession with that of 1981 (see Joyce and Lomax 1991). The earlier recession was particularly deep in the UK, as the exchange rate became overvalued due to monetary tightening and the rise of oil exports, but it was not preceded by rapid increases in leverage of the private sector. Hence, for example, the business failure rate in 1991 was twice as high as in 1981, and at 2.3 per cent stood considerably higher than at any time over 1966–90 (Chart 2.12). This can be attributed to a number of factors, but notably the higher gearing of companies at the outset of the 1990–1 recession (Charts 2.1–2.11). Among the further mechanisms of fragility, one can highlight the following.

(a) Effects on other companies

Although the linkage cannot easily be proven statistically, it seems likely that the high business failure rate in turn had consequences for related companies in the way outlined. In addition, slow payment of trade credit was widely cited as a *cause* of failure, with large firms effectively transferring their straitened circumstances to smaller suppliers via slow payment. Finally, failures in sectors such as property have worsened prospects for remaining firms, although banks, aware of the problem, have sought to avoid realizing their security at excessively low prices.

(b) Effects on public expenditure

As regards social-security payments, higher payments were made to the unemployed in respect of mortgage interest[15] than was the case in the earlier recession (though the rise in unemployment *per se* was comparable). Mortgage foreclosures, at a record 75,500 (0.8%) in 1991, imposed a further burden on the state, to the extent that individuals needed rehousing.

(c) Effects on economic policy

The slow response of the economy to monetary tightening, but the sizeable long-term impact, is consistent with the views of monetary transmission after financial liberalization outlined in Sect. 3. As regards the further policy response, there is no evidence that the UK compromised the thrust of its macroeconomic policy to allow unduly for the

[15] Half of interest is paid for 16 weeks; the whole plus any arrears thereafter.

effects of financial fragility—at least up to the time of writing, the commitment to hold sterling in the ERM band has been overriding. This should in turn have the beneficial consequence of retarding any recurrence of the syndrome of overborrowing.

(d) Cyclical effects on saving and investment

There was a parallel retrenchment by both the household and corporate sectors, which has been apparent for the former in a sharp increase in the saving ratio; for the latter in reduced investment, employment, stock-building, and dividend payments; and for both a marked reduction in borrowing (although the corporate sector found it difficult to reduce its financial deficit, which had reached historically unprecedented levels at the end of the preceding boom). Such a reaction probably made the recession deeper than it would have been in the absence of highly geared balance sheets.

(e) Effects operating via the financial system

Given the rapid slowdown in credit expansion (for example, domestic bank lending growth fell from 34 per cent in 1989 to 6 per cent in 1991), there was a great deal of discussion of a possible 'credit crunch', or sharp reduction in the supply/increase in the cost of credit (Budd 1990 offers a balanced analysis). Evidence for this was, however, weaker than for a sharp reduction in demand for credit, for the reasons detailed above. Despite sizeable loan losses, necessitating provisioning of around 1.5 per cent of domestic assets in 1991, the large banks retained Basle risk-adjusted capital ratios of above 8 per cent, so did not have to contract their balance sheets. However, there was clearly an increase in margins and perhaps also in the cost of credit, especially for small companies. In addition, there was a reduction of capacity in the banking sector as US and Japanese banks, themselves affected by capital constraints, partly withdrew from the market.

(f) Volatility of asset prices

The 1991 recession was accompanied by unprecedented falls in nominal house prices (3 per cent in 1990, 1 per cent in 1991) as well as considerable declines in commercial property prices (11 per cent in 1990, 10 per cent in 1991). The national average fall in house prices also masked much larger regional declines, notably in the South-East. In contrast, although real house prices fell in 1981 too, nominal prices did not, in a context of rapid inflation. Because of high loan/value ratios in earlier years, of up to 100 per cent, a significant proportion of mortgage foreclosures were cases where property prices were below the value of the outstanding loan ('negative equity'). This pattern entailed sizeable loan losses for mortgage lenders themselves, and also for insurance companies which would often insure the 'top-slice' of a high-leverage loan. There were also fears that sale of repossessed houses would put further downward pressure on house prices. Meanwhile, difficulties in commercial property, arising both from the recession itself and the preceding boom in construction, entailed marked losses for the banking sector, that necessitated provisioning.

(g) Bank insolvency

While there were no cases of 'core' institutions being threatened by failure, there were some difficulties among small banks, which in turn led to heightened caution among depositors and lenders in wholesale markets. Several building societies had to be merged with larger institutions when loan losses resulting from earlier imprudent lending cast their liquidity or solvency into question.

Conclusions

This section has outlined a number of ways in which failures in the corporate or household sector—the primary manifestation of financial fragility—can impinge directly on the wider economy, without the occurrence of widespread bank failures and financial crises. Evidence for the UK, as well as that for Canada, Australia, and Norway elsewhere in this volume, Japan, and the USA in the references quoted, shows the potential importance of these mechanisms.

Given that these difficulties arise from externalities in debt markets (agents choosing their gearing do not take macroeconomic implications into account), there would seem to be a role for public policy. Specific policy implications arising from fragility in the corporate and personal sectors were given in the conclusions to Chs. 2 and 3. In each case preventative policies are distinguished from means to mitigate consequences once it has arisen. Some overall points can also be made. Generally, in order to *prevent* fragility from arising, there may be a need for at least fiscal equality between debt and other forms of finance. Second, given that overborrowing was often encouraged by perceptions of low real interest rates in the context of inflation, a rigorous anti-inflation macroeconomic policy is further justified. Moreover, since rising asset prices often encouraged a further spiral of borrowing, policy-tightening to counteract such an increase, even at a low level of general inflation, may be justified. Third, given the danger that borrowers (particularly households) may not understand the risks involved, various incentives to improve information would seem to be justified.

In order to offset fragility's *consequences*, adequate prudential supervision of financial institutions is crucial. However, as noted, the appropriate macroeconomic policy response to fragility is more problematic. It was suggested above that given overgearing, use of monetary policy to avoid a recession was undesirable, as it might lead to moral hazard, with 'validation' of high leverage. But once a recession does occur, the arguments are more evenly balanced. It is at least evident that automatic stabilizers of fiscal policy should be allowed to operate. There are incentives also to use monetary expansion to boost the economy via depreciation and lower interest rates. But this may only resolve the fragility problem by leading to inflation, reducing the real value of debt, and again generating moral hazard. There are hence arguments for accepting a period of sluggish growth as balance sheets adjust, to avoid the need to reconquer inflation and to counteract moral hazard. That said, the authorities must stand ready for appropriate action if real interest rates become too high, or if financial fragility rapidly degenerates into financial crisis and 'debt-deflation' (Ch. 5, Sect. 3), as occurred in the Great Depression (Ch. 8). Such action might need to include both monetary and fiscal expansion. These comments suggest that authorities need to tread a fine line in judging the current state of the economy during such recessions.

It is suggested that the patterns described form a particularly fruitful area for further research, both at a theoretical and empirical level. In particular, a greater focus is needed on household indebtedness as a trigger for fragility, and not merely corporate debt, as prevails in the US literature on these matters. Transnational experience (e.g. in Canada, Japan, Norway, Australia, the USA, and the UK) could also be compared and contrasted in more detail. Third, it would be useful to estimate equilibrium gearing ratios, to enable one to assess the amount of adjustment in saving/expenditure that would be needed to reach them.

In the next four chapters the book turns to the issue of systemic risk in financial markets, in which one aim is to assess the nature of the link with financial fragility. In addition, it should be noted that some of the theories relating to financial crisis outlined in Chs. 5 and 7 cast further light on the mechanisms generating financial fragility itself. For example, they suggest that high and volatile inflation may predispose an economy to overindebtedness in an inflationary upturn, and overtightening of credit in a deflationary downturn (Ch. 5, Sect. 4); that financial fragility in the context of falling prices (debt deflation) may lead the economy into a severe downward spiral (Ch. 5, Sect. 3); that a form of 'disaster myopia' on the part of financial intermediaries may help to explain overlending (Ch. 5, Sect. 7); that rising interest rates may have a severe impact on credit availability via asymmetric information and agency costs (Ch. 5, Sect. 8); and that increased competition and new entry in credit markets may lead to heightened risk-taking, even if the probability of 'disasters' is correctly gauged (Ch. 7).

Appendix: Public Debt and Financial Fragility

This volume quite deliberately avoids a detailed assessment of issues relating to public debt; in advanced countries at least, the direct linkage to financial fragility is absent, for the government can always tax or print money to repay debts incurred in its own currency.[16] However, it is worth noting in passing some of the more indirect ways in which changes in public borrowing can cause difficulties for other sectors.

(i) Interest rates

If an increase in public-sector debt drives up real long-term interest rates (whether due to effects on the balance of investors' portfolios or their fears of monetization), then other borrowers may find themselves priced out of long-term bond markets. This will in turn make them more dependent on volatile shorter term sources of funds, whose interest rates will themselves be strongly affected by any monetary tightening the authorities may need to apply, and/or credit rationing by banks.

(ii) Exchange rates

Rises in public debt may in the 'large country case' lead to a sharp appreciation of the exchange rate, as was seen in the US in the early 1980s. Such an appreciation amounts to a monetary tightening, and may cause increased fragility, particularly for exporting industries.

(iii) Tax

To the extent that agents do not foresee effects of current government borrowing on future taxes, and leverage themselves during the boom that may follow a fiscal expansion, they may find that increased taxation to repay the public debt impinges on their cash flow at the time it is most needed to pay interest on their private debt.

[16] For issues relating to public debt, the interested reader should consult, inter alia, Barro (1974), Roley (1983), Blinder and Stiglitz (1983), Hutchinson and Pyle (1984), Friedman (1984), Bispham (1986), and Eisner (1986), Wallace (1981).

(iv) Foreign currency debt

In the case of ldcs, as discussed in Chs. 6 and 7, debt was incurred in US dollars (largely) by the public sector. The adjustment needed to repay the debt had deleterious effects on the private sector; economies had to be geared to exports and run at a lower growth rate to generate foreign currency to repay debt. Also, if the authorities defaulted on international debt, the private sector would probably find itself also excluded from credit, whatever its own reputation in the international markets.

(v) Automatic stabilisers

High levels of government indebtedness and structural budget deficits may reduce the ability of the government to run a higher deficit during recessions, thus stabilizing the economy—particularly if it fears the reactions of foreign investors to such behaviour. In cases of moderate indebtedness, the government may hesitate to carry out discretionary loosening of fiscal policy, and in severe cases it may need to offset the automatic stabilizers (unemployment benefit etc.). The increase in size of such automatic stabilizers (as well as the financial-sector safety net, discussed in Chs. 5–8), is a key reason why fragility and instability have not generated deep recessions since the Second World War (Summers 1991).

(vi) Fiscal and monetary policy

To the extent that a lax fiscal policy makes it difficult to stabilize the economy via further fiscal expansion or contraction, the whole burden of stabilization is likely to fall on monetary policy. Interest rates may need to be more volatile than otherwise, heightening tendencies to overleveraging and inflation when expansion is needed, and provoking default and the risk of financial instability (Ch. 5) when tightening is required.

5

The Economic Theory of Systemic Risk

Turning from financial fragility to systemic risk, the next two chapters seek to make an initial[1] assessment of the causes, nature, and consequences of instability in contemporary financial markets, by means of an examination of the features of six recent periods of financial disorder, in the light of the various theoretical approaches to financial crisis that have been proposed in the literature. To what extent did financial instability follow directly from financial fragility in the non-financial sectors, with defaults by companies or households progressively weakening the balance sheets of financial institutions? Or were risks other than credit risk primarily responsible? Were the periods of financial instability 'unique events' or can common features be discerned? How well do the predictions of the theoretical paradigms fit the actual data? This chapter provides the theoretical background, while Ch. 6 offers an empirical assessment.

Before commencing, it is appropriate to clarify terms. 'Systemic risk', 'disorder', or 'instability' are used to describe a disturbance in financial markets which entails unanticipated changes in prices and quantities in credit or asset markets, which lead to a danger of failure of financial firms, and which in turn threatens to spread so as to disrupt the payments mechanism and capacity of the financial system to allocate capital.[2] Such patterns should be distinguished from turning-points in the trade cycle (though they may sometimes coincide); equally the theories of the monetary transmission mechanism (see Miles and Wilcox 1989; Goodhart 1989) have many parallels with theories of financial disorder, but should none the less be seen as distinct (Ch. 4). It should be noted that use in the title[3] of the term systemic risk rather than crisis to cover the events of the past two decades is deliberate, and attempts to contrast these events which, though serious, did not lead in themselves to macroeconomic depressions, widespread financial collapse, and dysfunction of the payments mechanism, with prewar crises that did entail such results (see Ch. 8 for an assessment of certain true crises). In this the book follows Schwartz (1986)

[1] Ch. 7 outlines a possible alternative approach based on industrial-organization theory.

[2] It is of course a matter of judgement whether particular instances give rise to systemic risk. There is room for argument whether some of the events discussed in Chs. 6–8 were not of importance to the financial sector as a whole—or, alternatively, whether those noted in Chs. 2–4 may have threatened the financial as well as the non-financial sectors.

[3] In the text we use terms more loosely for the sake of brevity.

who described recent events as 'pseudo financial crises', although it disagrees with her conclusion that all such pseudo crises were matters of little import.

The chapter now outlines the principal theoretical approaches to financial crisis. The first two introductory sections cover, respectively, the concept of contagious runs on financial institutions and markets, and the aspects of financial regulation which seek to protect against such events. We then assess two 'traditional' views of financial crisis, which attempt to explain exclusively the totality of financial crises, namely the financial fragility and monetarist approaches. These are followed by five more recent paradigms which seek to clarify the mechanisms involved in crises, namely rational expectations, uncertainty, credit rationing, asymmetric information/agency costs, and aspects of the dynamics of dealership markets.

(1) Bank Runs

It is essential to begin with a discussion of contagious runs, since they are the principal identifying factor for crises. In terms of the classification of risks to banks set out in Ch. 4, Sect. 8, the focus here is on liquidity risk—inability to obtain funding to finance operations—though it may be linked to interest-rate and credit risk. Although most of the analysis covers banks, it is suggested that the concepts can also be applied to other financial institutions and even securities markets.

The question why banks are often vulnerable to runs and panics, particularly in the absence of a safety net of deposit insurance or lender-of-last-resort facilities,[4] has been addressed rigorously by Diamond and Dybvig (1983). By pooling risk, banks are able to provide liquidity insurance to risk-averse consumers facing private liquidity risks (i.e. they do not know when they will require liquidity, but prefer the higher returns associated with long-term investment to hoarding cash). In other words, banks offer the possibility of early redemption of deposits at a fixed rate; they offer returns superior to hoarding cash, as funds are on-loaned for fixed investment projects, but returns are below those on illiquid direct investment, reflecting the 'insurance' provided. This pattern is held to imply that banks provide 'optimal risk-sharing'. Meanwhile, reflecting the preferences of borrowers carrying out the long-term investment projects, banks' assets are long-term and illiquid, except for a small liquid proportion to meet normal demand for withdrawals;[5] hence banks engage in maturity transformation.

[4] See the discussion in Sect. 2.

[5] A criticism of the paradigm, rectified in Diamond (1984), is that it does not specify the nature of bank assets. His analysis of delegated monitoring and the importance of private information (Ch. 1, Sect. 4) offers an additional reason for assets to be illiquid and information on bank assets imperfect.

In this context, the risk-sharing deposit contract may give an incentive for panic runs by depositors, even if the bank is solvent; this is because of the 'first come first served'[6] process whereby claims are distributed to depositors. Until the bank declares closure it must meet withdrawals on demand. But once the run exhausts liquid assets, it must close on liquidity grounds; and its ability to borrow liquidity in normal circumstances is at most equal to the value of capital. Once the latter is exhausted, the bank is likely to be insolvent, due to the need to dispose of illiquid assets at 'distress' prices. After closure, depositors join a pool of creditors who may or may not be met in full (implicitly, depositors face variation in the effective seniority of their claim). Therefore, there is an incentive to be first in the queue, and the risk that others may withdraw can cause a panic regardless of the underlying financial position of the bank.

Such runs can, according to Diamond and Dybvig, be provoked by any event, however extraneous, but including runs on or insolvency of other banks. Such an effect might be particularly potent for banks which are creditors of the bank in distress. Runs are also likely when the equity of banks is a small proportion of balance-sheet totals, as depositors' fears of moral hazard increase, assuming managers' actions cannot be perfectly monitored (L. J. White 1989). And, more generally, in the presence of asymmetric information, which arises from banks' creation of non-marketable assets, runs may be triggered by any event that makes depositors change their beliefs about banks' riskiness. These[7] might include leading indicators of recession, or a decline in net worth of a particular class of borrowers. Runs may be particularly likely when such bad news follows a period of rapid growth in credit, when the leverage of banks and borrowers is most extended ('bad news and high leverage', see Calomiris and Gorton 1991). It may also involve failure of other, particularly large, institutions where there is a suspicion that balance sheets are similarly weak and undiversified. Again, the non-marketable nature of bank assets means a bank cannot easily prove otherwise. Payments system failure may provoke runs on banks unable to settle their accounts. Finally, outstanding contingent guarantees that banks may issue (e.g. back-up lines of credit) may aggravate effects of liquidity problems, since beneficiaries may exercise their claims at the same time as banks are in difficulty.

Runs can lead to economic disruption in various ways. To the extent that these are externalities, the bank concerned does not take them into

[6] Technically, as well as this 'sequential service' feature, there is a need for incomplete markets, i.e. agents are not allowed to trade claims on physical assets after their preferences for consumption have been realized. But, as noted in Ch. 1, banks specialize in lending to sectors where contracts are incomplete, owing to fixed costs and asymmetric and/or private information.

[7] These arguments, in effect, identify some of the factors outlined in more detail in the theories of financial crisis described in the later sections of this chapter.

account in its own portfolio decisions, and they thus constitute an a priori basis for public intervention. First, there is interruption of production as banks call loans, hence assets are prematurely liquidated, while optimal risk-sharing is disturbed. Such effects are particularly severe for those agents in the non-financial sector who have relationships with failing banks, and/or can only obtain credit from banks due to the latter's unique role as monitors and evaluators of loan contracts (i.e. those lacking reputation or too small to pay the fixed costs of capital market issue, as discussed in Chs. 1–3). The effects are of course magnified if failure provokes contagion to other banks or more generalized panics. As noted, contagious runs on banks may be provoked by any failure, because when there is uncertainty over the value of non-marketable assets (i.e. loans)[8] public perception of the health of the system is influenced by failures at individual banks.[9]

Effects of bank failures are further aggravated if there is also closure of securities markets, as then even agents having alternative sources of debt finance may find those sources closed. Meanwhile, as banks contract credit, the money supply may fall and real interest rates rise, thus discouraging spending and increasing pressure on fragile borrowers. In the extreme case of a flight to cash, the banking reserve base will contract, threatening further contraction of bank assets unless Central Banks intervene (see Sect. 4). Widespread bank failure is also likely to disrupt the payments mechanism (Corrigan 1987; Folkerts-Landau 1991). In a striking experiment, Humphrey (1986) showed that the failure of a major US bank might leave up to 50 banks with net settlement obligations at the end of the day in excess of their capital. Repetition of the experiment on a different day gave similar results for a comparable number of *different* banks, showing the unpredictable nature of this risk.

All of these costs are additional to costs that may arise in any bankruptcy, as outlined in Ch. 2 (such as costs of reorganization and social losses from breaking up unique bundles of assets).

As discussed in Sect. 2, the way to counteract runs and panics is for the authorities to provide a 'safety net' such as deposit insurance or lender-of-last-resort facilities, to remove fear of loss on the part of depositors, while enforcing capital adequacy standards and direct controls on risk-taking to

[8] Such contagion may be particularly strong if banks are linked by interbank loans, although in practice, given lack of timely data on exposures, most contagion in interbank markets has occurred as a result of uncertainty over the overall strength of balance sheets, rather than direct exposures (see Ch. 6, Sect. 1).

[9] Indeed, some authors would go further and suggest that panics are a rational means for depositors to ensure adequate monitoring, in that they force banks to resolve asymmetric information by collective action among themselves (i.e. monitoring each other and closing the insolvent). See the discussion in Calomiris and Gorton (1991). However, this argument abstracts from the superior solution of establishing a Central Bank (Goodhart 1987), with which banks will share information with greater confidence than with each other, and whose fulfilment of this role may promote market confidence more generally.

avoid exploitation of the subsidy that such (mispriced) insurance provides.[10] An important additional factor in protecting the wider economy from financial disruption is the automatic stabilizer: government expenditure rises relative to tax revenue in a downturn.

It is suggested that the Diamond and Dybvig (1983) paradigm, although most closely related to commercial banks, can also apply to investment banks or non-financial companies, to the extent that they rely on short-term financing, have a mismatch between assets and liabilities, and that there is imperfect information about the quality of their assets. Suppliers of short-term credit may 'run' from such institutions when rollover is due.[11] Moreover, although the paradigm focuses on retail depositors (and hence recommends deposit insurance), it is equally if not more applicable to wholesale depositors who lack such protection. In theory, if information about bank-specific risks is perfect, such a run could not generalize in a wholesale market (such as that for certificates of deposit) where bank debt is traded, as risk would be correctly priced (Gorton 1991). But experience suggests that markets discriminate imperfectly among banks, and/or apply quantity rather than price rationing of credit in cases of heightened risk (see the discussion in Ch. 6, Sect. 1). Finally, following the corporate finance theory of Chs. 1 and 2, runs are more likely when there are many than when there are few creditors; the latter can avoid free riders—and are also less likely to escape with their assets intact.

'Runs' may generalize further to securities markets. Some discussion of market crashes is given below under the paradigms of rational expectations (Sect. 5) and of dealer market behaviour (Sect. 9). But, as suggested by Bingham (1991*a*), one can also see them in terms of Diamond and Dybvig (1983) runs from a market. A liquid asset market can be seen as providing optimal risk-sharing from the security holder's point of view. Such liquidity depends on all other holders not seeking to realize their assets at the same time. If doubt arises over the future liquidity of the market, it is rational to sell first, before the disequilibrium between sellers and buyers becomes too great, and market failure supervenes. Such losses of liquidity, especially in short-term debt markets, may have externalities similar to bank failures, e.g. if there is a class of creditor raising funds in such markets which does not have a clear alternative source of short-term funding. Bingham suggests a number of ways to sustain systemic stability in this sense, discussed in the conclusions to Ch. 6.

[10] As discussed below, if deposit insurance is mispriced, due to inability of insurers to gauge the risk of individual banks, it provides a subsidy to equity holders, which is positively related to leverage and portfolio risk (Osterberg 1990).

[11] What Guttentag (1989) calls a 'walk'.

(2) Financial Regulation against Systemic Risk

It is appropriate at this point to add a few relevant details regarding the regulation of financial markets as a protection against systemic risk. The discussion of regulation does not aim to be comprehensive; those interested are referred to texts such as Baltensperger and Dermine (1987), Miles (1988), Goodhart (1989), Gardener (1986), and Franks and Mayer (1989, 1990). Those familiar with the issues should pass on to the next section.

Financial regulation has two main objectives, protection of retail investors and protection against systemic risk, although there is some overlap (subsidiary motives include concern for monetary control and to maintain adequate levels of competition). The need for investor protection arises from information asymmetry, particularly those between retail clients and financial intermediaries, given the fact that such transactions are often one-off (e.g. buying a life insurance policy) and involve a large proportion of wealth. Systemic risk arises from the tendency for failure of one financial intermediary to generalize to the system as a whole, as outlined above. Note that a form of information asymmetry is also at the root of this problem, in that 'runs' can occur for solvent institutions, leading them to collapse from lack of liquidity, when investors lack information about performance of their assets, as is a normal feature of banks holding non-marketable loans on their books. Retail investors may be particularly vulnerable in this context, as they may lack the information that runs are under way until it is too late. They may also lack the information to make an ex-ante judgement on the safety of a bank. (The corollary is that increasing disclosure of information may reduce the risk of runs.)

The implication of Diamond and Dybvig (1983) in a world without regulation is that banks would frequently be subject to runs, and systemic collapses would also occur at regular intervals. Banks would need to hold large amounts of capital to generate confidence, with deleterious effects on the cost of intermediation. (Reputations, a club of banks, or evidence of diversification might also be used to this end.) This is indeed the picture of the USA in the late nineteenth century that can be derived from Friedman and Schwartz (1963) and Mishkin (1991), with the caveat that suspension of convertability by banks acting together would often nip a crisis in the bud. (The cost of expectations of this policy was that depositors would demand higher returns on bank liabilities.)

There are several lines of defence against systemic risk.[12] First, there are forms of public insurance of bank liabilities, namely the lender-of-last-resort and deposit insurance ('the safety net'). Second, there are

[12] Note that here we abstract from 'structural regulation', which as noted in Ch. 1, Sect. 5 (*b*) is seen as having excessive net costs in terms of efficiency, as well as helping at times to provoke systemic risk if it fails to adapt to changes in fundamentals.

forms of protection against bank failure which regulators can apply, implicitly providing protection for the insurer, namely capital requirements, direct controls on assets, checks on bank management, and on liquidity. We deal briefly with each in turn.

The *lender of last resort* can be defined in various ways; our preferred definition is of an institution, usually the Central Bank, which has the ability to produce at its discretion currency or 'high powered money' to support institutions facing liquidity difficulties;[13] to create enough base money to offset public desire to switch into money during a crisis; and to delay legal insolvency of an institution, preventing 'fire sales' and calling of loans.[14] The function may thus operate either via maintenance of liquidity in the system as a whole, or via help to individual banks (where the latter implicitly assumes that the authorities have a better judgement of the solvency of individual banks than the market has). An essential feature is that its operation should be uncertain for any particular institution in difficulties—the lender must decide whether systemic risk threatens on a case-by-case basis. Otherwise the lender is effectively a backup for any forms of risk-taking in the financial sector—depositors have no reason to monitor banks' risks—generating severe agency costs. Banks would then operate with less liquidity and capital than they would otherwise. A counterargument to such discretion is that, given the residual risk that banks will not be granted assistance, the possibility of contagious runs remains. And markets are in any case likely to assume that large banks are likely to be granted assistance, thus reducing incentives to monitor. In some cases, especially with a cohesive and oligopolistic banking system, banks themselves can proxy the lender of last resort (usually under the leadership of the Central Bank) by taking over failing banks or providing loans to troubled institutions. This may become more difficult to organize as competition and new entry increases.

Deposit insurance, as its name implies, provides a guarantee that certain types of bank liability are convertible into cash, thus removing the

[13] This function should be distinguished from the normal monetary policy operation of relieving money-market shortages, though both may occur through the same channel. Note that rescues can be performed using taxpayers' money as well as via creation of high-powered money.

[14] The most celebrated reference on the lender of last resort is Bagehot (1873), who recommended Central Banks to 'lend freely to solvent banks only at a penalty rate' to defuse a crisis. Modern variants (see the discussion in Guttentag and Herring 1987) tend to avoid the latter prescription, as a penalty rate might exacerbate the crisis, while the distinction between illiquid and insolvent institutions often proves difficult to make in the heat of the moment. Moreover, rapid closure of insolvent banks may wreak havoc in the payments system (see the discussion of Herstatt in Ch. 6). If the authorities save banks that prove to be insolvent, they face further difficulties in disposing of the assets of insolvent banks—a major problem in the resolution of the US thrifts crisis (Kindleberger 1991). Difficulties of selling assets rapidly also make the concept of solvency ambiguous, when a bank's solvency may depend on how rapidly its assets are disposed of (Summers 1991).

incentive for 'runs' on solvent banks by uninformed depositors. To avoid insuring all of the system (including wholesale depositors who should not suffer from severe information asymmetries), there are usually limits to coverage. But difficulties may arise; for example, in the case of large banks judged 'too big to fail', all depositors may be paid off; unlike the lender of last resort, deposit insurance cannot be used at the regulator's discretion, which thus generates agency problems; and workable means of relating premiums to risk, and thus preventing an implicit subsidy to shareholders, have proved difficult to devise—instead there are flat fees related to the size of balance sheets (see, e.g. Kane 1986; Baltensperger and Dermine 1987; Acharya and Udell 1992). All of these may lead to severe moral-hazard problems; a response in most countries (but not the USA or Italy) has been to restrict deposit insurance coverage severely, so it effectively only becomes a partial protection for small retail depositors. This induces a degree of monitoring and market discipline by wholesale depositors (although, as discussed in Ch. 6, Sect. 1, the effectiveness of such monitoring is limited, especially given imperfect information).

Note that both the lender of last resort and deposit insurance are assumed to be publicly provided, or at least co-ordinated, by the public sector. The difficulty of private provision rests on the inability of insurers to provide sufficient reserves to offer unconditional guarantees for the financial system as a whole, as well as on the difficulty of assessing the riskiness of banks' portfolios. Since the public sector has the power to tax and to create money, it can offer unconditional guarantees, at least for nominal amounts.[15]

A system in which the lender of last resort and/or flat-rate deposit insurance operate as the sole forms of protection against systemic risk, would be vulnerable to excessive risk-taking by banks, imposing heavy burdens on the regulator. Such tendencies may be particularly marked in the absense of 'structural regulation' limiting competition (Ch. 1, Sect. 5). Capital requirements and other types of prudential supervision seek to avoid these difficulties.

Capital regulations, which require a minimum ratio of shareholders' funds to liabilities or assets, can be seen as means of shifting the risks insured by the 'safety net' back to shareholders, who are the first to bear losses incurred by the bank. (As shown by Merton (1977), the value of flat-rate deposit insurance is increasing in asset risk and decreasing in bank capital.) There are strong parallels with the theories of debt and corporate finance developed in Chs. 2 and 3. A low capital ratio, in other words high leverage, increases the probability of bankruptcy and raises agency costs for debt holders (in this case proxied by the lender of last resort/deposit insurer). A higher proportion of equity can reduce these risks. Note, however, that shareholders' capital is not the first line of

[15] Particularly if money creation causes inflation, part of the real value of the guarantee may be recouped in 'inflation taxes'.

defence for a bank against defaults by borrowers. Correct pricing of risk,[16] backed by adequate diversification, screening, and monitoring, should ensure that capital resources are never called upon. Theories of financial crisis discussed in the following sections show how risk pricing may go awry.

Capital requirements can be related to the riskiness of banks' asset portfolios. This can be seen as a means of offsetting the mispricing of the safety net, by implicitly raising the premium on risky portfolios, as well as giving incentives for banks to price risk correctly. However, for this to be accurate, the authorities must correctly assess risk. This approach is the basis of the *Basle capital adequacy agreement*, which imposes internationally agreed weights on different types of risk, including off-balance-sheet risks, and requires that banks in countries subscribing to the agreement should maintain a ratio of 8 per cent capital to risk-weighted assets. The motivation for the agreement is to ensure both financial stability and competitive equality.[17]

Criticisms of Basle (see Hall 1988; McKenzie and Thomas 1988), have focused on features such as the following.

- The risk weights are crude, being e.g. the same for all non-financial companies, regardless of size and leverage.
- The rules cannot vary over time in response to known events such as oil shocks, or between countries to reflect the structure (e.g. risk sharing) and behaviour (e.g. interest-rate volatility) of financial systems. Yet all of these may affect the variability and correlation of rates of return on assets.
- If capital regulations force banks to hold more than their desired share of capital, they may give incentives to maximize risk within each category (e.g. private sector loans, mortgage loans) so as to maximize return subject to the constraint, especially given lack of risk related deposit insurance premiums.
- No account is taken of covariances between risks, indeed the requirement is the same for a single loan to a risky borrower, as for a globally diversified portfolio to borrowers in the same risk class. Hence the distinction between systematic and unsystematic risk (Ch. 1, Sect. 3*a*) is ignored. See also Schaefer (1987).
- Funding risk, e.g. the proportion of volatile wholesale deposits, is not covered by the agreement.
- Capital is measured at book value when market value may be more relevant to costs of issuing or rolling over uninsured deposits.
- Capital is defined to include items other than shareholders' equity (undisclosed reserves, discounted revaluation reserves, general loan

[16] Which facilitates buildup of reserves against possible loan losses.

[17] However, these objectives cannot be entirely divorced; in the absense of competitive equality regulators might be tempted into a destabilizing 'competition in laxity'; or if they were not, banks left at a competitive disadvantage might fail in a disruptive manner.

provisions, hybrid debt capital, and subordinated debt), some of which critics suggest would be difficult to realize at a time of heightened financial risk.

- The initial focus is on credit risk and not other types of risk, e.g. market risk arising from security positions.
- Countries are allowed a degree of discretion (above the minimum) in application of the rules.
- Other critics such as Kane (1990) would go further and suggest that such international agreements are inherently suspect, since regulators are under a shorter time horizon than taxpayers (the analogy is drawn with the second type of agency cost, arising from conflict between managers (regulators) and providers of external finance (taxpayers)). Regulators are seen as seeking to extend or defend their share of the market for regulatory services in the face of disturbances in the economic environment, subject to bureaucratic, market, and technological constraints. As such, the Basle agreement is seen as a form of cartel imposing costs on financial firms which they cannot escape by switching to other regimes. Ultimately, Kane is confident that market forces will reshape the result. Kane's critique may be seen in the US tradition of suspicion of regulation, which is seen as a wealth transfer brought about by a political process driven by well-defined interest groups.[18] Although this approach seems best suited to US political processes than elsewhere, in all cases it seems likely that there is a degree of 'regulatory capture', entailing such transfers, given the need for co-operation between the regulator and regulated.

Some of the criticisms are ill-founded in that they disregard the other aspects of *prudential supervision*, which correct some of the difficulties arising from relying on capital requirements alone. For example, the US approach, under the acronym 'Camel', covers not only capital but also assets, management, earnings, and liquidity. UK banks are supervised for large exposures to individual borrowers (but not sectors), thus correcting the weakness of the risk-asset approach for failing to penalize undiversified portfolios. UK supervisors also assess holdings of cash, future cash flows, and diversification of the deposit base; adequacy of provisions for bad and doubtful debts (including provisioning policy, systems for monitoring credit risk, arrears, and practices for taking and valuing security); systems for monitoring the bank's condition and risks; and that the management be fit and proper.[19] All of these provide backup for capital adequacy in protecting the safety net from the moral hazard it may generate.

[18] See Stigler 1971; Peltzman 1976.

[19] Note, however, that supervisors do not seek detailed control over institutions' behaviour and strategies—as this would itself generate liability for failures, and also because the authorities consider that they lack the information to price risk accurately themselves.

Note that, in addition to the specific controls noted above, supervisors are aided by the desire of banks to maintain reputations, and hence not to risk bankruptcy by taking excessive risks. Such a mechanism will be more effective when banks have market power and hence their franchises are valuable (see Ch. 7, Sect. 4).

The description in this section has been largely of banking regulation; however, capital adequacy is also applied to non-depository institutions, notably investment banks, which can also be exposed to forms of runs and whose failure may generate systemic risk (see OECD (1991) and the description of the equity market crash in Ch. 6). Moreover, an increasing focus is applied to soundness of financial infrastructure such as payments and settlements systems, failures in which can generate or spread liquidity crises and systemic risk as much as failures of institutions (see Corrigan 1987; Folkerts-Landau 1991; and the discussion of the Herstatt crisis in Ch. 6). And securities markets themselves, notably for short- and long-term debt, are felt to warrant increasing attention, as their importance as a source of primary liquidity for borrowers increases (Goodhart and King 1987).

(3) Debt and Financial Fragility

This approach regards financial crises as an essential component of the turning-point of the business cycle—a response to previous 'excesses' which can operate through a variety of financial markets. It extends the concepts developed in the earlier sections of the book to the wider economy and the financial sector, and postulates both a direct link from financial fragility in the non-financial sector to financial crisis, and reverse causality to non-financial activity. Experience of The Great Depression (Ch. 8) was the key background.

Fisher (1932, 1933) attributed the downturn in the business cycle to overindebtedness and deflation. The earlier upswing is caused by an exogenous event leading to improved opportunities for profitable investment (what Kindleberger (1978) called a 'displacement'). This leads to increased fixed investment, as well as speculation in asset markets for capital gain. The process is debt-financed, mainly by bank loans, which increases deposits, the money supply, and the price level. Velocity also increases, further fuelling the expansion. Rising prices reduce the real value of outstanding debt, offsetting the increase in nominal debt, and encouraging further borrowing. This leads to a state of 'overindebtedness', i.e. a degree of indebtedness which multiplies unduly the chances of being insolvent (or alternatively a state of indebtedness implying a negative present value of borrowers in a wide variety of states of nature). The parallels with financial fragility, as discussed in Chs. 2–4, are clear.

When agents have insufficient liquid assets to meet liabilities, a crisis can be triggered. Debtors unable to pay debts and refinance positions can be forced by creditors to liquidate assets ('distress selling'). If this is widespread, and in the absence of lender-of-last-resort intervention by the monetary authorities, it triggers further crises and a deep depression; distress selling by the whole community leads to falling prices, bank deposits declining as loans are withdrawn. Deflation increases the real value of outstanding debt. Creditors see the nominal value of collateral declining with prices so they call loans; the real debt burden of borrowers increases and they continue to liquidate.[20] Each individual hopes to be better off by liquidating but the community is worse off due to deflation. If nominal interest rates are 'sticky', real rates increase. Bank runs are triggered as fears for their solvency increase, especially as falling prices reduce companies' net worth and profits and lead to loan default.[21] Output and employment fall until bankruptcy has eliminated overindebtedness, or reflationary monetary policy is adopted. The process then repeats itself.

Minsky (1977, 1982) elaborated Fisher's approach, and introduced the concept of 'fragility', to attempt to clarify the problem of overindebtedness during an upswing. Fragility depends on; first, the mix of hedge, speculative, and Ponzi finance; second, the liquidity of portfolios; and third, the extent to which ongoing investment is debt-financed. Hedge financing occurs when a unit's cash-flow commitments to debt servicing are such that cash receipts exceed cash payments over a long period; speculative financing entails cash-flow payments over a short period that exceed cash-flow receipts; Ponzi finance occurs when a unit has interest portions of its cash-payment commitments exceeding net income. A Ponzi unit has to increase its debt to meet outstanding commitments for long periods. For speculative and Ponzi units, a rise in the interest rate can entail negative net worth and insolvency. Some commentators suggest the high risk implicit in Minsky's perhaps rather pejorative terms for these 'units' runs somewhat counter to the examples he gives; speculative units include banks, and Ponzi units include loans to finance construction projects. However, difficulties related to the latter in many countries, as discussed in Chs. 6 and 8, give pause for thought.

How does the mechanism operate? In the upswing, the demand for new investment leads to an excess demand for finance, which increases interest rates, though this is partly offset by monetary financial innovations (giving an elastic money supply and velocity) which increase the supply of finance for further investment. Higher interest rates generate

[20] Of course recent experience has shown that deflation of general prices is not a necessary precondition for a protracted debt crisis, especially if contracts are set in real terms (e.g. floating-rate debt), or *asset* prices collapse.

[21] One can distinguish two effects of a deflation, 'market/interest-rate risk', that the value of debt claims may change and 'credit risk' from bankruptcy. The former is symmetric, with creditors gaining and debtors losing (but as noted by Kindleberger (1991), creditors are 'slow to recognise their increase in income or wealth and unlikely to found new banks'). Meanwhile, credit risk affects the creditor with no offset for the debtor.

fragility via an increase in debt finance, a shift from long- to short-term debt, a shift from hedge to speculative or Ponzi finance, and a reduction in margins of safety for financial institutions. Further rises in interest rates[22] can cause a refinancing crisis with firms unable to roll over their debt, leading to Fisher's 'distress selling' cycle, unless the Central Bank intervenes. Minsky suggests that the cycle described is an intrinsic feature of capitalist economies, repeating itself as memories of previous problems fade (see also Sect. 7 below). An application to recent experience would of course stress factors such as deregulation, certain fiscal changes (e.g. on real estate), and theories of leverage as outlined in Chs. 2 and 3, as well as the cyclical upswing and financial innovation, as the motive forces. For Minsky, international transmission of crises was likely to occur via defaults on international loans.

Kindleberger (1978) stressed the importance of 'euphoria' in the upturn, which leads banks to make insufficient provision for risk, and also to a high degree of speculative activity among investors in asset markets. Asset prices start off in close touch with reality but become progressively more excessive.[23] Cutler *et al.* (1989) characterized this type of behaviour as 'positive feedback trading'—traders whose purchases respond to rising prices rather than falling or low prices. The reversal of this as the 'bubble' is punctured aggravates the downturn. Note that such assertions, as well as aspects of Minsky's theories, may imply departures from economic rationality. Kindleberger also noted further international transmission mechanisms, stressing psychological factors, linkage of stock markets, commodity arbitrage, and interest arbitrage, which by linking banking systems can offset the price-specie-flow mechanism;[24] a flexible exchange rate was seen as a conduit for international transmission of crises rather than a barrier.

Bernanke (1983), in describing the Great Depression (see also Ch. 8) suggested that, given a heavy burden of debt on borrowers and a risk of bank runs, fragility can generalize itself by raising the real cost of intermediation between lenders and some classes of borrowers. He suggests that his theory is consistent with Fisher's outline but, unlike Kindleberger and Minsky, retains the postulate of rational, market-constrained agents. Following the 'monitoring' theories of intermediation outlined in Ch. 1, Sect. 4, costs of intermediation include screening, monitoring, and accounting costs, as well as unexpected losses inflicted by defaulting borrowers. Meanwhile, most bank loans are non-marketable loans to idiosyncratic borrowers, unable to access bond markets. In a

[22] The cause of such increases (not spelt out by Minsky) could plausibly be increased inflation late in the cycle and the response of the monetary authorities thereto.

[23] Loans based on asset values in periods of speculative excess may of course be highly risky.

[24] That is, the mechanism whereby trade imbalances generate flows of money (specie) which induce macroeconomic adjustments to correct the imbalance.

crisis, fear of runs may lead banks to desire rediscounted or liquid assets, including government securities, and withdraw from their traditional loan markets, with an ensuing sharp decline in bank credit to those most dependent on it. Such an effect will be worsened as insolvencies grow, while solvent agents' collateral value deteriorates and (owing to deflation) real debt burdens increase. Given banks' advantages in credit supply such as accumulated information, expertise, and customer relationships, their withdrawal sharply impairs financial efficiency, even if other channels of credit seek to substitute. Following the 'commitment' paradigm, borrowers who have good records with their relationship banks will face higher prices or lower quantities of credit from outside lenders;[25] following the 'monitoring' paradigm, inability to convey private information credibly to other lenders and markets may lead to an inability to raise credit at all. Such an effect is likely to reduce aggregate demand, worsening the downturn; and once costs of intermediation have risen it may be a protracted period before they are reduced again. A parallel pattern may arise for international lending.

Besides the focus on the safety net—which could include wider sectors of the economy than purely banks[26]—the policy implications of the financial-fragility approach also include active use of fiscal policy and/or maintenance of the automatic stabilizers to counteract downturns, and limitation of tax advantages to debt relative to equity.

(4) The Monetarist Approach

Monetarists identify financial crises with banking panics, which may cause monetary contraction or may worsen effects of prior monetary contraction on economic activity. For example, Friedman and Schwartz (1963) noted that of six major contractions in the US over 1867–1960, four were associated with major banking or monetary[27] disturbances, although none have occurred since 1933. Banking panics were held to arise out of public loss of confidence in banks' abilities to convert deposits into currency. This loss was often caused by the failure of an important institution.

Given fractional reserves, attempts by the public to increase its cash holdings can only be met by a multiple contraction of deposits, unless there is a suspension of convertibility of deposits into currency or intervention of the authorities (e.g. open-market operations). A panic may lead to widespread bank failures, unless the Central Bank acts to expand the money supply. This is because sound banks are forced into

[25] See also Sharpe 1990.

[26] Note than US guarantees of mortgages, instituted after the Great Depression, are one example of this.

[27] The fact that financial crises can occur without bank failures is shown by experience of countries such as Canada in the Great Depression (Schwartz 1986).

insolvency by falls in the value of their assets, caused by attempts to respond to the scramble for liquidity. Failures in turn affect economic activity and lead to deflation via reductions in the money stock, as the deposit/currency and deposit/reserve ratios fall.

Bank failures in this paradigm may have macroeconomic causes. For example, according to Schwartz (1987), financial instability tends to arise from inflation. Changing relative prices may clearly cause localized difficulties e.g. in commodities markets. But general inflation is also considered damaging. Besides the fact that it may cause interest-rate instability, it also distorts lenders' perceptions of credit and interest-rate risk, both in up and downswings of price movements, contributing to excessive lending in one case and inadequate intermediation in the other. An asset portfolio which requires fixed rates of money payments might be distributed across low-risk assets ex-ante (i.e. ex-ante risk pricing is accurate), but an unexpected reversal of inflation could increase riskiness of bank assets and lead to insolvencies; ex-post quality of assets differs from ex-ante. This means a stable price level is the best way to avoid financial instability.

Of course, the introduction of deposit insurance does much to alleviate the dangers of bank panics, as it removes the public's fear for its ability to convert deposits into currency. But without a stable price level, moral hazard may be severe. International transmission from the monetarist point of view occurs via the price-specie-flow mechanism for fixed exchange rates. In their view, countries with flexible rates could avoid contagion.[28]

Cagan (1965) again suggested that panics were caused by failures of major institutions and declines in public confidence in banks, which led to contractions in the money supply. He noted the 'inverted pyramid of credit' resting on New York prior to 1914, the absence of emergency reserves provided by a Central Bank (and inadequacy of private clearing houses as lenders of last resort), and sharp outflows of money forcing banks rapidly to contract credit. He noted that crises did not tend to cause economic downturns as they tended to follow peaks in activity, though the attendant monetary contraction could aggravate the downturn. In addition, some panics occurred without severe downturns, some severe downturns without panics, proving that panics were neither necessary nor sufficient for a severe contraction.

The policy prescriptions of the monetarists are for a stable and predictable path for the money supply, but for readiness on the part of the authorities to expand the money supply in the case of crisis. Deposit insurance or a credible and precommitted lender of last resort are seen as essential to avoid runs or panics.

[28] For a further discussion of theories of international transmission see Bordo (1989).

As noted, the monetarist and financial-fragility approaches are long-established alternative approaches to interpretation of economic history (although in principle the mechanisms could be reconciled, e.g. if monetary tightening triggers a crisis in a financially fragile economy). It is useful to recapitulate the main differences between the theories, while noting that both offer partially similar policy recommendations (the lender of last resort/deposit insurance). According to monetarists, inflation may lead to heightened risk in lending decisions, as uncertainty over future cash flows (and, for floating-rate loans, interest payments) increases. However, the incidence of crises is usually after the turning-point of the cycle, as the downturn weakens banks' balance sheets, leading to runs and panics which may intensify the downturn. Monetarists assume risk is accurately priced ex-ante, whereas financial-fragility does not. Financial fragility theory assumes a buildup to a crisis over the upturn, with rapid growth of debt and a 'mania' during which investors switch from money to real or financial assets. Bubbles in asset markets are likely to occur, as prices deviate from fundamentals. Crises, which may include bank runs but also deflation of the asset bubble, occur at the turning-point and cause the downturn. Both theories associate crises with a flight to money, which can be offset by the lender of last resort, but fragility theory takes money to include other bank deposits (inside money) and not just cash. Monetarists would dispute the idea that a flight to inside money can endanger the payments system, as other banks receiving inflows can recycle them back to solvent banks in difficulties.

Monetarists do not rule out asset price bubbles, although they do not see a necessary connection with the business cycle. Rather, they deny that loss of wealth associated with asset-market crashes, non-financial bankruptcies, and failures of individual banks are financial crises. Instead, 'financial crisis' is reserved for a shift to money that leads to widespread runs on banks. Monetarists go on to suggest that recent periods of financial instability (discussed in Chs. 6 and 8) have been 'pseudo financial crises', because a crisis would not have supervened even in the absence of lender-of-last-resort assistance (which in the event was just a bailout that was inefficient and/or led to inflation). On the other hand, the monetarists insist on the need for a credible and committed safety net for the financial system to prevent panics, and assert that this has been effective in the UK since 1866 and the USA since 1933 (see Ch. 8). So a great deal rests on the judgement that this commitment would have effectively prevented crises even if it had not been operational in the recent episodes.

Recent work on financial instability has tended to reflect a synthesis of financial fragility and monetarist views, emphasizing rising vulnerability of debtors but also runs on banks or financial markets, and potential for contagion and systemic risk. The current analysis adopts a similar approach.[29] We now go on to discuss five recent theoretical contributions, which elaborate and expand aspects of the traditional theories, without necessarily attempting to supplant them.

(5) Rational Expectations

Some attempts have been made to model crises in a rational-expectations manner. According to such models, manias (as stressed in financial-fragility approaches) are viewed as rational speculative bubbles, runs (the key monetarist conduit) are a speculative attack on a price-fixing scheme, and a panic is a run whose timing is imperfectly foreseen. However, as discussed below, those emphasizing the importance of uncertainty in crises would tend to dismiss such models (while acknowledging rational expectations to be an extremely fruitful approach to financial market behaviour more generally). Their use may be more appropriate in foreign exchange crises (Krugman 1991); such forex crises are not the focus of the current analysis, although they may be an indirect cause of financial instability (via the authorities' interest-rate reaction), or its consequence.

As discussed by Flood and Garber (1982), when expectations are rational in the sense of Muth (1961), agents' anticipations of price movements are mathematical expectations, conditional on an information set that may include structural knowledge of the economic model underlying the process concerned. However, if the expected rate of market-price changes influences the current market price, as is normal in asset markets, there is no unique expression for agents' expectations. Although there is only one market equilibrium condition, solutions are required for two endogenous variables—market price and the expected rate of market-price change. Under such conditions a bubble can arise. As agents using rational expectations do not make systematic prediction errors, a positive relation between price and its expected rate of change implies a similar relation between price and its actual rate of change. In these conditions, expectations can drive prices independently of fundamentals: a price bubble (though of course a bubble cannot be defined independently of the definition of the fundamental price behaviour).

Definitions of a rational bubble (Blanchard and Watson 1982) typically incorporate an assumed probability that the bubble will remain or crash. While the bubble lasts, the average return must exceed the risk-free rate

[29] Hence we agree with Schwartz (1986) that financial distress at Lockheed (1971), Chrysler (1979), and New York (1975) were in no way potential financial crises, but suggest that Penn Central (1970), UK Secondary Banks (1973), Herstatt/Franklin (1974), and the Debt Crisis (1982) clearly were.

to compensate for the risk of a crash. This will be true *a fortiori* for risk-averse agents; indeed, as the probability of the crash may increase over time, the price will have to increase exponentially to compensate both for the increased probability of a fall and for the larger risk in holdingan asset. (This theory may be contrasted with Kindleberger's looser definition of 'euphoria' where asset prices progressively lose touch with the fundamentals in an 'irrational' manner.)

Runs are also explicable in terms of rational expectations (Flood and Garber 1982)—a run being an event that terminates a price-fixing scheme. An agent (e.g. a bank) may be ready to buy or sell an asset at a given fixed price (i.e. fixes the price of deposits in terms of government currency). The viability of the scheme depends on the bank holding a stock of the asset, i.e. its liquidity. If rational depositors see the price fixing as temporary, and that prices will rise eventually (they will take a capital loss on their deposits), they will draw down the stock (of reserves) backing the price-fixing scheme. Alternatively put, they draw down the stock when the net worth of the institution is exhausted. If the stock is depleted rapidly, this is a run (leading to closure), although all depositors (having perfect foresight) are paid off without loss. The theory can be extended by introducing calculated risks to allow losses to depositors (panics), but only to the extent that a sudden event led *directly and proportionately* to real losses exceeding the net worth of the institution. (Compare the discussion of uncertainty in Sect. 6.)

Similar analyses have been applied to national foreign-exchange reserves in a currency crisis, when the authorities seek to maintain a fixed exchange rate (Flood and Garber 1984; Obstfeld 1986). Once reserves reach a critical level, rational speculators attack the currency, exhaust the reserves, and force a transition to floating. More recent work has extended to managed floats (Krugman 1991), whereby 'news' obtained from reactions of monetary authorities to changes in exchange rates can lead rational investors to cause a sudden jump in the exchange rate. The distinction from systemic financial crises may lay in the much greater credit risk and asymmetric information in the latter, as well as uncertainty more generally, as discussed in the next section.

(6) Uncertainty

Economic uncertainty, as opposed to risk, was suggested by Knight (1921) to be central to economic activity. Meltzer (1982) pointed out its importance in understanding financial crises. Uncertainty pertains to future events not susceptible to being reduced to objective probabilities, and also provides opportunities for profits in competitive markets. These aspects are discussed in turn below. Meltzer notes that events not susceptible to probability analysis are excluded from rational-expectations models of decision-making and optimal diversification of risks. Rational-expectations models have not in his view provided a basis for reliable predictions concerning behaviour of macroeconomic financial prices, nor have they provided convincing explanations of financial crises (see also Benink 1991).

Uncertainty reflects the changing economic environment, in which the random element is not well represented by stationary probability distributions. Hence the future is not knowable either precisely or probabilistically (inferring from past data). Uncertainty applies also to events whose implications resist purely objective analysis, such as wars, major changes in policy regime, financial crises, and their economic consequences. These alter the economic environment in a way that cannot easily be anticipated, diversified, or hedged against.

There is no precise economic theory as to how decisions are made under uncertainty. Uncertainty may be ignored (if events are felt to have a sufficiently low probability and information is costly to obtain). Alternatively, subjective ex-ante probabilities may be applied, together with a risk premium to cover unspecified adverse events. In each case, people tend to watch others and do not deviate widely from the norm in terms of factors taken into account and weights given to them. When the crowd is wrong ex-post, there is the making of a financial crisis, but there is no objective basis to prove before the event that the crowd will be wrong.[30] (Herding may be rationalized to some extent in finance if all (large) banks expect to be rescued in a systemic crisis, whereas one bank going alone in a different direction would be allowed to go bankrupt: Price 1987)

In terms of opportunity for profit, uncertainty rooted in change was suggested by Knight to be its main source in competitive markets. If all probabilities were known and risks diversified, profits would be bid away. Profits are earned by innovating and seeking opportunities where there is uneven information and uncertainty. These processes (which Shafer (1986) noted are similar to Schumpeter's 'creative destruction of innovation' (1942))[31] increasingly characterize financial markets. Whether the process leads to crisis depends on the form of the 'destruction'. It may not if innovators take market share from inefficient firms, risks are correctly priced, and firms are adequately capitalized—or indeed if innovation facilitates dispersion of risk to those best able to bear it. But it may, if deteriorating balance-sheet quality follows the innovation process (for example, via risk concentration) or if financial intermediaries fail to

[30] The point was also made by Keynes (1931), who noted that 'a "sound" banker, alas, is not one who forsees danger and avoids it, but one who, when he is ruined, is ruined in a conventional and orthodox way, along with his fellows, so no one can really blame him.'

[31] Indeed, in an earlier work, Schumpeter (1934) suggested financial crises themselves might have beneficial consequences, even if they affected the non-financial sector, because they free economic resources to move to more productive uses.

understand the properties of financial innovations (and hence underprice risk).[32]

These more adverse patterns are quite likely to obtain initially, when behaviour of innovations over the cycle is not yet known, and competition tends to narrow margins. Uncertainty is likely to be increased by this innovation process, and hence it may be greatest in unregulated markets like the euromarkets where innovation is untrammelled by restrictions on product design. When uncertainty is reduced in one area and profits are competed away, innovation may recur, exposing the market to new uncertainties. (See also the discussion of innovation and risk in Bank for International Settlements 1986*a*.)

An increased level of uncertainty may lead to a loss of *confidence* and hence runs and panics on financial institutions or collapse of liquidity in securities markets (it is notable that confidence plays no role in a rational-expectations model with stationary probabilities). Confidence increases as innovators receive profits and their practices are emulated. Adverse surprises, given uncertainty and imperfect information, may trigger shifts in confidence and hence runs which affect markets *more than appears warranted by their intrinsic significance*,[33] because they lead to a rethinkin of decision processes as well as to decisions themselves. This helps explain the wide variety of proximate causes of financial crises.

Policy recommendations based on the lessons of the uncertainty approach (Shafer 1986) include reduction of uncertainty by avoidance of unstable macroeconomic policy (and also micro—for example, sudden changes in the level of assistance to particular sectors such as agriculture). To check risky behaviour of financial institutions, that can lead to crisis if uncertainty worsens, it is argued that supervisors and markets may need greater influence over intermediaries. As well as acting through traditional capital adequacy and asset-quality examination, supervisors should have greater power to reorganize financial firms which are acting in an unsafe manner, though such a policy is of course difficult to implement at a suitably early stage. The power of markets to check (via high costs of credit) any risky behaviour of financial institutions can be increased by more disclosure and the limitation of depositor protection to retail depositors (by imposition of a low threshold).

(7) Credit Rationing

Although in many ways based in the financial-fragility approach, as well as incorporating the lessons of uncertainty theory, some recent work

[32] Risk premiums on new financial instruments may in any case be harder to set accurately, because there is no experience of their behaviour in recessions.

[33] e.g. runs on banks which, unlike in the Flood and Garber (1982) paradigm, lead to losses out of proportion to proximate events.

(Guttentag and Herring 1984*a*) on rationing of credit, together with relaxation of credit standards during periods of calm, casts further light on financial crises distinct from the mechanisms outlined above. In particular, unlike Minsky and Kindleberger, it assumes rationality of agents under normal cyclical circumstances, while showing how uncertainty can lead to mispricing of risk. The model is developed in some detail, as it also constitutes the framework for the analysis of 'excessive competition' in Ch. 7. Essential background for the approach are the economic theories of price and quantity rationing of credit as developed in the standard capital asset pricing model and in the work of Stiglitz and Weiss (1981) respectively; an outline of these was given in Ch. 1, Sect. 3.

Guttentag and Herring (GH) offer a model in which financial crises are characterized by an abrupt increase in the extent of credit rationing, following a period when rationing constraints have been loosened excessively; they also suggest that for uncertain events, such as financial crises, lenders' perceptions of risk (subjective probabilities) may deviate from reality (objective probabilities), owing to competition as prudent lenders are undercut; and that psychological and institutional mechanisms may explain such 'disaster myopia'.

More formally, assume a creditor makes loans of L at interest i, while borrowers undertake real investments with a stochastic real return R. If the return is insufficient to pay the loan, the lender can claim all the returns of the investment project plus borrower's capital K to repay the loan. If the borrower's capital is insufficient to fill the gap, the lender makes losses on the loans. Nature draws investment returns from a cumulative distribution F(R, w), where w indicates project-specific risk mediated by appropriate diversification to remove unsystematic risk, and hence leaving largely cyclical elements. The distribution is defined from zero to a maximum return R_M. The probability of loss is then:

$$\Pr(R < (L(1+i) - K)) = F((L(1+i) - K), w) \tag{5.1}$$

so a loss to the lender is more likely if the contractual amount due rises (due to higher indebtedness or higher interest rates); if borrowers' capital falls; or if the distribution of investment returns shifts adversely. But there may also be unusual circumstances where nature draws investment returns from a 'disastrous distribution', with returns at or near zero (oil shocks, abrupt changes in monetary policy regime, wars, etc.). As explained above, these are subjects of uncertainty rather than risk. The subjective probability that nature will draw from this distribution is π, where $0 \leqslant \pi \leqslant 1$. Where $\pi > 0$, the subjective probability of loss is

$$\Pr(R < (L(1+i) - K)) = (1-\pi) F(L(1+i) - K, w) + \pi \tag{5.2}$$

a weighted sum of the objective probability that nature will draw an unfavourable outcome from the project specific distribution F(L(1 + i) –

K, w) and the subjective probability nature will draw from the disastrous distribution π.

As regards the project-specific distribution, it is suggested that 'shocks' if repeated frequently enough (e.g. the cycle) will be priced into the risk premium on loans, and/or determine the degree of equilibrium quantity rationing of credit. GH suggest that these premiums will accurately reflect risk, because unfavourable outcomes are sufficiently frequent for lenders adhering to subjective probability distributions different from the objective to suffer losses, and have to withdraw from the market. In contrast, market participants do not know the uncertain distribution of disastrous outcomes, nor can it be inferred from history, and hence subjective and objective probabilities of lenders may not converge. *Competition may drive prudent creditors from the market* as those charging risk premiums for low probability hazards lose business to those ready to disregard it—there is no market mechanism to ensure such risks are correctly priced.[34] This insight clearly depends on the degree to which relationships link borrowers and lenders—strong relationships could enable the latter to charge higher rates even in the face of a competitive challenge. It also assumes a liberalized and competitive rather than regulated and/or oligopolistic system. Note under some circumstances competitive pressure can come from the deposit side as well as the loan side.

GH's main explanations for this phenomenon of *disaster myopia* are psychological and institutional. The hypothesis is that creditors' expectations in the case of these uncertain possibilities is characterized by three psychological mechanisms, the 'availability heuristic', the 'threshold heuristic', and 'cognitive dissonance'.[35] The availability heuristic is employed when a person calculates probabilities by the ease with which instances are brought to mind—which depends in turn on the time which has elapsed since the last occurrence and the intensity of the experience.[36] At some point after the occurrence of a previous crisis, the subjective probability of occurrence becomes so low it is treated as zero. This is an example of the threshold heuristic, a rule whereby the scarce resource of managerial attention is allocated. A third factor may be cognitive dissonance, which comes into play when new information becomes available to suggest that, contrary to prior assumptions, a serious hazard does exist. The mechanism protects decision-makers' self-esteem when information arises that casts doubt on the wisdom of past decisions, and leads them to ignore or reject the information. For example, just

[34] Such tendencies might be aggravated by competition for market share, or 'predatory pricing' aimed to drive competitors from the market; see the discussion in Ch. 7.

[35] See, e.g. Tversky and Kahnemann 1982; Simon 1978.

[36] e.g. in assessing probabilities of defaults by ldcs, the ease with which decision-makers could imagine such events would decline as the period since the last default in the 1930s lengthened and as fewer managers who experienced the 1930s remained active.

before the debt crisis (see Ch. 6) in 1980–1, evidence accumulated that ldcs were likely to experience difficulties, but most banks ignored the signs or explained them away, and supported their opinion with new loans.

These biases may be reinforced by institutional factors, namely the short periods over which performance of loan officers is evaluated, the rapidity with which staff change position, and the weakness or absence of measures of risk-adjusted rates of return. There may also be an asymmetry between outcomes for managers and shareholders, due to salary bonuses. Profits may accrue to managers—losses are paid by shareholders. Since there are agency costs, shareholders cannot induce managers to act in shareholders' interests. These may lead again to the disregarding of low-frequency events or 'disaster myopia'. Agency costs may also arise between banks and supervisors (as explained in Sect. 2 above). These factors may operate more rapidly at times of intense competition in financial markets (Ch. 7).

Meanwhile, in an obvious extension to the equations above, the probability of the lender becoming insolvent is

$$\Pr(R < (L(1+i) - K - K_c)) \tag{5.3}$$

where K_c is the lender's capital, so capital adequacy is a crucial buffer to enable lenders to remain solvent. A further refinement relates to the treatment of borrowers in relation to their capital. At a very high level of borrowers' capital ($K = L(1+i)$), pledged as collateral (assuming its value is stable), borrowers can repay loans even if disaster supervenes, and no risk premium is necessary. At the other extreme, if capital tends to zero there will be severe moral hazard, as the borrower has incentives to take risks and the optimal response to lenders is credit rationing by quantity (this resembles the net asset approach to moral hazard, discussed in Ch. 1, Sect. 2). Between these points are two boundaries, at one of which borrowers are charged a risk premium, and at the other price rationing changes to equilibrium quantity rationing. These boundaries are flexible and depend on the subjective probability of a shock as outlined above, both in terms of the project-specific risk and the subjective probability of a disastrous outcome. (Meanwhile the *objective* probabilities clearly also depend on the degree of rationing.)

This hypothesis may explain why, during periods when no major shocks occur in an expanding economy, capital positions may decline and creditors become more vulnerable to shocks. They lend to borrowers with low capital, allow outstanding loans to rise, and allow their own capital to fall with no increase in the subjective probability of their insolvency (capital ratios decline via implicit decisions in an expanding economy, as growth in asset valuations exceeds growth in retained earnings). One would expect to observe these tendencies in such phenomena as declining spreads on debt claims and a lack of diversification[37] of claims, with frequent 'large exposures' or risks concentrated in one class of customer.

While subjective shock probabilities decline in the way shown, capital ratios decline, default premiums fall, and actual vulnerability increases, as outlined above. However, perceived vulnerability does not increase (i.e. confidence does not decline) till a 'shock' to confidence occurs. Once such a shock has occurred, a further shock of non-crisis proportions may be sufficient to cause a sharp increase in credit rationing, entailing an actual crisis. Thus, as in the uncertainty approach, confidence is crucial and shocks may have consequences that exceed their intrinsic significance. A shock will have a more serious impact on the risk premium, the higher the initial level of the subjective probability of disaster ('vulnerable' conditions are more susceptible to crises than 'benign'). An increase in subjective probability also has a greater effect on credit rationing for weakly than strongly capitalized borrowers—hence 'tiering' whereby the range of default premiums paid by risky borrowers rises, and a significant proportion are quantity rationed.

According to GH, a financial crisis is a condition in which borrowers who in other situations were able to borrow freely are unable to borrow at any rate, while others who were formerly 'prime borrowers' face heavy default premiums. In terms of the model outlined above, a significant proportion of agents have capital positions below the 'minimum' for price-rationing, which may reflect either a sharp increase in subjective probabilities of a crisis, or the occurrence of a shock that has reduced capital positions. Correspondingly, many prime borrowers become 'risky' and are price-rationed. For newly quantity-rationed borrowers, outstanding loans may be above the level lenders find acceptable, so no new loans are made and creditors take steps to reduce outstanding loans. When many lenders have previously made short-term loans in response to (perceived) low probability hazards, 'runs' from debtors—including banks—may occur.[38] Units subject to runs encounter liquidity problems that may spill over contagiously to other similar units. It is not possible to dampen a run by offering to pay higher interest rates, because moral hazard means that for a quantity-rationed borrower the loan rate is already at the point to maximize the lender's return, and/or insolvency probabilities are too high to make an offer to pay higher rates acceptable.[39]

Policy recommendations based on the GH analysis are for direct control of bank capital ratios (i.e. prudential supervision), but with the

[37] On the other hand, as pointed out by Shafer (1986), there may often be a danger of excessive reliance on diversification rather than detailed credit analysis, especially in securitized markets where borrower-lender relationships are unimportant.

[38] The main exception is when there is only one creditor and when exposures are so large that pressures for public action are strong.

[39] i.e. interest rates may be viewed as a risk indicator; see Ch. 6, Sect. 1.

proviso that additional mechanisms may be needed to prevent 'disaster myopia'—in this context insufficient risk weights.[40] Fixed risk weights, as in the Basle agreement (Sect. 2), may be of assistance in this context, though it is also important that prudential supervisors remain vigilant to risk-taking (e.g. concentration of risk). The onus is also on the banks to evolve strategic-planning structures to offset the pressures, arising from the agency costs outlined above, which drive the bank towards short-termism (Guttentag and Herring 1984*b*). A major step would be a means whereby they could 'learn by experience', despite turnover of staff.

An extension of the credit-rationing paradigm by Bond and Briault (1983*a*) differentiates between types of borrower. It emphasises the 'control' aspects of credit rationing (see Ch. 1), which may operate more successfully in the case of corporations than sovereign borrowers. Their argument starts from the observation that banks cannot directly control the actions of borrowers, especially when they have many banks (lack of conditionality). In this context, when banks are concerned about the borrowing policy of an existing debtor, they are likely to apply quantity rationing of credit to future lending rather than price rationing, given the incentive and adverse selection problems of increasing price rationing. Such quantity rationing is initially likely to be in the form of shorter maturities rather than quantity limits. For non-financial companies, this is an adequate signal of loss of bank confidence; they understand it means that less borrowing should be undertaken and/or less risk-taking, because of the possibility of bankruptcy (and recovery of assets) if credit lines are withdrawn altogether. Sovereigns do not face the bankruptcy constraint, and repudiation of debt would involve banks in irrecoverable loan losses. Given this balance of self-interest, the influence of shortening maturities on sovereigns is likely to be slight. The authors concluded that, given these structural features of banking markets and the inability to impose conditionality, a central role for banks in sovereign lending was inappropriate. But the problem may generalize to corporations which are large in relation to banks, which can access bond markets or where bankruptcy costs are significant (Dome Petroleum, AEG, Olympia and York).

(8) Asymmetric Information and Agency Costs

A further approach to financial crises seeks to reconcile monetarist and financial fragility approaches, and is strongly based on the theory of the debt contract outlined in Ch. 1. It is much akin to the credit-rationing approach, particularly in its emphasis on capital/net worth, but not in its focus on overlending or disaster myopia. It also allows a key role for stock-market crashes, following the financial-fragility theory, but counter to the monetarist approach.

[40] See also Flemming 1982.

As noted in Ch. 1, recent work on debt and financial structure focuses on differences in the information available to parties to a financial contract, and difficulties that can arise when borrowers know more about their credit risk than do lenders. If lenders cannot distinguish good from bad risks, they will charge a rate that reflects average quality of borrowers, thus excluding some high-quality borrowers. Meanwhile, as in the 'equilibrium quantity rationing' paradigm, lenders may choose to ration credit rather than raise interest rates, in order to avoid adverse selection (Stiglitz and Weiss 1981) and a sharp exogenous rise in rates can lead to a collapse in credit extension (Mankiw 1986).

In this context, Mishkin (1991) suggested a number of mechanisms whereby these problems can cause financial instability. First, if interest rates rise due to monetary tightening or merely to balance the credit market, adverse selection may increase sharply, giving rise to a substantial decline in lending. Second, heightened uncertainty, such that lenders find it harder to screen borrowers, increases adverse-selection problems. It is suggested that in each case the impact is greatest on borrowers whose credit quality is difficult to ascertain—who are likely to be low quality (although, following Diamond and Dybvig 1983 (Sect. 1), this may also include banks, given their non-marketable assets). Hence an indicator of adverse selection is an increase in the credit-quality spread[41] in bond or commercial-paper markets (for companies) or certificates of deposit (banks).

Again, as noted in Ch. 1, collateral is a means whereby asymmetric information problems may be reduced (as the lender is then confident of recovering his loan even if the borrower proves to be of low quality). But this means that a decrease in the valuation of assets (e.g. a stock-market crash provoked by a change in future profit expectations, or the rate at which they are discounted), by lowering collateral values, sharply increases adverse selection for lenders. Again, this will impinge more on low-quality borrowers for whom there is asymmetric information.

A fourth mechanism operates via moral hazard. Given asymmetric information and incomplete contracts, borrowers have incentives to engage in activities that may be to their advantage, but which harm the lender by increasing risk of default. In particular, there may be an incentive to carry out projects with a higher mean return but also higher risk.[42] The agency problem is greater when borrowers have low net worth as they have less to lose from default. Net worth could decline due to stock-market crashes, as above, as well as due to an unanticipated

[41] That is, the differential of the current secondary market yield of a private sector security over the riskless rate. Ch. 6 assesses trends in these spreads.

[42] Other types of moral hazard may include embezzlement, expenditure on perks, undertaking unprofitable investments that increase borrowers' power, or merely not working hard.

disinflation or deflation that redistributes wealth from debtors to creditors. Such effects are plausibly greater for low-quality firms that have low net worth before such crises supervene.

Bank failures may have an important role to play in this context, given the comparative advantage of banks in solving agency problems (Ch. 1, Sect. 4). Relevant considerations include expertise in information collection, giving superior ability to screen and hence reducing adverse selection; ability to engage in long-term relationships with a general reduction in agency problems; and lower cost monitoring and advantages in enforcing contracts, reducing moral hazard. Bank failures or other developments reducing their role in intermediation[43] (as in Bernanke's argument in Sect. 3) may thus reduce credit availability. As noted in Sect. 1, contagious runs affecting solvent banks are another example of the effects of asymmetric information, and one consequence may be for banks to protect themselves by increasing reserves as a proportion of assets, inducing a contraction in loans relative to deposits. With no Central Bank intervention, a bank panic may also decrease liquidity and hence raise interest rates, compounding the adverse-selection and moral-hazard problems discussed above. If there is a prolonged fall in the money supply, there may be deflation with further adverse credit-market consequences.

(9) Dynamics of Dealer Markets

This final section offers a brief summary of aspects of recent developments in the theory of dealer (market-maker) market structure and dynamics. It focuses on reaction to asymmetric information, increases in which may lead to market collapse.[44] Although the emphasis is on secondary (trading) markets rather than primary (issue) markets, and hence not directly related to availability of debt, there are likely to be important transmission mechanisms linking failure of secondary markets to difficulties in raising funds. Much of this section comprises an introduction to basic concepts; those already familiar should skip it.[45]

Three types of market structure can be distinguished. First, there may be *open outcry*, where prospective buyers and sellers call out prices for a given quantity of the goods in question. Second, there may be an *auctioneer* who arranges flows of goods for sale and organizes bidding for each article in turn. However, the best way of dealing with irregular flows

[43] These may include credit controls or interest-rate ceilings.

[44] Although not strictly a theory of financial crisis—its original application was to thinly traded equities—details are felt of sufficient importance to warrant inclusion in this chapter.

[45] Those seeking a more detailed introduction are referred to Goodhart (1989) and his references.

of new orders is often for some market participants to take the role of *market makers*: buying and selling on their own account, increasing or reducing their inventories in the process, at announced bid (buy) or ask/offer (sell) price. This is typical of financial institutions trading in money, bond, forex, and most equity markets.[46] The main points of the theory of dealer markets that are relevant in the present context are as follows.

Influence of inside/asymmetric information on the bid–ask spread. A market maker is an institution ready to buy an asset at a given bid price and sell it at a higher ask/offer price. It provides (to buyers and sellers) the services of immediacy or insurance against price fluctuations arising from random order flows. To be able to satisfy sellers of the asset, the market maker must have an inventory of the asset in question, together with access to finance of such inventories; the spread must obviously cover the cost of finance.

Particularly in the case where the asset consists of securities, there is a 'market' risk of a capital loss on the inventory through unforeseen changes in prices. Indeed, if a market maker announces his purchase and selling prices, any change in demand or supply will leave him exposed to risks, e.g. of needing to rebuild inventory at higher prices than those at which he sold or holding a larger volume of lower priced assets.

The dealer will face a set of customers who are more or less informed about fundamentals relative to him. In this context, market makers need to charge a higher spread than would otherwise be the case on the regular flow of 'liquidity' orders from relatively uninformed customers,[47] to offset losses made on dealings with 'informed' or 'insider' traders whose orders reflect private information on changes in fundamentals.[48] Note that it is their knowledge relative to the dealer that is crucial. Hence any stimulus that increases information asymmetry (Sect. 8) will increase the proportion of 'insiders' from the market maker's point of view, while an improvement in the quality of publicly available information will have the opposite effect. The greater the volume of liquidity customers relative to insiders, the lower the spread required. The more the insiders, the less the quoted spread will reflect the realized return of the market maker, as his purchases (sales) are followed by lower (higher) prices following the informed traders' deals. Even if there are no informed traders, prices

[46] Ho and Saunders (1981) suggest one can also see banks as market makers in money, making bids on given terms for funds from depositors and offering loans to borrowers. The difference of bid-and-ask prices is then the interest-rate spread. However, as outlined in Ch. 1 and Sect. 1 of this chapter, banks have other functions in payments, maturity transformation, and monitoring of loans. We suggest treating banks as market makers would omit too many of these relevant aspects, and hence prefer to treat them separately.

[47] Reasons why such individuals may wish to trade could include portfolio adjustment for hedging purposes (Madhaven 1990), uninformed speculation, or to realize wealth for consumption.

[48] Obviously, if incurring such losses the dealer may also restrict quantities at which he is prepared to deal.

may tend to move systematically against market makers. This is because, as risk bearer, the market maker lowers ask-and-bid prices after a purchase, since he is less anxious to buy extra shares to increase his inventory position, and is more anxious to sell the shares he has just acquired. And vice versa for sales (Stoll 1985).

The size of the spread determined by these factors[49] will in turn influence the willingness of buyers and sellers to enter the market, and hence the volume of trading, which may in turn influence the spread. This leads on to the further issue.

Can inside/asymmetric information prevent a market operating? There are sizeable fixed costs in organizing markets, and volumes of 'liquidity' trading may respond inversely to costs of transacting. The costs of trading depend in turn largely on the bid–ask spread, related to the volume of uninformed regular deals. As uninformed trade rises, profits from a given bid–ask spread increase; new entry and increased competition among market makers reduce the spread, encouraging more liquidity trading (insider traders will not be affected—they will always trade when they know equilibrium values are outside current bid–ask spreads). A market's success will be self-reinforcing. This may explain current developments in financial markets, where trading tends to concentrate in certain dealer markets, as well as reducing the need for physical locations for markets (Davis 1990*c*).

Successful markets are often characterized by assets with a homogenous standardized quality, whose information is publicly available (government bonds, money markets). They may work even better with some price volatility, which may encourage yet more trading (uninformed speculation and defensive hedging). Indeed, expected stability of prices can cause asset markets to fail.

But markets may also enter adverse spirals leading to market failure (Glosten and Milgrom 1985). A relative increase in insiders, which may, for example, result from the various stimuli reported in Sects. 3–8, leads market makers to widen spreads to avoid losses. This discourages liquidity traders, who withdraw, increasing adverse selection. Some dealers may cease to operate. Once the insiders are too numerous and if their information is too good, bid and ask prices may be too far apart to allow any trade.[50] Since a wide spread in turn prevents the insider from revealing his information by trading, shutting down the market will worsen subsequent adverse selection (i.e. the proportion of insiders

[49] Those mentioned are not the only determinants. There will also be resource costs to the provision of market making services such as labour and office space, as well as a profit margin. Market makers may also carry out additional functions, which may be charged for separately or bundled with costs of market making. Market makers may enjoy monopoly rents which will be reflected in a larger spread.

[50] This assumes liquidity trade is endogenous; it not, there will remain a small number of trades.

relative to liquidity traders) and widen the spread further. The market will stay closed until 'the insiders go away, or their information is at least partly disseminated to market participants from some other information source'.[51]

It is suggested that these types of spiral may arise in a normally well-functioning securities market; an initial increase in asymmetric information, perhaps caused by the mechanisms identified in the earlier sections, leading to a widening of spreads which drives away liquidity traders. The secondary market, in effect, ceases to function. The associated decline in liquidity of claims is likely to increase sharply the cost of raising primary finance in such a market (i.e. there will effectively be heightened price rationing of credit), or it may even be impossible to gain investor interest at any price (quantity rationing). However, following the logic of the 'credit rationing' and 'agency cost' paradigms outlined above, increases in information asymmetries may in any case have direct effects on primary markets (including those for bank loans); the above analysis can hence be seen as complementary rather than a substitute.

Conclusions

Seven approaches to financial crises have been outlined, which seek to explain how financial instability may be triggered. Although partly substitutes (particularly the monetarist versus financial-fragility and rational-expectations versus uncertainty approaches) these approaches are also to some extent complementary. Uncertainty, credit rationing, and agency costs may add to understanding of how crises triggered by the earlier macroeconomic mechanisms are transmitted through the financial system. The theory of dealer markets shows the impact of information asymmetry, that again may be caused by external factors, in secondary markets. Even the main macro theories may illuminate each other: a monetary tightening could help trigger a collapse of a financially fragile economy. Finally, the credit-rationing and agency-cost approaches make some attempt at general reconciliation.

Note that the theories also cast further light on financial fragility in the non-financial sector. In particular, the patterns described in the financial-fragility, credit-rationing, and agency-cost approaches are clearly evident in the discussion of corporate and personal default in Chs. 2 and 3, and in the wider implications of fragility noted in Ch. 4.

[51] Madhaven (1991) suggested this implies that circuit-breakers such as market closure are ineffective. An auction may be needed to restart the market.

6

Financial Instability 1966–1990

In this chapter we test the theories outlined in Ch. 5 against evidence from six periods of financial instability since 1973, namely the UK secondary banking crisis of December 1973, the Herstatt crisis of June 1974, the advent of the Debt Crisis in August 1982, the crisis in the FRN market of December 1986, the equity market crash of October 1987, and the US thrifts crises of the 1980s.[1]

Background on wholesale financial markets—in which most of the crises occurred—is provided in Sect. 1. In Sect. 2 the events of the periods of disorder are outlined. Three crises took place largely in international markets; one linked international and domestic; the other two were purely domestic. It is relevant to note that virtually all occurred in unregulated[2] or liberalized financial markets. Sect. 3 sets these crises in the context of the long-run behaviour of prices and quantities in the financial markets with a graphical illustration of the 1966–90 period. The behaviour of key economic indicators as well as market prices and quantities surrounding these events is examined in more detail in Sect. 4. These sections permit a qualitative evaluation in Sect. 5 of the theories of crisis. The results also cast light on the behaviour of financial markets under stress and give indications of appropriate policy responses. Sect. 6 draws together the conclusions, suggesting which aspects of the various theories are relevant under current conditions and noting potential implications for policy.

It should be noted that the empirical approach of the chapter is largely qualitative, in that a degree of causation is inferred without rigorous statistical tests, albeit with theoretical support; in addition, the analysis does not probe the extent to which a combination of circumstances has occurred without precipitating a crisis. In support of this approach, it is suggested that a more rigorous empirical approach using econometrics is difficult to employ given the infrequency of crises. (A tentative econometric analysis of the precursors of financial instability is provided in Appendix 2

[1] Certain other crises of recent decades are omitted from the main analysis. However, a brief summary of features of selected further crises is given in Ch. 8.

[2] International markets are generally free from regulations on entry, innovation, or activities, although institutions are generally supervised by home regulators and benefit from a 'safety net'. Features of euromarkets are summarized in Davis (1992*b*).

at the end of this chapter.) However, the limitations of the analysis need to be borne in mind.

(1) Wholesale Market Structure and Dynamics

As an introduction, it is noted that many of the events occurred or entailed behaviour in wholesale money markets, whether in the domestic or international financial markets. It is therefore useful to begin by outlining certain features of these markets. The key wholesale market in the present context is the international interbank market, although the US domestic markets for commercial paper and certificates of deposit have also played a role in certain episodes of financial instability. We introduce the main features of the instruments before going on to discuss aspects of behaviour. The bulk of the latter focuses on the interbank market, although part of the analysis generalizes; certain separate considerations relating to the other markets are also noted.[3]

Briefly, the *international or eurocurrency interbank market* is an offshore[4] market for non-negotiable (and hence illiquid) bank deposits, usually of a fixed term of under six months (though a significant proportion is at call, i.e. a day's notice, and certain time deposits can be liquidated at a penalty). The main participants are major international banks (1,000 in the mid-1980s), although non-banks are not excluded.[5] Interbank lending in the US domestic market is largely carried out in the Fed Funds market, where banks borrow and lend excess reserves among themselves.

Certificates of deposit (CDs) are large-denomination, negotiable, fixed-interest time deposits, again usually with a maturity of up to six months. They are generally held by non-banks such as industrial companies and money-market mutual funds. Wholesale CD markets exist both in the US domestic and euromarkets. However, although the CD market has been of major importance for most of the period studied (1966–90), it is relevant to note that, since the late 1980s, the US domestic wholesale CD market has been partly replaced[6] as a source of bank funding by issues of fixed-rate *deposit notes*, having a maturity of 18 months and more and generally swapped into floating rates.

[3] For an overview of current US and international money markets see Stigum (1990).

[4] Hence not subject to domestic *structural* regulations, although banks are *supervised* by domestic authorities.

[5] In practice, companies and institutional investors often prefer the liquidity offered by CDs and other short-term securities.

[6] Underlying factors included weakening of bank creditworthiness after the debt crisis (Sect. 2) and the Continental Illinois débâcle (Ch. 8), which weakened the market; development of interest-rate swaps, which facilitated use of deposit notes; deregulation of deposit rates, which increased banks' ability to attract retail deposits; changes in reserve requirements, which meant they fell to zero at maturities over 18 months; and decreasing profitability for dealers in CDs. The last point underlines the key role of market makers to the viability of markets (Ch. 5, Sect. 9).

Finally, *Commercial Paper* (CP) is a form of short-term unsecured negotiable debt issued by non-banks, notably industrial and finance companies. Bank holding companies may also issue. Often there is a backup bank line of credit, to cover the risk that rollover of such debt might be impossible (and hence necessitating fire sales of illiquid assets). The main investors are money-market mutual funds. As for CDs, a euromarket counterparty has developed (euronotes).

Moving on to market functions and behaviour, in the *international interbank market* trading serves several functions.[7] First, for any bank the inflow and outflow of funds from deposits or loans will not always match, and interbank lines form an alternative to holding liquid assets. Since such precautionary balances can be reduced, transactions costs can be lower. Second, there are intramarginal transfers of liquidity from one bank to another. Since depositors may often prefer to hold funds with larger rather than small banks, the latter often need to borrow via the interbank market to finance their lending. Third, interbank trading may be a means of geographical diversification to banks in countries such as the USA where there are restrictions on branching. Fourth, international interbank lending may be necessary to enable the currency composition of deposits to match that of loans. Finally, one can identify a global liquidity distribution function whereby the international interbank market channels funds between market centres.

In this context, banks may be viewed as carrying out screening and monitoring of other banks, which is broadly similar to non-bank loans (Ch. 1, Sect. 4). The main differences are as follows (see Saunders 1987; Moffett 1986). Continuous assessment of credit risk between individual banks is costly and difficult, given lack of information about the borrower's portfolio, and also time-consuming in a market relying on ease and speed. The usual method is to establish mutual credit lines, to minimize cost and delay in transactions. Such lines will encapsulate longer term credit assessments, based on factors such as reputation, size, capital, nationality (given 'country risk' in the international markets, including presumed access to a lender of last resort), whether the bank supplies funds two way to the market, as well as perceptions regarding assets. The line will set a risk premium and also a quantity limit. Such quantity rationing may be rational in the sense of Stiglitz and Weiss (1981)—Ch. 1, Sect. 3—as in lending to another bank the bank accepts the risk of the other's portfolio in the context of imperfect information. Reflecting country risk and/or other identifiable differences between banks, price and quantity limits may also be divided into groups or 'tiers'. The continued dominance of the international interbank market over other forms of crossborder financing—at least till 1990[8]—suggests banks retain

[7] See also Ellis 1981; Bank for International Settlements 1983; Johnston 1983; Jeanneau 1989; Lewis 1991. Many of the features generalize to domestic interbank markets.

[8] Recent evidence suggests that markets in derivative products, notably forward rate agreements and interest rate swaps, are beginning to overhaul the interbank market, as they are viewed as fundamentally more efficient means of managing interest-rate risk, leaving

comparative advantages over securities markets here (although the scope of the market also entails an intrinsic advantage in terms of diversification).

As long as banks' credit standing is not in doubt, the international interbank system efficiently directs funds from surplus to deficit banks. But given the size of the overnight market, as well as facilities for early withdrawal of deposits, flows of funds can change rapidly. If deposits are switched from international to domestic markets it can continue to function. But in a crisis funds may not be available if depositors switch deposits between different banks or classes of banks (i.e. groups that are easily distinguished).

This may be a particular risk if maturities are short and information is imperfect. Indeed, Grunewald and Pollock (1985) have argued that, unlike the equity market, which prices risk over a continuum, the interbank/ money market is a rationing device that reacts discontinuously to risk. A borrower is either sound and can borrow at market rates, or cannot borrow at all. Such withdrawals of interbank deposits may cause losses to a bank, affect solvency and liquidity, and make other banks unwilling to lend. The alternatives are then sale of assets or bankruptcy. In crises, the behaviour of the interbank market may also lead to systemic problems, given that the quality of one bank's balance sheet is related to others it lends to.

Reasons for these patterns may lie in the structure of interbank trading as outlined above. Following the logic of equilibrium quantity rationing of credit, the willingness of a borrowing bank to pay more for funds (because it is finding them difficult to obtain) may actually lead to it being refused funds at any price, because in the context of information asymmetry, the request is seen as an adverse signal about its creditworthiness. At times of stress, for example following receipt of adverse news regarding credit risk or country risk, such judgements may also be applied to whole 'tiers' of similar banks, generating what amounts to contagious runs.

Such behaviour generalizes to other markets, notably domestic interbank markets in countries such as the UK,[9] and in some degree to the US domestic CD and CP markets. For example, CDs and CP also exhibit tiering at times of stress, and may feature forms of 'run' from issuers or groups of issuers. Investors are likely to have undisclosed 'lines' or limits to exposure (obviously these are usually one way). But there are also

interbank deposits purely as a funding instrument (Lamfalussy 1992). This could also be partly a consequence of the initial focus of the Basle Agreements on credit risk rather than market risk. Such off-balance-sheet exposures may heighten problems of imperfect information over risk of institutions.

[9] In the UK, interbank lines may be committed, i.e. guaranteeing access to funds for a fixed period in return for a fee and (usually) a series of covenants, or uncommitted, i.e. on a discretionary or best efforts basis. The latter may become unavailable at times of stress, while the former may become more difficult to roll over. Note that in neither case need there be firm 'relationships', although these cannot be ruled out; the focus is rather on 'control'.

arguments that CD and CP markets may be more unstable than the interbank market; institutional investors and corporate treasurers, who are the main investors in the CD and CP markets, may be even more prone than banks to 'run' from issuers or markets in difficulty given their fiduciary responsibilities; they perceive money-market assets as short-term, liquid, and low-risk; they have less detailed information about the credit risk than banks; they are subject to more stringent performance criteria; and they have no relationship reasons to maintain the viability of a given market or borrower. For traded instruments, 'herding' by institutions may give rise to volatility of market prices, generating market risk. As securities markets, the CD and CP markets may also be subject to adverse spirals in market liquidity, as market makers react to asymmetric information (Ch. 5, Sect. 9) although experience, for example during the 1987 crash, has shown the US CP market's liquidity to be extremely robust. This may relate partly to the number of liquidity traders.

Some authors like Wolfson (1989) argue that the development of wholesale money markets such as the interbank market has been both a symptom and a cause of greater instability in the banking sector. The suggestion is that, after the Second World War, banks in the USA (and UK) had large holdings of liquid government bonds, which could be sold in order to provide for liquidity needs and/or to increase lending. The rundown of these holdings reduced banks' ability to manage assets and accommodate loan demand, especially when money was tight.[10] In 1961 the negotiable certificate of deposit was introduced, with a secondary market for its resale (and contemporaneously, the international and UK interbank markets developed). There thus developed rapidly the technique of liability management, purchasing liabilities to meet needs for funds. Given the nature of the market as outlined above (as well as domestic US problems arising from interest-rate ceilings), liability management entailed increased risk. And as will be seen, wholesale market 'runs' played an important part in several of the crises discussed below. Some have argued that the increasing use of securities markets by banks for their funding requires the authorities to act as 'market maker of last resort' to prevent market collapse at times of stress.

Moreover, the OECD (1991) suggest that investment banks may be particularly vulnerable to wholesale-market runs, because they lack (presumed) access to a lender of last resort; they have significant short-term money-market funding requirements which may account for a large proportion of their capital (e.g. for financing leveraged buyouts, 'bought deals' in primary bond markets, or positions in secondary markets) and no stable retail deposit base: their financing needs change from hour to hour and hence they need flexible funding from a variety of sources; and their

[10] Wolfson notes that a parallel rundown occurred for companies, prompting the initial stages of the debt buildup discussed in Ch. 2.

trading interrelationships with other investment banks are close and complex (across a variety of instruments, markets, currencies, and time zones).

In such conditions a creditor may not know his exposure to a particular investment bank, nor can the investment bank calculate its exposure to another, at least intra-day or to the counterparties of others. 'In a crisis (such as a sharp fall in securities prices) this ignorance about the full extent of exposure to individual institutions itself generates anxiety, and may lead lenders and fellow traders to assume the worst about institutions perceived to be in the weakest state' (OECD 1991: 16). Then, if institutions face funding problems they need to sell securities, aggravating existing downward pressure on prices and devaluing other assets. Or market liquidity may have declined sharply so 'liquid assets' are unsaleable (compare Ch. 5, Sect. 9). An illiquid investment bank could thus rapidly become insolvent, bringing others down in its wake (and the crisis then spreads to the banking and payments system). Note also that many of the points generalize to the investment-banking activities of commercial banks.

(2) Six Episodes of Financial Instability

This section offers an account of the main features of the six periods of financial disorder analysed in this chapter.

(a) The UK secondary banking crisis 1973[11]

At the end of 1973, several small banks and other financial institutions in the UK faced increasing concern over the quality of their assets. This led in turn to difficulties in obtaining rollover of short-term money-market liabilities. The Bank of England, fearing a generalized crisis of confidence, organized a rescue operation (the lifeboat) with the aid of the major commercial (clearing) banks. The rescue operation continued for several years, as a number of the banks that initially appeared illiquid proved to be insolvent. But a systemic crisis was avoided.

The secondary banks emerged during the 1960s, and their main business was lending funds obtained in the wholesale money markets—themselves a relatively recent development at the time—to sectors such as commercial property. The latter had been shunned by the major clearing banks both for reasons of risk and because the clearers were subject over this period to either the operation or the threat of credit controls. As a result, they tended to reserve credit for established business customers. The establishment of secondary banks was at the

[11] See Reid 1982; Bank of England 1978; Corrigan 1990.

time a relatively easy process, with little examination of the 'fitness and properness' of the institution or its managers, and little formal prudential supervision.

The abolition of credit controls on all UK banks in the reform of 1971—'Competition and Credit Control' (CCC)—sharply increased competition in the banking sector, which together with a relaxation of macroeconomic policy contributed to a rapid increase in lending, a stock-market and property boom. The main clearing banks took advantage of the liberalization to lend to the sectors previously dominated by the secondary banks. Meanwhile, the secondary banks' own balance sheets expanded rapidly, balancing money-market liabilities with long-term loans, largely to property and construction companies.

The authorities acted in 1973 to reduce demand and the rising inflation that had accompanied it, by raising interest rates and tightening fiscal policy. These led to sharp falls in share and property values, aggravated by the advent of the oil crisis. These in turn weakened the balance sheets of secondary banks—whose assets were often secured on such collateral. Deposits began to be withdrawn. To address what was assumed to be a liquidity crisis, the Bank of England sought mechanisms that would avoid direct money creation or interest-rate reduction (as this would counteract the thrust of policy). Instead, the clearing banks were persuaded to pool funds for a 'lifeboat' operation to save the financial system from the consequences of widespread failures of the secondary banks, with the Bank providing 10 per cent. The intention was to recycle deposits which had been transferred from secondary banks to safer havens at the clearers. Eventually, twenty six banks were supported by up to £1.3 bn in loans. In addition to the lifeboat, the Bank and clearers sought to obtain additional funds from shareholders of secondary banks; shareholders were persuaded to agreed to dilution of their holdings; creditors were pressured to forego rights to foreclosure; in some cases, 'relationship' banks supported their secondary-bank customers; and direct assistance was provided by the Bank in the form of credit agreements.

In the course of the rescue, it became increasingly apparent that many banks faced insolvency and not illiquidity. But most depositors were protected, except for some who were shareholders. The Herstatt crisis of 1974 (see below) made the Bank sensitive to avoid any default on euromarket loans. The secondary banks who were assisted were obliged to reduce their operations; several were acquired by other institutions, including the Bank itself. Both the Bank and the clearers made losses (totalling around £150 mn), although some were later recouped. The crisis was a major stimulus for the 1979 reform of supervision, which considerably increased scrutiny of those applying for banking licences; increased resources were also allocated to supervision and a deposit protection scheme was set up.[12]

[12] Covering 75% of the first £20,000 deposit at the time of writing.

(b) Herstatt 1974[13]

As noted in Sect. 1, the eurocurrency interbank market is one of the largest components of international banking business. Johnston (1983) reported that in the early 1980s two-thirds to three-quarters of banks' total crossborder liabilities were in the form of claims with other banks (this pattern is also believed to have held in the 1970s).

The interbank market grew rapidly in the early 1970s—foreign currency interbank credits to European BIS reporting banks rose from $9 bn in 1970 to $21.8 bn in 1974.[14] In this context, in 1974, losses by several banks were linked to rash foreign-exchange dealing and inadequate appraisal of risks. After the generalized floating of exchange rates in the early 1970s, many commercial banks expanded their foreign-exchange positions. For example, currency instability increased the demand for forward cover for non-bank firms. Since contracts could not always be matched in the forward markets, banks would often accommodate their customers by 'covering' themselves by spot exchange transactions plus eurocurrency interbank borrowing. At some banks, internal controls were clearly inadequate, leading to concentration of risk; in other cases, dishonest dealers rigged the market to their own advantage. Traders often responded to unanticipated exchange-rate changes by taking further positions in the hope of recovering losses—but often increased them. The 1973 oil-price increase heightened volatility of markets and disrupted patterns of capital flows. Several banks were caught by unexpected depreciation in some currencies together with a tightening of US monetary policy. For example, Franklin National bank in the USA failed in May, as following announcement of sizeable losses on forex trading, it was subject to runs. In the international interbank market, it lost $700 mn in liabilities, and $900 mn from domestic non-bank depositors. Foreign-exchange losses also occurred at Lloyds Bank in Lugano, the Bank of Belgium, and Westdeutsche Landesbank. But the worst failure was at Bankhaus Herstatt in June 1974.

Herstatt had been established in 1955, had 50,000 customers, and had assets of DM 2.0 bn. In the early 1970s, in common with many other banks, it built up its foreign-exchange business, and the risks it took were the direct cause of its insolvency. A particular cause of controversy was the way in which the crisis was handled. The bank was closed abruptly by the German supervisory institution, and the Bundesbank ceased to clear for its account, at a time when it was heavily engaged in spot forex transactions. This left many payments it had promised over the previous two days in suspense, especially those to New York, whose business day was only beginning. As reported in Corrigan (1990) 'when Chase Manhattan, Herstatt's correspondent bank received word of the closure, it decided not

[13] See Johnston 1983; Corrigan 1990.
[14] Source: Bank for International Settlements 1975.

to honour $620m in payment orders and cheques drawn on the account. Banks that had paid into Herstatt were denied the countervalues due to them'. Payments problems increased: Lepetit (1982) notes

> In the Herstatt affair, it seems the German authorities wanted to teach speculators, as well as banks dealing with speculators, a lesson. But the US clearing system nearly collapsed with Herstatt on 26 June 1974; the CHIPS computer was switched off, and it was necessary for the clearing US banks to barter checks during the whole night and afterwards to use the impossible device of conditional transfers.

The Herstatt crisis raised questions about banks' international exposure and operations. Initially, confidence fell in the interbank market, and many banks began to assess their interbank lending in much more detail. They tended to discriminate sharply between the credit standings of different institutions, causing interbank interest rates to experience marked tiering. Interbank deposit rates indicated the existence of at least six tiers[15] of banks in the euromarket, and the range of rates also expanded significantly. Up to six weeks after the failure of Bankhaus Herstatt, only the strongest European and US money-centre banks (prime borrowers) could raise interbank funds at pre-existing spreads. Substantial tiering existed in other cases, with premiums as high as 2 per cent being faced by 'risky' Japanese and Italian banks and certain smaller banks which relied heavily on interbank funding. It is reported that they were virtually excluded from the market, suggesting some degree of quantity rationing also. Depositors moved funds from the eurocurrency market to national markets, the London euromarket shrank temporarily in mid-1974, and interest rate-differentials between the euro and the US domestic markets widened sharply (see Chart 6.2).

For a while, there was widespread concern for the stability of the international banking system. As reported in Mayer (1982), the minutes of the US Fed Board of Governors (1974: 41–2) state that:

> There was widespread concern in financial circles that such evidence of financial difficulty at a few firms might represent the tip of the iceberg . . . Lenders responded . . . by tightening their credit standards. In the squeeze that followed, many lesser-rated borrowers found their access to security markets partially or completely curtailed, and they were forced to fall back on standby lines of credit at banks. Since banks experiencing these unexpected loan demands were also finding it necessary to pay sharply higher costs for . . . funds, they increased their own loan rates . . . Stock prices . . . fell dramatically during the spring and summer period of maximum financial strain. The composite stock index of the New York Stock Exchange . . . at the low was nearly 50 per cent below the record high reached in early 1973.

Consequently, in September 1974, the Central Bank governors of the G10 and Switzerland expressed their commitment to the continued stability of

[15] Arguably, such a large number of tiers approximates to a continuous distribution.

the international markets.[16] This move did not guarantee automatic lender-of-last-resort intervention, to prevent moral hazard, but did indicate the willingness of Central Banks to intervene in a crisis. The absence of further banking failures also helped to stabilize the eurocurrency market by early 1975. Meanwhile, the Central Banks had also learnt the importance of timing of closures in a global market, and the potential fragility of payments system, where 'Herstatt Risk' remains an important concept, and a test for the robustness of any new systems, to date (Kamata 1991).

After 1974, banks in the euromarket made more use of back-and-forth interbank trading, and set interbank lines and limits with much greater care. Limits on the amounts or maturities of loans to any particular bank were related to the borrower's net worth or another quantitative guideline—as they arguably should always have been. However, by the late 1970s, the typical interbank market range of rates was reduced to only about 25 basis points overall. Memories were short. In contrast with the situation in 1974, concern was expressed at the narrowness of the range, and it was suggested that market liquidity had created abnormal compression, with potential for a further crisis. As shown below, the crisis when it came was largely concentrated in the syndicated credits market.

(c) The debt crisis 1982[17]

During the 1970s, inflation in many countries rose well above the accepted norm; freely floating exchange rates were widely adopted by industrialized countries; nominal interest rates were volatile and sometimes very high, though real rates were often negative (Chart 6.6); and there were substantial changes in the pattern of wealth holding, largely because of sharp increases in the price of oil relative to other commodities and manufactured goods. Many countries increased their demand for external finance. Meanwhile, the OPEC surpluses were invested through the banking system[18] and not in securities markets[19]—a major difference from earlier periods of international lending such as the late nineteenth century and 1920s.[20] Partly as a result of these developments, the syndicated credit became the preferred means for international lending by banks. (A eurocurrency syndicated-credit represents a loan or credit facility, generally at

[16] Their statement read 'while it is not practical to lay down in advance detailed rules and procedures for the provision of temporary support to banks facing liquidity difficulties, the means are available for that purpose, and will be used if and when necessary'.

[17] See Johnston 1983; Bond 1985; Dicks 1991.

[18] Though some banks built up holdings of eurobonds financed by these deposits.

[19] However, as noted by Bond and Briault (1983*b*), it would be wrong to see banks as mere 'recyclers' of funds. First, the correlation between ldc loans and OPEC deposits is highly imperfect. Second, banks evidently bid aggressively for deposits and also for loans.

[20] For an analyses of the interwar debt crisis see Eichengreen and Portes (1985).

floating rates, which is arranged on behalf of a borrower from another country and is made by a consortium of banks.) The syndicated credit enabled banks to cope with the demands made on the financial system during the 1970s, by mobilizing substantial quantities of funds with little complexity or delay. However, viewed in retrospect, the simplicity of syndicated credits may also have drawn into international lending a wider range of banks than would have been ideal, while many were made at excessively fine spreads, i.e. there was a form of bull market and slippage in credit standards.

An outline of the debt crisis must commence a significant time before 1982.[21] Following a period of disruption over 1974–5, partly associated with the Herstatt crisis discussed above, conditions in the syndicated-credits market began to ease in 1976, with lower spreads for prime borrowers and a higher average loan size. Lower spreads[22] and longer maturities for other borrowers followed in 1977 and 1978. Many borrowers began to tap the syndicated loan market regularly, and a much wider range of borrowers entered the market, including heavy borrowing by ldcs. Feldstein (1991) notes that in some countries such as the USA, the authorities actively encouraged banks to undertake such lending, as an adjunct to foreign aid. Some borrowers renegotiated or refinanced loans which had been taken out under tighter conditions. Virtually all borrowers were able to negotiate successively finer terms. By 1979 the following conditions were established: high levels of lending, low spreads, little consideration of capital or ability to pay of borrowers, a wide range of borrowers of varying credit quality obtaining loans (but a concentration of loans in Mexico, Brazil, Argentina, and South Korea).

Why did spreads not rise to cover risk, as debt burdens rose? Briault and Bond (1983*b*), Folkerts-Landau (1985), and others point to such factors as an increasing focus on the part of banks on balance-sheet growth rather than just profitability; the shift from asset to liability management; the ability to cross-subsidize international business from profits made in oligopolistic domestic markets and from the 'insurance' provided by banks to depositors via their—often inadequate—capital; regulatory insurance of banks by deposit insurance/lender-of-last-resort (moral hazard of which may have been heightened in some countries by official encouragement to lending); lack of knowledge of the extent and maturity of external debts; misjudgements of ldcs' debt-servicing ability in the context of historically low real interest rates, related in turn to rapid inflation; servicing ability was often lowered by ill-judged macroeconomic policies, with overvalued exchange rates, fiscal deficits, and monetary laxity (Dornbusch 1986); misjudgement of the risks of the potential

[21] Bond (1985) offers a detailed account of the behaviour of the market over the 1970s and early 1980s.

[22] Johnston (1980) noted a negative relation between growth of volume of lending and euromarket spreads over this period, and attributed it to portfolio adjustment.

correlation between sovereign risks when economic conditions deteriorated; and the intensity of competition in the market, which kept spreads low.

The oil shock of 1979–81, and subsequent slower world economic growth, damaged prospects for developing countries. The cost of servicing debt rose sharply as unanticipated alterations to US monetary policy in late 1979, aimed at reducing inflation (the shift to a system of targeting non-borrowed reserves), lifted dollar interest rates to unusually high levels and the dollar appreciated strongly. As debt-servicing difficulties emerged—borrowers were only able to meet high debt-servicing costs by sizeable increases in borrowing—market confidence was increasingly undermined. Spreads rose for non-prime borrowers, maturities shortened, and the number of 'new' credits fell. The debt crisis effectively began with the 'shock' of Mexico's sudden suspension of external debt servicing in August 1982 (due to a lack of 'control' by banks over sovereigns, assets could not be directly recovered in the case of such suspension (Ch. 5, Sect. 7)). Borrowing subsequently became more difficult for a number of heavily indebted countries, particularly in Latin America (i.e. quantity rationing applied strongly). However, Central Banks intervened to prevent a crisis in the interbank market by persuading creditor banks to roll over their claims on Mexican banks (Price 1987) and the Fed relaxed monetary policy, reducing interest rates sharply.

The level of 'spontaneous' syndicated lending (loans syndicated normally in the market) fell sharply after the middle of 1982, and remained low throughout 1983 and 1984. The level of loans to OECD borrowers did not alter significantly, but Latin American and Eastern European borrowers virtually disappeared as takers of 'spontaneous' credits (though the latter returned to the market during 1984). Even when 'unspontaneous' lending[23] is included, the market downturn is still evident. Ldcs themselves suffered a prolonged economic slowdown in the aftermath of the crisis.

In terms of realized spreads, the effect on general syndicated credit market conditions was only temporary, with the increase in average spreads in the latter part of 1982 reversed in the first half of 1983 (Chart 6.3), and no clear evidence of shorter mean final maturities. However, the syndicated loans market demonstrated an increasing tendency to be a source of funds only for favoured borrowers such as OECD corporations who were price-rationed, while all others were quantity-rationed (at zero), and thus did not affect observed spreads. This was shown by the relative stability, from the start of 1982, of both average spreads and mean final maturities for those borrowers still having access to the

[23] Not syndicated freely, but arranged with a predetermined group of banks for predetermined amounts, based on banks' existing exposure and backed by official support programmes.

market. From mid-1983, there were even signs of slightly improved conditions for such borrowers, with spreads falling and maturities lengthening. By 1987, developing countries, evidently still quantity-rationed, accounted for 10 per cent of syndicated lending, while Eastern bloc countries, which withdrew entirely from the market by the end of the year, accounted for only 2 per cent. Over 1982–90 most syndicated credits were arranged by companies in OECD countries (Allen 1990).

The crisis left a number of banks technically insolvent, i.e. the losses from writing off non-performing ldc loans exceeded capital, often several times. However, the authorities sought to prevent default, for fear of runs by uninsured wholesale depositors and a financial crisis. Instead, they allowed the loans to be recorded at book value on balance sheets; required[24] banks to lend money to cover interest payments and to roll over existing loans (after initially providing it themselves); demanded that provisioning against loans be built up and capital ratios be maintained. This policy of forebearance was largely successful—by 1990 most of the banks had made provisions for substantial losses, thus facilitating acceptance of lower interest rates and writedowns of principal with ldcs. This outturn contrasts with the US thrifts case discussed below, where forebearance led to excessive risk-taking.

On the other hand, some commentators would suggest that there *were* adverse consequences for the lenders. In particular, following the debt crisis, banks' lower credit standing and higher insurance and capital costs (as well as the effects of deregulation on the cost of deposits) led to a higher cost of funds relative to major companies. Consequent disintermediation may have led to a pattern of riskier lending (for example, to commmercial property) as well as desire for balance-sheet growth, which was one factor that led to the financial-fragility problems outlined in Chs. 2 and 3. Meanwhile, Feldstein (1991) notes that if credit had been provided via securities markets, the adopted solution would not have been possible—although this would in any case have caused less risk to the financial system than concentration of debt in the form of bank loans.

(d) The crisis in the FRN market 1986[25]

The origins of the market in floating-rate notes (defined as medium-term securities carrying a floating rate of interest that is reset at regular intervals in relation to some predetermined market rate) lie in the 1960s when banks used them as a means for raising short- or medium-term funds to support their international lending operations. However, a major spur was given by the debt crisis (outlined above), which led to a sharp

[24] This was necessary to avoid 'free rider' problems of banks demanding repayment of old loans without providing new funds, which would have led to a collapse of the repayment and lending process.

[25] See F. G. Fisher 1988; Muehring 1987; Federal Reserve Bank of New York 1987.

decline in new lending, as well as in inflows of funds to international banks. As a substitute for syndicated loans (in bank's asset portfolios and as a liability of sovereigns), FRN issues grew particularly strongly over 1981–5, while the fixed-rate eurobond market was relatively subdued. The innovation of perpetual FRNs was also popular. The main issuers of FRNs were governments and banks (companies preferred to issue in the fixed-rate markets). Banks sought to issue FRNs as subordinated and/or perpetual debt in order to increase their capital bases, but also were attempting to reduce the degree of maturity mismatch in their international lending. Banks, notably in Japan, also emerged as major investors in the FRN market, holding a large proportion of paper outstanding.

The FRN crisis began with sharp price falls in December 1986 in the perpetual sector, which have been blamed on factors such as investors' re-evaluation of the equity characteristics of these instruments; fears that the supervisors, notably in Japan, would deduct any holdings of bank-issued FRNs by other banks from the latter's capital (thus making investment unattractive); excess supply of bonds, considering the size of the investor base; underpricing of issues in relation to risk; and false expectations of liquidity given the size of the market. At the outset of the crisis, it was expected that the problem might be resolved by an issuing hiatus, followed by adjustment of terms (F. G. Fisher 1988). But large underwriting exposures undermined the market. Rumours of heavy selling became self-fulfilling and prices went into free-fall as market makers withdrew, thus increasing potential losses for remaining traders. Short selling worsened the situation.

A similar crisis hit the much larger dated sector a month later, yields soared, and issuance became virtually impossible. Although the difficulties of the perpetual sector helped to trigger this, the problems of fears of new supervisory rulings, oversupply, and illusion of liquidity were also present in the dated sector. As described by Muehring (1987) the market had been subjected to relentless downward pressure on yields, which fell below Libor in 1986. This tended to exclude banks as investors (given that their ability to buy FRNs is premised on borrowing funds at Libor) although they held 80–90 per cent of extant bonds. Lead managers tried to compensate for low spreads with innovations which relied largely on risky interest-rate plays, while trading also increased sharply in an attempt by investors to maintain profits—and helped further to compress spreads. Underwriters and investors assumed that risks in the market were limited due to the coupon reset mechanism and built up large positions, failing to note that profits were largely a function of the bull market conditions. (There was an illusion of safety in liquidity.) Last, it was assumed that an investor base existed beyond the banking sector. This was not the case, so short-term speculative demand was mistaken for genuine end-buyers. After the crisis more and more market makers withdrew and liquidity continued to decline. Both the perpetual and dated FRN markets were largely moribund for the rest of the decade, except for some development of mortgage-related issues.

(e) The equity market crash 1987[26]

Macroeconomic antecedents: During 1987, participants in financial markets became increasingly concerned with the persistence of large current-account imbalances between the USA, Japan, and Germany. The fear was that the imbalances would lead to investor reluctance to hold dollars, entailing downward pressure on the dollar, and higher US interest rates. In addition there was some increase in world inflation expectations, associated both with a strengthening in commodity prices, and with the build-up of liquidity in countries such as the UK and Japan with appreciating currencies; the latter was partly a result of official intervention to stem the dollar's decline following the Louvre accord. As a result of fears of inflation, monetary policy was tightened in several countries. Market concern was compounded by the limited macroeconomic policy co-ordination that had been achieved. Although the Louvre accord did help stabilize exchange rates during the first three quarters of 1987, little progress was evident on adjustments to fiscal policy, particularly in the USA and Germany. Adverse US trade figures for July and August sharply reversed the weak improving trend which had prevailed since the spring, with damaging effects on market confidence and (in combination with tighter monetary policy) on interest rates. For example, short-term US interest rates rose from 7½ per cent at the end of September to 9 per cent just before the crash. Furthermore, the failure to achieve sustained reductions in current-account imbalances was highlighted by renewed and public policy discords between the USA and some other countries in mid-October.

Portfolio imbalance: A notable feature prior to the crash was the widening yield gap between government bonds and equities in the USA, Japan, and the UK. The main theoretical determinant of equity values is the discounted present value of expected future dividends.[27] The market's valuation of these dividends will depend on the relative attractiveness of alternative investments, such as bonds. Allowing for risk differentials, the returns on the two assets should tend to equalize over time. The widening of the differentials after 1986, at a time when inflation was relatively constant—equity yields falling as prices rose, bond yields rising with inflation expectations, and tighter monetary policy—implied the need for a portfolio shift at some point to re-establish more normal differentials. In the absence of a sharp fall in bond yields, such shifts can

[26] See Bailey *et al.* 1988; Brady 1988.

[27] Though corporate asset values may also play a part, notably in Japan.

require extremely large changes in equity prices. The fall in equity prices may have represented such a portfolio shift.

A speculative bubble? An explanation of the strong rise in equity prices in 1987 may be couched in terms of a deviation from the fundamental determinants of value. The reasons for the overvaluation of equities are difficult to identify, but may have included falls in the number of shares outstanding, owing to buybacks and management buyouts in the United States; development of programme-trading techniques such as 'portfolio insurance' that offered institutions confidence that gains could be protected against a crash; lower transactions costs and higher turnover, that fostered an impression of increased liquidity; and the merger wave in many countries. Falling interest rates, buoyant economic prospects, and strong monetary and credit growth also fuelled share price growth. More generally, in the UK and USA, but particularly in Japan,[28] a speculative bubble may have occurred. The key *underlying* factor was the belief that overpriced shares would always find a buyer at current prices and that the level of liquidity would always be the same. Speculative bubbles throughout history have tended to deflate extremely rapidly, as did the 1987 bubble on 19 October.[29]

Information failure in the market for liquidity is held by some observers to be a key complementary explanation (Gennotte and Leland 1990; Grundfest 1991). The suggestion is that the US market suffered during the crash from a lack of information about a spike in demand for short-term trading activity—related in this case to passive programme traders—as well as uncertainty about fundamental values. The markets were uncertain about the size of expected demand for liquidity, the reason why some traders were selling, and price levels at which buying interest might reappear. This caused a sharp rise in the price of liquidity—it became expensive to buy the immediate right to sell shares—as bid-offer spreads widened and prices fell. Proponents of this view suggest that better information about the size and composition of market demand for liquidity might reduce the incidence of crashes.

Systemic risk arose largely from the difficulties of investment banks, notably in the USA and Canada. On the one hand, several investment banks were left with large tranches of devaluing international equity after they had applied 'bought deal' techniques to primary equity issues. But more generally, to keep the US stock market and index futures market open, brokers needed to extend massive amounts of credit on behalf of their customers to meet margins calls. By noon on 20 October, two houses alone had $1.5 bn outstanding. There were fears of commercial banks

[28] However, for the Japanese market, a greater crash occurred in 1990.

[29] It is notable that the consensus at the time was that the price falls were not *proportionate* to the macroeconomic changes immediately preceding the crash (as rational expectations would predict) but *greater than appeared warranted*, suggesting a rethinking of decision processes (as the uncertainty approach would predict).

cutting credit lines to securities houses, with potential systemic consequences for the markets and associated payments and settlements systems. Only a Fed announcement that ample liquidity would be provided (as well as pressure on banks to keep credit lines open to brokers, backed up by discount loans)[30] eventually calmed the markets. In the longer term, provision of liquidity by Central Banks—expanding the money supply and reducing short term interest rates—may have helped offset effects of the crash on activity.

There were also 'fragility' implications for the non-financial sector, as the equity market crash had sharp consequences for quantities and prices of credit in capital markets. In the US the yield spread on commercial paper over Treasury bills had increased over the year prior to the crash, indicating heightened risk, although the corporate bond spread was relatively stable. Given high levels of leverage in the corporate sector, together with disruption to financial markets, a number of companies had difficulties obtaining financing. But more generalized fragility—notably among equity holders in the household and financial sector—was avoided. Margin requirements preventing individuals buying stock with borrowed funds may have been important in this respect. And life insurers and pension funds—having long-term liabilities as well as volatile assets—are not subject to runs in the way banks are; although there was also little hint of risks to banks in the CEJ countries with large equity holdings.

The consequences of the crash for borrowers in debt markets are illustrated by the behaviour of the eurobond market, where issuance fell sharply and there was marked tiering of yields to sovereign and corporate borrowers, the latter finding themselves virtually excluded from the markets. Fears of recession led to sharply increased default premiums on heavily indebted corporate issuers, while the most heavily indebted were quantity rationed (for example, Bell Resources had to abandon proposed issues). Issuance of equity-warrant bonds, which had been the mainstay of the eurobond markets in previous quarters, virtually ceased, given the lack of attractiveness of the equity component. Problems in the eurobond sector, aggravated by the stock-market turmoil, as well as a sharp increase in inflows to banks on deposit of funds withdrawn from the securities markets, left banks flush with funds. This, and the lack of alternative opportunities for income, probably contributed to strong competition among banks in the credit markets, which provided an alternative source of funds to borrowers excluded from the securities markets. The competitive terms attending new syndicated credits, and the reduced attractiveness of other means of obtaining finance, also increased the appeal of credits to borrowers. The equity-market crash was initially felt

[30] By 21 Oct. US commercial bankers had increased lending to investment banks and ordinary investors by $7.7 bn.

to have discouraged syndicated lending on such financings as leveraged buyouts and takeovers, but they soon rebounded in 1988.

A detailed description of the effects of the crash on the euromarkets, which illustrates the heightened linkages between markets in the current financial framework, and the links between secondary and primary markets, is given in Appendix 1, at the end of this chapter.

(f) The US thrifts crises[31]

US savings and loans institutions (or thrifts) are a long-established form of mutual bank, which in the 1980s were subject to two linked crises, a 'maturity mismatch' crisis at the beginning of the decade and a 'loan quality' crisis in the mid- to late 1980s. However, it is suggested that the genesis of these events lies several decades further back.

In the tightening of regulation and compartmentalization of the US financial system which ensued after the crises of 1929–33 (see Ch. 8), thrifts were assigned responsibility for provision of residential mortgages (usually long-term, at fixed rate) while interest-rate ceilings were imposed on bank deposits. Such a system sought to provide stability and protection for the institutions. But problems arose as the regulatory structure came to conflict with economic conditions. Already in the 1950s and 1960s, interest rates were occasionally high enough to result in disintermediation of deposits to market instruments such as Treasury bills, but in practice rates soon fell and the high denomination of bills limited depositor interest. Imposition of ceilings on thrifts' own rates—at their own request—in 1966, prevented their liability rates exceeding asset yields.

In the 1970s the problems became more serious as, first, under pressure from inflation, interest rates rose above the deposit ceilings (typically around 5 per cent depending on maturity) for long periods and, second, the development of money-market mutual funds enabled small depositors to shift to money-market instruments. Thrifts thus suffered increasingly from liquidity problems. To prevent such disintermediation, interest-rate ceilings were progressively raised, while the institutions switched heavily into wholesale funding (after being permitted to issue unregulated Money Market Certificates, with a denomination of $10,000, in 1978). This, however, exposed a serious problem of interest-rate risk owing to the mismatch between the existing stock[32] of fixed-rate long-term mortgage assets (often at low interest rates) and high-interest short-term floating-rate liabilities. This effect was particularly severe after US monetary policy was tightened in 1979 (while the recession also increased bad debts). Net worth, earnings, and capitalization declined and failures increased.

[31] For a summary see A. P. White 1989; Bellanger 1989.

[32] Raising rates on new mortgages was of little avail in stemming the problems.

Rather than seeking orderly closure of the whole industry while net worth remained positive, the authorities sought to enable thrifts to continue in business, in the hope that eventually profitability could be re-established, as new mortgages at higher interest rates replaced old unprofitable ones. Guttentag (1989) suggests this was due to three underlying factors: first, a belief that the shock and the industry's exposure was not the industry's fault; second, inadequate supervisory resources to deal with so many insolvent firms; third, lack of political will to deal with a deferrable problem—especially since action would probably deplete the deposit insurance fund. The problem was deferrable because confidence was retained and insolvent institutions were allowed to continue operating.

In acts of deregulation dated 1980 and 1982, thrifts were allowed to diversify assets away from long-term home mortgages in the hope of speeding the return to profitability, and capital standards—which would otherwise have led to closure or balance-sheet shrinkage—were relaxed. The level of deposit-insurance coverage was increased in 1980. Finally, as regards interest-rate controls, they were further eased as permission was granted for issue of high-interest/low-denomination, money-market deposit accounts in 1982, and interest-rate ceilings were finally abolished in 1986. As noted by L. J. White (1992) these changes increased the *opportunities* (related to assets), *capabilities* (related to liabilities), and *incentives* (related to capital) for risk-taking by thrifts in the early 1980s.

Heightened risk-taking was indeed the response, as many thrifts tried to grow out of their problems by rapid expansion, diversifying into high-yield and high-risk assets such as land, development, construction, and commercial real estate as well as 'junk bonds',[33] although there was also considerable expansion in traditional fields of mortgage lending. Risk was often concentrated in narrow types of business as well as geographically. Real estate was particularly favoured due to generous depreciation provisions in the tax code at the time. Growth tendencies were particularly marked in the South-West, which experienced an oil-related boom over 1983–5. Depositors were content to finance such ventures, given the generosity of US deposit insurance,[34] despite increased credit and interest-rate[35] risk. With low capital standards and limited liability, equity holders had little to lose, particularly for thrifts that were technically insolvent (438 in 1984). Managers, who had often entered the industry *de novo* or taken over faltering institutions, had little reputational or monetary capital at risk. And reductions in supervisory budgets, as well as disruptive reorganizations, over this period meant monitoring of these trends was highly imperfect.

[33] See Ch. 2.

[34] Which covered 100% up to $100,000 per bank—hence rich depositors and even pension funds could hold $100,000 deposits with many banks in total safety.

[35] To the extent that funding of long-term fixed rate assets was by short-term liabilities.

After declines in commodity prices in 1985–6, as well as overbuilding *per se* and tightening of tax laws, the office real estate market began to collapse, and many of the other speculative loans proved non-performing.[36] In combination with low capital ratios, insolvency was widespread—thrifts were unable to sell remaining mortgages on secondary markets to pay off depositors. There was also evidence of insider abuse, fraud, mismanagement, and unsound banking practices, such as inadequate credit appraisal, at many of the insolvent institutions, although pursuit of higher yields via acceptance of high risk was probably the overriding factor. Such problems were compounded by the fact that the deposit insurer (FSLIC) lacked the resources to wind down all the insolvent thrifts, which were thus left to operate while taking ever-increasing risks.

Pauley (1989) recorded that at the end of 1988, 360 thrifts were insolvent according to 'generally accepted accounting principles' (GAAP) and another 150 had negative GAAP capital after deducting goodwill. A further 292 had GAAP net worth of under 3 per cent of assets (compared with the Basle capital standard of 8 per cent). In combination with those already closed or merged, assets of these institutions amounted to $540 bn. The policy response has been to guarantee deposit-insurance liabilities[37] and set up a corporation (Resolution Trust) to acquire ailing thrifts, closing them or selling them to other institutions. Meanwhile, remaining thrifts were subjected to tighter capital standards and limits on types of investment. Reserves were required against risk of future defaults on higher risk assets—which in turn reduced ability to meet the new capital standards.

The second thrifts crisis occurred without runs, except in Ohio and Maryland in 1985 when a panic took place among depositors with privately insured thrifts. In Ohio this was triggered by failure of a government securities firm[38] with which a large saving and loan had sizeable investments. The losses exceeded the capital of the thrift and the reserves of the private guarantee fund, generating contagious runs. The institutions concerned had to be closed by the state governor till they could obtain federal deposit insurance. It was notable (Gilbert and Wood 1986) that the Federal Reserve was unable to stop the run by offering liquidity assistance to the institutions, implying a sharp focus of US depositors on the deposit-protection aspect of the 'safety net'. The Maryland panic was broadly similar; losses at the largest institution provoked runs on all privately insured thrifts. In neither case was there a run on federally insured savings and loans.

[36] Banks were not immune to these problems—there were notable difficulties in Texas and New England (on the latter, see Tannenwald 1991).

[37] The danger of not doing this could have been loss of faith in insurance of banks, and hence widespread runs and failures.

[38] Related to inadequate operational procedures, fraudulent activities, and excess in the agreed repurchase/government securities markets.

(3) Prices and Quantities in the Financial Markets 1966–90

In order to assess the periods of instability in a comparative manner, and to evaluate economic theory in the light of them, it is useful to complement description with data which allow one to pinpoint the precursors and effects of the various periods of disorder on prices, quantities, and other economic indicators. This is provided in the charts in this section and the tables in Sect. 4. The charts set the crises in context by providing indicators of prices and quantities over the whole period, thus allowing times of crisis to be contrasted with more quiescent periods. The tables in Sect. 4 focus on developments immediately surrounding the crises. It should be noted that frequent use of US and dollar markets data in Sects. 3 and 4 is not aimed to imply that these patterns were solely observable in dollar markets or the USA. They were common elsewhere (see Ch. 8); but the USA was the predominant economy, and US domestic and eurodollar were the key financial markets for most of the period covered.

Chart 6.1 shows short-term interest rates in US dollars, while Chart 6.2 shows the differential between the risk-free rate (US Treasury bills) and other rates of the same maturity. A detailed description of these markets and their relationships is given elsewhere (see Stigum 1990; Jeanneau 1989; and the description in Sect. 1). Suffice to say that commercial paper

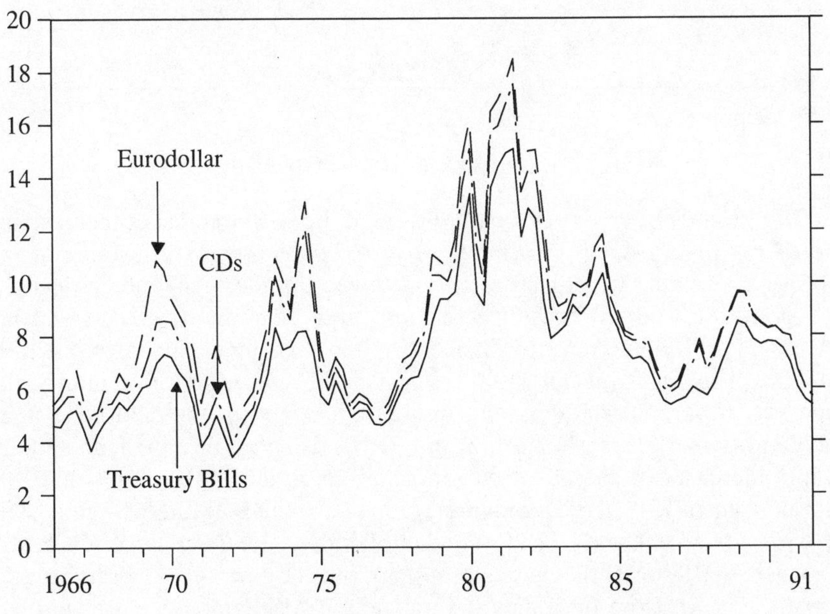

Chart 6.1. US$ short-term rates (%)

(USCP) rates indicate risks to the domestic corporate sector, certificate of deposit (USCD) rates risks to the domestic banking sector, while the three-month eurodollar rate (Libor) shows the risks in the eurocurrency interbank market (where in each case risks may include liquidity and other risks as well as credit risk). The charts indicate a long-term convergence of rates in these markets as integration of financial markets has proceeded. As well as relativities, Chart 6.1 illustrates the periods of tightening of US monetary policy (when short rates increased), notably over 1972–4, 1978–80, 1980–2, and 1987.

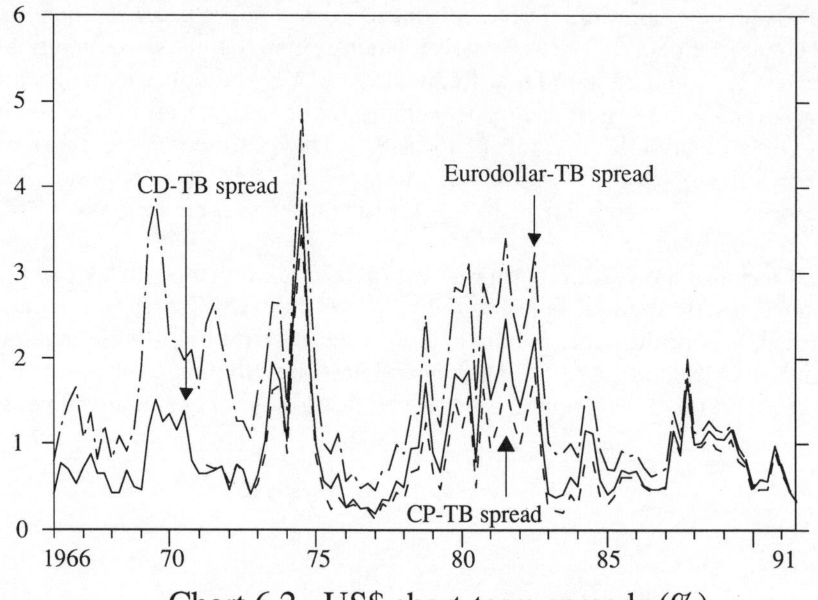

Chart 6.2. US$ short-term spreads (%)

The periods of crisis are clearly visible in both charts, as an increase in rates on private-sector liabilities *vis-à-vis* public-sector risk-free rates. These are related to an increase in perceived liquidity risk and credit risk of domestic and eurocurrency claims, and also often to declines in Treasury bill yields due to 'flights to quality' or loosening of monetary policy. The crisis of mid-1974, which was centred on the interbank market, is particularly apparent, though the effects of the debt crisis and the equity-market crash (but not the FRN crisis) are also evident. Other rapid increases in spreads occurred as a consequence of failures in 1970 (Penn Central), 1980 (silver market), 1984 (Continental Illinois), and 1990 (Bank of New England). The first and third of these are described in Ch. 8.

Chart 6.3 shows the average spread over Libor of new syndicated credits, drawn from the Bank of England's ICMS database. As would be expected, spreads for ldcs generally exceed those for OECD countries, although, naturally, *realized* spreads do not reflect the exclusion of many countries from the market after 1982. These are, of course, spreads at issue, so when there are no loans, there are no observations. The widening of spreads after the Herstatt crisis and associated macro-economic problems is clearly visible. There was then a long-run decline in spreads after this peak in 1974. The major crisis in the credits market (the debt crisis) is clearly visible in the pattern of spreads for ldcs over 1982–3, but it had almost no effect on realized spreads for OECD corporations. The rapid decline in spreads for ldcs after 1983 reflects quantity rationing of countries felt to be poor risks. In contrast, the crises of 1986 and 1987 appear to have had very little effect on realized spreads in the credits market, which for OECD borrowers continued an apparent long-term decline.

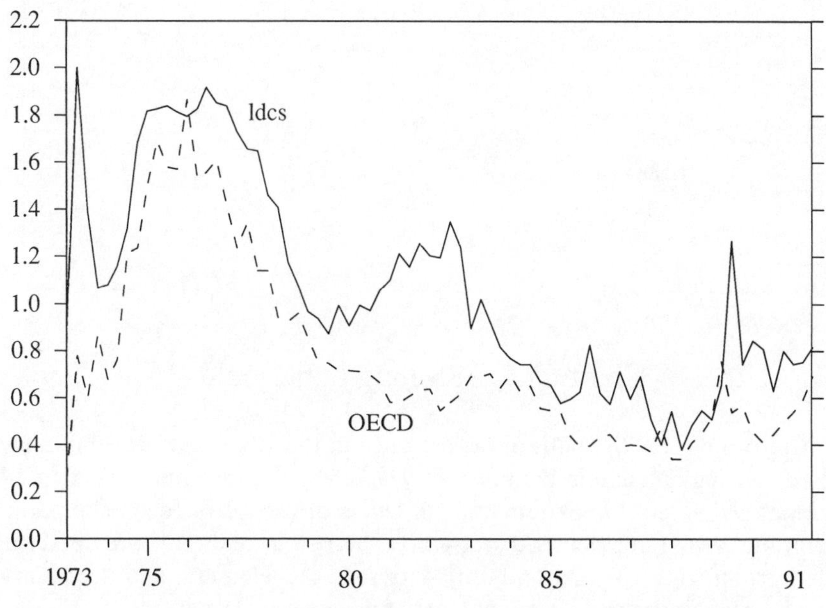

Chart 6.3. Spreads on syndicated credits (%)

Chart 6.4 shows secondary market yields for eurodollar and US domestic bonds of roughly ten-year maturities, Chart 6.5 the differential of euro and domestic corporate over US treasury rates. The earlier crises of 1974 and 1982 are clearly apparent in the eurobond market; by contrast, the FRN crisis and the crash are revealed in only minor increases in secondary-market spreads for private-sector issuers. Meanwhile, US corporate spreads relate largely to the cycle (Davis 1992*a*). It is notable that yields on US government bonds (Chart 6.4) barely changed in 1974, while over 1979–82 they increased sharply, and again in 1987–8.

Obviously these changes are related to US domestic conditions (expected inflation and the relationship between supply and demand of domestic bonds) rather than financial crises as such, though unstable financial conditions can also increase yields required on government bonds if there is a flight to short-term assets.

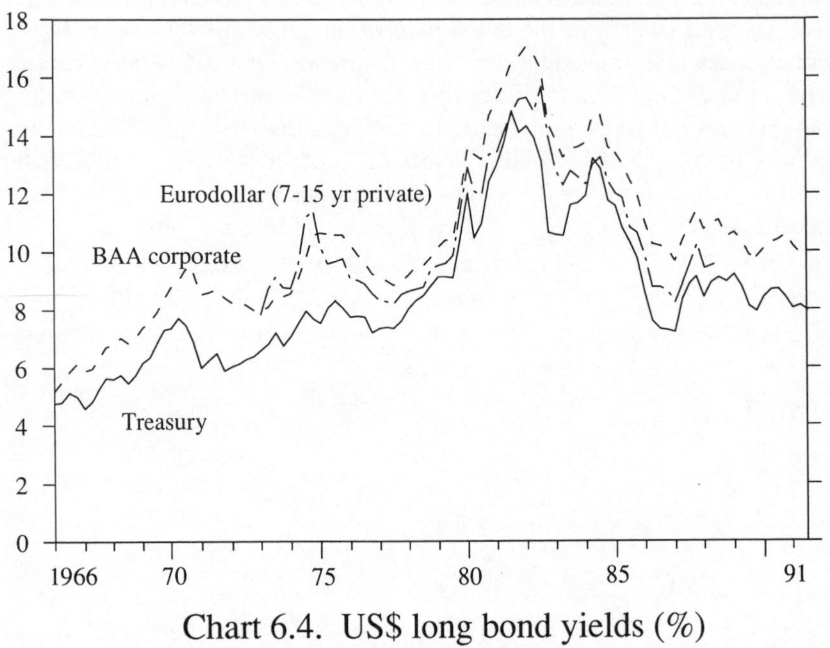

Chart 6.4. US$ long bond yields (%)

Chart 6.6 gives the pattern of real rates in the USA (calculated crudely by deducting inflation in the previous year). The negative rates experienced in the 1970s, and the extremely high levels of the 1980s (even compared with the 1960s) are clearly discernible. The rise in real rates provided the background for the ldc and thrifts crises; the Herstatt and secondary banking crises occurred in the context of negative real rates.

Chart 6.7 shows spreads in the UK domestic markets corresponding to those shown in the US and eurodollar sectors. During 1973 it is clear that interbank–Treasury bill differentials were extremely high (at other times they have been negative),[39] while the long corporate–government spread was also rising sharply. Although the debt crisis affected UK banks, the short spread's response was less marked than in 1973. Meanwhile, the long spread appears counter-cyclical in the 1980s.

[39] Believed to relate to UK money-market operating procedures.

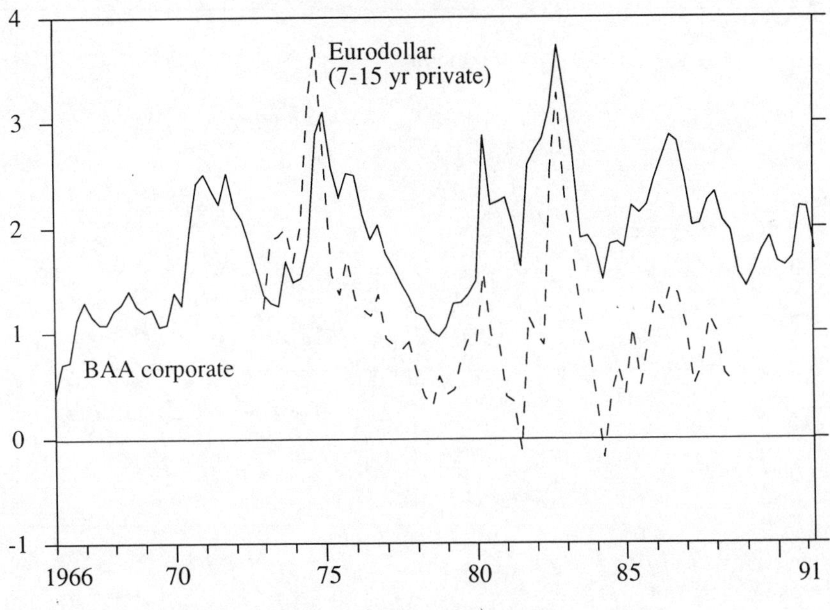

Chart 6.5. US$ long bond spreads (%)

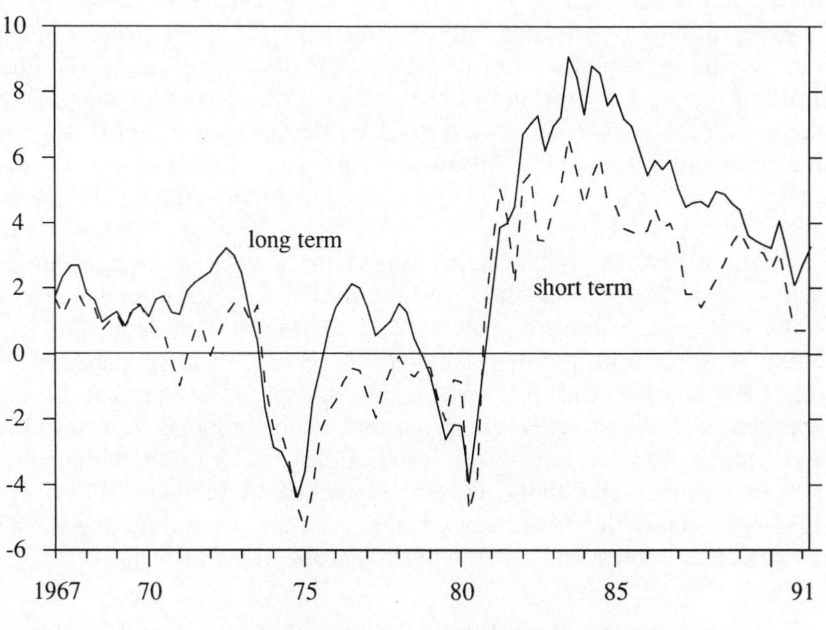

Chart 6.6. US$ real rates (%)

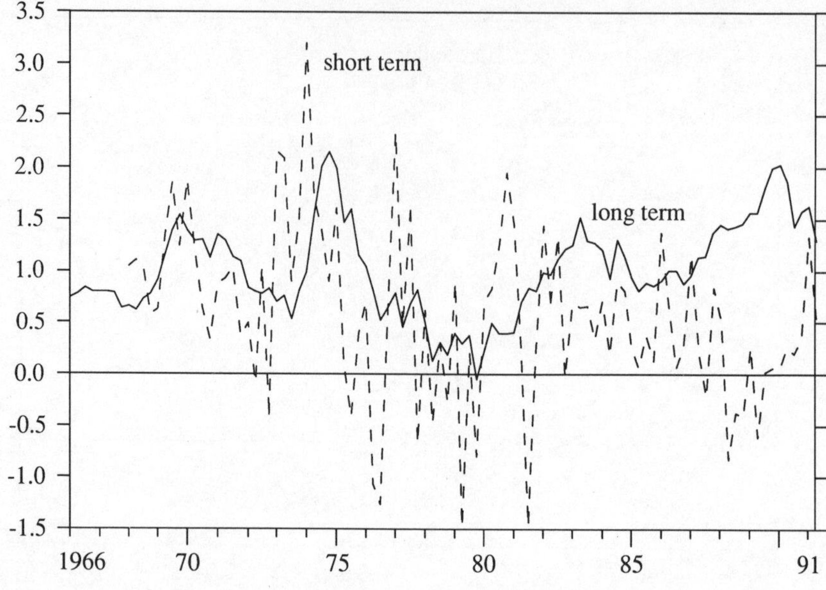

Chart 6.7. UK long and short spreads (%)

Chart 6.8 shows annual changes in equity prices in the UK and US markets. The occurrence of the 1973 crisis in the UK amid a bear market is clear; the debt crisis also followed declining US share prices (largely due to the recession), while the crash of 1987 is apparent for both markets. Chart 6.9 illustrates the behaviour of the secondary dated FRN market during 1985–8. The steady decline in discounted margins[40] prior to the crisis and huge increase in spreads afterwards is evident. It is notable that a second sharp increase in spreads occurred after the equity-market crash.

Charts 6.10–6.11 give an impression of total volumes of euromarket activity over 1972–91. In Chart 6.10 the decline in total gross issuance in 1982, after steady growth since 1975, is particularly evident. This was almost entirely reflected in volumes in the credits market. The crisis in the FRN market and the ensuing dormancy of the market is also apparent. Finally, the effects of the crash on the eurobond market and its subsequent recovery can be discerned. Chart 6.11 reveals the composi tion of euromarket activity: the dominance of credits over 1972–4 and 1978–82, and their subsequent replacement by fixed-rate bonds, the growth of euronotes, and the growth and decline of the FRN market.

[40] A measure of the rate of return on an FRN relative to an index rate (Libor) calculated by discounting future cash flows on a money-market basis.

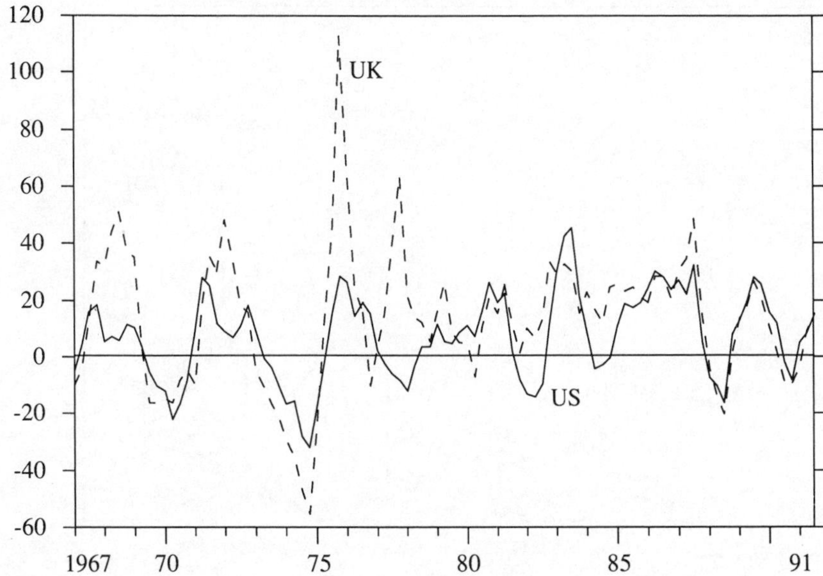

Chart 6.8. Growth of US and UK share prices (%)

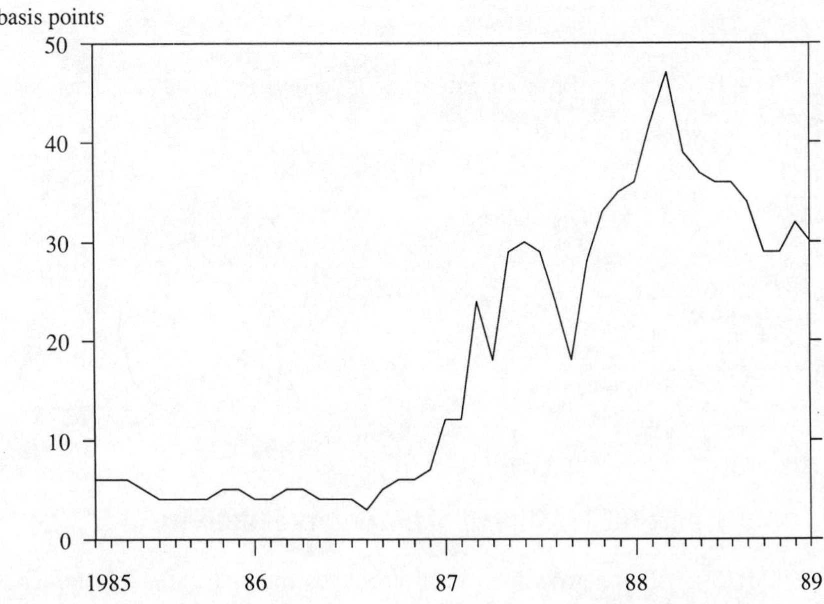

Chart 6.9. Discount margins for US bank FRNs

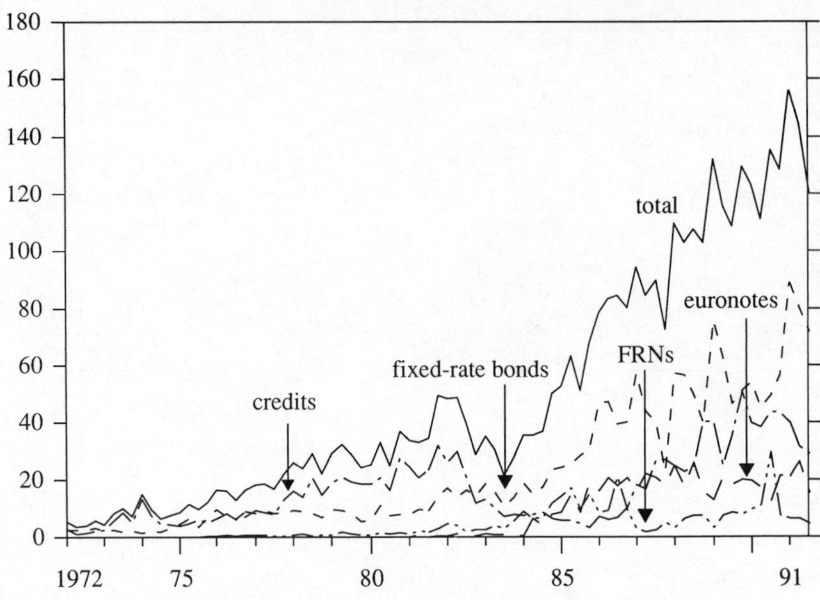

Chart 6.10. Gross euromarket volumes ($ bn)

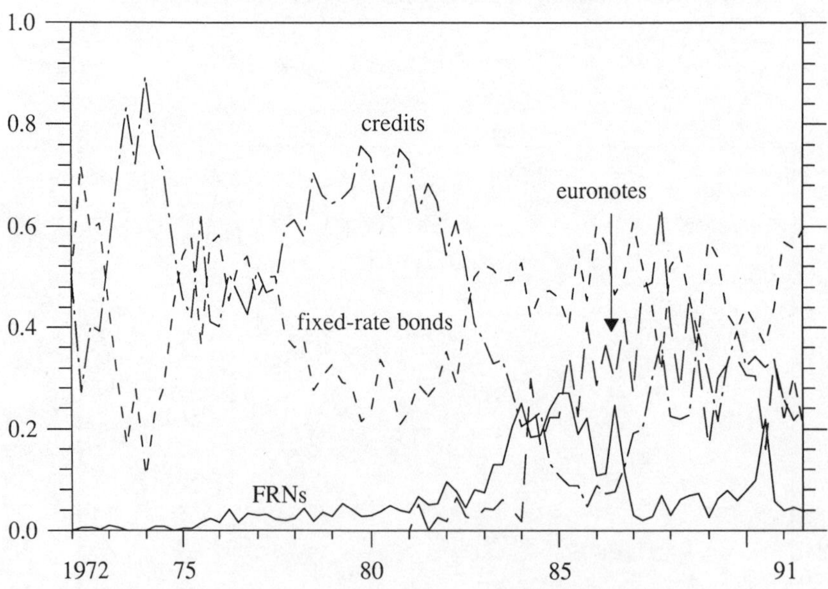

Chart 6.11. Shares of euromarket activity

Chart 6.12 shows growth in total credit to the non-financial domestic sectors (public, corporate, household) in the UK and US domestic markets as a proportion of GNP. Rapid growth in credit is apparent in the

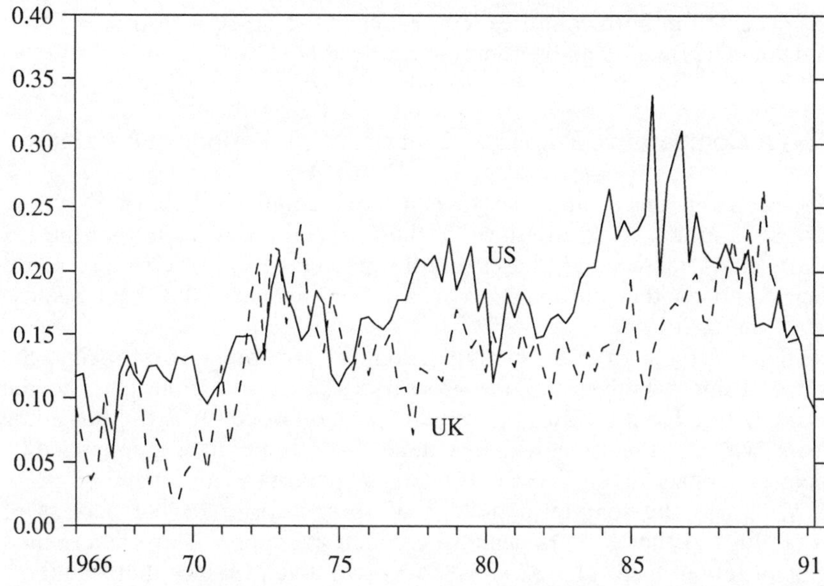

Chart 6.12. US and UK credit expansion/GNP

Table 6.1. Growth of indebtedness (indices)

Years before crisis	t−4	t−3	t−2	t−1	t
International					
1974 (growth of interbank market)[a]	100	152	201	217	232
1982 (growth of ldc debt)[b]	100	124	152	180	200
1986 (growth of FRN market)[c]	100	109[e]	244[e]	398	502
1987 (growth of US corporations' debt)[d]	100	115	127	142	156
Domestic					
1973 (secondary banking)[f]	100	113	167	331	523
1980 (US thrifts)[g]	100	117	133	148	165
1986 (US thrifts)[g]	100	117	140	152	163

a Outstanding foreign currency interbank credits (reporting banks). Source: BIS Annual Reports.
b Evolution of non-OPEC ldc's external indebtedness. Source: BIS Annual Reports.
c Stock of FRNs outstanding. Source: BIS Annual Reports.
d US corporations' total liabilities. Source: US flow of funds.
e Estimated.
f Lending to property, construction, other financial and HP.
g Balance sheet of savings and loans institutions—assets.

UK prior to the secondary-banking crisis, as well as prior to the later thrifts crisis in the USA. Most recently, a marked decline in credit growth has occurred in both countries, consistent in each case with the recession and financial fragility in the non-financial sectors (Ch. 4).

(4) A Comparative Empirical Analysis of the Periods of Instability

The tables in this section describe in more detail the behaviour of key economic indicators at the times of the financial crises. Note that the US thrifts crisis had several phases and no specific period of crisis. Here we focus both on the 'mismatch' crises of 1980 and also the 'loan quality' crisis, dating it 1986.

Tables 6.1–6.4 examine potential longer term precursors to financial crises. Table 6.1 illustrates the growth of debt outstanding prior to the crises. The table illustrates the rapid expansion of credit in the preceding years, which as the accounts above have illustrated (and as emphasized by theories of financial fragility) were an integral part of the crises themselves.

What was the long-term pattern of spreads prior to the periods of instability? Although data cannot be conclusive (spreads are determined by a variety of factors), Table 6.2 offers tentative evidence that standards of risk appraisal were relaxed on each occasion. Interbank spreads in

Table 6.2. Indicators of risk pricing prior to crises

Years before crisis	t−5	t−4	t−3	t−2	t−1	t
International						
1974: interbank spreads[a]	n/a	n/a	2.4	1.3	2.2	3.1
1982: spreads on new ldc credits[b]	1.6	1.3	1.0	0.9	1.1	1.0
1986: spreads on FRNs for banks[c]	—	0.23	0.19	0.14	0.17	0.19
1987: spreads on corporate borrowing[d]						
credits	0.6	0.6	0.7	0.4	0.4	0.3
bonds	0.8	0.63	0.02	0.09	0.29	0.99
Domestic						
1973: money markets[e]	0.9	1.3	1.0	0.8	0.3	1.7
1973: bond spreads[f]	0.7	1.25	1.28	1.21	0.82	0.7
1980: money market[g]	0.67	0.28	0.37	1.03	1.15	1.63
1980: mortgages[h]	1.1	1.3	1.4	1.2	1.8	2.3
1986: money market[g]	1.89	1.66	0.46	0.84	0.57	0.54
1986: mortgages[h]	2.7	3.1	2.1	1.4	1.8	2.5

a Eurodollar 3 month rate less US Treasury bill rate.
b Average spread over Libor of syndicated credits to ldcs.
c Average spread over Libor in primary eurodollar dated FRN market for US bank debt.
d OECD corporations; spread over Libor for US dollar credits; over US treasury bonds for eurodollar bonds.
e UK interbank–Treasury bill differental.
f Spreads of UK corporate bonds over gilts.
g US CD–Treasury bill spread.
h US fixed-rate mortgages less government bonds.

1972–3 were below those in 1971; spreads on credits to ldcs and on bank FRNs (except in 1986 itself) declined before their respective crises. Corporate borrowing, at least on syndicated credits, was made on progressively more generous terms prior to 1987. Spreads fell in domestic markets prior to 1973 and 1986 too, except for US mortgages prior to 1986 (1980 was an exception—as noted, the main cause was mismatch on existing loans, not overlending *per se*). Nor were these patterns only observable in the markets where the crises occurred; for example, as noted in Sect. 2, interbank margins fell sharply in the 1970s prior to the debt crisis.

Table 6.3 illustrates patterns in banks' capitalization, an important concomitant of vulnerable situations, as highlighted by theories of credit rationing. The capitalization of banks in both the UK and USA declined prior to the 1974 crisis; in 1982 UK banks' capitalization fell while that in the USA remained low. In contrast, in 1986 and 1987, crises which had little impact on commercial banks, capitalization increased. The stronger capitalization of banks in recent years is partly a result of the tightening of prudential regulation and associated increases in required capital ratios. Such regulation should in principle make banks more resilient to the type of crisis outlined in this book. In domestic markets, UK banks' capital declined prior to the secondary-banking crisis; and the exceptionally low level of US thrifts' capital in the 1980s is apparent.

Table 6.3. Commercial banks' capital ratios

Years before crisis	t−4	t−3	t−2	t−1	t
Euromarket					
1974: US banks[a]	6.6	0.4	6.1	5.8	5.7
1974: UK banks[b]	7.7	7.6	7.3	6.8	6.4
1982: US banks[a]	5.8	5.8	5.8	5.8	5.9
1982: UK banks[b]	8.0	7.7	7.4	6.9	6.9
1986: US banks[a]	5.9	6.0	6.1	6.2	6.2
1986: UK banks[b]	6.9	7.3	6.9	8.5	8.9
1987: US banks[a]	6.0	6.1	6.2	6.2	6.9[c]
1987: UK banks[b]	7.3	6.9	8.5	8.9	8.5
Domestic					
1973: UK banks[b]	7.9	7.5	7.0	6.3	6.5
1980: US thrifts[d]	5.6	5.5	5.5	5.6	5.3
1986: US thrifts[e]	3.7 (3.0)	4.0 (3.1)	3.8 (2.8)	4.4 (3.3)	4.5 (3.4)

a All insured commercial banks, capital plus reserves/assets.
b Major UK banks' capital-asset ratios (1974–primary book capital/asset ratio).
c Estimated.
d Net worth/assets ratio–regulatory accounting principles.
e Net worth/assets ratio–regulatory accounting principles (generally accepted accounting principles).

Sources: OECD 1987; Revell 1980; Llewellyn 1988; A. P. White 1989.

Table 6.4 shows shifts in regime prior to financial crises, the effects of which were acknowledged to be important at the time of the events (see Sect. 2), and effects of which on systemic vulnerability are highlighted by theories emphasizing uncertainty. The shift from fixed to floating exchange rates and the US switch to monetary targeting based on non-borrowed reserves both increased volatility in markets, though the latter was probably more important for its effect on the level of interest rates. Anticipation of announcement of new measures for banks' capital increased volatility in the FRN market. The case for a regime shift in equity markets in 1987 is less clear cut, but the data show that there were increases in volatility which coincided with the widespread introduction of market innovations such as portfolio insurance (as well as the bull market itself). In the domestic crises, the UK Competition and Credit Control liberalization increased the volatility of interest rates (as well as unleashing debt growth). For the thrifts the initial crisis relates to the same change in US monetary policy as the debt crisis; a higher mean and variance of interest rates with which they were unable to cope. The second crisis was partly triggered by the collapse in primary product prices.

Tables 6.5 and 6.6 examine some factors often held to be directly associated with financial crises. Thus Table 6.5 shows share-price movements before (and after) the crises, as highlighted by the financial-fragility and agency-cost approaches. Each euromarket crisis except 1986 was associated with a sharp downwards movement in share prices—most obviously the crash of 1987, which was centred on the equity market. This entailed declines of 20–30 per cent in world share prices, and followed a sharp upward movement in share prices over the previous year, which many have characterized as a speculative bubble. The 1974 and 1982 crises followed sharp falls in share prices over the previous year. In 1982 an extremely strong recovery in share prices followed the crisis (48 per cent), but in 1974 prices were flat for the following year. The secondary-banking crisis—but not the thrifts—also occurred in a bear market. These data suggest that share price weakness may, directly or indirectly, be associated with disorder in financial markets. Whether it is a causal factor rather than an indicator of deteriorating economic conditions is of course less clear, though declines in equity prices tend to entail strong quantity-rationing in new issue markets, thus aggravating funding problems for those quantity-rationed in credit markets. Also, effects on net worth of falling share prices (and correlated increases in other asset prices) may affect access to credit, by aggravating agency problems (Ch. 5, Sect. 8). Tables 6.6–6.8 illustrate some other potential causal factors.

First, real monetary growth was low or declining prior to the 1974, 1982, and 1987 crises in the euromarkets, as well as the UK secondary-banking crisis, suggesting a degree of monetary restraint by the authorities (given

Table 6.4. Shifts in regime prior to financial crises

Date	Event	Indicator	Statistics	Prior period	Following period
May 1971[a]	Shift fixed–floating exchange rates	$/DM exchange rate	Mean	3.82	2.98
			Coefficient of variation	0.05	0.12
October 1979[b]	Change in US monetary policy	US Treasury bill rate	Mean	8.29	12.32
			Coefficient of variation	0.16	0.17
December 1986[c]	Expectations of Basle agreement re bank FRNs	US bank FRN discount margin	Mean	4.75	24.58
			Coefficient of variation	0.23	0.31
November 1986[d]	Introduction of programme trading techniques	US share prices	Mean	131.9	162.6
			Coefficient of variation	0.07	0.08
July 1971[e]	Introduction of competition and credit control	UK Treasury bill rate	Mean	7.2	7.2
			Coefficient of variation	0.10	0.37
January 1986[f]	Collapse of commodity prices	$ oil price (1982 index)	Mean	84.4	47.5
			Coefficient of variation	0.02	0.30

a Observation periods: June 1968–May 1971; June 1971–May 1974.
b Observation periods: Jan. 1976–Sept. 1979; Oct. 1979–Aug. 1982.
c Observation periods: Jan.–Dec. 1986; Jan.–Dec. 1987.
d Observation periods: Nov. 1985–Oct. 1986; Nov. 1986–Oct. 1987.
e Observation periods: Jan. 1969–June 1971; July 1971–Dec. 1973.
f Observation periods: Jan.–Dec. 1985; Jan.–Dec. 1986.

Table 6.5. Share price[a] movements and financial crises (% changes)

Crisis	12 months prior	1 month prior	1 month after	12 months after
International				
1974 (June)	−14.3	0.0	− 7.8	+ 2.9
1982 (August)	−15.4	0.0	+11.7	+48.1
1986 (December)	+20.0	+ 1.4	+ 6.4	− 3.1
1987 (October)	+18.0	−12.1	−12.5	1.0
Domestic				
1973 (December)	−35.1[b]	−17.8[b]	− 1.5[b]	−51.5[b]
1980 (December)	+23.8	+ 0.07	− 0.4	− 7.3
1986 (December)	+20.0	+ 1.4	+ 6.3	− 3.1

a US Standard and Poor's 500-share
b FT–30 share index

the prevailing level of inflation), and concurring with the descriptions in Sect. 2. Thus, in 1974 real M1 fell in three of the four quarters, ending with the crisis period; in 1982, real money fell in the four quarters before the crisis; in 1987, real monetary growth was negative in the period of the crisis, having decelerated consistently over the previous four periods. In the UK in 1973, real monetary growth had fallen from 15 per cent to 11 per cent prior to the crisis; US monetary policy was consistently tight over 1980–2 for the thrifts, with the marginal reserve requirement increased in spring 1980. The FRN crisis and the later US thrifts are exceptions: monetary growth was consistently rapid over the preceding year. The FRN crisis was a localized rather than general macroeconomic phenomenon; the later thrifts crisis was driven more by regional and regulatory factors, although the dollar appreciation up to the end of 1985 did entail a monetary tightening.

Table 6.6. Developments in US monetary growth prior to crises

Crisis	US monetary growth (M1) (real, change on same quarter a year before)				
	t–4	t–3	t–2	t–1	t
International					
1974 (Q2)	2.8	− 0.3	− 2.4	− 3.5	− 5.0
1982 (Q3)	3.2	− 1.4	− 1.0	− 0.2	1.3
1986 (Q4)	8.5	8.7	10.0	11.1	14.3
1987 (Q4)	14.3	12.0	7.2	3.8	− 1.5
Domestic					
1973 (Q4)	15.0[a]	13.1[a]	10.9[a]	13.6[a]	11.2[a]
1980 (Q4)	− 5.1	− 6.0	− 9.0	− 5.8	− 5.1
1986 (Q4)	8.5	8.7	10.0	11.1	14.3

a UK monetary growth

Consistent with the money data, short-term interest rates (Table 6.7) were increased before the 1973, 1974, and 1987 crises, and were high prior to the debt crisis. (Real rates, in contrast, were quite low except in 1982 and 1986, suggesting cash-flow effects for debtors—or other types of risk than

Table 6.7. Official short-term interest rates prior to crises

Crisis	Nominal (and real) US federal funds rate, quarterly				
	t−4	t−3	t−2	t−1	t
International					
1974 (Q2)	7.8 (2.2)	10.6 (3.7)	10.0 (1.6)	9.3 (−0.6)	11.3 (0.7)
1982 (Q3)	17.6 (6.7)	13.6 (4.0)	14.2 (6.6)	14.5 (7.6)	11.0 (5.2)
1986 (Q4)	8.1 (4.6)	7.8 (4.7)	6.9 (5.2)	6.2 (4.5)	6.3 (4.9)
1987 (Q4)	6.3 (4.9)	6.2 (4.1)	6.7 (2.8)	6.8 (2.6)	6.9 (2.5)
Domestic					
1973 (Q4)	7.1[a] (0.3)	8.9[a] (1.4)	8.7[a] (0.1)	9.7[a] (1.5)	12.0[a] (2.0)
1980 (Q4)	13.6 (0.9)	15.0 (0.8)	12.7 (1.9)	9.8 (−3.1)	15.9 (3.3)
1986 (Q4)	8.1 (4.6)	7.8 (4.7)	6.9 (5.2)	6.2 (4.5)	6.3 (4.9)

a UK bank rate

credit risk—were most important.) As for the economic cycle (Table 6.8), the data show that in the euromarkets, the 1974 and 1982 crises came several quarters after the turning-point in GNP. The FRN and equity-markets crises came amid rapid economic growth—as did the later thrifts crisis for the US economy as a whole (rather than regions). The timing of the euromarket crises in relation to the cycle suggests that they were not causal factors in relation to GNP; if anything the contrary (i.e. weakened economic activity may have created the conditions in which the crisis could occur). In contrast, the UK secondary-banking crisis and the initial US thrifts crisis occurred closer to the turning-point.

Table 6.8. Developments in real GNP prior to financial crises

Crisis	Real US GNP growth, change on same quarter a year before				
	t−4	t−3	t−2	t−1	t
International					
1974 (Q2)	5.4	4.1	3.1	0.1	0.2
1982 (Q3)	3.4	0.3	−2.7	−2.2	−3.3
1986 (Q4)	3.8	4.0	3.4	2.5	2.3
1987 (Q4)	2.3	1.8	3.1	4.1	5.1
Domestic					
1973 (Q4)	4.6[a]	9.5[a]	5.4[a]	5.4[a]	3.2[a]
1980 (Q4)	0.3	1.3	−0.8	−1.4	0.3
1986 (Q4)	3.8	4.0	3.4	2.5	2.3

a UK GNP growth

Table 6.9. Changes in the flow of lending during crises (%)

	Change in gross flow	Quarter of crisis on previous year[a]	Following year[a] on quarter of crisis	Year beginning crisis on previous year
International				
1974 (Q2)	Credits	− 8.6	− 40.8	−38.0
	Fixed-rate bonds	+ 15.2	+ 60.7	+ 43.8
	FRNs	—	—	—
	Interbank claims[6]	− 44.8	− 57.8	− 82.7
1982 (Q3)	Credits	− 25.7	− 49.2	− 50.0
	Fixed-rate bonds	+ 28.3	− 17.2	+ 19.4
	FRNs	− 43.7	+ 62.5	+ 16.4
	Interbank claims[b]	+ 37.4	− 75.5	− 44.1
1986 (Q4)	Credits	+ 78.1	+117.4	+214.4
	Fixed-rate bonds	− 7.1	− 9.4	− 5.3
	FRNs	− 31.2	− 68.0	− 75.1
	Interbank claims[b]	+120.4	− 34.4	+ 66.1
1987 (Q4)	Credits	+ 49.4	− 3.5	+ 39.7
	Fixed-rate bonds	− 40.0	+101.1	+ 9.5
	FRNs	+ 23.5	+ 17.0	+ 30.2
	Interbank claims[b]	− 17.5	− 45.0	− 43.4

Domestic				
1973 (Q4)	UK lending to property, construction, finance houses and other financial[b]	+ 13.1	− 93.6	− 59.1
	Other bank lending to UK residents[b]	+ 1.0	+ 1.4	+ 11.4
	Domestic private bond issues[b]	− 47.7	− 88.2	− 86.3
		1979–1980	1980–1981	1981–1982
1980	US thrifts' asset accumulation[b]	− 7.2	− 32.0	+ 59.0
	US banks' asset accumulation[b]	− 12.8	+ 11.5	+ 1.8
	Domestic private bond issues[b]	+ 15.1	+ 12.5	+ 13.7
		1984–1985	1985–1986	1986–1987
1986	US thrifts' asset accumulation[b]	− 48.6	+ 5.5	+ 13.8
	US banks' asset accumulation[b]	+ 19.9	+ 0.9	− 32.7
	Domestic private bond issues[b]	+ 52.3	+ 61.5	− 10.1

a quarterly averages
b net flow

Tables 6.9 and 6.10 show quantity and price developments in the major markets at the times of the crises. Regarding the euromarkets, as might be expected, Table 6.9 shows that the markets directly concerned in the crisis were worst hit in each case: interbank claims fell by 45 per cent in the quarter of the crisis of 1974, compared with the previous year; credits by 26 per cent in 1982, FRNs by 31 per cent in 1986, and bonds by 40 per cent in 1987. It is also evident that in 1974, 1982, and 1986 the crises were prolonged in the market concerned; there was no rapid recovery. Thus, interbank claims declined by a further 58 per cent in the year following the 1974 crisis, compared with the quarter of the crisis itself; credits by a further 49 per cent in 1982, and FRNs by 68 per cent in 1986. In contrast, the fixed-rate bond market recovered strongly in the year after the crash (doubling issuance), showing that the crisis was rapidly overcome and its effects largely concentrated in the fourth quarter of 1987. In domestic markets, the sharp fall in UK lending to property and construction, as well as other financial institutions, in 1973, is evident from Table 6.9. As for the thrifts, longer term data shows a sharp deceleration in lending during the 'maturity mismatch' crisis not echoed elsewhere, and in the year before the 'credit quality' crisis.

Table 6.9 also gives indications of effects in other markets. Did quantities decline (suggesting systemic dimensions) or increase in order to substitute for the worst-hit market? Patterns for the earlier crises suggest some degree of contagion (though of course general economic conditions also affected issuance). The secondary-banking collapse extended to the bond market, but did not strongly affect bank lending more generally—although intervention by the authorities may have helped to sustain bank credit. In 1974, the euro credits market declined sharply along with interbank claims over all the sub-periods analysed. By contrast, fixed-rate international bond issuance remained buoyant, largely due to activity in foreign bond markets (the eurobond market was severely depressed). In 1982, there was an initial increase in fixed-rate bond issue and interbank claims in the quarter of the crisis, but comparing the year beginning the crisis with the previous year, only the fixed-rate bond market showed any increase (the beginning of the securitization process). The FRN crisis appeared to be more localized. In the quarter of the crisis, credits and interbank claims increased sharply, while fixed-rate bonds declined marginally. Over the longer term, similar patterns were observable. Again, in 1987, activity in the credits market increased sharply, while bond issuance plunged, and issuance of FRNs also recovered. Over the following year, there were increases in all but interbank claims. Finally, there appears to be no strong relationship between lending by thrifts and other sectors.

These data suggest that in no case was contagion pervasive (though of course not all borrowers could freely substitute between markets). One can none the less distinguish between 1973/74/82 on the one hand and

1986/87 on the other, in that a greater substitutability between instru ments (i.e. a lesser degree of contagion) is apparent during the later crises, possibly because the markets were more developed—or con versely that systemic effects were more muted in these cases. Saunders (1987) also found little evidence of contagion *between* groups of banks in the interbank market in the euromarket crises of the early 1980s.

Table 6.10 shows in more detail the price responses to the crises, for example, the sharp increase in Libor relative to US Treasury bills (illustrating stress in the interbank markets) in 1974. It is notable that secondary-market yields on fixed-rate bonds and (to a lesser extent) spreads on new syndicated credits also increased over this period, suggesting a degree of contagion[41] between markets and concomitant price rationing of credit. The UK secondary-banking crisis also had clear effects on interbank spreads, spreads on trade bills, and corporate bonds.

The other crises are less clear-cut in terms of price responses. During the debt crisis, average realized spreads on syndicated credits did not increase, suggesting the existence of quantity rationing of credit to account for the decline in lending shown in Table 6.9. Fixed-rate bond yields increased, suggesting concerns over default risk, but the increase in borrowing over the year of the crisis suggests there were still willing investors and borrowers at these rates. Finally, although interbank claims declined sharply, there was no strong increase in Libor compared with the US Treasury bill rate. As with syndicated credits, this may imply some quantity rationing. For the 1986 crisis, there was little detectable effect in markets other than the FRN market.[42] (Some slight upward pressure on spreads on credits is also apparent.) Table 6.10 also shows the sharp contrast between the period before and after the crisis. In October 1987 the increases in yields on fixed-rate bonds is apparent. Pricing in the credits market appears unaffected, but Libor relative to US Treasury bills increased sharply from 1 to 1.9 per cent, perhaps reflecting perceptions of risks in international banking relative to domestic government paper. It is notable that the US Treasury bill rate itself fell sharply after the 1987 crisis, reflecting relaxation of monetary policy and the flight to quality by investors. A similar pattern is evident after the advent of the debt crisis. Finally, since the US thrifts crisis is less clear cut in terms of timing, it is omitted from the table.

[41] The alternative hypothesis in the credit market, that funding costs rather than the shock were responsible for higher margins on syndicated credits, was found weaker in empirical work by Johnston (1980).

[42] There is a striking contrast between secondary-market FRN discount margins prior to the 1986 crisis (7 basis points) and primary-market issue spreads on FRNs to the same class of institution (20 basis points). This may show the high degree of speculative activity in the market.

Table 6.10. Changes in interest-rate relationships during crises (%)

Month	t−12	t−3	t−2	t−1	t	t+1	t+2	t+3	t+12
International									
1974 (June)									
credits[a]	0.1	0.3	0.5	0.5	0.7	0.6	1.3	0.9	1.2
fixed-rate bonds[b]	1.8	1.8	1.9	2.0	2.2	3.0	3.1	3.6	1.2
FRNs[c]	—	—	—	—	—	—	—	—	—
interbank[d]	1.6	1.2	2.3	3.3	3.9	5.7	4.8	4.0	0.9
US Treasury bill rate	7.2	8.0	8.2	8.4	8.2	7.8	8.7	8.4	5.2
1982 (August)									
credits[a]	1.0	0.9	1.1	0.9	1.0	0.9	0.9	0.9	0.7
fixed-rate bonds[b]	− 0.3	0.9	0.7	1.6	2.8	3.2	3.7	3.2	1.1
FRNs[c]	—	—	—	—	—	—	—	—	—
interbank[d]	3.3	2.4	3.3	2.5	2.5	3.6	2.7	1.7	0.9
US Treasury bill rate	15.6	12.2	12.1	11.9	9.0	8.2	7.8	8.0	9.4
1986 (December)									
credits[a]	0.3	0.3	0.4	0.3	0.6	0.3	0.6	0.6	0.3
fixed-rate bonds[b]	1.3	1.2	1.3	1.4	1.4	1.2	0.9	1.0	1.2
FRNs[c]	0.03	0.06	0.07	0.07	0.07	0.12	0.12	0.24	0.38
interbank[d]	0.9	0.7	0.7	0.6	0.7	0.6	0.7	0.8	0.1
US Treasury bill rate	7.1	5.2	5.2	5.4	5.5	5.5	5.6	5.6	5.8

1987 (October)									
credits[a]	0.4	0.7	0.2	0.3	0.3	0.4	0.3	0.4	0.3
fixed-rate bonds[b]	1.3	0.8	0.7	0.6	0.9	1.4	1.2	1.3	0.6
FRNs[c]	0.07	0.32	0.28	0.25	0.2	0.32	0.38	0.36	0.28
interbank[d]	0.7	1.0	1.0	1.1	1.9	1.6	2.1	1.2	1.2
US Treasury bill rate	5.2	5.8	6.0	6.4	6.4	5.8	5.9	5.7	7.3
Domestic									
1973 (December)									
corporate bonds[e]	0.75	0.66	0.87	0.56	1.01	0.8	0.92	1.27	2.18
trade bills[f]	0.4	2.0	1.5	1.4	2.2	3.5	2.3	3.4	2.0
interbank[g]	– 0.4	0.9	—	—	1.5	—	—	3.2	0.9
UK Treasury bill rate	8.5	11.3	11.0	12.9	12.8	12.4	12.2	12.4	11.3

a Average spread over Libor (US dollar credits)

b Secondary market–private sector eurodollar bonds minus US treasuries

c Secondary market–discounted margin over Libor (US banks' dollar FRNs). The discounted margin is a measure of return from an FRN relative to that on its index rate (Libor), calculated by discounting future cash flow on a money market basis.

d 3 month eurodollar rate less US Treasury bill rate

e UK corporate–government bond yield differential

f Trade bill–Treasury bill differential

g Interbank–Treasury bill differential

Table 6.11. Summary of features of periods of instability

	International crises				Domestic crises		
	1974	1982	1986	1987	1973	1980	1986
Monetary							
Prior monetary tightening	yes	yes	no	yes	yes	yes	(no)
Occurred beyond cyclical peak	yes	yes	no	no	no	yes	no
Banking panics	yes	no	no	no	yes	no	no
Aggravated downturn	no	yes	no	no	yes	(yes)	no
Caused reduction in money supply	no	no	no	no	no	no	no
Financial Fragility							
Prior 'displacement'	(no)	yes	(no)	(no)	yes	(no)	yes
Accumulation of risky debt	yes	yes	yes	(yes)	yes	no	yes
Occurred at cyclical peak	no	no	no	no	yes	no	no
Speculation	yes	yes	yes	yes	yes	no	yes
Distress selling in credit markets	no	no	(yes)	no	yes	no	no
Deflation/increased real rates	no	no	no	no	no	no	no
Rational expectations							
Bubble in asset/security prices	no	no	yes	yes	yes	no	yes

Uncertainty							
Regime shift	yes	yes	yes	(yes)	yes	yes	yes
Competitive innovation	no	yes	yes	yes	(no)	(yes)	no
Evidence of crowd psychology (low risk premiums)	yes	yes	yes	yes	yes	no	yes
Credit-rationing							
Declining risk premia	yes	yes	yes	yes	yes	no	yes
Declining 'capital ratios'	yes	yes	no	yes	yes	yes	yes
Increased quantity rationing	yes	yes	(yes)	(yes)	yes	no	no
Long-term quantity rationing	yes	yes	(no)	no	yes	no	no
Increased price rationing	yes	yes	yes	yes	yes	no	no
Concentration of risk	(yes)	yes	(yes)	yes	yes	yes	yes
Intense competition between intermediaries	yes	yes	yes	yes	yes	yes	yes
Agency costs							
Rising risk premiums before crisis	yes	no	no	(yes)	yes	no	no
Falls in asset prices	yes	yes	no	yes	yes	no	yes
Disinflation	no	yes	no	no	no	yes	no
Dynamics of dealer markets							
Cumulative collapse of liquidity in secondary markets	no	no	yes	(yes)	no	no	no
General							
International transmission	yes	yes	yes	yes	no	no	no
Intervention of authorities	(yes)	yes	no	yes	yes	yes	yes
Contagion between markets	yes	yes	(yes)	yes	yes	no	no

(5) The Theory of Crises Viewed in the Light of Empirical Evidence

This section assesses the realism of the theories of financial crisis in the light of the six periods of instability outlined and illustrated in Sects. 2–4 above. The results are summarized in Table 6.11. These suggest that while all of the theories have important contributions to make to the understanding of recent financial disorder, none are all-embracing and a form of synthesis would seem to be called for. Some attempt at this is made in the concluding section of the chapter.

(a) Financial fragility

Some but not all of the mechanisms highlighted by this approach seem validated by the evidence. Apart from the initial thrifts crisis, there clearly was rapid accumulation of debt in each case; interbank positions in 1974, third-world debt in 1982, FRNs in 1986, corporate debt in 1987, debt of property and construction in the UK in 1973 and in the USA in 1986. The nature of the risk concerned differs of course; in most of the crises, concerns were centred on credit risk; the earlier thrifts crisis was largely a question of interest-rate risk; in the FRN crisis market and liquidity risks were perhaps crucial (none of the banks who had issued FRNs had any financial difficulties); in 1987, it was a mixture of all types. Again, these accumulations were accompanied by speculation. 'Speculative' underwriting exposures were a particular problem during the crash, while the secondary-banking and later US thrifts crisis was directly related to speculative lending. Foreign-exchange speculation caused the 1974 crisis. The ldc debt crisis arguably also had a speculative side, banks always wishing to earn spreads, while expecting to be able to exit at the next rollover date (despite the fact that borrowers needed new credits to cover their interest-payment obligations). The same false expectations of liquidity of course helped to create the conditions for the equity-market crash. The FRN market collapsed after speculators had become the main holders. Finally, there was in most cases evidence of declining risk premiums. Adopting Minsky's terminology, some of the episodes could at least partly be characterized as speculative or Ponzi financing.

On the other hand, apart from the secondary banking and initial thrifts, the crises did not tend to occur at cyclical peaks and thus possibly help cause the following downturn. This may imply that risk premiums were sufficient to cover 'normal' cyclical patterns but not uncertain events. But it may partly be due to the policy response (for example, the loosening of monetary policy in 1982 and 1987). This may also account for the absence of widespread distress selling and of deflation with concomitant increased real rates. Equally, wealth effects on consumption, which were widely feared in 1987, turned out to be minor, perhaps because investors had not fully taken into account the previous rise in share prices. As regards a 'displacement', for the domestic crises, one (but not the only) trigger was often a change in regulation: CCC in the UK; deregulation of thrifts' rate ceilings[43] and then lending powers for the USA. In the international crises, the existence of a prior 'displacement', triggering rapid growth in debt and of accompanying monetary innovation is more debatable. Arguably the 1974 crisis was triggered by the 'displacement' of the switch to floating exchange rates. The period of the debt crisis opened with the displacement of the oil shock, though its precise links to the crisis (the need for balance-of-payments financing) are less direct than in the theories of financial fragility. The relevant 'displacement' for the other crises is less clear, though it might be suggested that securitization was a key factor. Innovations with significant monetary effects have been a feature of the 1970s and 1980s (money-market mutual funds in the USA; high-interest cheque accounts in the UK). The former was of particular importance in the earlier thrifts crisis.

(b) The monetarist approach

It can be argued that rapid inflation did underlie some of the periods of instability outlined. In particular, rapid inflation in the 1970s reduced real interest rates, encouraging ldc borrowing and leading to mismatch problems of US thrifts. Inflationary pressures helped generate property booms in the UK (1973) and USA (mid-1980s).

Again, the influence of monetary tightening[44] on the international crises of 1974, 1982, and 1987 and domestic crises of 1973 and 1980, together with the fact the 1974 and 1982 crises occurred *after* cyclical peaks (see Table 6.6) lends at least partial credence to monetarist views of financial crisis. However, it is less clear that the crises *caused* a reduction in the money supply, thus aggravating the contraction. The nearest to this may have been in 1974, when the reduced supply of short-term interbank credit may have influenced the price of credit (syndicated credits) to final users.[45] The debt crisis may have worsened the recession of the early 1980s, due to the effects on global demand of the reduced

[43] Although retail deposits were not deregulated till after the crisis, the crucial move in the mismatch crisis was perhaps the 1978 deregulation of money-market certificates.

[44] Necessitated, according to monetarist views, by inflation caused by earlier monetary laxity.

[45] However, Johnston (1980) suggested that the crisis itself (i.e. heightened default and liquidity risk) was the main underlying factor, prompting the communiqué by the G10 governors in Sept. 1974 outlining their commitment to continuing stability of the markets (while not committing them to lender-of-last-resort intervention).

ability of ldcs to purchase imports, and indirectly due to monetary contraction arising from the cutoff of credit. The UK secondary-banking crisis probably worsened the cyclical situation in 1973–4. Loosening of monetary conditions generally helped to prevent adverse macroeconomic changes after the 1987 crisis.

Bank panics were not a feature of most of the crises, though the withdrawal of deposits from UK secondary banks and insolvency of Herstatt in 1974 (and the accompanying collapse of Franklin National in the US domestic markets) had many of the features of a panic. The lack of panic may again be partly attributed to the role of Central Bank intervention, particularly in 1982 and 1987 when the bankruptcy of some borrowers was feared. On these occasions, relaxations of monetary policy also helped to offset any tendency for monetary contraction. It was the initial absence of strong intervention in 1974 that led to the Herstatt crisis, and necessitated the statement by Central Banks in September that they stood ready to offer support to the international markets. The US thrifts crises and ldc debt did not generally involve panics, owing to deposit insurance and the practice of forebearance in leaving non-performing loans on balance sheets at book value.

(c) Rational expectations

As noted above, several of the crises had features resembling speculative bubbles and runs. However, particularly in the case of bubbles, it is less clear that they were 'rational' in the sense that returns increased exponentially in order to encourage risk-averse individuals to remain in the market concerned. The bubbles (for example in 1987) are more reminiscent of irrational bubbles, where agents were prepared to remain in the market regardless of the pattern of excess returns, so long as they were not strongly negative. A degree of irrationality may have been present, which manifested itself in the belief that the fundamentals had changed—and that the agent would always be able to exit first (the illusion of liquidity). Such hypotheses are of course difficult to test formally. Rational-expectations theory of runs again seems somewhat too precise to characterize the respective crises, given that seemingly trivial causes led funds to be withdrawn (from lower rated banks in the interbank market, the FRN, and equity markets) and in each case many lenders/investors were left with disproportionately large losses. Only in the later US thrifts could it be suggested that speculation was in some degree 'rational', given the low capitalization of firms and protection of deposit insurance. Note, however, that this generally negative view of rational expectations in financial crises is not aimed to imply that agents in financial markets do not usually take all relevant information into account—rather that given uncertainty and imperfect information, rational choices ex-ante may still lead to crises ex-post—and ex-ante irrationality cannot be ruled out.

(d) Uncertainty

Most of the mechanisms outlined in Ch. 5, Sect. 6 under the heading of uncertainty had a role to play in these crises: a shift of regime with unforeseen consequences, evidence of crowd psychology in lending, and competitive innovation.

In terms of a regime shift, the regulatory changes in domestic markets were a key stimulus to the 1973 and 1986 crises; the direct cause of the 1974 crisis was the shift from fixed to floating exchange rates, the dynamics of which were unforeseen by market participants. Similarly, the banks prior to the debt crisis, and thrifts prior to their mismatch crisis, did not foresee the possibility of a second oil shock, the deep recession, and the new US monetary policy which drove up interest rates so sharply and increased their volatility. The evidence of a regime shift is weaker for the FRN market; the problem was rather uncertainty of the potential dynamics of the market that was already in existence, though expectations regarding the Basle guide-lines may qualify as a partly unforeseen influence. Finally, and again rather tenuously, the crash showed an unforeseen possibility for equity prices to fall suddenly by a large proportion, thus weakening the asset backing (and increasing the debt/equity ratio) of corporations with international debt outstanding, as well as financial intermediaries holding large equity positions.

Reduced risk premiums for uncertain events, which could be characterised as 'herding', was evident in each episode: lending to property and construction in 1973 (UK) and 1986 (USA); lending on the interbank market in 1974 without careful assessment of credit risk and risky practices in foreign-exchange markets; similar risky lending to ldcs, even when new loans were needed to pay interest on existing ones; launching of ever-greater volumes of FRNs at lower and lower spreads; and the crowd psychology of an equity-market bubble and speculative debt finance dependent on high equity values. In each case lenders (or intermediaries) were comforted by the knowledge that others were making the same judgements, and/or they assumed risk was diversifiable; in each case they were proved wrong, and risk premiums proved too low in retrospect. Only for thrifts in 1980 was there no such movement; instead, economic developments made safe loans risky for the lenders, given the nature of their funding.

Innovation played a key part in the international crises of the 1980s—and in most cases there was a flaw in the market's understanding of the innovation. In the case of the debt crisis, the main innovation was the syndicated credit together with sovereign lending itself[46] as outlined; the securities-market crashes of 1986 and 1987 were even more fundamentally linked to innovation, which provided at least part of the driving force behind the move to crisis conditions. The FRN market, as noted, was characterized by a wide variety of innovations which attempted to compensate for declining spreads.[47] Investors may have failed to understand market or liquidity risks in the market, or even the nature of the instrument. The equity-market crash has been linked to numerous innovations (programme trading, portfolio insurance) which gave rise to an illusion of liquidity. Similarly, in the eurobond market any illusions of liquidity on issues of less than top quality or featuring financial innovations were shaken by turbulence at the time of the crash. Effects of innovation were less clear in the other cases, though the development of money markets was a vital precursor to secondary banks and Herstatt; and the advent of money-market mutual funds in the 1970s aggravated the disintermediation problems suffered by the thrifts.

(e) Credit rationing

Like uncertainty, credit rationing has been a widely observed feature of recent financial crises, generally following an earlier relaxation of credit standards. Increased risk premiums (i.e. price rationing of credit) for classes of institution affected is evident from the charts and tables, as spreads over risk-free rates increased. There is also, however, some evidence of quantity rationing for lower quality institutions. This was evident for secondary banks in 1973; also in the interbank market after 1974, while many banks were subject to price 'tiering', the lowest class often finding themselves excluded from the market altogether. Similarly, in 1982, the most indebted ldcs were excluded from the granting of voluntary credits. The decline in interbank lending despite rates being constant may also suggest quantity rationing. In contrast, deposit insurance ensured thrifts were not rationed in the 1980s, and could continue making speculative loans.

In the later crises, quantity rationing was again evident. The FRN market virtually closed for new issues in 1986, as did the equity-warrant eurobond sector in 1987, and only top-quality borrowers could gain access to the straight eurobond sector. Brokers and securities houses with equity

[46] In terms of Bond and Briault 1983*a* (Ch. 5), the market failed to understand the control implications of sovereign lending.

[47] See Mason 1986.

exposures initially faced severe quantity rationing of bank credit. However, banks in 1986 and corporations in 1987 did not find themselves excluded from credit altogether, but instead shifted to other, more expensive, markets, namely the straight bond and euronote markets in 1986 and the syndicated credit and domestic bond and loan markets in 1987. Again, such quantity rationing as there was only remained for a relatively short time. Though these partly reveal the lesser severity of these crises, notably in respect of credit risk, they also suggest a declining segmentation of the markets, which makes a closing of all sources of credit for a borrowing sector less likely.

Guttentag and Herring also highlight declines in borrowers' and lenders' capital ratios together with concentration of risk—somewhat more precise forms of Minsky's 'fragility'. Declining capital ratios for banks were certainly evident prior to the secondary-banking, Herstatt, ldc, and thrift crises, especially if risks are correctly weighted. Low capitalization exacerbated the crises when they did occur. Concentration of risk was also apparent, particularly in the secondary-bank, thrifts, and ldc debt crises, although especially for ldcs it was not recognized as such. In the initial thrifts crisis, such concentration was effectively enforced by regulation which locked them into their specialization in long-term fixed-rate housing finance. Again, in the equity-market crash, there were concerns over heavily indebted corporations (especially those involved in speculative takeover plays) as well as security brokers and investment banks that had taken on concentrated risks (such as large underwriting exposures). However, international banks were in a much stronger condition in 1986 and 1987, thanks to pressure by supervisory authorities to improve capital ratios. Intense competition between intermediaries was also present in each crisis and helped to prompt risky behaviour.

Finally, the fact that monetary tightening and credit rationing (and/or shifts to more expensive markets) were both features of the 1973, 1974, 1982, and 1987 crises lends some credence to the Greenwald and Stiglitz view of the monetary transmission mechanism (Ch. 4, Sect. 5).

(f) Asymmetric Information and Agency Costs

The distinctive features of agency-cost theory highlighted in Table 6.11 are increases in risk premiums *prior* to the crises, collapses in asset prices, and strong disinflation or actual deflation. The data suggest that at least one of these features was generally present, except for the FRN crisis, thus lending some support to the agency-cost approach. Rises in risk premiums, notably for banks, were marked even before the crises of 1973 and 1974, thus arguably indicating increasing vulnerability. Sharp falls in share prices preceded or accompanied the 1973, 1974, 1982, and 1987 crises, while collapses in commodity and property prices triggered the secondary-banking crisis and the thrifts' 'loan quality' crisis of 1986. Finally, the strong disinflation of 1979–82 in the USA underlay the ldc debt crisis and the thrifts' 'interest rate mismatch' crisis.

(g) Dynamics of dealer markets

A final theoretical contribution in Ch. 5 relates to the determinants of behaviour of dealer markets in the presence of asymmetric information. The informal description of the FRN crisis suggests it was triggered by various bearish fundamentals (rumours of supervisory rules), re-evaluation of the characteristics of the instrument and excess supply of bonds in relation to end investors; 'large underwriting exposures undermined the market . . . rumours of heavy selling became self-fulfilling and prices went into free-fall as market makers withdrew . . . worsening losses for remaining traders'. The closeness to the Glosten and Milgrom (1985) description is striking. It is evident that the crisis did not arise from general perceptions of credit risk, but rather that in the circumstances of declining trading and perceptions of information asymmetry, remaining as a market maker became increasingly unprofitable. Hence liquidity collapsed. The associated rise in yields demanded on the instrument meant that primary market activity also became unviable, i.e. there was a form of contagion from secondary to primary markets.

Elements of a Glosten/Milgrom adverse spiral were clearly also present in the crash, as in the description of a sharp rise in the price of liquidity, following uncertainty about the size and nature of expected demand—dealers were uncertain how much would be 'liquidity' trade and how much 'insider' trade. But, as noted, the systemic risk went much wider, and by several other transmission mechanisms. The description of the eurobond market's behaviour at the time of the crash (Appendix 1 at the end of this chapter) again indicates the validity of the mechanisms highlighted by the theory of dealer markets.

(h) General issues

We conclude with observations on issues common to several of the theories. For example, international transmission was a feature of each euromarket crisis (the crises were not confined to one national market). This is partly to be expected; the euromarkets are an important conduit for international capital flows; they also involve commercial and investment banks from all the major countries, which if involved in similar business would all be hit in a systemic crisis. The effects of the debt crisis are an example of this. Transnational effects of financial crises are also, however, increasing due to the growing integration of domestic and international markets, with the same borrowers, intermediaries, and lenders active in each. This has reduced the insulation of domestic markets from shocks originating in international or other domestic markets, as the 1987 crash illustrated. On the other hand, lack of contagion between markets in recent years may imply that internationalization—and development of hedging—enables shocks to be more widely diffused and dissipated.

Intervention by the authorities was highlighted by most of the theories as the immediate solution to financial crises when they occur. These were not felt to be events that the market can sort out painlessly for itself. Decisive intervention (by the US Fed and other Central Banks) was particularly apparent in the equity-market crash, but was also evident after the debt crisis and the 1974 débâcle. The lifeboat in 1973, regulatory changes, and 'bailouts' for thrifts were the response to the domestic crises. Only the FRN crisis was felt sufficiently localized to blow itself out.

Lastly, in terms of contagion between markets, it was shown in Sect. 5 that this was a feature of all the international crises to some extent, although in the FRN crisis it was largely confined to the market itself (effects of the perpetual FRN market on the dated market) and in no case were all the markets simultaneously affected. Nevertheless, the 1974 interbank crisis accompanied sharp declines in syndicated credits, which, though partly resulting from the macroeconomic situation, also resulted from the loss in confidence in international markets and banks' funding difficulties. The debt crisis also closed the eurobond market to ldcs and led to sharp falls in interbank claims; the crisis in the eurobond markets in 1987 was itself a result of contagion from the equity markets, though contagion to other euromarkets and to domestic government bond markets was more muted. The secondary-banking crisis, in its cyclical context, may also have caused contagion; the thrifts crises were more insulated.

Conclusions

Subject to the limitations of the qualitative approach adopted, the analysis of Chs. 5 and 6 offers several types of conclusion; first, it allows one to assess whether the crises were 'unique events' or have common features; second, it allows one to analyse the link between fragility and systemic risk; third, it allows one to evaluate theories of financial crisis under current conditions: which factors should be highlighted, which discarded, and whether a synthesis is possible. This allows an assessment to be made of implications for the authorities and market participants. The data and descriptions presented in Ch. 6, informed by the theoretical summary in Ch. 5, suggest that the crises studied were not unique events but had discernible common features. Perhaps the most important of these common features of financial instability in the past two decades were the following:

- They followed rapid accumulation of debt and substantial speculation in assets; crowd-like behaviour among lenders, declining risk premiums, and concentration of risk were features of this accumulation.
- They followed a shift in regime which had unforeseeable or unforeseen consequences (i.e. not merely a cyclical downturn).
- Structural changes in financial markets leading to heightened competition often preceded the crises (Ch. 7).
- Innovation was often an important concomitant, as were declining capital ratios of lenders and borrowers.
- They often followed a period of monetary tightening (necessitated by inflationary pressures) and/or recession.
- They were accompanied by sharp increases in price and quantity rationing of credit, but this did not always prevent rationed borrowers from obtaining credit elsewhere.
- They sometimes entailed a collapse of liquidity in securities markets.
- For crises in the euromarkets, international transmission was strong and rapid.
- Contagion between markets was limited—in no case were all markets strongly affected.
- Action by the authorities prevented the crises from having serious systemic and macroeconomic consequences, although in some cases (notably the US thrifts) the cost of doing so has been immense.

As regards the link from financial fragility to systemic risk, the analysis suggests that it is close but not simple. In particular, transmission of fragility in the non-financial sector to financial institutions requires low capital ratios, low risk premiums, and lack of diversification of claims. The later US thrifts and the ldc debt crises are good examples. This suggests one reason why financial fragility discussed in Chs. 2 and 3 has not led to widespread systemic risk is that bank capital ratios have been maintained and (except in the USA) risk diversified across the economy. But there remains a question whether the safety net, arguably extended in the USA in 1990 to monetary policy, encourages debt accumulation on a 'ratchet' basis that will lead eventually to a genuine crisis (Wolfson 1989; Kane 1985) or rapid inflation (Friedman 1990). Moreover, experience of smaller countries such as Norway, Australia, and Sweden (Ch. 8), shows how fragility can in some circumstances lead directly to systemic risk.

Meanwhile, the FRN crisis shows that securities-market failure at least does not require financial fragility in a traditional sense. The market collapsed without any perceived increase in credit risk of the (major global) banks which had issued claims; it was more a case of dynamics of dealership markets reacting to asymmetric information, which in turn paralysed the primary market. (The discussion of the eurobond markets in the wake of the crash (Appendix 1 to this chapter) again shows how market-maker behaviour can influence primary activity.) The earlier US thrifts crisis resulted largely from interest-rate risk and not credit risk.

Turning to a review of theory, a synthesis would stress the monetary and 'fragility' precursors of financial crises, while emphasizing the role of uncertainty in the conditions for crisis, the likelihood of credit rationing, often arising from asymmetric information/agency problems, or declining secondary-market liquidity, as a consequence of such crises, and the importance of intervention.

Put more precisely, a synthesis of the theory of financial crises applicable to conditions in contemporary financial markets, drawing on economic theory and recent experience, should offer predictions regarding the preconditions, causes, nature, and consequences of financial crises. For example, a long period of relatively calm conditions with intense competition between financial institutions, increasing and concentrated debt accumulation at increasingly low risk premiums (partly as a consequence of these), financial innovation, and declining capital ratios may constitute the *preconditions* for a financial crisis. Deregulation often figures as a precondition in domestic markets but at most indirectly in international markets. Supervisory pressure to maintain capitalization and prevent excessive risk-taking may help to prevent unstable conditions from arising, while forebearance on such matters may aggravate them. The crisis may be *triggered* by a tightening of monetary conditions and the unforeseen consequences of a shift in regime (including the unforeseen properties of financial innovations). It may be accompanied by a sizeable deviation of asset values from their fundamental determinants (a speculative bubble). The crisis may *entail* runs, panics, or declines in asset values which lead to sharp increases in price and quantity rationing of credit, as well as reductions in liquidity of securities markets.

However, it may not *lead* to strong contagion between markets, further monetary contraction, and economic recession, although to prevent these effects the authorities may have to intervene firmly and decisively. Not that such intervention is always required. Some crises are localized enough not to offer systemic risks, either because the institutions involved are sufficiently robust or because the market concerned is relatively unimportant. Indeed, some would argue that minor crises may be salutary in leading intermediaries and the authorities to tighten up control and supervision. What the theories appear to omit is a role for structural change in financial markets as a forerunner of crisis. This issue is dealt with in Ch. 7.

The analysis of this paper has implications both for the authorities and for market participants in deregulated financial markets (drawn mainly from the recommendations of the theoretical paradigms).

For *supervisors*, it is suggested that the common features of financial crises identified above could be of assistance in helping to assess when heightened vigilance and examination of financial institutions' balance sheets are required. Theory and experience suggest that such examinations could cover not only capitalization but also concentration of risk, implications of innovations, indirect exposures, and potential liquidity of intermediaries' assets and liabilities (both loans and securities) in crisis situations (Guttentag and Herring 1988). Given that supervisory regimes covering many of these aspects have been developed and refined recently (including enhanced international co-operation), the possibility of serious crisis may be judged to have been reduced. However, some additional factors could also be considered. In particular, there could be a greater focus on macroeconomic indicators of crisis, such as growth of debt, gearing of creditor sectors, asset prices, and aggregate spreads. Other relevant factors include intensity of competition, the strength of control mechanisms over borrowers, and vulnerability to crises in other national and international markets.

Moreover, supervisors still need to be vigilant to ensure not only that the institutions they supervise are not becoming subject to 'disaster myopia' but also that they are not becoming complacent themselves, accepting prevailing judgements of risk which may have become distorted by a period of calm and intense competition. A possible indicator of such myopia is declining risk-premiums (Table 6.2). Fixed rules, e.g. risk-weighted capital adequacy, offer some discipline against this, although not a complete one, as long as other aspects of supervision remain discretionary. Thirdly, market-based systems to reduce information asymmetries and hence risk (reduced depositor protection to ensure adequate risk monitoring by wholesale depositors, rating agencies, and greater disclosure) may have a useful role to play. Fourth, given the link to financial fragility, an equalization of the tax treatment of debt and equity to reduce tendencies to overindebtedness will help minimize systemic risk. Finally, as shown by the US thrifts, forebearance may be far costlier than immediate closure.

Securities market regulators need to be aware that financial instability may affect them as well as banks, and that markets may be a more general transmission mechanism of instability to banks. Two main types of problem have been noted: collapse of liquidity in securities markets and failure of a major institution (although links between them are also possible). The first may be minimized by developing robust market structures (via encouragement of standard instruments, as well as policy to reduce transactions and related costs), the second by appropriate capitalization. Both will be helped by stable macroeconomic policy and—according to some commentators—use of a 'market maker of last resort'. Bingham (1991*a*) notes that robustness will also be increased by inducing dealers to monitor one another, while actions to spread the cost of safety-net operations across them will be of assistance in this context.

For *macroeconomic policymakers*, the relationship of crises to shifts of policy regime and turning-points in the tightness of policy implies, first, the need for policy to seek to avoid conditions, such as rapid inflation or a currency crisis, which may necessitate such sudden shifts or tightening of policy. Second, should such changes be required, there is a need for vigilance for financial stability. Third, knowledge by market participants that the lender of last resort is available if needed is crucial. Herstatt became far worse due to lack of confidence in the safety net, although generally its presence prevented 'true' crises on the lines of 1866 in the UK and 1933 in the USA (Ch. 8).

Of course, its use should be sparing and bank management (and their shareholders) who have made mistakes should always be sacrificed. Otherwise the existence of the lender of last resort may actually induce the development of financially fragile conditions that its use is aimed to counteract. Moreover, care is needed in distinguishing cases of illiquidity from insolvency. Seeking to save the US thrifts via liquidity assistance, for example, would entail shovelling Central Bank resources into a bottomless pit. Again, use outside the banking sector, to assist investment banks or securities markets, may generate moral hazard, though it clearly should not be ruled out. In addition, policymakers must bear in mind that in certain circumstances, such as a depreciating currency, a broad-based lender-of-last-resort-response with lower interest rates may not be easily sustainable (Summers 1991). Nor may it be desirable in the context of rapid inflation.[48] The potential for such a dilemma makes alternatives such as use of commercial banks as proxies, as well as sound prudential policy to minimize the need for intervention, all the more essential.

For *market participants*, several of the same implications apply as for regulators. They need to examine market conditions frequently in the light of the factors identified above, perhaps by use of strategic planning divisions, in order to assess the likelihood of crisis situations and the consequent appropriateness of their pricing of risk (Guttentag and Herring 1984*b*). How assured are their credit lines? How strong is their asset backing? Has their exposure to credit or liquidity risk been increasing? Again, a closer focus on gearing, asset prices, etc., at a macroeconomic level in relation to historic experience, may be a useful

[48] Sterilization of the monetary impulse once the crisis is over may blunt some of the adverse macroeconomic effects.

indicator of whether risk is being underpriced. Depositors and investors also need to be aware of potential risks—though as noted above this may require limitation of depositor protection and of moral hazard created by intervention. Private rating agencies may have an important role to play in monitoring firms' exposures, as well as taking a longer and broader view. However, there will always be limits to the benefits of disclosure due to inherent difficulties in assessing bank portfolios.

Although financial crises by their nature are rarely foreseen, often being triggered by a seemingly extraneous event, this synthesis of the economic theory of crises offers material for econometric investigation of the causes of financial crises. The rather *ad hoc* results in Appendix 2 (at the end of this chapter) suggest a role for monetary tightening, the cycle, rapid credit expansion, and bond spreads, consistent with the theories discussed in the text. In addition it is suggested that qualitative analysis of conditions in financial markets at a given time in the light of the results can be fruitful in offering certain pointers for vigilance. For example, in an earlier work on this issue, dating from 1989,[49] the author concluded that the following were of potential concern:

- the level in private-sector indebtedness, particularly in the UK and USA but also in other countries, beyond the range of historic relations with income and/or asset valuation,[50] as discussed in Chs. 2 and 3.
- the tendency of investment banks to take on large exposures, often of a sizeable proportion of their capital, during LBOs and other transactions.
- low spreads on syndicated credits for OECD corporations (see Chart 6.3).
- the rise in global inflation and the need for tightening monetary conditions.
- the intense competition among financial intermediaries (partly as a consequence of excess capacity), which often focuses on market share rather than profitability of transactions, as discussed in Ch. 7.[51]

An analysis of broad prospects as seen from the time of writing (early 1992) is provided in the conclusion.

Appendix 1: Euromarkets during the 1987 Crash[52]

Following the crash, the volatility in global equity markets rapidly spread to the *eurobond market*. Syndication activity came to a standstill while

[49] Davis (1989)

[50] See also Davis (1987) and references therein.

[51] See also Davis (1988*b*) and references therein.

[52] This section was originally prepared by J. G. S. Jeanneau, and previously appeared in Davis (1989).

trading in the secondary market was very thin. In the week ending 24 October, new issues in the international bond markets amounted to just \$1.4 bn compared with a weekly average of near \$4 bn over the previous year. As was the case in most bond markets around the world, secondary-market eurobond prices and yields fluctuated violently on 20 October as collapsing share prices led to a reassessment of fixed-income securities. Prices of long US Treasuries, which dropped to 88 on 19 October because of the uncertainty caused by the crash, rose to 99 on the next day to close at 95. During that week yields on 30-year Treasuries fell from 10.5 per cent on the 19th to 9.9 per cent on 26 October as investors moved to the relative security offered by government fixed-income markets and Central Banks injected liquidity in the financial system. The sharp price swings made it extremely difficult for dealers to quote realistic prices, and volatility in the eurobond market also made it difficult for investors to evaluate spreads, leading them to require higher risk premiums, and causing most euromarket yield curves to steepen. Dealers reported difficulty in launching new eurodollar bond issues (which are mainly swapped) because of the wide disparity in yields between eurobonds and domestic government bond markets.

The crash had the immediate consequence of reducing *liquidity* in the eurobond markets and accentuated the problems of oversupply. Because of the small size of issues relative to those in domestic markets it had always been difficult to keep eurobonds liquid, and volatility left traders without recourse to their usual methods of evaluating bonds and protecting their inventories; volatility made it virtually impossible to assess yield spreads and harder to hedge by selling US Treasuries short, because of the drying up of stock lending by US investors to investment banks. As a result of the lower liquidity, differentials widened, deal sizes were curtailed, and bid/offer spreads widened. For example, the most liquid sovereign issues, which traded in \$5 mn blocks at bid/offer spreads as low as 10 basis points before the crash, saw block sizes reduced to \$1 mn on 30 basis point spreads.

The collapse of equity prices brought activity back to the *swap market* although most transactions were in the secondary market. The bond market rally led corporates to try to arrange low-cost fixed-rate funding in exchange for floating-rate funding. Asset swappers also entered the market in order to take advantage of the widening spread between euro-issues and domestic government bonds. The substantial price declines suffered by a number of corporate euro-issues meant that it was relatively cheap for swappers to purchase bonds producing a high yield in exchange for lower yielding bonds. Swaps could then be rearranged on the basis of these newly acquired bonds. However, the US dollar primary swap market made little use of the available windows owing to a number of factors: first, absolute swap rates fell sharply in line with domestic government markets but the excess of supply over demand for fixed-rate funds pushed swap spreads to record high levels; second, bond yield volatility made it hard to hedge positions; third, hedging problems were compounded by the inability of dealers to borrow Treasuries because holders were concerned about the creditworthiness of investment banks and therefore demonstrated a strong preference for retaining them; fourth, the lack of issues on the euromarket failed to provide counterparties on the fixed-rate receiving side; and finally, the swap market was destabilized by concerns about counterparty risk. By the end of November, swap spreads had returned to pre-'Black Monday' levels but primary-market activity remained minimal.

Overwhelmed by orders to sell, the largely London-based market for dollar-denominated *Japanese equity warrants* came to a standstill for a day and a half. The major market makers had little choice but effectively to cancel trading in the days following the crash, because a significant proportion of the underlying stocks on the Tokyo stock exchange had moved to their limits and were not traded. Average warrant prices fell from an index value of 409[53] in the week prior to the crash to 192 (a 53 per cent decline) by the end of the following week. Trading reopened with much wider spreads (from 75 basis points to 2 percentage points) and with reduced lot sizes (from 50 to 25 warrants). The stock-market crash led to a massive sell-off of Japanese equity warrants by foreign investors. Japanese investors and institutions reportedly purchased most of the warrants because they were more optimistic about local equity prices than were foreign investors. As a result, much of the warrants market, traditionally based in London, effectively shifted in Tokyo. The primary and secondary markets for Swiss franc convertible bonds, mainly used by Japanese companies, also dried up. The major market makers agreed to halt trading as some bonds fell to steep discounts of as much as 25 per cent below a par issue price. Yields on some convertible bonds which had been issued with coupons as low as 25–50 basis points at par moved up to reach almost 6 per cent, higher than equivalent maturity straight Swiss franc denominated bonds.

In the *weeks following the crash*, only a handful of top-rated sovereign and supranational borrowers were able to take advantage of the international rally in fixed-income markets. The lesser liquidity of eurobonds (which has always been a feature of this market) caused eurobond prices to lag behind domestic issues and spreads to widen significantly over their domestic equivalent as yields generally fell (although this was somewhat less pronounced for top-rated sovereign issues). The same phenomenon occurred for corporate bonds, more particularly for second-ranking corporates, and meant that domestic markets offered less expensive

[53] Cresvale Index.

financing for all but top-quality issuers. Initial uncertainty over the economic situation also caused a sharp widening of corporate–government spreads in both domestic and eurobond markets. While eurobond activity weakened, some domestic bond markets such as the US market saw very strong issuing activity in the weeks following the crash as issuers took the opportunity offered by bond market rallies to lock in cheap fixed-rate funding. Because of the prevailing exchange-rate uncertainty, the marked tiering of funding costs according to credit quality, thin secondary-market trading, and the resulting lower liquidity, the fixed-rate bond sector remained depressed in spite of the fall in short- and long-term interest rates. Nevertheless, by mid-November, the situation had become calmer and primary and secondary-market activity more orderly. The higher yield available on eurobond issues (especially eurodollar paper) began to attract some investors away from their domestic markets. By the end of the quarter, even Japanese warrant prices had improved by significantly more than the underlying share prices on the Tokyo stock exchange (index value of 305 at the end of December), while trading lots and spreads reverted to more normal levels.

Appendix 2: Prediction of Systemic Risk: A Simple Econometric Test

In order to assess the precursors of financial instability, econometric tests were carried out to find the determinants of an indicator of turbulence in banking markets, namely sharp increases in the spread on short-term bank liabilities. Results were generated for an international spread (Treasury bill–eurodollar or 'TED') and US domestic spread (certificate of deposit–Treasury bill spread).

The independent variable is the probability that there will be a sharp rise in the spread of short-term bank liabilities (interbank offer rate/certificates of deposit) over the risk-free rate (Treasury bills). Historically, such increases have been a major indicator of financial instability (Chart 6.2); for example, for the eurodollar spread, rises of over 50 basis points occurred in the following quarters:

69 Q1		79 Q3	
69 Q2		79 Q4	
70 Q2	Penn Central	80 Q4	
73 Q1		81 Q3	
73 Q3		82 Q3	debt crisis
74 Q2	Herstatt/Franklin	84 Q2	Continental Illinois
74 Q3	Herstatt/Franklin	87 Q2	
78 Q4		87 Q4	crash

Estimation employed the logit estimator, where probability of crisis, P = 0 for periods when the spread did not rise 50 basis points and P = 1 when it did. The dependent variable is log (P/1 − P). The independent variables were entered as four lags in a general equation, differenced for stationarity where appropriate, then being restricted to those which remain significant. The independent variables chosen were the following:

Short-term and long-term spreads (dependent spread and long bond quality spread—BAA corporate less Treasury bond) *and changes in share prices*; these proxy the 'agency cost' hypothesis, that heightened vulnerability of borrowers and asymmetric information tends to precede an actual crisis.

The level of interest rates and real monetary growth to show the effects of monetary tightening on the probability of crisis.

Economic growth to give the relationship to recession.

Credit expansion to show whether crises occur in the context of rapid expansion in credit that comes to a abrupt halt.

Note that in a logit framework the lagged dependent variable cannot be defined (it would take the log of zero) and therefore the framework is not a full vector autoregression. Results—taking a generous approach to statistical significance—were as follows ('t' ratios are in parentheses):

International

$$\log\left[\frac{P}{1-P}\right] = \underset{(2.9)}{-4.23} + \underset{(1.7)}{0.86}\text{ short spread}_{t-4} + \underset{(1.8)}{1.7}\text{ long spread}_{t-2} - \underset{(2.5)}{2.56}\text{ long spread}_{t-4} + \underset{(1.8)}{1231}\log\left[\frac{\textit{credit expansion}}{\text{GDP}}\right]_{t-1} - \underset{(1.9)}{47.8}\,\Delta\log\left[\frac{\text{MI}}{\text{P}}\right]_{t-1} + \underset{(2.9)}{100.5}\,\Delta\log\left[\frac{\text{MI}}{\text{P}}\right]_{t-4}$$

$R^2 = 0.18$, log likelihood = −37.3, correct predictions = 86%

Domestic

$$\log\left[\frac{P}{1-P}\right] = \underset{(2.2)}{-4.69} + \underset{(1.5)}{1.65}\text{ short spread}_{t-3} - \underset{(2.5)}{6.15}\text{ long spread}_{t-1} + \underset{(2.1)}{5.19}\text{ long spread}_{t-2} - \underset{(1.2)}{1.74}\text{ long spread}_{t-4} + \underset{(2.7)}{2964}\log\left[\frac{\textit{credit expansion}}{\text{GDP}}\right]_{t-2} - \underset{(2.0)}{100.9}\,\Delta\log\left[\frac{\text{MI}}{\text{P}}\right]_{t-3} + \underset{(2.4)}{119.1}\,\Delta\log\left[\frac{\text{MI}}{\text{P}}\right]_{t-4} - \underset{(1.4)}{75.9}\,\Delta\log\left[\frac{\text{GDP}}{\text{P}}\right]_{t-4}$$

$R^2 = 0.41$, log likelihood = −22.4, correct predictions = 93%

The consistent results are that high short spreads, rapid credit expansion, and decelerating monetary growth tend to precede periods of instability. These are consistent with a number of the theories outlined in Ch. 5, notably the agency-costs, financial-fragility, and monetarist approaches. In the international estimate there is also a clear relationship between increases in the long spread and crises. In the domestic case, recession enters, albeit at a low significance level, while the relation with the long spread is more complex: a saw-tooth pattern seems to emerge. This could reflect a different timing of the crises in domestic as opposed to international markets.

7

Systemic Risk and Financial Market Structure

Chs. 5 and 6 identified a number of features common to most periods of financial instability in recent decades, including debt accumulation, unanticipated shifts in policy or regulatory regimes, financial innovation, monetary tightening, credit rationing, and international transmission. These observations were felt to validate to some extent the various theories of financial crisis that have been proposed in the literature, in particular those emphasizing financial-fragility, monetary, uncertainty, credit-rationing, and asymmetric-information/agency-cost aspects of crises. On the other hand, no one theory was able to explain financial instability; features of several had to be jointly present in order for a situation of financial instability to arise.

This chapter explores the hypothesis that many of the factors underlying heightened systemic risk can be adequately subsumed in an industrial organization framework, with particular reference to the role of an intensification of competition among financial intermediaries following market developments which reduce entry barriers. The analysis is set largely in terms of commercial banking, but is also applicable to other types of intermediary, notably investment banks. The approach seeks both to encompass the mechanisms highlighted by existing theories of financial crisis, particularly those relating to uncertainty and imperfect information, and also to extend them by focusing on certain structural aspects that have hitherto been generally neglected by theorists, and which can be discerned in many, if not all, cases of financial instability. (In other words, it seeks to *complement* and not *substitute* for the analysis of Chs. 5 and 6.). It is suggested that the hypothesis could provide additional policy recommendations and also useful leading indicators of potential situations of instability as well as fragility, both for regulators and for market participants themselves. Such results may be of particular relevance, given the rapid changes occurring in many financial markets, notably in certain EC domestic markets after 1992, and in Eastern Europe as former command economies liberalize.

It is noted that the potential importance of the linkage from easing of entry conditions to financial instability is well known to practitioners, for example Broker (1989), writing for the OECD Expert Group on Banking, noted that 'the painful experience of some countries (following deregulation) suggests the need for safety measures to ensure the stability of the system by preventing competition . . . becoming destructive'. Suzuki (1987) noted the absense of 'destructive competition' among Japanese financial institutions during the high growth period prior to 1973. But the dynamics of competition amongst intermediaries in financial markets following reduction in entry barriers are rarely assessed analytically or discussed in contexts other than deregulation, when in fact a wide variety of developments, including innovation and technical progress, as well as sharp changes in demand for credit itself, can lead to changes in entry conditions to financial markets.

The chapter is organized as follows: Sects. 1 and 2 respectively assess the relevant aspects of the theories of financial crisis, and briefly introduce recent developments in the theory of industrial organization. In Sects. 3 and 4, a synthesis between these approaches is developed which explores the transmission mechanisms between changes in entry conditions and systemic risk. Evidence for the mechanisms highlighted in the synthesis, drawn from the various periods of financial instability of recent decades, is presented in Sect. 5, while in Sect. 6 consideration is also given to features of periods of new entry and intense competition when instability did not develop. The final section draws together the conclusions, suggests implications for regulatory policy, and highlights the potential uses that could be made of the mechanisms outlined, as well as suggesting some areas where reductions in entry barriers may require heightened vigilance by regulators and market participants.

(1) Theories of Financial Crisis

A comprehensive literature survey is provided in Ch. 5. Here, at risk of slight repetition, we offer a selective summary, with emphasis on the role of structural changes in patterns of intermediation in the development of crisis situations. Do changes in competitive conditions among intermediaries have a role to play?

Theories emphasizing *debt and financial fragility* consider financial crises to be a key feature of the turning-point of the business cycle, a response to previous 'excesses' of borrowing which can operate through a variety of financial markets. Amongst the key components of the theory are, first, the concept of a displacement—an exogenous event leading to improved opportunities for profitable investment—and, second, monetary financial innovations which partly offset increases in interest rates caused by excess demand for finance during the fixed investment boom. However, sharp increases in demand for credit mean interest rate increases eventually occur, which leads to 'fragility'. Features of fragility include an increase in debt finance, a shift from long- to short-term debt; a shift from borrowing which is adequately covered by cash flow to borrowing not covered at all by it; a heightening of speculative activity in asset markets; and a reduction in margins of safety for financial institutions. Further rises in interest rates, perhaps due to policy tightening, lead on to financial crisis.

There is clearly little explicit consideration of market structure. Declining risk premiums, for example, are held to be purely cyclical phenomena, though the involvement of structural factors in the process, e.g. the setting up of new credit institutions during the upturn which disappear in the crisis, is not ruled out, and financial innovation is explicitly recognized as an important component. Apart from this, however, the theory is consistent with an unchanged industrial structure of financial markets during the development of financial fragility.

The *monetarist* approach emphasises banking panics, that may cause monetary contraction. Banking panics arise from a public loss of confidence in banks' abilities to convert deposits into currency. This may be caused by failure of an important institution, which may in turn stem from failure of the authorities to pursue a steady and predictable monetary policy. However, the approach does not take the further step back to assess how a key bank could get into such a vulnerable condition. The underlying assumption seems again to be of a relatively static financial market structure.

Theories of crisis focusing on *uncertainty* define it as pertaining to future developments not susceptible to being reduced to objective probabilities[1] (e.g. financial crises) and also providing opportunities for profit in competitive markets. Responses to uncertainty, for example by lending officers in banks, may be to apply subjective probabilities to uncertain events plus a risk premium. But agents often tend to judge such probabilities by the actions of others (i.e. herding) which can lead to financial instability if the crowd proves to be wrong. Meanwhile, supernormal profits can only be earned by innovation when there is uneven information and uncertainty. This may lead to crisis if deteriorating balance sheets follow the innovation process or firms fail to understand the properties of innovations (perhaps due to lack of experience). Uncertainty itself may thus be raised by the innovation process. In the presence of uncertainty, adverse surprises may trigger shifts in confidence, affecting markets more than appears warranted by their intrinsic significance: hence a crisis.

In this paradigm, the process of competition is highlighted, as well as the interactions between players. But there is no precise description of the links between levels of uncertainty, competition, and innovation. Does heightened competition increase uncertainty (other than via innovation?). Are uncertain events largely exogenous to market processes or endogenous?

[1] Or, alternatively and more loosely, to which expectations can only be applied with extreme difficulty.

Paradigms of *credit rationing* suggest financial crises are characterized by abrupt increases in rationing. Extending the theories stressing uncertainty outlined above, a further distinction is made between 'normal' systematic risks, such as recession, and financial crises—the latter being subject to much greater uncertainty as outlined above. In the case of recession, it is suggested that risk pricing is accurate, because unfavourable outcomes are frequent enough to ensure an over-optimistic intermediary is driven from the market (this does, however, assume a suitably long time horizon). But for financial crises and other uncertain events there is no such presumption; competition may drive prudent creditors from the market, as they are undercut by those disregarding the likelihood of financial crisis for reasons of ignorance or competitive advantage.

As well as competition, various psychological factors underlying this pattern of 'disaster myopia' may be identified, notably a tendency to calculate probabilities by the ease with which past occurrences are brought to mind, which declines with time, as well as institutional factors such as short periods over which loan officers are assessed, and asymmetry of outcomes for managers and shareholders. These tendencies, which imply declining *subjective* probabilities of shocks during periods of calm, may lead to declining capital positions, loosening of 'equilibrium' price, and quantity rationing of credit, and hence increased *objective* vulnerability of creditors to shocks. Subjective and objective probabilities may thus during a period of calm drift further and further apart, until a shock caused by an uncertain event leads to an abrupt increase in credit rationing, triggering a crisis, as lenders become aware of their imprudence.

Again, in this paradigm there is some discussion of competitive conditions in markets. The existence of imprudent creditors, which eventually forces others to emulate their short-termism, is an important part of the process; but it is not specified whether they are new entrants, nor is there any discussion of the extent to which innovations and other changing demand and supply conditions may influence the process. Nevertheless, we consider the credit rationing framework to be a useful one, and employ it in Sects. 3 and 4 to clarify the nature of the developments made by the industrial analysis.

Asymmetric-information and agency-cost theory, as outlined in Ch. 5, is not applied to structural change in the financial system, although, as discussed below, agency costs *per se* are important components of the transmission mechanism outlined here from heightened competition to instability. *Dynamics of dealer markets*, again, discuss behaviour of secondary markets in response to changes in relative information, rather than competitive conditions among intermediaries *per se* (although their withdrawal can help destabilize the market).

In sum, extant theories of financial crisis tend to suggest a potential importance for changing industrial structure and levels of competition, but generally do not specify them explicitly. Most of the theories are consistent with a steady-state financial system, subjective to various cyclical, monetary, or other (largely exogenous) shocks. Can theories of industrial organization help further to illuminate the nature of financial crises? We now go on to outline potentially relevant points.

(2) Recent Developments in Industrial Economics and their Application to Financial Markets

While traditional industrial economics (Bain 1956) tends to distinguish perfectly competitive from oligopolistic markets by reference to barriers to entry such as economies of scale, the new industrial economics, as it is often termed, lays stress on the important of sunk costs as an entry barrier to markets, i.e. costs which cannot be recovered in leaving the market (for a summary see Mayer 1985). If there are sunk costs, entry can always in principle be deterred by incumbents. Sunk costs may develop over time (e.g. by reputation, relationships, and expertise) or may be created by means of strategic competition (product differentiation, advertising, etc.). Regulations preventing entry can be conceptualized as an extreme version of such barriers. In contrast, economies of scale are not seen as an entry barrier, because in the absence of sunk costs another firm, perhaps in a related sector, can set up production and enter the market in a hit-and-run manner (the 'contestable markets' paradigm). Seeming oligopolists can be disciplined by this potential competition to act in a perfectly competitive manner, while in a market without economies of scale, a decline or elimination of sunk costs may tend to a perfectly competitive market *per se*.

Davis (1988*b*) applied these concepts to the primary eurobond market and suggested that they offered useful insights into market behaviour among financial intermediaries (for a summary see the Appendix to this chapter). However, what is most crucial at this stage is an understanding of these paradigms *per se*. For this reason, we now go on to discuss the approaches of contestable markets and strategic competition in somewhat more detail (features of standard perfect competition, which are also an important component of the argument, are taken as known). We also note the potential importance of non-profit-maximizing behaviour (managerial theory of the firm). Those already familiar with these theories should move on to Sect. 3.

According to the theory of *contestable markets* (see Baumol 1982 and the review in Spence 1983) many seeming oligopoly situations may be characterized by competitive behaviour on the part of existing firms, because of the potential for new firms to enter in a 'hit and run' manner in response to excess profits. Contestable markets may thus benefit both from efficient industrial structures and competitive behaviour. In order to induce competitive behaviour there has to be an absence of significant lags between a decision to enter and entry occurring, an instant response of demand to changing prices, and an absence of losses on exit due to *sunk costs* (for example, capital specific to the industry that cannot be used if the firm decides to withdraw). The entrant knows that if the incumbent has sunk costs, it will always be worth the incumbent's while to deter entry.

According to this theory, economies of scale need not be a barrier to entry; firms can produce at minimum efficient scale for a short period and sell (storable) output over a long period. Obviously, if there are neither economies of scale nor sunk costs, the paradigm collapses to that of competitive equilibrium. Entry into oligopolistic industries is often assumed to be easier for established firms in related industries than for new firms, given the frequent importance of economies of scope (joint costs); such 'cross entry' is typically ignored in the more traditional approach but is obviously important in financial markets. The degree of 'contestability' will of course change over time with shifts in parameters such as demand, technology, and regulation. Some have argued that contestable markets typify deregulated financial markets such as that for residential mortgages in the UK (see Davies and Davies 1984), although deregulation alone may not be sufficient to eliminate the importance of sunk costs as barriers to entry.

Others, in contrast, have suggested that the 'contestable markets' approach may perhaps be best regarded as a benchmark or welfare standard, as well as being valuable for highlighting the role of sunk costs. They would argue that not many markets in the real world fit the assumptions, notably that there are no sunk costs (or that they are equal between entrants and incumbents) and that an entrant can come into a market and set up at full scale before existing firms respond to changing prices (see Shepherd 1984). Where sunk costs such as expertise, relationships, and reputations[2] are important, as in most financial markets (Ch. 1), demand will not respond instantaneously to prices. Nor are firms identical, as the theory implicitly assumes. We outline two alternative theories of firm behaviour in the presence of sunk costs.

A key element in a dynamic approach to industrial analysis is recognition of the *discretion* of firms to deviate from short-run profit maximization, particularly in the case of multiproduct firms in situations of oligopoly (such as banking and finance in many countries). As well as from

[2] In financial markets, these may constitute the principal asset of the intermediary itself.

sunk costs themselves, which offer excess profitability, enabling currently unprofitable activities to be cross-subsidized, discretion arises from the divorce of ownership from control in public companies, which enables managers to change the objectives of firm behaviour. This is the familiar form of agency costs for providers of external finance introduced in Ch. 1. Such behaviour is limited by the possibility that the share price of a firm that is not profit maximizing will decline, the firm be taken over, and the managers sacked. In the financial sector, deregulation has permitted more 'discretion' to firms to merge and to enter new markets,[3] although to the extent that it reduces entry barriers, it has also tended to reduce excess profitability from oligopoly, which was a source of discretion.

It has typically been assumed in *managerial theories* (such as Williamson 1970) that, given discretion, managers will aim to maximize an objective such as sales revenue growth, which enters the managerial utility function, rather than profit maximize in either short or long run. In the context of the discussion of Chs. 1 and 2, there are agency costs weakening shareholders influence over managers. Such problems may be particularly severe in oligopolistic and relatively uncompetitive financial sectors, where managers benefit from a great deal of 'free cash flow' and are not subject to the takeover sanction—often at the authorities' insistence. Indeed, behaviour of financial institutions (seeking growth in balance-sheet size or market share) suggests that managerial utility maximization may be a common objective. On the other hand, substitutability of profit and growth should not be exaggerated. Profits are likely to be essential for growth, given the use of retained earnings to invest in extra capacity and—particularly in financial markets—the need to accumulate reserves in order to maintain capital adequacy, and cover losses due to default.

The focus in the 'new industrial economics' (see, for example, Tirole 1989) is rather different from the managerial theory of the firm literature, in that discretion is used for strategic purposes (where a 'strategic move' is one designed to induce another player to make a choice more favourable to the strategic mover than would otherwise occur) and the principal goal of managers is again assumed to be (long-run) profit maximization. The following paragraphs show applications of the theory of *strategic competition* to entry deterrence.

The traditional theory of industrial structure ('limit pricing') suggested that price or output levels of the incumbent could discourage entry, whereby existing firms sell as a price level just below that at which an entrant can obtain adequate profits. This may be unrealistic, as the incumbent firm may reduce its output in the event of entry. Instead, in order to deter entry, the incumbent(s) typically vary instruments that

[3] And some intermediaries remain protected from takeover.

have a lasting and irreversible effect on cost or demand conditions—that create sunk costs. The incumbent commits himself to a course of conduct that would be detrimental to an entrant. Short-run profit maximization is traded for the long-run benefits of avoiding entry.

On the cost side there could be overcapitalization, such that the output produced by the incumbent could have been produced more effectively with a low level of capital, or more variable factors of production. The same may hold for research expenditure, where high levels may offer a credible threat to entry.[4] By a further strategic move, a firm may be able to raise rivals' costs, for example by setting high wage rates in the industry. Pre-emptive patenting is a fourth approach on the cost side that could be used in strategic entry deterrence; though patents tend to lack force in finance, as products are easily copied in such a way as to avoid infringing patents. Finally, if there are *intertemporal dependencies* of cost—the 'experience curve' whereby a firm's cost level is a declining function of its cumulative output (experience itself being a sunk cost)—then even price or output choice can deter entry. An application to financial markets is accumulation of information regarding borrowers and market dynamics, which helps reduce risk of loss.

On the demand side, firms may act strategically by advertising, product differentiation, or brand proliferation to deter entry. Again, there may be intertemporal dependencies on the demand side, arising from sunk costs such as relationships and a reputation built up by being first or by being 'trustworthy' (Radner 1986). Again, there is a clear relation with the theory of debt outlined in Ch. 1. It should be emphasized that entry barriers built up over time in this way need not be due to active planning on the part of the firm, but may result from historical accident due to short-run profit-maximizing behaviour (Salop 1979). The analysis, which applies to cases of perfect information on existing firms' behaviour, can be extended to *imperfect information*, i.e. informational asymmetries such that the entrant is unable to predict the incumbent's responses. In such cases, limit pricing may be used to deter entry since the potential entrant is *ex hypothesi* uncertain about the cost level of the incumbent. An incumbent may signal with a low price to indicate efficiency, whether he actually is efficient or not. *Predatory pricing* in cases of imperfect information, i.e. selling at price below marginal cost, may be a worthwhile way of building up a reputation as a committed fighter for markets, thus deterring competition, especially if the incumbent is active in a series of markets.

[4] We note that strategic considerations will not always induce firms to overinvest to deter entry; depending on the possibility for the incumbent to invest after entry and the reaction function, underinvestment may instead be optimal (Fudenberg and Tirole 1984). However, in our view the importance of intertemporal features such as reputation, relationships, and expertise in financial markets are likely to make strategic overinvestment optimal in many cases.

In application of these concepts to the behaviour of intermediaries in the primary eurobond market, Davis (1988*b*) found that the market shared both contestable and non-contestable features (see Appendix). Of course, one aspect of financial market conditions not tested in the eurobond market is that of stuctural regulation, prevalent in domestic markets, which can act similarly to sunk costs as a barrier to entry or activity. Equally, while strategic mechanisms such as innovation and product differentiation are stressed in the discussion above as a barriers to entry, they may also act as a means of entry if a new firm, for example, uses an innovation to help it gain a clientele from other firms.

(3) An Industrial Approach to Financial Instability

Bringing these analyses together enables one to outline an approach to financial instability based on the industrial dynamics of competition in financial markets, which both encompasses most of the features outlined in the theories of financial crisis (Ch. 5) and extends their analysis by explicit discussion of structural features. Evidence is presented below (Sect. 5) which indicates the relevance of some of the mechanisms discussed for recent periods of systemic risk.

The approach is developed in detail below, but its essential features may be summarized as follows: periods of financial instability, which may culminate in crises, are often preceded by changes in conditions for entry to financial markets. Such developments lead to heightened competition in the market concerned, whether due to actual new entry (tending to perfect competition), effects of potential new entry on the behaviour of incumbents (heightened contestability), competitive responses of incumbents to the threat of entry (strategic competition), or indeed 'managerial' growth maximization. Such heightened competition may provoke reductions in prudential standards (which may be manifested in lower prices and higher quantities in credit markets, as well as declining capital ratios), especially in the absence of appropriate prudential supervision. This in turn can lead on to financial instability. In effect, the market may overshoot the level of competition which is sustainable in long-run competitive equilibrium, and various market imperfections and distortions (many of which are discussed in the existing literature on financial crisis) can be adduced to explain this.

(a) Declining sunk costs of entry

The new industrial economics, as summarized in Sect. 2, stresses the importance of irrecoverable costs as barriers to entry, which prevent the achievement of competitive equilibrium (in the absence of economies of scale) or contestable markets (given economies of scale). In the presence of sunk costs, prices in equilibrium may exceed competitive levels, as incumbents gain supernormal projects from their protected situation (often, but not necessarily, with the aid of collusion). In capital markets, this might be manifested in high underwriting costs of new issues; in banking markets by large spreads between deposit and loan rates. In each case credit availability might be below equilibrium levels.

Such an equilibrium may be disturbed by any developments which change the sunk costs of entry, and thus lead to heightened potential for entry. In unregulated markets (such as the euromarkets), sunk costs might decline due to product innovation by entrants (which enables them to overcome barriers arising from the reputation of incumbents with existing products); establishment of new markets (such as wholesale or interbank markets) which offer funds to banks lacking branch networks to collect retail deposits; technological advance, that may reduce the need to set up subsidiaries in a major centre; and market developments that devalue the advantages built up over time by incumbents (e.g. loss of reputation due to a debt crisis, or new types of borrower with whom they lack established relationships). Note that each of these entails a shift in demand conditions or market technology. Similar factors will apply in domestic markets, with one important addition, namely the possibility of structural deregulation.[5] In effect, this may change 'sunk' costs of entry from infinity (where regulation bars entry) to a low level at which entry becomes attractive. In this case, underlying demand for financial services, which was suppressed by regulation, comes to the fore. Note again that, in each case, 'entry' need not be from outside—it may be between market segments by existing firms, or remain a threat rather than a realization.

(b) Results of declining sunk costs

Following the discussion in Sect. 2, consequences of lower entry barriers can be outlined for three cases: no economies of scale or sunk costs after the barriers fall; economies of scale and no sunk costs; economies of scale and a reduction in sunk costs. However, as discussed in (c) below, all are likely to have similar consequences for market behaviour.

First, in the absence of economies of scale and of sunk costs, in the new state of the world, heightened competition is likely to arise via actual new entry, which drives prices and quantities of credit from an imperfect towards a perfectly competitive level. Alternatively, in the presence of

[5] However, authors such as Kane (1984) and Steinherr (1990) suggest that, even in domestic markets, technological change has been the primary force for financial change—deregulation has been reactive to such pressure. And Lamfalussy (1992) suggests that without technical changes and shifts in underlying demand conditions, the opportunities offered by deregulation might not have been exploited to such a degree. A number of the examples of financial developments outlined below and in Ch. 8 confirm these hypotheses.

economies of scale, but lacking sunk costs of entry, potential competition will lead the incumbents to adopt prices and quantities similar to those in competitive equilibrium, i.e. the contestable markets paradigm will apply. Third, when sunk costs are reduced but not eliminated there will again be some effect on prices and quantities; both entrants and incumbents are likely to engage in strategic competition, varying instruments that have a lasting effect on supply and demand conditions and which seek to change the behaviour of competitors. As in other industrial markets, this may include innovation or product differentiation (so as to reduce the niches available to entrants), overcapacity, and higher factor costs. In the presence of imperfect information, price competition may also take on strategic aspects. More generally, predatory pricing or even price wars may be used in order to seek to influence rivals' behaviour. Any prior collusive agreements are likely to be weakened or destroyed in such cases.

It is suggested that competition in financial markets is likely to exhibit features of all three of these paradigms (see the discussion of the primary eurobond market in the Appendix). On the one hand, there is likely to be new entry following declines in sunk costs, which will reduce profitability for all intermediaries. Prices of financial services are likely to fall. But as suggested in Ch. 1, Sect. 4, there remain some economies of scale, for example those resulting from risk pooling, and hence the number of firms may be limited. Finally, some advantages for incumbents related to sunk costs (such as reputation, relationships, private information, and expertise) are likely to remain. They are likely to engage in some strategic competition to defend their positions, such as predatory pricing. Although such behaviour is not totally successful (their profitability declines) it may succeed in confining new entrants to certain segments of the market and in maintaining a distinction between leading incumbent firms, who retain large shares of the market, and new entrants whose share is relatively small.

(c) Consequences of increased competition

The effects of heightened competition are similar in each of the cases outlined above: declining profitability, lower prices, and increased quantities. In financial markets, lower profits entail reduced ability to maintain capitalization as a cushion against shocks, while lower prices and increased quantities may entail provision of loans at lower risk premiums or to riskier borrowers. Such effects may be traced for both banking and securities markets.

At a most basic level, in a banking market where credit is rationed by price (see Ch. 1, Sect. 3), an increased availability of credit is likely to entail lower risk premiums throughout the market. Given a downward-sloping demand curve, borrowers who were previously inhibited from taking on any or more credit for reasons of cost may increase their borrowing. Such a tendency may be particularly marked if new intermediaries price at below market-clearing levels in order to gain initial market share in the face of the various advantages of reputation, information, etc. enjoyed by incumbents. But lower prices and increased quantities are also likely to arise in cases of heightened contestability (as entrants reduce prices in response to the threat of entry) and via strategic competition (such as predatory pricing by incumbents).[6] Heightened competition is also likely to lead to a shift in bargaining power from the intermediary to the borrower; the former may be forced to accept lower profits to keep relationships, preserve its reputation, and maintain the value of information it has collected about a firm.

Loosening of credit rationing is also likely for borrowers who are initially in a situation characterized by quantity rationing. On the one hand, any tendency for slow adjustment of rates to market conditions (with consequent disequilibrium quantity rationing of credit) is likely to be eliminated. More seriously from the point of view of risk and profitability, a situation characterized by equilibrium quantity rationing (resulting from asymmetric information between borrowers and lenders) is also likely to be disturbed. New entrants seeking market share, or incumbents seeking to reinforce their own positions, may seek to satisfy the credit demands of those who are quantity rationed, although rationing was a profit-maximizing strategy in the pre-entry situation. It is likely that the boundary between those who are price rationed and those quantity rationed will shift in favour of the former, although information on those previously rationed remains imperfect and/or their capitalization or collateral is inadequate. Such a tendency will be particularly marked if new credit markets (e.g. junk bonds) become available to those previously confined to banking markets, since equilibrium quantity rationing depends on the existence of some market segmentation. Note that loosening of equilibrium quantity rationing may entail increased risk although risk *premiums* remain the same or even increase, so long as quantities increase.

Competition may also have an effect on the liabilities side of balance sheets. Banks will compete more aggressively for deposits, reducing the spread between deposit and loan rates. Prudent banks will need to follow their more aggressive competitors, or lose their deposit bases. Such competition may sharply reduce profitability, as higher rates are paid on the whole stock of deposits and not merely at the margin.

[6] We note that the cases of contestability and strategic competition are not always easy to distinguish. Reversibility of price reductions, success in preventing entry, and concomitant increases in innovation and other instruments of strategic competition may indicate the latter.

The discussion above is set largely in terms of banking, but similar arguments may apply to securities markets. Heightened competition is likely to lead to a reduction in underwriting margins in primary markets, which thus increases risk. Securities houses may take on greater risk, so as to obtain a greater share of the fees involved in bond issuance; for example, by undertaking bought deals, where the lead manager takes the whole of a new issue on to his books, before selling it on to investors. (Bought deals may also act as a barrier to undercapitalized firms, i.e. their introduction may itself be a form of strategic competition.) Secondary-market dealers may reduce bid/offer spreads and raise quantities at which they are ready to trade, hence increasing vulnerability to changes in fundamentals. They may also run exposed positions on their own accounts.

Finally, heightened competition may lead financial-market participants to reduce their capitalization. If the mean return to capital when operating in a prudent manner is reduced sharply by new entry, there may be a temptation to increase leverage, thus offering a higher mean return at a cost in terms of greater risk of bankruptcy. In many cases the intermediary will have little choice, as competition reduces profitability from which capital may be built up.

(d) Need competition cause instability?

One objection may immediately be posed to any attempted linkage between the above description of the industrial behaviour of financial markets and financial instability, namely the existence of a competitive equilibrium in which financial firms make normal profits, risks are adequately covered in loan pricing/underwriting margins and capital adequacy is maintained. In such an equilibrium, risk premiums would be sufficient to cover losses over the economic cycle, and borrowers for whom information or collateral were inadequate would be quantity rationed in an equilibrium manner. Any excess intermediation capacity would be eliminated as returns to equity fell, and capital would be reallocated. It might be thought that the shift to such an equilibrium from an imperfectly competitive or oligopolistic market (where insufficient credit was advanced and intermediaries gained monopoly profits) should not be a cause for vigilance, but instead a pure welfare gain, at least if one abstracts from any financial fragility in the non-financial sector (Chs. 2–4).

However, although there may be benefits when comparing different equilibria, the benefits may be at least partly offset by losses in the transition. The reasons why it may be the case, especially if prudential supervision is weak or absent,[7] are basically the factors outlined in the

[7] However, instability cannot be ruled out even in the case of firm prudential supervision if regulators are misled by uncertainty into disregarding low probability hazards.

'uncertainty', 'credit rationing', and 'agency cost' approaches to financial crisis, as well as aspects of the theory of finance outlined in Chs. 1 and 2.

Because of factors such as the importance of information and uncertainty in financial markets, several of which arise from the nature of the debt contract (Ch. 1), the effect on declining market power on the value of bank franchises; certain features of newly competitive markets *per se* (short time horizons, competition for market share, oligopoly dynamics) and any inadequate or ill-directed regulation (including any tendencies to retard removal of excess capacity), financial markets for which entry barriers are sharply reduced may be prone to levels of competition which prove, at least ex-post, to be excessive. This may entail risk premiums below those needed to cover losses, excessive leverage, and a relaxation of prudential standards. In such conditions, banks may be particularly vulnerable to runs leading to bankruptcy. Because of externalities between financial firms such as contagion, as well as the key role of banks in monitoring loans in the presence of asymmetric information for borrowers unable to access other types of finance (Ch. 5, Sect. 1), such potential failures that arise from excessive competition are a public policy issue in a way that they are not in other industries.

In addition, although examples of their operation in other industries, such as retailing and estate agency, are common,[8] such problems of excessive competition are usually worked out by merger and size adjustment. There may also be some bankruptcies, but they may not be as widespread as in the financial sector.[9] A basic reason is the heightened risk of contagious runs, given liquid liabilities and illiquid assets of financial institutions, as outlined in Ch. 5, Sect. 1. An additional reason for this distinction may be that, in other industries, creditors have a strong incentive to monitor firms' management as pressures on their solvency increase. Indeed, creditors' monitoring should encourage an orderly process of exit and discourage owners from recouping their losses by continuing to invest in the industry. In finance, the responsibility is largely taken by the regulators, who as discussed below may have inadequate resources or may seek to avoid exit of firms to bolster their own positions. A further distinction may be between primary and secondary markets. The analysis below is largely set out in terms of primary markets; however, analogies for dealer markets can generally be envisaged. In Sect. 6 the issue of competition among market makers in London after Big Bang is assessed. Why were disruptive bankruptcies avoided?

[8] Nevertheless, some of the features noted above—e.g. problems of information, uncertainty, and inadequate regulation—are particularly marked in financial markets.

[9] Externalities arising from contagion and counterparty risk following bankruptcies of non-financial firms cannot be ruled out, of course (Ch. 4, Sect. 1), and counterparty risk may affect financial institutions if they are already vulnerable.

(e) Excessive competition in financial markets

Given the importance to the chapter of the link from competitive adjustment to instability, it is worthwhile to clarify its nature more formally. We would suggest that one way to formalize the concept of excessive competition and the ways in which it comes about is to use the framework of credit rationing and 'disaster myopia' as presented by Guttentag and Herring (1984*a*) (GH). As detailed in Ch. 5 and recapitulated in Sect. 1, the nub of their argument is that the background to financial crises is often an excessive loosening of price and quantity rationing of credit; that unlike normal cyclical developments ('project-specific risk'), where risk is correctly priced, for uncertain events such as financial crises there may be a tendency for underpricing of risk (subjective and objective probabilities of crises to deviate), owing to competition as prudent lenders are undercut; and that additional psychological and institutional mechanisms may also help explain the 'disaster myopia' phenomenon. It is of course also essential that the non-financial sectors be receptive to increased credit. Reasons why this may be so are outlined in Chs. 2 and 3.

The GH analysis provides an introduction of the excessive competition concept and suggests excessive competition can occur autonomously during a period of calm, though a crucial ingredient is 'imprudent creditors' who force others to emulate their short-termism. We suggest that an industrial analysis, integrating the lessons of the other theories of crisis, provides a broader and more convincing set of underlying factors and transmission mechanisms, and Sect. 5 points to identifiable counter parts to them in recent periods of financial instability. Indeed, the GH analysis itself may be best interpreted in industrial terms. Imprudent creditors can only undercut in the presence of low sunk costs, where loans must be priced similarly by all lenders, i.e. loans from all lenders are seen as identical. Were this not the case, the prudent could protect themselves by charging higher rates or quantity rationing. And one way of motivating the prudent/imprudent distinction is in terms of incumbents and entrants. The next section outlines the transmission mechanisms one by one, relating them in each case to the GH framework developed in Ch. 5. We note that several or all of them may be simultaneously operative.

Before commencing, some assumptions are needed regarding capital adequacy regulations. Why do they not restrain banks from 'excessive competition? First, equity markets may be as bullish about prospects as banks themselves, and hence provide the necessary equity. Second, rapid growth generates retentions, even if these will be negated later by need for provisions. Third, in some cases capital regulations may *stimulate* risk taking (Ch.5 Sect. 2). Fourth, regulators may not be aware of excessive competition in their calculations—an issue discussed further below.

(4) Structural Reasons for Overshooting

(a) Information

As discussed in Ch. 1 (see also Chant 1987), banks may be characterized as

> monitors and enforcers of loan contracts . . . managing risk is performed by acquiring non-marketable securities for which the institution takes the responsibility for screening information about the borrower. The value of these assets is specific to the institution . . . which has gained the information required . . . and understands the problems with respect to enforcement. These dimensions of the customer relationship must be built up over time. The value of these claims would be less for an outside party who has not gained the knowledge embodied in the customer relationship.

To the extent that new entrants can induce borrowers to switch away from established credit relationships or offer extra credit (by offering lower prices), such information-based linkages will be weakened and existing information devalued. Conceptually, new lenders may be seen as 'cannibalizing' existing market information and structure, to the detriment of existing lenders. In terms of theories of intermediation (Ch. 1, Sect. 4), monitoring is weakened and it is also possible that 'commitment' breaks down. Despite this, however, new lenders are still likely to lend on the basis of inadequate or asymmetric information during the initial stages. They have no time or reputation to develop 'commitment' relations and must perforce rely on 'control'. Thus, for both types of lender, entry may lead to a lowering of credit standards.

In terms of the framework developed in Ch. 5, Sect. 7, excessive competition arises from imperfections in lenders' knowledge of the risk factors relating to the project-specific distribution, namely the amount borrowers have outstanding to all creditors, and especially for new entrants, the distribution of project-specific returns. These lead to a deviation of subjective and objective probabilities of shocks. Lenders may expose themselves to both unsystematic and systematic risk as a consequence.

(b) Uncertainty

Uncertainty may be increased by new entry. Incumbents may be unable accurately to predict the responses of new entrants to changing conditions, and their existing knowledge of market dynamics will be rendered less useful. Entrants, inexperienced in the market, will face even greater uncertainty. Unaware of the dynamics of supply and demand in the market, they may be prone to herd-like behaviour, all lending to the same type of client. When the market itself is new, all firms will face uncertainty.[10]

More generally, the effects of uncertainty discussed in the theories of financial crisis summarized in Ch. 5 will be heightened when the industrial structure of the market becomes fluid. For example, it was noted how competition may cause firms to make inadequate provision for uncertain events such as financial crisis, because firms making such provisions are undercut by those disregarding such possibilities for reasons of ignorance or competitive advantage. New entrants may be particularly prone to such undercutting. Sufficiently short time horizons may even make firms disregard the better anticipated systematic risks such as the economic cycle in their risk appraisals, thus again, via the process of competition, helping to reduce the prudential standards for the whole market. Hit-and-run entry, as predicted by the theory of contestable markets, must by its nature have a short time horizon.

Again, theories of financial crisis stressing uncertainty noted that profits are earned in competitive markets by innovating where there is uneven information and uncertainty. But instability may follow heightened innovation if it leads balance sheets to deteriorate and/or if intermediaries fail to understand the properties of their innovations. Tendencies for innovation are heightened during periods of intense competition in markets as firms attempt to use innovation to gain a stable clientele, and it was noted above that innovation and product differentiation is a key instrument for strategic competition by both incumbents and entrants. Meanwhile, even if the innovator is able to control risks, his profits may draw in unsophisticated firms at just the time when returns are falling and risks increasing (Corrigan 1990).

In terms of the GH framework, the general case of uncertainty is a reduction in the subjective probability of a disastrous outcome relative to the objective probability, which is provoked by these various mechanisms and may also entail the psychological effects described by GH. But it may go further and lead to an unjustified reduction in subjective expectations of unfavourable project-specific/cyclical outcomes. This may especially be the case for hit-and-run entrants who disregard the long term, for new entrants in general, and for all participants in new financial markets (e.g. for innovative products) and newly deregulated markets, where cyclical patterns have not yet been established. It is relevant to add that the deviation of subjective and objective probabilities helps to explain a potential paradox in the paradigm suggested here, namely that, given

[10] In practice, most of the crises discussed below occurred in existing markets, though new markets often played a role in facilitating entry (e.g. by improving possibilities for funding).

falling sunk costs, entry occurs but, despite an (objective) deterioration in market conditions, no exit until it is too late.

(c) Features of industrial competition

Besides the features outlined above, which are of particular importance in financial markets, there are several more general features of competitive processes that may cause overshooting of competitive equilibrium. Firms earning normal profits on their existing products may all be simultaneously attracted to situations offering potential for growth, but individual firms are unable to predict in advance whether rivals will follow. Such tendencies will be particularly marked if there is no clear ordering of firms in terms of likelihood of success. Once investments are sunk, entry decisions may be difficult to reverse. Moreover, if there are sunk costs, firms may find it optimal to stay in the market for some time even if they make losses, as they will lose sunk costs of reputation etc. if they leave.[11] During this period they may be vulnerable to adverse conditions in financial markets.

Competition for market share as stressed by managerial theories of the firm—an approach frequently adopted both by entrants and incumbents, or in new and developing markets—may lead to cumulative reductions in market prices until it is checked by losses for participants and withdrawal or retrenchment. Such competition may persist if some participants can cross-subsidize[12] their operations from others making excess profits elsewhere (i.e. there is a market failure elsewhere) and they are relatively immune to takeovers, as is the case for banks in most countries. As well as in prices, such competition may be manifested in strategic moves (excessive innovation, r&d, or product differentiation) which, given the mechanisms outlined above, may also have systemic consequences.

Implicitly, competition for market share entails disregard not only for the probability of disaster but also a degree of undercutting of the profit-maximizing response to the project-specific/cyclical distribution. Evalua tion of loan officers over a short period on the basis of current lending performance, as highlighted by GH, is typical of market-share-oriented financial institutions, as in the UK in the late 1980s. The project-specific distribution will not be disregarded in the long run, since market-share competition implies a desire to remain in the market rather than risking bankruptcy; but disregard in the short run may be enough to cause difficulties.

[11] There are analogies with trade-theoretic behaviour of exporters attempting to break into a market (see Dixit 1987).

[12] i.e. provide funding to a loss-making operation at terms cheaper than those attainable in the capital market.

(d) Regulatory features

An appropriate response to excessive competition in financial markets includes more stringent prudential regulation, as discussed in Ch. 5 and in the conclusion to this chapter. Thus even maintenance of a pre-existing regulatory regime may be insufficient to counteract it. In addition, inadequacies in regulation may heighten tendencies to excessive risk-taking. For example, if deposit insurance covers all deposits, and premiums do not adequately reflect the relative risks of different types of institution, it may promote undercapitalization and risk-taking by intermediaries, even if they are profit maximizing rather than seeking market share.

Overshooting may also be caused by excessive provision of lender-of-last-resort facilities. If it is known that all firms getting into difficulties will be saved, competitors (in particular, new entrants) will have incentives to take excessive risks, ignoring the externalities imposed on other intermediaries (who may help finance the lender of last resort) and on the lender of last resort itself. Moreover, lenders in the interbank market may not have the correct incentives to discriminate between banks (by price or quantity rationing) and discourage risk takers.[13]

Third, innovations that may lead on to financial instability may themselves be responses to regulations such as credit or interest-rate ceilings. Eisenbeis (1986) suggests CDs and off-balance-sheet activities should be seen in this light—although their use by banks not subject to such regulation (e.g. in the UK), and the fact that their use has no general association with instability, runs counter to his thesis.

Fourth, regulators may seek to prevent 'non-systemic' failures or retard exit of institutions in their sector, partly to protect their own reputations, thus leaving firms with low equity to pursue high-risk strategies (Kane 1991). It may also be inappropriate and destabilizing to retain regulatory restraints on incumbent firms when new entrants are not subject to them, and hence the end result of competition is to leave the incumbents inviable.

In the regulation case, excessive competition can arise *despite* knowledge by lenders of the true probabilities of shocks in the project-specific/cyclical case and even the distribution of disastrous outcomes. Low capitalization relative to risk is the consequence. Implicitly, moral hazard due to regulation leads lenders to seek risk in the same way as for uncapitalized borrowers in the case of private-sector lending (Ch. 1), where need to curtail risk gives rise to incentives for quantity rationing by lenders.

[13] Though this is partly also an information problem.

(e) Value of bank franchises

Extending this analysis, it has been shown by Keeley (1990) that deregulation may lead directly to incentives for risk-taking by financial institutions. The mechanism follows the logic of corporate finance theory. In a regulated market, where banks have a degree of market power in making loans, the bank's charter (franchise, licence) is a capital asset (since it allows the bank to make excess profits). Deregulation, which facilitates new entry, or which liberalizes rate-setting on bank liabilities, reduces the value of the charter, especially for banks in protected local markets that rely on non-price competition to attract funds. Technological change facilitating disintermediation via securities markets will have similar effects. Abstracting from local markets, such effects may also impinge more heavily on the value of charters when banking systems have an atomistic market structure (e.g. the USA) than when they are oligopolies (Europe), and for foreign than for domestic banks.

When charters are valuable, banks have incentives not to risk failure by reducing capital or increasing asset risk, if (as seems likely) transfer of charters is costly or impossible (i.e. there are high bankruptcy costs). However, to the extent that lender-of-last-resort or mispriced deposit-insurance protection is present, there is a partial offset to this, stimulating risk-taking till the marginal value of the put option associated with the safety net equals the marginal loss from losing the charter. Conversely, when charters have low value there are incentives to take risks *independent* of the moral hazard created by the safety net. In other words, the argument as regards levels of risk-taking is not dependent on the safety net, but the latter makes overshooting more likely.

The concept of the franchise may be broadened to include the various sunk costs built up by incumbents in financial markets identified above, notably relationships, reputation, and expertise. The devaluation of these (unsaleable) assets can lead to excessive risk-taking similar to devaluation of franchise. In terms of the framework, the incentives identified here can lead to excessive competition despite knowledge of the project-specific/cyclical shocks.

(f) Previous market situations

It is appropriate to consider at this point whether a distinction should be made between different types of competition and market structure prior to reduction of entry barriers, and the way in which entry barriers are removed. Are firms that were previously uncompetitive (e.g. in domestic markets) more prone to excessive competition than those in competitive markets (e.g. the euromarkets)? Is deregulation more likely to provoke risk-taking than other types of easing (technological progress, innovation, new markets)? These are partly empirical questions, addressed in Sect. 5 below, but some considerations can be suggested.

On the one hand, firms used to operating in uncompetitive markets may be more cautious in entering new markets than more competitive rivals. On the other hand, they are also likely to be X-inefficient and may thus find it hard to adapt to sudden changes in competitive conditions. They may be of inefficient size, having previously been protected; this means failures or consolidation are likely. They may have poorly developed credit monitoring.[14] The process may entail incentives to risk-taking as franchises are devalued. Furthermore, as regards deregulation, in the short term, uncertainty is likely to be greatest in the case of deregulation of a previously uncompetitive market, because the dynamics of supply and demand in a competitive situation are totally unknown. In contrast, a decline in barriers to entry in an established competitive market at least occurs in the context of known competitive behaviour. 'Disaster myopia' may occur in each case, but for deregulation there may also be ignorance of the cyclical behaviour of loan losses. In the medium term, given the changes likely to arise from new entry itself as outlined above, it may be wrong to distinguish these cases.

(g) Summary

Sections 3 and 4 have sought to develop a framework for analysing the development of financial instability based on an industrial-organization approach to the process of competition between financial intermediaries. Broadly, it suggests that declining sunk costs of entry may lead to increased competition, which due to various imperfections and market failures may become excessive in relation to long-run competitive equilibrium and lead on to financial instability.

While being distinct in its primary focus on structural aspects, the framework also seeks to encompass the mechanisms and predictions of existing theories. Thus *uncertainty*, imperfect information, features of regulation, as well as more general aspects of the competitive process, are among the mechanisms that help lead competition to become excessive after declines in entry barriers. Such competition is likely to lead to reductions in *credit rationing*, entailing increased *debt growth*, as well as reduced capitalization, which leaves the financial system vulnerable to shocks such as abrupt *monetary tightening*, which increase *agency costs* of lending. These may provoke sharp increases in *credit rationing* and collapses in liquidity in *dealer markets*.

[14] See Bank of Japan 1991*b*.

(5) Financial Instability: A Re-examination

In this section the evidence of the various recent periods of financial instability discussed in Ch. 6 is briefly reappraised to judge the realism of the mechanisms identified in Sects. 3 and 4. To avoid excessive repetition, the accounts are abbreviated—the reader is referred back to Ch. 6 for a complete assessment. We note that there are many other recent examples of similar episodes, in countries such as Norway, Australia, New Zealand, Canada, and Spain. Several of these are outlined in Ch. 8.

(a) The secondary-banking crisis

A number of industrial features can be discerned in accounts of the UK secondary banking crisis (see Reid 1982). For example, the sunk costs of entry to banking markets were diminished by the development of wholesale money markets, which reduced the need for banks to develop a retail deposit base and an expensive branch network. Moreover, the deregulations of 1958 (liberalization of fund raising) and 1971 (Competition and Credit Control) eased access of the secondary banks to wholesale funds *per se* and funds from UK clearing banks, respectively. These reductions in entry barriers precipitated the development of secondary banks, while granting of licences was also at the time a relatively unregulated process. The scale of new entry can be judged from the fact that 87 new firms obtained banking licences in 1967–70 and a further 46 in 1970–3.

The development of secondary banks permitted increased and concentrated lending to property and financial companies, which had previously either not existed, or whose demand for funds had been credit rationed for reasons of risk and regulation (direct controls on bank credit). There was thus evidence of 'herding' to a new group of borrowers where, due to lack of relationships, information links, etc., entry barriers were low. However, once the market developed, and following the 1971 deregulation, clearing banks themselves also began to lend to property companies, as part of the more general expansion of their balance sheets. (This could also be seen as a form of strategic competition: pricing low to compete with new entrants.) Leverage of borrowers increased sharply; many loans were backed by assets such as equities and property which proved in retrospect to have unsustainable market values. Following the monetary tightening and general economic crisis of 1973–4 such collateral devalued rapidly.

The collapse of the secondary banks was at the centre of the crisis. They had, arguably, lent on inadequate information regarding systematic risk, i.e. the vulnerability of their loans in the case of a normal cyclical downturn (though it could be argued that the oil crisis was an unprecedented occurrence), as well as taking on unsystematic risk by concentrating their risks, not building adequate capital, and relying on what proved to be unstable sources of funding in the wholesale markets.[15] As new entrants to the deposit market with no market power, they would also lay little value on depreciation of their banking franchises.

(b) Herstatt

This 1974 crisis can be viewed on two levels: the interbank market which funded the banks concerned and the forex market in which the initial losses were made. The rapid development of the international interbank market entailed rapid new entry to the market, thus compressing spreads,[16] while the relative novelty of the market itself and lack of experience by lenders probably led to inadequate appraisal of risks. Certainly, the reaction of lending banks in the interbank market to the crisis—where information was imperfect to discriminate sharply between risk classes, and where information was more readily available to limit the amounts or maturities of loans to a particular bank to their net worth or other quantitative guide-lines—were policies that prudent lenders should have carried out in any case. Evidently, desire to increase assets and market share had driven spreads too low and led lenders to disregard the potential for instability.

In the forex market, the switch to floating exchange rates increased opportunities for profit (as non-financial firms sought forward cover) thus attracting new entrants and leading existing firms to increase their exposures. Given technology and the availability of interbank wholesale funds, sunk costs of entry were evidently low, and competition for business was fierce. Extremely risky practices,[17] such as banks covering forward transactions by spot transactions plus eurocurrency borrowing, were common. On the one hand, it appears that many banks failed to understand the dynamics of the forex market: perhaps understandably, given the long history of fixed rates. On the other hand, heightened competition was a factor driving them to make little allowance for risk. The crisis was precipitated by failure of the Herstatt bank in Germany, due to foreign-exchange losses, following unexpected depreciation of

[15] See Ch. 6, Sect. 1.

[16] See e.g. Brimmer and Dahl (1975), who discussed the expansion of US banks' overseas branch networks after introduction of the Voluntary Foreign Credit Restraint Programme (1965–74), which restricted foreign lending from head offices in the United States. Claims on foreign banks by US overseas branches rose from $6.1 bn in 1969 (20% of assets) to $61.1 bn in 1974 (40% of assets). The authors also noted 'the competition to place funds in the interbank market led to a significant narrowing in lending margins, and this had a significant adverse impact on the profitability of the foreign branches'.

[17] Which could also be seen as strategic innovations.

some currencies and a tightening of US monetary policy. That the problem was more widespread is shown by the fact that many other banks also suffered losses.

(c) The debt crisis

The growth of lending to ldcs in the 1970s again showed many of the features outlined above. The development of the syndicated credit reduced the sunk costs that banks needed to incur in order to enter the international markets, as a single deal could involve many banks with only one set of documentation, credit appraisal, etc. Small banks could rely on credit appraisal and monitoring made by larger banks having relationships with borrowers. Meanwhile, the deposits of oil exporters after 1973 provided a ready source of funds and the deficits of oil importers led to sharp increases in the demand for external finance.

All these features encouraged rapid new entry to the market, after it had recovered from the disruption of 1974–5 associated with the Herstatt crisis. An account of the development of indebtedness (Johnston 1983) illustrates the relaxation of standards of risk appraisal which followed:

> Spreads for prime borrowers began to decline in 1976 while loan size increased; lower spreads and longer maturities for other borrowers followed in 1977 and 1978. Many borrowers began to tap the market regularly, and a wider range of borrowers entered the market, including ldcs. Some borrowers renegotiated or refinanced loans taken out under tighter conditions, despite increasing ratios of debt to exports.

A number of accounts note the industrial-organization features that underlay these patterns. Bond and Briault (1983*b*) suggest that during the 1970s banks competed aggressively for deposits and loans, stimulated by factors such as an increasing focus on balance-sheet growth rather than merely profitability; a shift from asset to liability management; the ability to cross-subsidize international business from profits made in oligopolistic domestic markets; misjudgement of the risks, notably the potential correlation of sovereign risks in a recession, the lack of conditionality to sovereign debtors, and the potential for tightening of US monetary policy. One reason risks may have been misjudged was that participants in syndicates were often new entrants lacking adequate information, who were willing to leave risk appraisal to the lead bank, while the latter, having a small share of the risk and gaining fee income from the deal, had incentives to underplay the risk. Moreover, the growing intensity of competition itself tended to reduce spreads (suggesting sunk costs were low). Finally, banks were misled by the short maturities of their loans into believing that they could always reduce or eliminate their exposures at the next rollover date (an 'illusion of liquidity'). This was dependent on other banks filling the gap, which in 1982 they proved unwilling to do, in the wake of the worsening of market conditions culminating in the Mexican default.

(d) The crisis in the floating-rate note (FRN) market

The invention of the floating-rate note long predates the bull market and crisis that occurred in 1986, but a major spur to development of the market was given by the debt crisis, which led to sharp declines in syndicated credits, necessitating development of markets in substitute instruments (as well as for banks themselves to rebuild their capital by issuance of subordinated debt). Increased demand led to new entry of investment banks as intermediaries; competition to offer finer terms to borrowers led to downward pressure on yields, which fell below Libor in 1986. This tended to exclude banks as investors, since their interest in FRNs was premised on obtaining Libor (at least over the medium term) although they held 80–90 per cent of extant bonds. This pattern suggests intermediaries lacked information on the investor base or otherwise failed to understand the underlying behaviour of the market.

Lead managers sought to compensate, by innovation (as well as employing innovation as a means of strategic competition between themselves), which relied on risky interest-rate plays, while heavy trading by investors in an attempt to maintain profits further compressed spreads. Intermediaries (and investors) assumed risks were limited by the coupon-reset mechanism and built up large positions, failing to note that profits and liquidity were largely a function of bull market conditions. The market entered a crisis at the end of 1986, with falling prices, a collapse of liquidity and a complete halt to new issues following the rumours of new capital adequacy guide-lines (deducting holdings of bank FRNs from bank capital), excess supply of bonds, re-evaluation by investors of the equity characteristics of perpetual FRNs, and perceived illiquidity of innovative products. (All of these could be seen as causing heightened information asymmetry.)

(e) The equity-market crash

The crash itself may be seen largely as a speculative bubble in asset markets, and as such it was partly divorced from the type of changes in industrial structure stressed above, (though it is notable that in the USA it was preceded by strategic innovations such as portfolio insurance, which were promoted heavily by investment banks aiming to attract institutional investors such as pension funds to their fund management services, and may have given investors 'illusions of liquidity'). However, systemic risks associated with the crash arose from debt claims, and events in these markets did have an industrial angle. We assess first underwriting exposures, and then leveraged situations.

One of the principal concerns of the markets at the time of the crash was associated with underwriting exposures, notably following the sale of part of British Petroleum by the UK government. US and Canadian investment banks, seeking market entry, undertook 'bought deal' type underwriting, despite the considerable length of time over which the risk would be held, namely one week compared with less than a day for normal deals, and their rather low capitalization in relation to such risks. Such firms appeared ready to sustain considerable risk to enter the market and gain the sunk cost of a reputation for successful underwriting (it should be noted that sub-underwriting is not possible in the USA). As a result of their exposures to rapidly devaluing unsold equity, commercial banks threatened to cut credit lines to the securities houses concerned. The situation was aggravated by heavy requirements for credit by securities houses more generally, on behalf of customers to meet margin calls. Only the intervention of the Fed (the announcement that liquidity would be provided) and the UK announcement of a support price for BP helped to calm the markets.

A second feature of debt markets prior to the crash was the rapid build-up of debt by the corporate sectors of a number of countries (see Ch. 2). Associated developments included the development of the junk-bond market (which reduced the incidence of equilibrium quantity rationing in banking markets), wider access to eurobond markets by firms of low credit quality, and innovative debt-financing methods such as the leveraged buyout, all of which were introduced as part of a process of strategic competition and new entry by investment banks, and to a lesser extent commercial banks. These changed market conditions led to further increases in competition among suppliers of funds, and to what proved in some cases to be inadequate risk appraisal.

The main casualties of the crash in terms of leveraged firms were those whose loans were backed by (overvalued) equity claims, typically following acquisitions undertaken during the speculative period. Some found themselves quantity rationed in credit markets and a few had to default. But generally the price of debt increased and many borrowers were driven to more expensive markets (bank lending rather than bonds).

(f) The US thrifts crises

The initial crisis for thrifts (1980–2) was caused largely by the effects of changes in US monetary policy and adverse economic conditions on a heavily regulated industry, where risks were heavily concentrated on the intermediaries (funding fixed-rate loans with floating-rate deposits).

However, an important industrial feature was the growth of money-market mutual funds, whose entry to the deposit market was facilitated by declines in sunk costs resulting from technology, as well as deregulation and growth of money markets. Because their rates were not subject to ceilings, these provided important competition for the thrifts when monetary tightening drove up interest rates, effectively disintermediating them from deposit markets. As a result of thrifts' initial problems, deposit rates were deregulated, as were lending powers (thrifts were empowered to offer adjustable-rate mortgages and non-housing loans). Capital standards were relaxed.[18] Lower interest rates also afforded some relief.

A further, more serious, crisis followed, beginning in 1985–6. Although the collapse of primary product price was a key factor in this,[19] thrifts evidently also lacked the expertise and information required to lend prudently outside their traditional fields (even if one excludes those thrifts which deliberately sought risky loans as a gamble, prompted by the moral hazard offered by deposit insurance). In particular, they financed the high volume of what proved to be speculative real-estate investment, which both proved unprofitable itself and drove down the prices of existing real estate, often below the value of mortgage debt. They also invested heavily in junk bonds. Again, this is an example of new and undercapitalized entrants to markets (when barriers to entry caused by regulation are removed) acting in a herd-like manner, concentrating risk, demanding inadequate risk premiums, and operating price rationing of credit when quantity rationing might have been more appropriate. It also reflects the response to excessive safety-net protection, and the devaluation of franchises given increased competition.

(g) Summary

The industrial features of the crises discussed above, and numerical evidence on entry are summarized in the tables. They show that most of the industrial features highlighted here were present in each case, and new entry was rapid. Three caveats are in order. First, we note that, depending on the nature of the cost function, some entry without systemic implications can be expected to arise normally with economic growth. A judgement must be made whether actual entry exceeds this level; however, a reasonable benchmark may be entry in relation to longer term patterns of entry, which in all sectors has been fairly slow. Second, there will come a point when a new intermediary is sufficiently

[18] The chief federal regulator (the FHLBB) had jurisdiction over the FSLIC insurance fund, which was inadequately financed. The FHLBB also had a close promotional relationship with the thrift industry. Capital forbearance, rather than thrift closures (which would have caused FSLIC bankruptcy) was the resulting policy.

[19] Regionally concentrated balance sheets (due to geographic restrictions on expansion) made institutions vulnerable to such changes.

Table 7.1. Industrial aspects of financial instability

	Secondary banks	Herstatt	Ldc debt	FRNs	Crash	Thrifts
Reduction in entry barriers due to:						
deregulation	Yes	—	—	—	—	Yes
innovation	—	—	Yes	Yes	Yes	Yes
new markets	Yes	Yes	—	—	—	—
technology	—	Yes	—	—	Yes	Yes
developments in existing markets	—	—	Yes	Yes	—	Yes
New entry of firms	Yes	Yes	Yes	Yes	Yes	Yes
Entry of new market by existing firms	Yes	—	—	—	—	Yes
Lower prices in credit markets (declining risk premiums)	Yes	Yes	Yes	Yes	Yes	Yes
Low or declining capitalization	Yes	Yes	Yes	—	Yes	Yes
Higher quantities in credit markets (increasing indebtedness of borrowers)	Yes	Yes	Yes	Yes	Yes	Yes
Exploitation of safety-net protection	—	—	—	—	—	Yes
Low value of banking franchises	Yes	—	—	—	—	Yes

established that some of the imperfections (information and uncertainty) specific to new entry may cease to operate. In our judgement this requires experience of a full cycle, i.e. longer than the period shown. Third, entry is of course not the only feature highlighted in this chapter as indicating increased competition. In contestable markets, prices may fall without entry occurring; strategic competition may be manifested in heightened innovation, etc., as well as predatory pricing. There may also be 'managerial' competition for market share by existing firms.

Table 7.2. Indicators of market entry prior to instability

	Years	t−5	t−4	t−3	t−2	t−1	t
Secondary banking[a]	1973	+29	+29	+12	+12	+11	+11
Herstatt[b]	1974	+27	+26	+12	+17	+17	+ 4
Debt crisis[c]	1982	+ 7	+15	− 7	+ 6	+57	−23
FRN[d]	1986	+15	−10	− 3	+25	+ 1	− 9
Crash (loans)[e]	1987	−25	−72	−16	−28	+ 5	+45
Crash (bonds)[f]	1987	+13	0	− 5	+19	+15	− 6
Thrifts	1986[g]		(*)				

a New authorizations of banks (interpolated).
b Net increase in number of US banks with overseas branches (source: Brimmer and Dahl 1975)—data for other countries not available.
c Net increase in book runners in syndicated credits to ldcs.
d Net increase in lead managers in FRN market.
e Net increase in book runners in syndicated credits market.
f Net increase in lead managers in eurobond market.
g In this case there was new entry to non-traditional markets (adjustable-rate mortgages and non-housing loans) by the whole thrifts sector due to deregulation, which occurred at t−4(*).

(6) New Entry without Instability

It is relevant also to consider the features of periods of deregulation and new entry that occurred without provoking instability among financial institutions and markets, to see what distinguishes them. The *mortgage market in the United Kingdom* was traditionally the preserve of the building societies, banks often having been constrained from expansion into this market by direct controls on lending. However, the abolition of such controls in 1979–80, together with the loss of lending opportunities elsewhere (due to the debt crisis and domestic economic downturn) led to rapid entry by the banks. Once permitted to enter by deregulation, banks found it easy to vary their scale of involvement in mortgages via transfer of staff (i.e. they could easily exit from the market as well as enter, implying low sunk costs and contestability). Given new technology and innovations of credit scoring and securitization, new centralized mortgage lenders (without branch networks) were also able to gain access to the market.[20] New entry led to increased gearing of mortgage borrowers and (given increasing house prices) extremely rapid growth in mortgage debt outstanding (Ch. 3).

Although there was new entry and growing debt, and (as noted in Chs. 3 and 4) this sector has been the locus of considerable financial fragility for the personal sector, several features of this market may have helped prevent generalized instability for financial institutions. First, both existing firms and new entrants were adequately capitalized (as well as being subject to firm supervisory oversight), thus affording a protection against loan losses and reducing incentives to make excessively risky loans. Insurance companies in many cases stood ready to guarantee the 'top slice' of loans. Second, mortgage interest rates remained higher than wholesale costs of funds to a greater extent than they had in the 1970s when credit was rationed (since credit had previously been 'disequilibrium'[21] quantity rationed, new entrants did not need to offer significantly lower rates to gain business). Risk premiums were thus maintained. Mortgage loans are in any case variable rate, in common with deposits, so there is no mismatch, unlike the thrifts, though credit risk remains. Third, supply constraints on housing helped prevent rapid falls in house prices even when policy was tightened, although some falls have occurred, as noted in Ch. 4. Fourth, apart from the deregulation of building-society lending in 1986, neither group of institutions was shifting radically into new areas of business in which they might be unaware of the dynamics. Finally, banks often already had relationships with customers to whom they were making mortgage loans. Such failures as have occurred have tended to be new institutions lacking experience and relationships or small institutions seeking rapid growth. Most of these features contrast with the US thrifts crisis.

Big Bang in the City of London entailed the entry of international banks and securities houses to the UK stock exchange, which together with the abolition of separation of agency and market making led to creation of a large number of integrated securities operations. There was evidently excessive entry in relation to potential market capacity, because most firms were soon making losses, while the relative success of previous incumbents suggests a role for sunk costs related to intertemporal advantages and strategic competition.[22] However, despite the crash and the initial reduction in the stock of gilts, firms up to 1992 either remained in the markets or withdrew quietly without any disruptive bankruptcy or systemic risk.

A number of features may help explain this situation. First, the firms have always been adequately capitalized and firmly supervised. Many are

[20] Callen and Lomax 1990.

[21] See Ch. 1.

[22] The case is similar to that of eurobond issue discussed in the Appendix.

subsidiaries of international firms with profitable (oligopolistic) business elsewhere. Most firms entered by acquisition of existing firms and hence did not suffer from poor information on entry. Many had experience of dealership elsewhere, such as US and Japanese investment banks, or firms active in the secondary eurobond market.

Finally, and perhaps more tentatively, outturns suggest that for experienced and diversified firms, risks in secondary-market trading may be better controlled than those in primary issuance or bank lending (which helped provoke most of the crises discussed above).[23] This could be conceptualized in terms of position risk (where a 'position' is a holding of financial instruments, whether long (positive) or short (negative)). In primary debt markets (underwriting) and in banking (loans) such exposures are common, and (in the case of banks) long term, although diversification, hedging, and risk pricing should offer protection. In contrast, market makers tend to unwind positions as rapidly as possible; and they tend to hold balanced long and short positions, which removes undiversifiable risk. While losses are frequently made, they can often be recouped rapidly (e.g. after the crash). Particularly in a market where entry is restricted and hence there are some monopoly returns, there may also be longer term cross-subsidization of 'good times' and 'bad times'.

Not that experience shows that secondary dealing is riskless; cases of losses especially by new and inexperienced entrants are common, usually due to their ignoring position risk. Cases of UK and Japanese corporate treasurers indulging in dealership (Tateho Chemicals, Allied Lyons) are notorious. Herstatt is another example. It can be suggested that, with the risk of runs and contagion, acceptance of such position risk can pose a particular danger for commercial banks (which are increasingly active dealers in markets such as securities, forex, swaps, futures, options, and forward-rate agreements).

The key features distinguishing the deregulation of UK mortgages and Big Bang thus appear to be adequate capitalization, firm supervision, and reasonable levels of information for entrants. However, it cannot be ruled out that absence of instability may also result from a fortuitous absence to date of sufficiently severe shocks in these markets (the crash notwithstanding).

Conclusions

This analysis offers the following conclusions, which complement those of Ch. 6:

[23] In the Glosten and Milgrom (1985) paradigm noted in Ch. 5, the market collapses because liquidity traders and market makers withdraw, not because the latter have gone bankrupt.

- Many of the factors which are held in theory to underlie the development of systemic risk can be analysed in the context of theories of industrial organization, while industrial organization can itself contribute to further understanding of the genesis of instability.
- Examination of situations of instability reveals that a number of the factors highlighted were both present and helped to explain aspects of its development such as the growth of debt and declining risk premiums.
- Notably, one can trace reductions in entry barriers, due to such factors as deregulation, innovation, new markets, technological advance, and developments in existing markets, followed by actual new entry of firms, entry of new markets by existing firms, competition for market share, predatory pricing, and other competitive responses by incumbents to the threat of entry.
- Consequences are as predicted by the theory as outlined, namely declining risk premiums, increasing indebtedness, and (generally) low or declining capitalization.
- The transmission mechanism between entry and instability includes features such as lower levels of information, heightened uncertainty over market responses, and herd-like behaviour among lenders, as well as the more general consequences of heightened competition in terms of prices and quantities.
- Even when instability has not resulted, it is suggested that the industrial approach illuminates some supply-side reasons for development of fragility in the non-financial sectors.

Given the results, it is relevant, first, to consider how excessive competition can be prevented—or its effects minimized—while retaining the benefits of efficient markets. Obviously, risk can be minimized by extremely strict structural regulation, such as market segmentation, and direct controls on prices and quantities of credit, but this may cause inefficiency which more than offsets gains in terms of risk reduction.

The main conclusions for regulation are largely similar to those in Chs. 5 and 6, namely that some form of 'regulatory' insurance such as the lender of last resort and deposit insurance remains vital to prevent systemic risk, but to prevent associated moral hazard it is necessary to enforce prudential regulations such as capital adequacy requirements together with direct limits on risk exposures of those involved, e.g. limits on large exposures or concentration of risk on particular borrowers. There is an important additional element, namely that closer monitoring of banks is needed following structural change, to the extent that it increases incentives to take risks. Regulatory structures developed during periods when competition was restrained may be quite inadequate.

In addition, some form of learning mechanism, so that previous mistakes are not repeated, would be useful both to supervisors and participants. As for other mechanisms for controlling and monitoring risk, credit-rating agencies may have an important role to play complementary to the regulatory authorities in assessing financial fragility. Finally, a central risk office may help overcome inadequate information on lending to individual customers—if all lenders co-operate. As noted in Ch. 1, these are more common in the less competitive bank-dominated countries than Anglo-Saxon financial systems.

As well as buttressing various approaches to regulation, the results may also be of direct use to regulators and to market participants. Although the regulatory mechanisms noted above should in principle be effective against 'excessive' competition, even if it were not detectable ex-ante, some problems may arise. First, late detection of such a situation may require regulation to impose higher costs than early detection; second, the implications of changing prices and quantities may on occasion be ambiguous; and third, there may be a tendency ('disaster myopia') whereby perceptions, even of regulators, may be distorted by a period of calm financial conditions (or competition itself) so that they accept prevailing judgements of risk and thus fail to detect excessive competition. In effect, regulators are also subject to a deviation between subjective and objective probabilities of crisis. To avoid the problem of late detection, a leading indicator should be useful, while to interpret changing market conditions, and to help prevent disaster myopia, even an additional coincident indicator (in addition to prices and quantities of credit themselves) should be of assistance.

It is suggested that a sharp focus on the industrial dynamics of competition in financial markets can provide such indicators, supplementing the microeconomic and macroeconomic indicators highlighted in the conclusion to Ch. 6. Note that these are system properties that may help predict problems in (some) individual institutions. Their use implies a greater focus on system properties than may occur at present. First, changes in sunk costs of entry must occur in advance of associated entry, while even the latter is likely to take time before it impacts on prices and quantities of credit. These suggest that such changes have leading indicator properties and will signal that changes in capitalization etc. should be monitored particularly rigorously.[24] Second, even if not detected in advance, changes in sunk costs of entry and associated new entry or other adjustments may help regulators to interpret changes in prices and quantities such as rapid growth of lending and declining spreads (e.g. the extent to which they are likely to be associated with deteriorating information, heightened uncertainty, and associated overshooting of competitive equilibrium, rather than being an orderly

[24] Of course, the indicator has qualitative and not quantitative properties. The time lag between changes in entry conditions and crisis in the examples given above is highly variable.

removal of oligopoly rents). Third, by offering an extra indicator, focus on industrial dynamics may help minimize disaster myopia. Finally it should be noted that in each case it is important for regulators to understand the market structure and type of competition (and hence sunk costs, economies of scale, and associated technology) in each of the markets for which they are responsible, as this will influence the way in which the various transmission mechanisms and excessive competition *per se* will manifest themselves.

Going beyond use of traditional regulatory instruments, a number of analysts (Kane 1991; Wojnilower 1991) suggest the authorities should seek to monitor excess capacity in financial markets and try to remove it, before it leads on to excessive risk-taking by firms no longer able to operate profitably.[25] Changes in entry conditions give advance warning that excess capacity may be about to arise, before the adverse consequences supervene.

Furthermore, due to the close relationship highlighted between structural change and fragility in the non-financial sector, the results may also be of assistance to macroeconomic policymakers. For example, observation of increased credit growth, together with heightened structural change, may indicate that credit is being directed to increasingly vulnerable borrowers, rather than being part of the normal process of economic growth, and that this may cause difficulties in the next downturn.

Use of the results need not be confined to ongoing regulation and macro policy. The design of policies of deregulation, as well as of responses to new developments, may be aided by consideration of market dynamics. For example, will opening up some currently uncompetitive EC markets as the Single Market develops—when Europe will witness both cross-border and functional deregulation—lead to fragility and instability? Monitoring of entry and other structural adjustments to change may help prediction. Second, how should Eastern European countries liberalize? Sudden elimination of entry barriers may not be the most appropriate solution, unless strong safeguards against systemic risk are in place.

Appendix: The Industrial Economics of the Primary Eurobond Market

Davis (1988*b*; 1992*d*) assessed whether theories of industrial organization offered insights into the *behaviour of the primary eurobond market* in the 1980s. It is useful to recapitulate some of these conclusions in the context

[25] Measurement of such excess capacity is of course likely to be a problem.

of this chapter, to enable the reader to assess in more detail the contribution industrial economics can make to analysis of financial-market behaviour. More generally, a number of the features highlighted generalize to the behaviour of international syndicated bank lending and institutions in 'Anglo-Saxon' financial systems—but not to those of Germany and Japan (see Ch. 1, Sect. 5).

Davis concluded that, on the face of it, the market appears to have many of the features of a contestable market. On the side of contestability, capital costs, in terms of dealing rooms, finance for underwriting, expertise, etc., may be high, but those specific to eurobonds are rather low, because they can be adapted from other sectors such as corporate bonds. There are a wide variety of well-capitalized firms and investment banks ready to contemplate entry. Entry can be rapid, as can withdrawal. It is thus clear that contestable market features help to explain some of the behaviour of firms in the eurobond market, i.e. that it is highly competitive, especially within the individual currency sectors, despite the market structure.

It is, however, harder to explain purely in the context of the theory of contestable markets why some firms' eurobond operations have continued to be successful while others have been unable to establish themselves, why there has been no significant decline in market concentration over time despite continual new entry, and why profitability has declined so steeply. Certain features of eurobond market structure, interpreted in the light of other aspects of the new industrial economics, may help to explain these tendencies. There may be significant entry barriers to the upper echelons of the industry, resulting from intertemporal dependencies on the demand and cost side and from strategic competition. Dealing first with intertemporal dependencies, the advantages of established firms may include accumulated expertise, reputation, and relationships. Offered the same price for an issue, borrowers will choose an existing firm, given their reputation for successful launches, to avoid all the disadvantages in terms of future borrowing costs should an issue fail. Similarly, investors tend not to deal with a new house if they are doubtful about its tenacity—and skilled market staff will not join a firm even for high salaries if they are unsure whether it will remain in the market.

Recent experience suggests that these advantages of existing firms can only be offset if there is a large savings surplus in the home country, where entrants have strong relationships with investors, where there is a desire and ability to invest in euromarket instruments and/or a lower cost of capital. For much of the 1980s, this was the case for Japanese firms (Aliber (1984) suggested this factor also enabled Japanese banks to undercut US banks in the eurocurrency markets). These enable such entrants to charge a lower price than incumbents at the same profit margins. Implicitly, there are two types of new entry, one with a secure customer base wishing to increase its portfolio share of eurobonds, and one assuming 'speculatively' that business can be taken from other houses or that a suitable share of any incremental business can be obtained. This would explain the pre-eminence of various investment banks over the years and the inability of many new entrants to gain profitability. Implicitly, exit costs exceeded costs of entry, largely due to the sunk costs of contacts, reputation, and privileged access to information on market movements (on the demand side) and expertise (on the cost side) built up over time.

In addition, incumbent firms have actively carried out *strategic moves*. They have, in effect, invested in excess capacity, though whether this was deliberate or accidental is harder to judge. Predatory pricing has been widely used by both incumbents and entrants to the eurobond markets. Development of specialized expertise, for example in swaps, is a further form of strategic investment. Established firms tended to scoop up the talent in the market which is still in second-tier houses—without which they found it difficult to survive. The introduction of 'bought deals' by certain houses led to a significant increase in capital requirements.

It may be suggested that competition in provision of market analysis and in research and development was also aimed at increasing market share and discouraging entry. Strong and timely market analysis may enable a firm to retain its investor base. Such analysis by some firms obliged others to gather similar information to protect themselves, or attempt to enter the market. Such duplication is arguably a deadweight cost to society. Meanwhile, the invention of new financial instruments may enable an institution both to make initial gains by charging high fees and, by virtue of its developing expertise, to make long-term excess profits. Even if high prices are not charged, an innovation may give an investment bank an advantage in gaining mandates, which may enable losses to be converted into 'normal' profits. Again, the private benefits to the successful innovator may exceed social benefits even if the latter are positive, because many innovations, particularly on the product development as opposed to the process/new technology side, do not offer strong benefits to investors aside from existing instruments. In some cases they may worsen the situation for market participants by reducing liquidity. The large potential private benefits to innovation lead to a high and perhaps excessive level of such innovation—including duplication of effort to the same end, at considerable resource cost.

The decline in profitability can also be explained by other factors relating to the *nature of trade* in the eurobond market between borrowers and intermediaries. Which side bears the larger sunk costs? Borrowers may find it in their interest not to break a relationship with an investment bank, as the latter may stabilize the bond price and maintain an orderly aftermarket, ensuring a good reception of future issues. If it seeks too low a spread, its issue may fail, thus damaging its chances of making further issues. On the other hand, rules of the AIBD require firms to make markets, and other firms may be ready to make markets in the relevant issue. Borrowers are increasingly sophisticated and thus have less need of information that the intermediary can offer, particularly as lead manager performance can be monitored in the grey market—i.e. information asymmetries are becoming less. Nor do they require a particular investment bank with whom they need to maintain a relationship. Indeed, borrowers having a high reputation among investors are increasingly ready to deal with several firms rather than merely a 'house' bank. The investment bank wishes to maintain relationships in order to ensure future business, to preserve its reputation, and to maintain the value of any information it has gathered about the firm in question—which is obviously unsaleable. Once these factors are taken into account, together with the tendencies to rapid new entry, intense competition, and the high elasticity of demand for eurobonds, it is evident that the balance of advantage is increasingly to the borrower. The investment bank is unlikely to be able to squeeze monopoly rent from a relationship. Similarly, the investor base of the market has tended to change from private account holders to institutional investors. They have considerable countervailing power against intermediaries, as placing power is an essential part of dealers' strength to win mandates and again institutional investors' sophistication entails symmetric information. It is more in the investment banks' interest to maintain relationships.

8

Ten Further Financial Crises

Given the focus of the analyses in Chs. 6 and 7 on six major periods on instability since 1970, it is useful to outline the events of other selected periods of crisis.[1] Such an approach serves several purposes; first, it indicates the generality or otherwise of the mechanisms outlined in a wider range of financial markets (common features of the events are summarized in Table 8.1); second, it may offer additional insights into the links between fragility and systemic risk; third, by offering a wider sample, it facilitates a broader analysis of the different types of crisis. Given the degree to which some of these events have been studied, the accounts are inevitably partial; further details can be obtained from the references.

(1) Overend Gurney (1866)—UK

The Overend Gurney crisis[2] is generally agreed to be the last major financial crisis in the UK. The company concerned was a large bank specializing in discounting short-term bills on behalf of commercial bankers, founded in the early nineteenth century from the amalgamation of two banks that had been active since the eighteenth century. Although in the early nineteenth century the company had been conservative in its operations, new management desiring rapid growth led to the firm becoming less circumspect in lending mid-century. From 1858 the bank started lending on bills of low credit quality and on unsound collateral. A more general shift of 1861 (the act authorizing limited liability) led to flotation of a large number of speculative non-financial companies. These in turn paid their contractors via the innovation of 'finance securities' on which discounts—and hence profits for Gurney and other discount houses—were large. In addition, Gurney accepted equity interests for what proved to be unrepayable loans advanced to ironworks and shipping companies, although only a few analysts were aware of these problems. Losses led to incorporation in 1865, in an attempt to attract capital.

[1] All but two are events of recent decades. For a longer term perspective, albeit in each case written with a particular theoretical approach in mind, see Kindleberger 1978, 1988; Friedman and Schwartz 1963; and Mishkin 1991.

[2] See Batchelor 1986.

But in early 1866, against the background of a rise in bank rate from 3 per cent at the time of flotation to 8 per cent at the end of 1865, there came the collapse of a firm of contractors, Watson, Overend and Co. and two other companies with which Overend Gurney had ties. These three drew on paper issued by each other and discounted with Overend Gurney. Further minor failures followed. On 10 May 1866, Overend was compelled to seek assistance from the Bank of England. The Bank refused, and on the same day Overend Gurney was declared insolvent.

Runs on all London banks followed the next day, as depositors, in particular country banks, sought cash (not merely transferring deposits to other banks). The Bank of England, drained of notes, hesitated over whether to make its usual purchases of newly issued government debt. This information made the panic far worse. 'No one knew who was sound and who was unsound',[3] as provincial bankers feared all discount houses—who also held finance securities—and London banks had equally poor balance sheets (a case of contagion in the presence of imperfect information) A number of basically solvent banks failed, as well as others who were genuinely bad risks. However, the next day, after a suspension of the Bank Charter Act which forbade the Issue Department to augment the note supply, the Bank gave assurances that it would freely provide support to the banking system, albeit at a high interest rate. This broke the panic. Commentators such as Schwartz (1986) suggest the Bank learnt from this that it had to accept the responsibility of being lender of last resort, freely providing funds to illiquid banks at a penalty rate, and the public understood that the Bank had accepted the responsibility. This has prevented the recurrence of such generalized panic in the UK.

As regards macroeconomic counterparts, real GNP was flat in 1866 and rose only 1 per cent in 1867, while real investment fell 9 and 12 per cent (Mitchell 1981). These data suggest that the crisis did not lead to a major economic collapse, though it may have prolonged the recession.

(2) The Stock-Market Crash and the Great Depression (1929–1933)—USA

Much ink has been spilt over economic and financial developments in the USA (as well as elsewhere) in the late 1920s and early 1930s; here we merely note some key economic developments, focusing on the USA, and summarize some of the arguments regarding cause and effect. Many of the latter actually stimulated the development of theories of financial crisis outlined in Ch. 5.

The 1920s saw a rapid economic expansion, which in combination with financial innovations such as investment trusts led to a stock-market

[3] See Batchelor 1986.

bubble. Stock-market speculation was financed by rapid increases in borrowing.

There was a large and broad-based expansion of private debt in the 1920s; outstanding corporate bonds rose from $26 bn in 1920 to $47 bn in 1928 (over 50 per cent of GNP). Small businesses and households increased indebtedness sharply; outstanding mortgages rose from $11 bn in 1920 to $27 bn in 1929.[4]

Monetary policy was tightened from mid-1928 onwards, to seek to curb the stock-market boom. Initially, higher nominal interest rates had little effect, as stock-market lending remained profitable, though general prices began to fall and demand began to weaken.

The stock-market collapse coincided with minor events such as the Hatry crisis in London; but it appeared more to be the deflation of a speculative bubble, where prices had departed from fundamentals.[5]

The crash led to a sharp tightening of credit, which was initially counteracted by the Fed as lender of last resort.

Industrial production began to fall sharply in 1929–30.

The fall in stock prices spread to commodities, which led to widespread default on international and domestic bank loans and depression in commodity exporting countries.

Beginning in 1930 there was a flight to quality in the bond market —cutting off a source of credit—and an increasing number of bank failures. The number of banks halved over 1929–33. As well as deteriorating loan quality owing to the recession, crash, and commodity price falls, banks suffered from cash withdrawals and from outflows of gold from the USA.

The nominal money supply contracted over 1931–3 while high-powered money increased, reflecting the flight to cash.

Prices fell sharply, increasing pressure on debtors holding debt contracts written in nominal terms, with the debt service/GNP ratio rising from 9 per cent in 1929 to 20 per cent in 1933.

Among debtors, insolvencies were severe for small businesses, farmers, mortgage borrowers, and state and local government. Only large corporations were relatively immune.

The wave of bank failures came to a climax in March 1933, resulting in a panic and closure of all banks. The Fed did not respond as lender of last resort, nor did the banks act as a 'club' to suspend cash payments to depositors, as they often had in the nineteenth century when the Central Bank did not exist (they now considered maintenance of stability to be the Fed's responsibility).

[4] Indeed, as noted by Taggart (1985), business debt was proportionately higher in the 1920s than the 1980s—not a reassuring precedent.

[5] See Galbraith (1954) for a highly readable account.

Among the causal factors, monetarists emphasise the contractionary monetary policy and decline in money supply; Keynesians note mainly an orthodox recession based on the multiplier/accelerator process, accompanied by higher interest rates following policy tightening; financial-fragility theorists focus on the rise in indebtedness, market bubble, crash, commodity price falls, and wave of bank failures.

As for the causes, there is disagreement over the transmission of the crisis. Three main explanations have been advanced to account for the transmission of bank failures to the macroeconomy (Haubruch 1990). According to the monetarist view (Friedman and Schwartz 1963; Hamilton 1987), the decline in the stock of money that resulted from the panic was the main cause. Without this, the failures might not have had major effects. For Keynesians (Temin 1976), the banking panics were part of the wider process that started with a decline in autonomous spending, and if they had not occurred the Depression would still have supervened. But for finance theorists (Bernanke 1983) the crisis affected the economy by reducing the quality of financial services, in particular the intermediation of credit. This entailing a rising cost and increased rationing of credit that made it difficult to continue or establish businesses or farms (see also Ch. 5, Sect. 2). Financial-fragility theory (I. Fisher 1932, 1933), in line with this, also emphasizes the effects of nominal debt contracts, the burden of which sharply increased the rate of business failures and hence of bank failures. Summers (1991) notes that all of these effects were aggravated by an absense of automatic stabilizers (i.e. increase in government expenditure relative to taxation in a recession). Before the Second World War, a 1 per cent decline in GNP generated a 0.95 per cent fall in disposable income, whereas since 1945 it has only generated a 0.39 per cent fall.

The Depression was, of course, a global rather than purely US phenomenon. Developing countries that had borrowed heavily in the 1920s, and/or were dependent on commodity exports, together with advanced countries that sought to maintain fixed exchange rates (such as France and Germany), were hardest hit.[6] A major feature in Continental Europe was failure of major universal banks such as the Austrian Kreditanstalt, owing to collapses in the value of their equity holdings. In addition, countries such as the USA, with a structure of small and poorly diversified banks, suffered more runs and panics than those with nationwide branch systems, such as Canada and the UK.

The US regulatory response was to tighten regulation of banks and thrifts. Entry controls were imposed, asset and liability composition restricted, capital requirements imposed, self-dealing restrictions tightened,

[6] Bernanke and James (1991) offer an international comparison of links from finance to the real economy in the Depression, focusing on the exchange-rate regime, deflation, and financial crisis. They suggest that banking crises significantly aggravated the downturns.

and deposit insurance was introduced. Besides seeking stability, some of these regulations sought to reallocate credit to 'socially desirable' purposes such as housing. Some analysts such as Kane (1985, 1986) and Wolfson (1989) attribute to these restrictions the difficulties US institutions underwent in the 1970s and 1980s in the context of high inflation and innovation (compare the discussion of savings and loans in Chs. 6 and 7).

(3) The Yamaichi Rescue (1965)—Japan[7]

A rapid expansion took place in the Japanese economy over 1958–61, entailing declining interest rates and growth in investment. Unsurprisingly, the stock market was buoyant, and securities houses expanded their business on the back of this by developing the innovation of investment trusts, which enabled individuals to participate in the boom. They also traded actively on their own account, financing stock purchases by borrowing from banks, finance houses, and the call market where the investment trusts placed their liquid deposits. Such borrowing was aided by a contract used to secure funds called 'unyo azukari', where, for a fee, retail customers allowed their securities to be used as collateral. Meanwhile, capitalization of the securities houses was rather low. Hence, as noted by Corrigan (1990), funds were sourced in a wholesale, collateral in a retail market.

A tightening of monetary policy in 1961 in response to a balance-of-payments deficit caused the stock market to peak in mid-year and start to fall. The securities houses sought to stem the fall by buying stocks, but further policy moves in 1963 (the US tax on capital outflows and the increase in Japanese reserve requirements) overwhelmed the effect of this. The securities houses set up a support operation for the equity market in 1964[8] to which the Bank of Japan lent ¥70 bn to buy stocks. But its resources were overwhelmed by sale of stock by investment trusts and of inventory by securities houses (i.e. free riding). A further holding operation, with an even larger loan from the Bank of Japan, again failed to stem the fall, and securities houses continued to suffer large losses. These resulted largely from interest payments on their loans which exceeded declining commission income, aggravated by losses on inventory. In May 1965 Yamaichi declared default on its loans, and although banks were willing to reschedule, the retail owners of collateral began to panic and withdraw their assets from 'unyo azukari' accounts for fear of loss. Such runs threatened to spread to other securities houses, while the banks remained heavily exposed to the securities industry. The response

[7] Source: Corrigan 1990.

[8] The Japan Joint Securities Operation.

was special access by Yamaichi to unsecured loans from the Bank of Japan channelled via the banks 'for maintenance and fostering of the credit system'. Another house also had to be supported. The longer term response was a tightening of regulation, with strict licensing of securities firms, separation of brokerage and dealing, high capital requirements, and segregated customer accounts.

(4) The Penn Central Bankruptcy (1970)—USA[9]

Although commercial paper (CP) markets—markets for short-term tradable liabilities of highly-rated companies—are long established in the USA, a crucial event in their evolution was the advent of the certificate of deposit (CD) in 1962, which led to a rapid expansion in US money markets and in the freedom of banks to bid for deposits and loans. As outlined in Ch. 6, Sect. 1, the CD facilitated development of liability management among banks. In the light of the expanded powers offered by CDs, banks proved eager to expand their business more generally, opening credit lines to other financial institutions and 'nurturing the epidemic growth of the commercial paper (CP) market, even though their generosity in granting the securing credit lines on which the market depended came at the expense of their own loan business'.[10] Meanwhile, experiences such as the credit crunch of 1966, which threatened to lead to a cut-off of business credit (as market rates exceeded CD ceilings) prompted non-financial firms to seek both committed lines of credit with banks and alternative sources of funds such as CP. Indeed, many banks formed holding companies to issue unregulated CP to circumvent CD interest-rate ceilings. Finally, a lowering of interest rates in 1968, partly to offset the fiscal tightening that year, led to an explosion of credit 'as lenders were encouraged to be more aggressive',[11] as well as rising inflation. Interest rates began to rise as monetary policy was tightened, but rather than operating strongly on demand for credit, the eventual blockage came on the supply side, as political pressures mounted on banks not to raise the prime rate further. Lending became unprofitable and growth of loans ceased in late 1969. Spreads on CP and bonds rose and the stock market fell sharply.

It was in the aftermath of this 'credit crunch' that Penn Central Transportation Company failed[12] and defaulted on its $200 mn outstanding CP. Issuance of CP declined sharply; companies unable to roll over their CP had to turn to banks to obtain credit; while companies found

[9] See Timlen 1977; Wojnilower 1980.
[10] Wojnilower 1980: 286.
[11] Wojnilower 1980.
[12] Failure followed a series of unsuccessful rescue attempts (Mishkin 1991).

borrowing in all markets more expensive. The authorities feared a wave of corporate bankruptcies; one ground for this was that lenders would ration credit owing to shortage of funds; the other was that they would particularly ration borrowers driven from the CP market, due to their inability to screen good from bad borrowers, since they lacked a relationship. The authorities' response was suspension of interest-rate ceilings on short-term CDs (to enable banks to obtain funds) and indications that the discount window was available for banks needing reserves to extend loans to companies. Large-scale business failures were avoided, though firms found their borrowing capacity sharply reduced, and the cost of credit increased.

(5) The Continental Illinois Bank Failure (1984)—USA

The Continental Illinois[13] bank, one of the largest US banks, suffered from non-performing loans arising from the ldc debt crisis and the weakness of commodity prices, after a rapid and concentrated increase in lending both to ldcs and the energy sector in the early 1980s. Partly due to the US regulations against interstate banking, it was also forced to rely heavily on wholesale deposits, 40 per cent of which were from the international markets, and 16 per cent domestic interbank deposits.

In 1984, after a period when the bank had to pay a higher price for its wholesale deposits, large depositors began to withdraw funds, as concern about the quality of its loan portfolio grew. The Penn Square failure of 1982 was important background to the crisis, as uninsured depositors suffered losses. The run started in the international interbank market, as Japanese, European, and Asian banks began to cut credit lines and withdraw overnight funding. Only later did US non-banks begin to follow. Such withdrawals reached $8 bn per day, outstripping liquidity and capital. The run continued despite an announcement by the Federal Deposit Insurance Corporation that all of the bank's liabilities were guaranteed. Fearing systemic risk if the bank failed—adverse rumours had already caused difficulties at Manufacturers' Hanover bank—the authorities instituted a major rescue operation. This entailed a $5.5 bn line of credit arranged by twenty-eight banks, $2 bn of new capital infused by the Federal Deposit Insurance Corporation and a group of commercial banks, and discount window funds from the Fed (with $4.5 bn in discounts being done in the week beginning 16 May). Partly as a result of this, there was no contagion to other institutions or markets. While the bank was not explicitly nationalized, the government placed a representative on the executive board of the bank.

[13] See Goldstein *et al.* 1991; Saunders 1987.

(6) The Canadian Regional Banking Crisis (1985)[14]

As outlined in Ch. 2, the Canadian economy entered a boom in the later 1970s and beginning of the 1980s, which led to heavy borrowing by firms active in energy and in agriculture. This came to an end in the recession of 1982 for the economy as a whole. But the primary sector failed to recover from the recession of 1982, and was doubly hurt by the weakness of commodity prices in 1985.

Among the banks that profited from the boom were a number of small regional banks including the Northland and Canadian Commercial (CCB) banks. They had expanded their lending with the assistance of wholesale money-market funding, and their exposure was concentrated on real estate and energy in Western Canada. In March 1985 CCB told the Bank of Canada that provisioning for loan losses, as required by the regulator, would wipe out its capital. Fearing a loss of confidence in the banking system if the bank were allowed to fail, the Central Bank assembled a support package of C$225 mn with contributions by the 'Big Six' major banks, the government, and deposit insurers as well as itself. The reason for rescue of the small bank rather than its closure seems to be fear that the public would overreact, especially as bank failures were rare in Canada and the US Ohio/Maryland thrifts crises (Ch. 6) occurred at the same time.

The Northland Bank had been receiving liquidity assistance from major banks since 1983, and its agreement for this expired in June 1985. It then turned to the Bank of Canada for liquidity, at the same time as the crisis at CCB. As the problems became public knowledge, retail depositors began to run both from the troubled banks and other similar institutions, while the major banks withdrew money-market support, leaving liquidity support to the Central Bank. A supervisory report in the September on the state of loan portfolios indicated insolvency, and the Central Bank withdrew support. All depositors were covered by the government, even beyond the insurance limit, partly 'because officials had encouraged investors to maintain deposits'.[15] The cost of this was C$900 mn. Some echoes of the crisis continued for the rest of the year to trouble small Canadian banks; Mercantile Bank of Montreal needed liquidity support and then takeover; Morguard Bank of Vancouver was also taken over; Continental Bank of Toronto suffered a loss in confidence when profits fell but was able to re-establish its reputation after a period of liquidity support by the Central Bank and major commercial banks.

[14] See Estey 1986.
[15] Corrigan 1990.

(7) The Collapse of the High-Yield (Junk) Bond Market (1989)—USA[16]

As noted in Ch. 2, US corporate finance in the 1980s was marked by a rapid growth in leverage, much of which was associated with the issuance of high-yield bonds. Whereas there had always been low-rated or speculative bonds on the market—often a result of loss of credit rating by firms ('fallen angels')—in the early 1980s, the investment bank Drexel Burnham Lambert set out to create a market for bonds that would have low credit ratings at issue. An additional stimulus was the decline in the private placement market, as life insurers sought greater liquidity (Crabbe *et al.* 1990). Initially, the market was largely a source of finance for small emerging companies which could not easily find credit from other lenders, while offering equity-like risks and rewards to investors seeking high yields. But the market also attracted takeover and LBO activity, often enabling corporate raiders to take over large companies from a small asset base. Drexel undertook to make markets in the securities, aided by certain savings and loans and insurance companies having close relationships with the firm.

Initially, other US investment banks sought to distance themselves from the market, but were eventually attracted by the high profitability of primary issuance activity. Savings and loans and insurance companies were keen investors, since the market offered equity-like returns together with the guarantees and security associated with bonds. Also, they were partly forbidden by regulation from investing directly in equities. Bush and Kaletsky (1990) suggest that junk bonds enabled such institutions to offer higher yields to retail investors and gain market share at the expense of more prudent competitors, thus increasing the onus on them to hold junk bonds too. It is a matter of controversy whether risk was underpriced in the market; while the yields seemed generous enough to compensate for realized defaults, these occurred in the context of a period of prolonged economic expansion.[17] High leverage, the high prices paid for companies (whose security thus depended on inflated asset values), and accounts and prospectuses based on an indefinite continuation of expansion, gave grounds for caution. It can be suggested, in effect, that junk bonds dispensed with the credit analysis[18] usually performed by banks, leaving investors to rely on liquidity and diversification to protect themselves. As discussed below, the former proved an illusion; as did the latter (given high defaults) to some degree.

By 1989 the market had reached a value of $200 bn and issues were still proceeding briskly. These included part of the financing of the $25 bn

[16] See Bush and Kaletsky 1990.

[17] The 1990–1 slowdown exacted a heavy toll of bonds, with default rates of 8.8 per cent in 1990 and an estimated 11.5 per cent in 1991 (Moody's 1991).

[18] Although in principle the lead manager should offer credit assessment, balance may have been affected by the attraction of the front end fee.

RJR/Nabisco takeover, the largest yet (see Borio 1990*b*). But the market was weakened by a number of factors. There was a default at Campeau, a Canadian conglomerate that had financed purchases of US retailers by junk bonds; the government's savings and loan bail out bill ordered thrifts to dispose of all junk bonds; and finally there was the failure of Drexel Burnham Lambert in early 1990. As a consequence, prices fell rapidly, liquidity collapsed, and new issues dried up—resemblance to the FRN crisis discussed in Chs. 6 and 7 was close. It is notable that the market failure occurred without a tightening of monetary policy or a recession, though the later slowdown in the USA weakened the market further. No intervention was felt necessary to rescue Drexel—whose failure was felt to pose no systemic threat—nor the market itself. Issuance was near zero throughout 1990, though a recovery was apparent by the end of 1991.

(8) Instability in Australia in the Late 1980s[19]

Except for a brief period in the mid-1970s, the Australian banking system was tightly 'structurally' regulated from the war till the early 1980s, with interest-rate controls on deposit and loan rates, limits on maturities of interest-paying deposits, portfolio regulations enforcing holdings of government securities up to a certain proportion of the balance sheet, requirements to hold special deposits with the Central Bank, and frequent imposition of credit ceilings. Entry controls had facilitated formation of an oligopolistic cartel which tightly rationed credit; such credit as was granted went only to the most creditworthy borrowers. Banks also cross-subsidized favoured classes of customer and did not compete directly for deposits. The credit rationing in turn minimised the need for supervision. But profitability was increasingly threatened by expansion of relatively lightly regulated non-bank financial institutions (such as building societies, merchant banks, and credit unions) which were free to innovate. This in turn led the tightening of monetary policy via credit controls to impinge ever harder on banks, for a given effect on the economy.

Deregulation removed the controls mentioned above, and led to reintermediation and a sharp increase in competition between banks, intensified by a cyclical upturn and entry of foreign banks to the market.[20] Banks turned from asset management to liability management in wholesale markets in order to fund expansion of lending, with the aim of protecting market share. Lending was to a much wider range of borrowers

[19] See Reserve Bank of Australia 1991.

[20] In practice foreigners made worse losses than domestic firms, highlighting the mechanisms favouring incumbents over entrants noted in Ch. 7.

in terms of credit quality, although mainly in the corporate sector. Banks lacked relationships in such lending. Equity markets provided banks with capital to back sharply increased assets. Loans were often secured on inflated prices of relatively illiquid assets—notably property, or no security at all, while spreads were low. Risks increased sharply, particularly with the banks' lack of experience in credit monitoring, and a decentralization of lending power to local managers. Supervisors were not geared to the extent of competition (although, in their defence, no depositors lost money, nor was the national safety net required). The result was escalating loan losses and bad debts. Such losses were aggravated when monetary policy was tightened in 1988/9.

Financial fragility led to a number of failures, some of which threatened to spread more widely. The State Bank of Victoria failed when its merchant bank subsidiary, Tricontinental, incurred A$2 bn losses: 70 per cent of its loans were bad—largely to construction, small business, and corporate raiders. Commentators saw it as an 'end lender' ready to take loans others reject. The state government was unable to bail out the bank, so it was sold to the nationalized Commonwealth Bank. The State Bank of South Australia had sought to grow rapidly in both domestic and international financial markets, with a particular focus on property transactions. The largest losses were outside its home area, in unfamiliar markets. The state government recapitalized the bank after its failure. Tasmania Bank was another state bank in difficulty (absorbed by the Savings Bank of Tasmania).

Perhaps the most serious problem arose from failure of the Pyramid Building Society, a private non-bank institution with AS2 ½ bn in assets, the second largest society. The society got into difficulties with commercial property lending, when prices slumped in Victoria. Also, it had funded assets at very high interest rates, with the profitability of loans arising from upfront fees—and hence growth; it had doubled in size over 2–3 years. Once rumours started, it began to lose deposits, with the state government eventually being forced to close it. Building societies that had not diversified from their traditional business faced much less acute difficulties in terms of profitability. Nevertheless, runs occurred at the same time as this crisis on two other former building societies, the Bank of Melbourne and Metway Bank, although the causes appeared to be unfounded rumours (i.e. contagion) rather than unsoundness.

It should be noted, however, that none of the major four national banks, with their strong retail deposit bases, got into difficulty. Notwithstanding large losses, all their Basle ratios remained over 8 per cent (average 9.7 per cent in 1991). Nor was overall confidence lost in the banking system; the difficulties were generally managed in an orderly fashion.

(9) The Swedish Finance Company Crisis (1990)[21]

As in many other countries, the Swedish banking sector was tightly regulated for much of the post-war period, with prohibitions on entry (no new banking licences were granted from 1945 to 1983), quantitative restrictions on credit, and exchange controls. Banks were obliged to hold a proportion of government bonds on their balance sheets, in the interests of cheap financing of the budget deficit; and credit was provided to the housing sector on a privileged basis.

The tight regulation of banking gave rise to growth of a non-regulated sector, the finance houses. Although these originated in the 1920s and 1930s, specializing in consumer and small company loans, in the 1970s and 1980s they expanded first into factoring and leasing, and then lending to small- and medium-size firms, circumventing controls on banks. Their number rose from 67 in 1970 to 292 in 1988, with assets of SEK171 bn.

Heavy regulation of banks also led to development of direct finance. The Swedes introduced a commercial paper market in 1980. Initiated by banks—the first deregulation was of CDs—it was further stimulated by issuance of short term Treasury bills in 1982. Industrial companies, housing finance institutions, and government agencies were heavy users of the market. By 1990 there were 270 programmes valued at SEK160 bn, making the market the third largest in Europe. Finance houses could not issue commercial paper, but required a bank to make markets in their promissory notes (company investment certificates, CIC). However, market participants considered CICs identical to CP, although banks were not obliged to provide backup liquidity, or make markets. Further deregulation of banks (Englund 1990) entailed, first, abolition of liquidity ratios—which were 50 per cent in 1983—followed by abolition of other controls, and the end of exchange controls in 1989.

The deregulation of finance created a structural expansion in markets which, along with the upturn of the cycle, caused an economic boom, rapid growth of the financial sector, and increasing asset prices. Banks grew particularly strongly, balance-sheet size increasing from 90 per cent of GNP in 1985 to 200 per cent in 1989. Mergers raised banks' competitiveness. Banks regained market share of consumer credit from finance houses, whose margins narrowed and whose numbers fell sharply. Many of the finance houses turned to higher risk lending, such as highly-leveraged commercial real-estate transactions and financing of investments in shares; banks supplied the bulk of their funds via CICs.[22] When

[21] See Bisignano 1991; Moody's 1991*a*.

[22] A similar pattern was apparent in Japan, where much speculative financing of real estate and equity markets was via lightly regulated 'non-bank banks', albeit largely funded by banks. A crisis on the Swedish scale has been avoided at the time of writing, although the authorities are concerned (Bank of Japan 1991*b*).

growth in asset prices faltered, a crisis occurred in the finance company sector at the end of 1990. The initial casualties were Nyckeln Holdings—which suffered severe credit losses when customers defaulted due to falling real estate prices—and Beijer Capital, its major shareholder, which was also highly leveraged. The proximate cause of Nyckeln's default, even before credit losses became known, was inability to roll over its CIC programme. After the failure, Beijer Capital's programme was cancelled by banks, and it failed. The sizeable and unprecedented losses to creditors of these firms caused a 'shock' that spawned rumours that several finance houses were in difficulties, and the CIC market dried up; banks refused to allow rollover. Many finance houses were forced to sell assets; others sought emergency bank loans. Three defaulted on their programmes. One underlying factor may have been inadequate monitoring of the finance companies' lending by the banks, which largely financed them and in a number of cases owned them. The crisis left banks nursing heavy losses. The Swedish Bank Inspectorate reportedly lacked resources and authority to supervise the companies.

The potential volatility of CP markets has strong parallels with Penn Central described above. This became even more apparent with the collapse of the broader commercial paper market which followed; for several months even well-managed non-financial companies, whatever their nature, found it difficult to raise CP. Whereas spreads had been very low prior to the crisis (10–15 basis points over the risk-free rate), suggesting inadequate credit appraisal, defaults led to an extreme flight to quality, with wide spreads and all but the highest quality issuers excluded. Some recovery in the CP market was apparent by July 1991. Meanwhile, the banking sector, facing increasing losses on property exposures, lurched into greater difficulties, similar to the pattern described below for Norway.

(10) The Norwegian Banking Crisis 1990–1991[23]

During the post-war period up to the mid-1980s, Norwegian banks were tightly regulated both in the quantity and price of credit offered. Financial deregulation, which came to Norway in 1984, with abolition of credit ceilings, sought to shift from this over-protected and isolated regime to one where banks, exposed to competition, would provide lower cost financial services, as well as becoming more efficient in anticipation of integration of financial services in Europe. This coincided with strong oil revenues and expectations of continuing real-income growth, boosted by expansionary macroeconomic policy, as well as deregulation of other

[23] See Solheim 1990; Fossli and Preston 1991.

aspects of the economy such as housing tenure and retailing. (Thus there were a number of 'displacements'). Banks responded by lending aggressively and expanding rapidly; lending was particularly focused on services, households[24] (consumer and mortgage credit, including home equity loans, via mortgage financing companies), construction, and commercial property (notably retail). Such an approach was encouraged by rapid increases in property prices and tax breaks to borrowers; all interest was deductible for households as well as companies; in addition, a law fixed households' borrowing rates to a certain maximum level, which ensured negative real rates, the circle being squared for banks by vast quantities of low-cost liquidity from the Bank of Norway. Also, formerly specialized institutions such as savings banks entered new markets, and foreign banks entered the credit market, but remained marginal players.

After the fall in oil prices of 1986 a recession began, while the government tightened policy to compensate for a devaluation. It fixed the exchange rate, in effect switching the regime from one of negative to positive real rates. Interest rates rose especially sharply for households, as the law restricting interest rates was abolished. The consequence was a prolonged slowdown, with consumption falling each year in 1987–9 and house prices declining 40 per cent over 1988–91, although lending continued to grow for some time after the downturn in GDP. The impact on banks came in two waves. First, new service companies with little asset backing began to default. But then the collapse in property prices led to growing credit losses by banks, particularly with the concentration of risk in this area (90 per cent of losses were on loans to companies rather than households).

It was apparent that banks, accustomed to an over-regulated system, could not cope in a fully liberalized environment. They lacked internal controls on lending; often separate loans could be obtained from different branches without the head office being aware of total exposure; and many loans lacked adequate collateral. Diversification was poor, partly as a result of the specialization of the economy in sectors such as oil and fish farming. Government agencies often lacked resources to supervise lending, and there were few means to check borrowers' credit quality. Meanwhile, securities trading turned in heavy losses during the 1987 crash.

One response to the losses was a series of mergers to remove excess capacity;[25] but profits were reduced by rationalization costs, while purchasers often discovered unexpected bad debts in the merged banks. Although difficulties began in 1987–8, notably affecting regional banks, the problems came to a head in 1990–1, as in 1990 the three main national banks made combined losses of over Nkr3 bn; by late 1991 their capital

[24] Indeed, the saving ratio was negative from 1985–8.

[25] e.g. the number of savings banks fell from 322 to 150 in 1980–9.

had fallen from Nkr7.4 bn in 1990 to 2 bn. The government set up a Bank Insurance Fund of Nkr5 bn in early 1991, but it was already half used up when Christiania Bank, the second largest, announced in October that third quarter losses would wipe out the bank's share capital. Losses on the real-estate portfolio, on equity holdings, non-performing loans, and restructuring costs were held responsible. The Central Bank announced that it would provide 'an ample supply of liquidity to Christiania and the rest of the banking sector'. A short time later, the largest bank declared it had insufficient capital to meet regulatory requirements. At the time of writing, the consequence seems likely to be effective nationalization of major banks.

Conclusions

This summary of ten further periods of instability confirms the generality of many of the features highlighted in Chs. 6 and 7 (see Table 8.1). In particular, accumulation of debt, speculation in assets, monetary tightening, and credit rationing/runs occurred frequently. In addition, changes in market structure, such as new entry, innovation, or changes on the demand side, often preceded the crises, whether a consequence of deregulation (Sweden, Norway, Australia) or a more autonomous development (1866, 1929, Japan, Penn Central, junk bonds). As well as buttressing the analyses highlighted in Chs. 5–7, the broader sample of crises offered by this chapter enables further similarities and distinctions between episodes of instability to be drawn.

(a) Securities market collapse (FRNs, junk bonds, Penn Central, Sweden)

A fully functioning primary debt securities market can suddenly dry up and cease to offer funds to borrowers, while secondary markets become much thinner, spreads widen, and prices plummet. It is suggested that these events constitute a syndrome similar to bank runs to which securities markets may be subject when under stress. Quantity rationing of credit becomes pervasive and liquidity dries up. This can be more or less serious for the economy, depending on whether borrowers have alternative sources of credit (FRNs), restricted alternatives (junk bonds, Sweden), or potentially none without action by the authorities (Penn Central). Note that the crash is in principle another example of such a collapse, although it was arguably not as much of concern for cutting off a source of (equity) finance as for the other reasons outlined in Chs. 6 and 7.

Table 8.1. Summary table

	UK 1866	USA 1929–1933	Japan 1965	USA 1970	USA 1984	Canada 1985	USA 1989	Australia 1989	Sweden 1990	Norway 1990
Debt accumulation	yes	yes	yes	yes	yes	yes	yes	yes	yes	yes
Asset speculation	yes	yes	yes	—	—	—	yes	yes	yes	yes
Concentration of risk	yes	yes	yes	—	yes	yes	—	yes	yes	yes
Regime shift	yes	yes	—	—	—	—	—	—	—	yes
New entry	—	yes	—	—	—	—	yes	yes	yes	yes
Innovation	yes	yes	yes	yes	—	—	yes	—	yes	—
Monetary tightening	yes	yes	yes	yes	—	—	—	yes	—	yes
Declining capital ratios	yes	yes	yes	—	yes	yes	yes	—	—	yes
Credit rationing/runs	yes	yes	—	yes	yes	yes	yes	yes	yes	yes
Contagion between markets	yes	yes	—	—	—	—	—	—	—	—
International transmission	—	yes	—	—	—	—	—	—	—	—
Action by the authorities	(yes)	—	yes	yes	yes	yes	—	yes	—	yes
Dysfunction of finance/ Economic collapse	(yes)	yes	—	—	—	—	—	—	—	—

Some of the general theories of rapid changes in credit availability as outlined in Ch. 5 are clearly applicable to these crises, notably the 'credit rationing' and 'agency cost' paradigms for primary markets, and the 'dealer market' approach to secondary markets. However, in Bank for International Settlements (1986*a*) it is suggested there are additional reasons for these events. A number of factors may prompt institutional investors to rush to sell assets in the event of a credit failure: the fiduciary role of investors; the fact that they see their holdings as short-run low-risk high-liquidity assets; that they may have less detailed information than would a bank to base a credit decision; and less of a relationship reason to support a particular borrower or keep a particular market functioning.

(b) Deregulation (Australia, Sweden, Norway, later savings and loans)

Several of the periods of instability followed an earlier deregulation of structural controls on financial markets, which led inexperienced bankers to overlend, resulting in difficulties when monetary tightening or recession supervened. Particularly in Scandinavia, prudential supervision was insufficiently developed to cope. Note, however, that only a minority of the crises can be traced so directly to deregulation—it is wrong to suggest that it underlay all of the financial difficulties of recent decades.

(c) Disintermediation and reintermediation (secondary banks, Sweden, Australia, earlier savings and loans)

Although indirectly related to deregulation in some cases, the cases where a financial sector develops outside the regulated sector are distinct. In the cases of the secondary banks, Sweden, and Australia, it was the disintermediating sector which got into difficulties as the main banks were deregulated and able to outcompete them on a level playing-field. In the case of savings and loans, the money-market mutual funds caused problems for depository institutions, owing both to interest-rate regulation and the nature of their balance sheets, while the funds remained viable after deregulation. It is notable that in Australia, the UK, and also Canada, the major banks remained stable despite difficulties elsewhere.

(d) Failure of a single large institution (Overend Gurney, Continental Illinois)

When an institution that is regarded by markets as being at the core of the financial system fails, it can trigger contagious failures out of proportion to its size, in a way that an 'outside' institution (as Herstatt seemed to be) may not. This explains the crisis in the UK in 1866 and the trouble US regulators went to in order to avoid failure of Continental Illinois in 1984.

Such a pattern leads commentators to talk of institutions that are 'too big to fail'; though the authorities seek to avoid such discussion, for fear of moral hazard.

(e) Commodities and property (secondary banks, later savings and loans, Canada, Australia, Sweden, Norway)

The frequency with which instability has been associated with lending to these sectors illustrates their heavy demands for capital and uncertain returns, given the extreme cyclical instability of prices. Lending concentration exposed banks to high levels of risk, both systematic and unsystematic. There are clearly also elements of Minsky's 'Ponzi lending', in that loans must come upfront, often long before cashflow from the projects become positive. Again and again banks have developed loanbooks with highly concentrated exposures to these sectors.

(f) International debt

Although the ldc debt crisis is the only international lending crisis covered here, it is relevant to note that such events have recurred frequently through history, with the debt crisis of the 1930s being a further prime example. There are often elements of the commodity crisis as outlined above, but added are the difficulties of sovereign risk incurred in foreign currency to often widely dispersed creditors. The bankers' current caution over Eastern Europe can be interpreted in the light of such experiences—though not their losses on domestic lending made since the debt crisis.

(g) Equity-market linkages (1929 crash, Japan, 1987 crash, Norway)

Although sharp declines in equity prices have been frequent events, difficulties for financial institutions seem to stem from particular associated patterns of circumstances. For example, difficulties may arise from innovations which enable institutions to profit from the boom, and entail debt exposures. Investment trusts in both 1929 and Japan, and the associated recycling of money back into the market, made their purveyors vulnerable when 'leverage went into reverse'. Meanwhile, the use of programme-trading techniques prior to the crash offered investors—including financial institutions—an illusion of liquidity and protection against declines in the market. Another phenomenon linking equity markets to financial instability is when there are equity holdings on banks' books, as in Continental Europe in the 1930s and the Norwegian events discussed above. Although losses in 1990–1 on securities holdings by Japanese banks did not appear (to date) to have threatened their solvency, the difficulties they cause for the capital adequacy of the banks is thought to be an important component of credit tightening and consequent financial fragility in the early 1990s.

It is suggested that these categories move in the direction of a 'typology' of financial crises. In combination with the more general features highlighted in Chs. 5–7, they should be of additional assistance to regulators or bankers monitoring developments in financial markets, in recognizing potential instability at an early stage. To such a typology can be added some of the distinctions already made in the text, for example between 'runs and walks' (withdrawal of immediate access to credit versus refusal to roll over longer term credits for firms in difficulty), 'quiet and noisy crises' (crises where losses are hidden and institutions allowed to continue versus those where they abruptly go out of business), and the concept of 'cyclical/financial-fragility' crises such as the Great Depression —and, to some degree, the situation in many advanced countries in the early 1990s.

Conclusion: Themes and Prospects

As interim conclusions have been presented after each main section of the book, it is more useful here to bring out some of the themes that have pervaded the work, to offer additional considerations relating to them, suggest further lines of research, and summarize certain key policy implications. A final section assesses prospects for the later 1990s. Will the issue of financial instability recede?

(1) Issues of Finance

(a) Debt

The analysis of the book should be sufficient to correct oversimplified views[1] regarding debt as a commodity like any other that were noted in Ch. 1 Sect. 1. But despite its complexity, problems of costs of default, lack of risk-sharing, and the known market failures to which it is subject, debt is clearly the most efficient instrument for many, if not most, financial transactions. It would thus be undesirable to enact policies restricting its usage in a general manner. It is, nevertheless, clearly unhelpful that most tax systems artificially stimulate debt finance beyond the level that is appropriate to its intrinsic merits. It also appears to be the case that, even abstracting from the tax system, agents are vulnerable to excessive use of debt, a phenomenon that has in turn stimulated many of the difficulties outlined in the book. In particular, financial institutions and private investors show repeated tendencies to underprice risk in debt contracts (ex post and sometimes ex ante), which in turn has been readily accepted by borrowers.

To the extent that these patterns are seen as undesirable, and particularly where they are seen as a consequence of lack of information or externalities, they give an a priori basis for government intervention. At present, this consists largely of financial regulation, but there remain policy issues regarding the optimal form of this regulation, discussed in Ch. 5 and Sect. 2 below. It could also be questioned whether further policy action is needed for the non-financial sector. As discussed in Sect. 3 below, there arise key issues in financial structure in this context, which,

[1] See also Stiglitz (1991), who refers to 'treating debt markets like those for tables and chairs'.

even if not amenable to policy action, should constitute an important background for policy deliberations on these matters. As regards topics for further research, there would seem to be a need for progress in relating the strong theoretical basis for the understanding of debt in equilibrium outlined in Ch. 1 to issues such as the complex nature of modern banking (Lewis 1991); a firmer empirical foundation more generally; and behaviour of loan and primary debt securities markets out of equilibrium.

(b) Equity

Although the book is about debt, equity is at least as relevant to the issues in hand. It has been shown that, given its superiority to debt in terms of risk-sharing, a greater proportion of equity in a balance sheet reduces risks of financial fragility, bank runs, and systemic risk. It does this largely by reducing the conflicts of interest between lender and borrower. There may also be a greater incentive to monitor the firm with equity than debt. On the other hand, given asymmetric information and the weakness of control mechanisms, there are also market failures in equity issuance that may be more severe than for debt, reflected in features such as the scope for overpricing new issues, and for diverting funds away from shareholders to suit managers' own objectives. The takeover sanction seems at most a weak counterweight.

While most of the discussion of equity focuses on non-financial companies, it has a number of implications for banks, which warrant further research. In particular, how do they overcome the market failures in equity markets to raise enough capital to grow (if retentions are insufficient)? Or, on the other hand, if retentions do suffice, are banks particularly subject to Jensen's problem of diversion of free cash flow (Ch. 2), despite their high leverage? How important is it that they are often protected from takeover? And to what extent is regulation responsible for the high leverage of banks? Why does leverage of banks (at least pre-Basle) differ sharply between countries?

A related policy issue, notably in Continental Europe, is how to stimulate use of equity finance more generally, so as to render the economy more robust. This is of particular importance if there is a decline in commitment/relationship banking. Fiscal changes may have an impact, but arguably a durable shift towards equity requires development of a funded pension system.

(c) Information

The problem of asymmetric or imperfect information lies at the root of the difficulties in both debt and equity financing, as well as explaining both the existence and the potential instability of banks. The problem provides a basis for a number of possible policy initiatives, such as disclosure requirements, compulsory credit ratings, collection of information regarding liquidity in securities markets, central risk offices, etc., although encouragement to institutions to collect their own information on credit risk, and vulnerability to crises, may be as or more fruitful. More generally, there are grounds for research in this area, notably in an assessment of the empirical as opposed to theoretical consequences of information problems.

(d) Agency costs

A particular theme in the discussion of corporate debt, and the wider implications of financial fragility, was the pervasive influence of agency costs on financial arrangements. For example, the higher sustainable debt ratios in relationship-banking countries are held to relate to the lowering of agency costs arising from various institutional arrangements. And if competition tends to cause such relationships to break down, it leads to an increase in such costs. A suggestion raised by the analysis of financial instability is that agency-costs analysis could provide further insight into the behaviour of financial institutions. For example, it could provide a better explanation of repeated periods of underpricing of risk and losses by banks. On the one hand, the safety net clearly generates agency costs (by bearing all or part of the risk to bank creditors and equity holders) which need to be offset by capital adequacy and banking supervision. But there may equally be conflicts between bank managers and lending officers, between banks and their owners and creditors, independent of the safety net. Explaining and modelling such effects would be a further advance towards understanding and controlling the processes that lead on to systemic risk.

(e) Risk

The asset pricing theory outlined in Ch. 1, Sect. 3*a*, and particularly the distinction between diversifiable (unsystematic) and non-diversifiable (systematic) risk is the core of finance theory. In the context of credit rationing it is important to note its shortcomings. (Can institutions observe and control risk, given adverse selection and moral hazard? Do they often mistake diversifiable for undiversifiable risk, as for example in the ldc debt crisis?) But the distinctions remain crucial to the overall analysis. Systemic risk is a form of undiversifiable risk *par excellence*, as is interest-rate risk. Liquidity and credit risk can be diversified to some extent (different sources of finance, lending to borrowers whose credit risk is uncorrelated), but frequently are not. Many issues are raised:

Do financial institutions, and borrowers in the non-financial sector, understand to a sufficient degree the benefits of diversification? Repeated patterns of risk concentration suggest either incomprehension or deliberate ignorance. Regulation may aggravate such patterns, if it constrains financial institutions to a narrow range of assets. And it was noted that the Basle agreement does not take covariances between asset returns into account.

And what of systematic risk? Is it understood that it can only be transferred or shared, and not eliminated? (A good example is the way the shift from fixed-rate to floating-rate debt shifts interest rate risk from creditor to debtor, but increases credit risk.) Hellwig (1991*b*) suggests that rather than safety *per se*, regulation should be aimed at an efficient risk allocation. Thus, any restrictions on the use of hedging instruments by financial institutions may constrain risk-sharing, thus making the allocation less efficient. Hellwig also questions whether time depositors should be entirely insulated from the consequences of interest rate risk. Again, systematic risks can be subdivided into those which are broadly predictable by probabilistic calculation (such as the cycle and most interest rate movements) and those subject to uncertainty (financial crises and changes in interest rate regime). It was suggested that the competitive process may enforce adequate pricing of the former but not the latter. Again, experience suggests that market forces may lead to inadequate coverage, even for the former—though not all economists would accept this. They would suggest it implies a form of irrationality: not taking account available information at the time of lending, that is contrary to the way financial markets behave. They would see any ex-post underpricing as due to an uncertain change in conditions and/or the presence of inappropriate government policy.

(2) Regulatory Issues

(a) The safety net

A general issue that has recurred frequently, both for financial fragility and instability, is the utility of the safety net (i.e. lender-of-last-resort and deposit-insurance facilities). How restricted should its use be? Clearly, in the case of the lender of last resort, it is a matter for the judgement of the authorities whether its use in a particular period of financial stress is needed to prevent systemic risk; the need for such judgement, as well as the need for uncertainty over the operation of the net, preclude any fixed rules.

But one might still suggest that its use could reasonably be restricted to financial markets and institutions on grounds of market failure; implicit extension to non-financial companies would not seem to be justified on these grounds, and would offer too little stability at the cost of excessive moral hazard. There remains an issue, however, whether financial markets as well as institutions need protection. A number of authors suggest that there is a need for a 'market maker of last resort', given increased use of direct financing, notably for maintenance of short-term liquidity.

There is a clear tradeoff in the financial sector between systemic stability and moral hazard. It would be useful to know the nature of it. In particular, what degree of moral hazard is prompted by each operation of the safety net? What is the effect of frequency of operation? Size of operation? Co-operation of private institutions in the rescue concerned? To what extent can moral hazard be counteracted by regulation, supervision, and capital requirements?

Following on from this, it would be useful to know the optimal form of the safety net, i.e. the lender of last resort as opposed to deposit insurance. The general issues are fairly well known. Deposit insurance should in principle be reserved for cases of insolvency and the lender of last resort for illiquidity, but in practice the distinction is hard to make. Deposit insurance, by being certain in its effects, may offer greater systemic protection, or alternatively it can be 'tuned' to protect only investors for whom credit appraisal is excessively costly. In the former case, the certainty can lead to excessive protection for risk-taking, especially as insurance is rarely priced according to risk, given intrinsic difficulties. Moreover, pressures to extend protection to all investors (especially when a large bank with 'systemic' dimensions is concerned) may be intense. The lender of last resort offers more flexibility and has sufficed for most countries other than the US; in such countries, deposit insurance has been strictly confined to depositor protection rather than being a bulwark against systemic risk. There remain difficulties, particularly with broad-based lender-of-last-resort responses which involve an increase in the money supply and lower interest rates, as they may face conflicts with other macroeconomic policy objectives, such as control of inflation or maintenance of exchange-rate parity.

A further backup is provided by the automatic stabilizers inherent in the fiscal system, which cushion the real economy against some of the consequences of financial instability. The analysis implies that such stabilizers are a valuable feature of an economy that should be left to operate and not deliberately counteracted. An additional consideration is whether the safety net can be privatized, e.g. by private deposit insurance and/or help by major institutions for the Central Bank in rescue operations, which may help to avoid the conflicts in macroeconomic policy outlined above. US experience suggests that private deposit insurance cannot be relied on for systemic protection (as in the case of Ohio and Maryland thrifts noted in Ch. 6). Meanwhile, UK and Canadian experience has shown that the major banks are more prepared to provide private-sector assistance with rescues, or recycling of funds, when there are entry barriers and a 'club' of banks. Such groups have a clear common interest in maintaining the reputation of the banking system, are few in number and easy to co-ordinate, have spare resources to devote to rescues, and can avoid 'free riding' by competitors who are unwilling to co-operate. Such clubs could also be seen as having an 'implicit contract' with the Central Bank, in return for benefits such as shielding banks from competition (Bingham 1991*b*). Increased competition following deregulation, as well as global integration, may reduce the cohesion of such 'clubs', and devalue implicit contracts, since the Central Bank can no longer deliver the former benefits.

(b) Prudential regulation

Prudential regulation, as noted, is an essential complement to the safety net if excessive risk-taking is to be avoided; the US thrifts offer the best example of the consequences of its absence. Many of the lessons have clearly been learnt, namely the need for capital adequacy to offer protection against shocks and minimize incentives to risk-taking, and the additional need for balance-sheet supervision to offset directly forms of risk-taking (large exposures), which may themselves be stimulated by capital adequacy regulation, notably in the absense of risk weighting. More contentious is the need for market-value based accounting by supervisors; there are obvious difficulties for non-marketable loans, but the risk of using book values is arguably much greater, as shown by the thrifts crisis. And at a deeper level, are there sufficient learning mechanisms to enable supervisors (and market participants) to learn from their mistakes, given rapid turnover of staff? To give one example, why did the Swedes not learn from the Norwegian banking crisis (Ch. 8) to limit property exposures of their banks? There may be excessive readiness to assume the current domestic situation is unique—again, this book seeks to show otherwise. Finally, it is suggested that structural and macroeconomic data may be a useful adjuct to normal regulatory procedures.

Meanwhile, even abstracting from issues of investor protection, the systemic risk in securities markets arising from failure of a major institution clearly requires similar prudential regulation of investment banks, adapted to their circumstances (position risk being more important than credit risk). But the risk of securities market failure due to liquidity crisis may also require the authorities to ensure robust market structures. There are a number of issues relating to capital adequacy, as outlined in

Ch. 5 and the conclusion to Ch. 6. At a most general level, it could be questioned whether rules as opposed to discretion are really appropriate—is risk systematically mispriced? Also, should risk weights be fixed? Counter-arguments in support of fixed weights and rules include the lack of information to the supervisors to maintain a more discretionary regime, the risk of competition in laxity to maintain competitive equality, the fact that rules are allowed to be tighter than Basle allows, and the benefits of fixed rules in preventing supervisory 'disaster myopia'. Some commentators would deploy an additional argument that, short of bank failure and systemic risk, some form of regulation should be used to offset tendencies to excessive borrowing that lead to financial fragility (i.e. operating on the demand for credit). Such an argument requires the borrower not to understand the risks, which is clearly the case for part of the household sector. The argument on the basis of externalities of default (Ch. 4) could apply to both persons and companies. But detailed regulation is clearly unviable; use of the tax system is more appropriate. Taxation of mortgage-interest payments is one proposal that has emerged in the UK. Improvements to availability of information to borrower and lender may also be helpful (see conclusions to Chs. 2 and 3).

(c) Financial liberalization

The role of liberalization in the growth of debt to the household sector seems fairly clear, as the latter has generally been the residual recipient of credit in the case of restriction. For companies, liberalization's role is less clear cut. The effects on corporate debt in many countries appear to arise via increased competition, lower profitability of lending, and blurring of boundaries between financial institutions, rather than liberalization directly. As regards instability, liberalization can lead to such a pattern via a number of channels, notably debt growth, heightened uncertainty, new and unfamiliar instruments, and entry of new and inexperienced institutions. But note that the euromarkets—the locus of several of the cases of instability cited above—developed independent of liberalization, indeed largely as a response to regulation elsewhere. Crises in the euromarkets tended to be triggered by technological change or shifts in demand for credit. Hence liberalization is not the only cause of instability, and equally, well-directed liberalizations may be carried through without instability (Ch. 7).

To the extent that liberalization has had deleterious consequences, the main question in the context of the book is whether the costs are still outweighed by the benefits, and how the costs can be reduced. Such a calculation needs to take into account as costs not merely the direct effects on default and systemic risk but also the broader externalities arising from financial fragility that were highlighted in Ch. 4. If they lead to heightened instability that requires greater use of the safety net, the adverse effects of this on risk-taking as well as direct costs (of saving thrifts etc.) need to be taken on board. On the other hand, the benefits may relate not merely to the lower cost and improved quality of financial services but also the heightened ability of the private sector to adjust balance sheets and any effects of heightened competition on the efficiency of the financial system and hence on the use of costly resources in performing its intermediation function (Colwell and Davis 1992). As noted in Ch. 1, the consensus (Blundell-Wignall and Browne 1991) is that liberalization has had net benefits. Others note that, even if there were net costs, developments such as globalization, technological advance, and the burgeoning of the euromarkets mean that deregulation cannot easily be reversed, especially in the absense of exchange controls.

As regards means of reducing costs of deregulation, liberalization of regulations restricting activities of financial institutions can reduce instability by offering alternative markets to firms whose principal activity is threatened by structural change. There is a case for 'consistent' rather than 'piecemeal' liberalization, as deregulation of one market together with maintenance of controls in another may give rise to instability. Furthermore, given the difficulties faced by firms unfamiliar with free competition, there may be a case for gradual rather than sudden liberalization, so long as it applies equally to different institutions. This is the Japanese approach, which contrasts with most other countries (Shigehara 1991), although such gradualism may only be possible if the process is begun before pressures become too intense. Banks may need to be 'taught' credit monitoring (Bank of Japan 1991*b*). More generally, costs of deregulation should be lower, the more efficient prudential regulation is—note that regulation needs to be tightened when markets are liberalized, and the costliest cases of instability have followed liberalization and loosening of prudential regulation.

Macroeconomic policy also has a key role to play. Comparative experience of financial fragility and systemic risk, especially those following deregulation, suggests that a policy generating long-term low and stable inflation and positive, but not excessive, real interest rates, and consequently avoiding the need for sudden changes in policy tightness, are crucial to avoiding instability. The German experience is a good example. But the Japanese conjuncture shows, that even when policy bears down firmly on general inflation, asset price booms, whether following deregulation or autonomous, can generate fragility. Policy may hence need to take asset price booms into account at an early stage. Finally, experiences such as those following the tightening of US monetary policy in 1979 (thrifts, debt crisis) suggest that if inflation does become established, it needs to be subdued gradually; attempts at sudden disinflation may trigger financial instability.

(3) Financial Structure and Behaviour

Some of the most interesting issues raised by a study of financial fragility and instability relate to the nature and behaviour of financial markets and their implications. They are, of course, not entirely distinct from the regulatory issues, which to some extent respond to them.

(a) Financial innovation

Innovation may be a response to financial regulation (a means to circumvent it), a response to liberalization (taking advantage of freedom), or of course an autonomous process, driven by technical change or market conditions. The crucial question in the present context is its influence on fragility and instability. As regards the former, a number of innovations may be classified as credit creating, in that their introduction entailed a relaxation of credit rationing, while very few have been equity creating, and there has been little technical progress in the crucial field of credit monitoring (although as markets work better, more information should be embodied in prices). Junk bonds and securitized mortgages were among the credit-creating innovations highlighted. It is, however, less clear that such innovations in themselves led to excessive borrowing, independent of the other factors highlighted. As regards instability among financial institutions, the main problem seems to have been misunderstanding, for example of the nature of innovations (perpetual FRNs), their potentiality (portfolio insurance), or mere lack of experience of how new markets may behave under stress (junk bonds, Swedish commercial paper). Lamfalussy (1992) also suggests that increasing exposures by banks to off-balance-sheet risks, (via swaps, forward rate agreements etc.)—which often exceed those to the interbank market—aggravate the problems of asymmetric information regarding banks' portfolios, both in terms of direct exposure and indirect exposures arising from linkages between markets and sectors. They thus increase the risk of runs. And because derivatives have increased linkages between market segments, disruption in one may more readily feed into others—generating systemic risk.

On the other hand, innovations that distribute systematic risk to institutions best able to absorb it, and/or spread it more widely across the financial system, may help to diffuse financial instability and prevent systemic risk. To the extent there is such diffusion, rather than concentration, such an explanation could be an important supplement to increased readiness to use the 'safety net' as an explanation for the lack of major crises since the war.

(b) Competition in financial markets

It is evident that a degree of competition between financial institutions and markets is required in order to obtain an efficient allocation of funds to final users, with a minimum of monopoly and X-inefficiency. However, aspects of the analysis in this book pose the question whether there is a sharp competition/instability tradeoff which should be treated carefully, or at least monitored closely by prudential supervisors. Such a tradeoff appears particularly acute in the initial stages of a transition to a competitive system, before the financial system has experienced a recession, although behaviour in the euromarkets implies that a syndrome of instability can also recur over the longer term. A particular problem arising in domestic markets may be weakening of relationship links between financial institutions and borrowers, which it is suggested may be an important component of the financial fragility and instability of recent years. The lack of such links in the euromarkets may be a factor underlying their vulnerability too.[2]

(c) Excess capacity

The issue of excess capacity in financial markets is clearly linked to competition, so long as it is not assumed that the market is always in long run equilibrium. Its definition is of course problematic: inadequate returns to equity from operating in a prudent manner is one possibility. Its orderly removal faces markets and regulators with serious challenges, to ensure it occurs through mergers or reductions in size of institutions, rather than disruptive bankruptcies. If some firms can cross-subsidize activities from profitable niches elsewhere, it may persist, while as sociated incentives for risk-taking, particularly for firms not benefiting from such situations, may inflict considerable instability on users of the market. Regulators may aggravate such problems, by seeking to impede closure of client firms.

Some analysts, such as Wojnilower (1991) would suggest that subsidies or other incentives to exit or merger are appropriate, at least in the highly atomistic market conditions typical of the US. Others, such as Tannen wald (1991), question the existence of excess capacity in certain financial markets, and suggest that recent banking losses have been consequences of cyclical changes which will correct themselves in an upturn (unless instability intervenes). In the light of such contrasting approaches, a challenge to researchers is to provide precise symptoms, definitions and measures of excess capacity, as well as indicators as to whether its removal will entail disruption of markets in any particular instance.

[2] Davis and Mayer 1991.

(d) Industrial structure of financial markets

Ch. 7 argued at length the view that a closer focus on structural developments is appropriate from the point of view of financial instability. This by no means exhausts the importance of the industrial-organization framework, however. To offer just one example, oligopolistic banking systems may have some additional features of relevance. At least when competitive pressures are moderate, they make it easier for a 'club' of banks to exist, exerting discipline over members and offering non-inflationary assistance to the lender of last resort in heading off crises. They may also be less vulnerable to failure than an atomistic system, even during periods of 'excessive competition', given diversification of sources of income.

These advantages need to be set against the standard efficiency arguments against market power in terms of supernormal profits etc. Second, oligopolies may be particularly vulnerable to a 'too big to fail' syndrome, where markets assume that authorities will eliminate any danger of bank failure, with adverse effects on moral hazard. Third, concentration on financial markets may increase the vulnerability of the markets in which the player is active to failure of a single institution. Some analysts suggest this is an emerging problem in international wholesale markets at the time of writing. Also oligopoly dynamics may lead firms to follow each other into new areas to maintain balance in their relationship, even if the consequences are losses (Big Bang), financial fragility (Australia), or heightened risk (ldc debt). Moreover, the dynamics of an oligopoly recovering from a period of excessive competition may entail sharper reductions in competition, with more deleterious consequences for the macroeconomy, than a similar situation in an atomistic market, where competition is harder to suppress.

(e) Wholesale markets

It would be easy to arrive at alarmist conclusions regarding the money markets, in particular the international interbank market, given their key role in many of the crises outlined. However, a more balanced view would suggest, first, that they clearly serve key economic functions, as outlined in Ch. 6, Sect. 1, and that the efficiency of the global financial system is accordingly enhanced; second, the striking feature of the markets is their robustness rather than their fragility, given the rarity with which serious difficulties have arisen (in the absence of the wholesale markets to absorb and diffuse shocks, the system might have been more unstable); and third, since retail depositors are sheltered by deposit insurance, any problems will inevitably be reflected in uninsured markets;

such instability that has arisen could be seen as a price worth paying to avoid moral hazard.

That said, there may remain certain policy issues. In particular, it could be questioned whether the Basle risk weight of 20 per cent on interbank exposures is too low. Second, the authorities need to be vigilant to detect any undue risk-taking in the markets. Third, the fact commercial banks simultaneously act as dealers or market makers in markets such as forex, swaps, securities, and derivatives products, as well as being principals in the interbank market, could lead to heightened contagion. And finally, there remains the tension between the desire to maintain stability via the lender of last resort, and the need to minimize moral hazard, that must be resolved on each individual occasion. Beliefs that major banks are 'too big to fail' in such well-informed markets could lead to significant underpricing of risk.

(f) Organization of finance

The contrast was made at an early stage of the book between 'Anglo-Saxon' financial systems and those in Continental Europe and Japan, where the latter tend to have closer links between lenders and (corporate) borrowers, and hence can sustain a high level of debt for a given level of default. While the latter are not immune to financial fragility, it would appear that such a system is less subject to the sharp disequilibrium shifts in indebtedness, that often give rise to fragility, than a more transactions-based financial system. Experience in the USA and UK compared with Germany certainly supports the hypothesis, although experience in 1990–1 in Japan runs somewhat counter.

If correct,[3] such a conclusion poses the question whether policy moves in the direction of such a structure are desirable, along the lines noted by Bisignano (1991) (such as promoting closer links between finance and industry). But it also raises the questions of how sustainable relationship banking is when exposed to competition (as, for example, in Norway), whether it is sustainable as securities markets grow and more information is disclosed and embodied in prices, and whether the gains are worth the costs of limiting competition. An interesting case will be Japan. Certainly the development of securities in Japan and/or access of Japanese firms to international markets in recent years was accompanied by sharp rises in debt, followed by financial difficulties in some cases. Will banks be content or able to rescue firms who have not patronized them in the previous upturn? Is the German system unique—and can it survive? Finally, and abstracting from such competition, there is the question whether the increasing coexistence of two very different approaches to financial

[3] An alternative hypothesis is of course that it is competition itself that causes instability and not structure.

market behaviour may lead to market instability, especially in securities markets where global agreements on market practices have not been reached (Bingham 1991*b*).

(4) Prospects

To conclude, we make a brief assessment of future prospects. A number of commentators have suggested that the 1970–90 period was historically unique, given the degree of turbulence in the macroeconomy and financial markets, combined with the switch from a regulated to a liberalized financial system. A number of considerations can be adduced.

On the one hand, it is true that the two decades saw much higher inflation than the historic norm, as well as low real interest rates in the 1970s followed by rather high ones in the 1980s. It is suggested in the text that these were all significant causes of fragility and instability, and that countries that did not suffer these shifts appear to have undergone a much lower degree of financial difficulty. Partly in response to inflation, macroeconomic policies have had to be very stringent at times (often after being excessively lax earlier on), thus compounding problems for over-indebted borrowers and their lenders. The authorities may be expected to seek to avoid these difficulties in coming years, given recent experience of them. Indeed, already at the time of writing, inflation rates are below 5 per cent in many OECD countries, though real rates remain high.

Meanwhile, financial intermediaries and borrowers have suffered sizeable losses and failures owing to their willingness to extend and accept credit. Financial innovations often showed unexpected behaviour in response to market disequilibria or recessions. Regulators, too, learnt a great deal about the behaviour of liberalized financial markets, whose operations differ radically—and often diametrically—from those of cartelised, segmented, and constrained sectors typical prior to the 1970s. They are also aware of potential for systemic risk arising from or via payments and settlements systems. Consequently, experience may be expected to imbue caution and greater understanding among players in financial markets, helping to impede a repetition of the excesses of the past two decades. Experience is buttressed by formal agreements to strengthen regulation, such as the Basle agreement on capital adequacy. Third, a number of factors may divert financing towards equity and away from debt. Tax systems in a number of countries, such as the UK and France, are becoming a great deal more neutral in their treatment of financing methods. The likely further development of pension funds in countries currently reliant on social security (Davis 1991*b*) may offer a significant fillip to the demand for equity. The development of an EC-wide securities market in the aftermath of 1992 may increase the access of European firms to equity finance.

On the other hand, a degree of vigilance against financial instability remains appropriate. The whole thrust of the 'disaster myopia' hypothesis (Chs. 5–7) is that memories of financial instability can rapidly fade, a process intensified by rapid turnover of staff and/or intense competition. Examples are the repeated pattern of overlending to ldcs in the 1930s and 1970s, and UK banks exposures to property in the early 1970s and late 1980s.

Some of the underlying conditions for financial instability continue to obtain. The level of competition among institutions and markets remains intense, with one of the root causes being continuing excess capacity. Technical advances continue to open up opportunities for shifts in the pattern of intermediation. As international interpenetration increases, notably in EC countries, such pressures may intensify. Such a process will also remove supplies of cheap funding for banks, which on the one hand reduces cross-subsidization of unprofitable operations, but on the other may increase incentives to take risks. As noted, such competition also weakens 'club' relationships between banks and Central Banks, potentially making maintenance of stability more difficult. Again, this weakening of 'club' relationships could be a marked feature of the EC, especially if full integration of financial systems goes ahead, posing a problem for a future European System of Central Banks.

Many financial markets remain heavily regulated, and may thus be particularly vulnerable to the behaviour patterns discussed in the text. Dornbusch (1991) points to possible difficulties in countries such as Korea, and in Greece and Spain after 1992, because 'at the pace at which liberalization is taking place, and capital markets are opened, regulation is in no way allowed to catch up with reality'.

The adverse state of balance sheets—both of banks and non-banks—in certain countries may take time to adjust, implying a prolonged period of financial fragility. Experience of Norway and Canada as outlined in the text could apply more widely. A general point here is that the immediate policy response to systemic risk (the lender of last resort) is well understood and generally effective, hence another Great Depression is unlikely. On the other hand, the appropriate macroeconomic policy response to problems of financial fragility (Ch. 4) that fall short of deflation or banking crises (as opposed to means of limiting fragilities' development in the first place) is less straightforward. Monetary expansion, for example, may cause inflation and moral hazard—and/or could be ineffective. Resolution may just require a period of sluggish economic activity while balance sheets adjust, with appropriate vigilance that the conditions do not suddenly deteriorate into a crisis.

Although monetary policy is now appropriately aimed at reducing inflation, as noted above, interest rate volatility cannot be ruled out, especially if there are errors in fiscal policy. The internationally-integrated financial system is highly intolerant of such mistakes, and may require large shifts in interest rates to offset them, with adverse consequences for securities markets and borrowers. The example of Sweden, forced to raise short rates by 6% in 1990 to protect the currency, is highly relevant here. Moreover, despite the 1991 recession in a number of countries, some commentators such as Lamfalussy (1992) suggest that since simultaneous downturn in all the major industrial countries has not been seen since liberalization and the growth of securities and derivatives markets began, the conclusion that the system is stable cannot yet be safely drawn.

Finally, while the trend to securities markets may be helpful in promoting equity financing, such markets also open new sources of debt to firms (and households via loan packaging), which US experience of the 1980s shows can lead borrowers into difficulties. Monitoring of securitized debt may be inadequate and/or risks mispriced. A number of instances have also shown that debt securities markets can show tendencies to instability similar to banks, which can in turn raise difficulties for firms that have broken their relationship links with banks. Indeed, relationship banking may itself be threatened by increased competition and development of securities markets. And as banks are left increasingly with the poorer credits unable to access markets, the risks on their books—and incentives to seek more—may increase.

Glossary

Adverse selection situation in which a pricing policy induces a low average quality of sellers in a market, while asymmetric information prevents the buyer from distinguishing quality. When it is sufficiently severe, the market may cease to exist.

Agency costs costs arising from the deviation between the agent's and principal's interests in an agency relationship. Includes both the costs to the principal of the behaviour of the agent and any expenditures incurred by the principal (or agent) in order to control the agent, such as monitoring expenditures by the principal and bonding expenditures by the agent. Two main types of agency problem are identified in this book, first the cost arising in the debt contract between debtors and creditors, and second the costs arising in the relationship between owners or managers of a firm and providers of external finance.

Agency relationship contract under which one or more persons (principals) engage another (the agent) to perform some service on their behalf which involves delegation of some decision-making responsibility to the agent.

Anglo-Saxon countries term used to refer to English-speaking advanced countries with developed capital markets as well as banks (UK, USA, Canada, Australia, NZ).

Bankruptcy a court-supervised process of breaking and rewriting contracts.

Basis point 1/100 of 1 per cent.

Basle agreements agreements among banking supervisors of the G10 countries to harmonize minimum standards of prudential supervision. Usually used to refer to their agreement on capital adequacy.

Basle risk weight weighting given to different types of exposure under the Basle agreement, in arriving at measure of risk-weighted capital adequacy. For example, loans to companies bear 100% weight, and hence need capital backing of 8%; mortgages bear 50%; interbank claims 20%.

Bearer security a security whose owner is not registered on the book of the issuer. Interest and principal are payable to the holder.

Bid–ask (or offer) spread the difference between the price at which a market maker is prepared to buy (bid) securities and that at which he is ready to sell (ask/offer).

Bought deal method of security issuance where the managing investment bank takes the whole of the issue on to its books at an agreed price, before selling it to investors.

Bridge loans short-term high-risk financing, used to fund a leveraged buyout or takeover until longer term financing can be arranged.

Broker agent bringing buyers and sellers together in exchange for a fee. Unlike a market maker, does not take a position.

Building society (UK, Ireland, Australia) form of mutual retail depository institution specializing in provision of secured finance for house purchase by the household sector.

Capital adequacy regulatory requirement for banks to maintain a certain ratio of shareholders' funds to assets.

Capital gearing debt as a proportion of assets.

CD (certificate of deposit) a negotiable certificate issued by a bank as evidence of an interest-bearing time deposit.

CEJ countries shorthand used to denote Continental Europe and Japan, whose financial systems contrast sharply with those in Anglo-Saxon countries (Ch. 1, Sect. 5).

Clearing House Interbank Payment System (CHIPS) a computerized network for transfer of international US dollar payments linking over 100 depository institutions which have offices or subsidiaries in New York City. Messages covering payments between the various depository institutions are entered into the CHIPS computer over the business day. At the end of each day, participants' net positions are settled through the Federal Reserve's funds transfer system.

Collateral assets pledged by the borrower in a debt contract, for the lender to seize in case of default (also called 'security').

Commitment informal, long-term, two-way, largely exclusive relationship between borrower and lender, hence 'relationship banking'. (Compare 'control'.) A loan commitment is a distinct concept: promise by a bank to provide a loan at specified terms.

Complete markets theoretical construct providing a full set of markets covering all present and future contingencies (e.g. ability to buy now an umbrella next Wednesday only if it rains).

Contestable market market in which there are no sunk costs of entry or exit, and hence incumbent firms behave as if they were in competitive equilibrium, even if there are economies of scale, owing to the threat of potential competition.

Control exclusive focus on the formal provisions of the debt contract in any transaction, hence 'transactions banking'. (Compare 'commitment'.)

Country risk risk relating to loans to borrowers based in a given country.

Coupon nominal payment due on a debt instrument, often expressed as a percentage of face value.

Covenant restriction on the behaviour of the borrower agreed at the time of issue of a debt instrument, breach of which allows the lender to claim default (often called an 'indenture').

CP (commercial paper) a short-term unsecured and generally marketable promise to repay a fixed amount (representing borrowed funds plus interest) on a certain future date and at a specific place. The note stands on the general credit-worthiness of the issuer or on the standing of a third party who is obliged to repay if the original borrower defaults.

Credit quality spread difference between the yield on a risk-free security and one which is subject to credit risk, but is otherwise similar (in terms of maturity etc.).

Credit rationing process whereby provision of debt to a given borrower is limited.

Credit risk risk that the borrower will fail to repay interest or principal on debt at the appointed time. Used interchangeably with default risk.

Default failure of the borrower to comply with the terms of the debt contract (breach of covenants; failure to repay principal; failure to pay interest).

Default risk as credit risk.

Deposit insurance provision of a guarantee that certain types of bank liability are convertible into cash.

Direct financing provision of external finance from saver to end-user via securities markets rather than financial intermediaries.

Disaster myopia tendency to disregard uncertain low-probability high-risk hazards.

Discount window facility offered by the US Federal Reserve allowing member banks to borrow reserves against collateral (usually in the form of government securities.)

Disequilibrim quantity rationing of credit rationing of credit by amount at a non-market-clearing price with excess demand of loanable funds, where among loan applicants who seem identical some receive credit and other do not. Arises either from government regulation or slow price adjustment.

Disintermediation diversion of funds that are usually intermediated into direct finance. May be used more narrowly to imply any shift away from banks to other intermediaries.

Duration average time to an asset's discounted cash flows.

Equilibrium quantity rationing of credit rationing of credit by amount in a situation where profit-maximizing lenders are unwilling to change the conditions under which loans are offered. Consequence of asymmetric information and incomplete contracts.

Eurobond international bond issue, usually in bearer form, underwritten by an international syndicate of banks and sold principally in countries other than that of the currency of denomination.

Euromarkets offshore markets where lenders and/or borrowers in financial contracts are from countries other than that of the currency of denomination of the contract. The principal markets are for eurobonds, syndicated euro-credits, euronotes and the eurocurrency interbank market.

Euronotes short-term promissory notes, usually with fixed maturities of up to a year, issued in the international capital markets in bearer form and on a discount basis; in mid-1980s generally underwritten (revolving underwriting facilities), later generally not (eurocommercial paper, medium-term notes).

Event risk risk a corporate bond will be downgraded owing to an unpredictable outside event, usually a leveraged buyout.

Expected return gain from holding a financial claim net of expected loss from default risk etc.

External finance finance that is not generated by the agent itself; debt or equity.

Financial crisis major collapse of the financial system, entailing inability to provide payments services or to allocate capital; realization of systemic risk.

Financial fragility a state of balance sheets which offers heightened vulnerability to default in a wide variety of circumstances. Used in this book to refer largely to difficulties of households, companies, and individual banks as opposed to the financial system as a whole (see 'systemic risk').

Foreign bond bond issued by a foreign borrower on a domestic market.

Forward rate agreement agreement between two parties wishing to protect themselves from interest rate risk. They agree an interest rate for a specified period from a given future settlement date for an agreed principal amount. The parties' exposure is the difference between the agreed and actual rate at settlement.

Free rider problem tendency for party to an agreement or transaction to take advantage of others' compliance, which reduces the incentives for others to comply; for example, in securities markets, disincentive to gather information about a borrower, owing to the ability of other investors to take advantage of it at no cost to themselves.

FRN floating-rate note; a medium-term security carrying a floating rate of interest which is reset at regular intervals, typically quarterly or half-yearly, in relation to some predetermined reference rate, typically Libor.

Futures contract an exchange-traded contract generally calling for delivery of a specified amount of a particular grade of commodity or financial instrument at a fixed date in the future. Contracts are highly standardized and traders need only agree on the price and number of contracts traded. Traders' positions are maintained at the exchange's clearing house, which becomes a counterparty to each trader once the trade has been cleared at the end of each day's trading session.

Gearing debt as a proportion of balance-sheet totals (used interchangeably with 'leverage').

Hedging taking an offsetting position in order to reduce risk, for example taking a position in futures equal and opposite to a cash position. A perfect hedge removes non diversifiable/systematic risk.

Herstatt risk risk in payments and settlement systems that disruption in one market will feed through into others that open later in the day.

Illiquidity generally, inability to transact rapidly in financial claims at full market value; more specifically, for a borrower, inability to obtain sufficient funds to service current obligations (compare 'insolvency').

Income gearing interest payments as a proportion of disposable income (US; interest burden).

Incomplete contracts debt contracts which do not specify behaviour of the borrower in all possible contigencies.

Insider party to a transaction having relevant information not available to the other party.

Insolvency state of balance sheet where liabilities exceed assets (compare 'illiquidity').

Intermediation process whereby end-providers and end-users of financial claims transact via a financial institution rather than directly via a market.

Internal finance finance generated within the borrower: retentions and depreciation.

Interest-rate risk risk arising from changes in value of financial claims caused by variations in the overall level of interest rates.

Junk-bonds high-yielding bonds that are below investment grade and are at times used in corporate take-overs and buyouts. Investment-grade securities are generally those rated at or above Baa by Moody's Investors Services or BBB by Standard & Poor's Corporation.

Ldcs less developed countries.

Lender of last resort an institution, usually the Central Bank, which has the ability to produce at its discretion liquidity to offset public desires to shift into cash in a crisis; to produce funds to support institutions facing liquidity difficulties; and to delay legal insolvency of an institution, preventing fire sales and calling of loans.

Leverage debt as a proportion of the total balance sheet (used interchangeably with 'gearing').

Leveraged buy-outs (LBOs) corporate acquisitions through stock purchases financed by the issuance of debt (which may include 'junk bonds').

Libor London Interbank Offered Rate. The rate at which banks offer to lend funds in the international interbank market.

Life cycle pattern of saving, borrowing, and consumption over a person's life; life-cycle hypothesis is of borrowing in young adulthood, repayment and saving in middle age, dissaving in old age.

Limited liability feature of corporations whereby equity holders cannot be held liable for losses in excess of the value of their shares.

Liquidation sale of a defaulting borrower's assets and distribution to creditors.

Liquidity constraint limits on borrowing preventing individuals from reaching desired level of consumption; in context of life cycle, preventing attainment of life-cycle optimum.

Liquidity risk risk of illiquidity as defined above.

Market maker intermediary in securities market that offsets fluctuating imbalances in demand and supply by purchases and sales on its own account, increasing or reducing its inventories in the process (ie taking positions), at its announced buying (ask) and selling (bid) prices.

Market risk risk that the value of marketable securities will change while the investor is holding a position in them. Sometimes used more narrowly to indicate systematic risk that cannot be eliminated by diversification.

Maturity time between issuance and repayment of principal on a debt instru ment.

Mezzanine finance high-risk bank finance of intermediate seniority in case of default.

Money markets wholesale markets for short-term, low-risk investments.

Money-market mutual fund open-ended collective investment vehicle investing in short-term, high-quality, liquid financial instruments (CDs, CP, Treasury bills).

Monitoring process whereby lenders check the behaviour of borrowers after funds have been advanced (compare 'screening').

Moral hazard incentive of beneficiary of a fixed-value contract, in the presence of asymmetric information and incomplete contracts, to change his behaviour after the contract has been agreed, in order to maximize his wealth, to the detriment of the provider of the contract.

Mortgage-backed bonds bonds traded mainly in the USA which pay interest semi-annually and repay principal either periodically or at maturity, and where underlying collateral is a pool of mortgages.

Net worth assets less debt, also called 'net assets'.

OECD Organisation for Economic Co-operation and Development, club of richest industrial countries, which currently has 24 members.

Option the contractual right, but not the obligation, to buy or sell a specified amount of a given financial instrument at a fixed price before or at a designated future date. A *call option* confers on the holder the right to buy the financial instrument. A *put option* involves the right to sell the financial instrument.

Panic pattern of contagious bank runs.

Perfect capital market theoretical construct featuring complete markets (see above), perfect information to all parties, no costs of default and ability of all agents to borrow freely at the going rate against their wealth, including future wage income.

Portfolio insurance method of computer-aided trading in equities which seeks to protect the value of a portfolio against declines in the market by means of transactions in stock index futures. Experience suggests it is unviable when too high a proportion of investors seek to use it.

Position holdings of financial instruments, whether in positive amounts (long position) or negative (short position), hence position risk: risks arising from such holdings, which are usually market/interest-rate risk but which may also include liquidity risk or credit risk.

Price rationing of credit equilibration of the credit market by means of the interest rate charged.

Price-specie-flow mechanism whereby trade imbalances generate flows of money (specie) which cause macroeconomic adjustments to correct the imbalance.

Primary market market in which financial claims are issued (compare 'secondary market').

Private placement issue of securities offered to one or a few investors rather than the public; not registered; usually very illiquid.

Programme trading term applied to types of computer-aided transaction strategies in securities markets.

Rational expectations hypothesis that investors and other agents in the economy act in the light of all the available information, including knowledge of underlying patterns of behaviour in markets.

Retail banking traditional forms of banking practice, where small deposits are aggregated within the same institution into large loans.

Risk danger that a certain contingency will occur; often applied to future events susceptible to being reduced to objective probabilities (compare 'uncertainty').

Risk pricing degree to which price of an instrument reflects the risks involved, allowing for diversification.

Run rapid withdrawal of short-term funds from a borrower (e.g. a bank), which exhausts its liquidity and leaves some lenders unable to realise their claims.

Savings and loan US retail depository institution, focused on lending long term for house purchase.

Screening process whereby lenders seek to detect the quality of borrowers before a loan is advanced.

Secondary market market in which primary claims can be traded.

Securitization the term is most often used narrowly to mean the process by which traditional intermediated debt instruments, such as loans or mortgages, are converted into negotiable securities which may be purchased either by depository institutions or by non-bank investors. More broadly, the term refers to the development of markets for a variety of negotiable instruments, which replace bank loans as a means of borrowing. Used in the latter sense, the term often suggests *disintermediation* of the banking system, as investors and borrowers bypass banks and transact business directly.

Seniority relative priority of a claimant on a defaulting borrower.

Settlement risk the possibility that operational difficulties in payments and settlements systems interrupt delivery of funds even where the counterparty is able to perform.

Shelf registration rule in US securities markets (dating from 1983) permitting a single registration to cover issue of securities at various times over two years, up to a specified amount. Increased the flexibility of US domestic markets.

Sovereign risk risk of lending to a given government.

Spread difference between the yields on two securities; usually refers in the text to the difference between yields on risky and risk-free debt. Also used for difference between bid-and-ask price offered by a market maker.

Strategic competition form of industrial behaviour, where firms carry out policies aimed to induce competitors to make a choice more favourable to the strategic mover than would otherwise be the case.

Strip financing form of financing which entails creditors holding a fixed combination of equity, and senior and junior debt.

Sunk cost costs incurred by a new entrant to a product market that cannot be recovered on exit.

Syndicated euro-credit loan facility, offered simultaneously by a number of banks, usually from more than one country, that sign the same loan agreement and stand equally in right of repayment.

Systematic risk risk that cannot be eliminated by portfolio diversification.

Systemic risk the danger that disturbances in financial markets and institutions will generalize across the financial system, so as to disrupt the provision of payment services and the allocation of capital; used interchangeably with financial instability or disorder.

Swap a financial transaction in which two counterparties agree to exchange streams of payments over time according to a predetermined rule. A swap is normally used to transform the market exposure associated with a loan or bond from one interest rate base (fixed term or floating rate) or currency of denomination to another; hence interest-rate swaps and currency swaps.

Thrift US savings and loan institution.

Trade credit credit granted by one non-financial firm to another.

Treasury bill. short-term negotiable debt issued by the government.

Unbundling separate pricing and sale of parts of a financial claim or service that are usually provided jointly.

Uncertainty term applied to expectations of a future event to which probability analysis cannot be applied (financial crises, wars, etc.).

Underwriter institution providing a guarantee of a certain price to an issuer of a security; may also manage and sell the issue, but these functions are separable.

Unsystematic risk idiosyncratic risk that can be eliminated by appropriate diversification.

Warrant long-term call option; e.g., equity warrant, instrument giving the right, but not the obligation, to buy shares at a given price at a specified time in the future.

Wholesale banking type of banking entailing forms of risk pooling external to the institution, e.g. use of interbank markets as sources of funds, splitting of participations in large loans.

Wholesale markets financial markets used by professional investors for instruments or transactions having a large minimum denomination.

Yield current rate of return on a security (for an irredeemable instrument, coupon as a proportion of market price; for a dated security, also takes into account investor's capital gain or loss over the period to maturity).

References

Acharya, S., and Udell, G. F. (1992), *Monitoring Financial Institutions*, Working Paper No. S–92–3, Salomon Center, New York Univ.

Aghion, P., and Bolton, P. (1992), 'An Incomplete Contract Approach to Bankruptcy and the Financial Structure of the Firm', *Review of Economic Studies*.

Akerlof, G. (1970), 'The Market for Lemons: Quality Uncertainty and the Market Mechanism', *Quarterly Journal of Economics*, 84: 488–500.

Aliber, R. Z. (1984), 'International Banking: A Survey', *Journal of Money, Credit and Banking*, 16: 661–95.

Allen, T. J. (1990), 'Developments in the International Syndicated Credits Market in the 1980s', *Bank of England Quarterly Bulletin*, 30: 71–7.

Altman, E. I. (1968), 'Financial Ratios, Discriminant Analysis and the Prediction of Corporate Bankruptcy', *Journal of Finance*, 23: 589–609.

—— (1984), 'A Further Empirical Investigation of the Bankruptcy Cost Question', *Journal of Finance*, 39: 1067–89.

Alworth, J. S. 'The Impact of Taxation on the Cost of Capital in Industrial Countries', mimeo, Bank for International Settlements, Basle.

Aoki, M. (1988), *Information, Incentives and Bargaining in the Japanese Economy*, Cambridge Univ. Press, Cambridge.

Asquith, P., Gertner, R., and Scharfstein, D. (1991), *Anatomy of Financial Distress: An Examination of Junk Bond Issuers*, Working Paper No. 3942, National Bureau of Economic Research

Auerbach, A. J. (1985), 'Real Determinants of Corporate Leverage', in B. M. Friedman, ed., *Corporate Capital Structures in the United States*, National Bureau of Economic Research, Univ. of Chicago Press.

Bagehot, W. (1873), *Lombard Street*, repr. 1962, Richard D. Irwin, Homewood, Ill.

Bailey, A. J., Davis, E. P., Exeter, J. J. M., and Jeanneau, J. G. S. (1988), 'Causes of the Crash', mimeo, Bank of England, London.

Bain, J. (1956), *Barriers to New Competition*, Harvard Univ. Press, Cambridge, Mass.

Baltensperger, E., and Dermine, J. (1987), 'The Role of Public Policy in Ensuring Financial Stability: A Cross-Country, Comparative Perspective', in R. Portes and A. Swoboda, eds., *Threats to International Financial Stability*, Cambridge Univ. Press, Cambridge.

Bank for International Settlements (1975), *Forty Fifth Annual Report*, Basle.

—— (1983), *The International Interbank Market: A Descriptive Study*, BIS Economic Paper No 8; Basle.

—— (1986*a*), *Recent Innovations in International Banking* (The Cross Report), Basle.

—— (1986b), *56th Annual Report*, Basle.

Bank of England (1978), 'The Secondary Banking Crisis and the Bank of England's Support Operations', *Bank of England Quarterly Bulletin*, 18: 230–6.

Bank of Japan (1991*a*), *Corporate Management Under Continued Economic Expansion*, Special Paper No. 199, Research and Statistics Dept., Bank of Japan.

—— (1991*b*), *Credit Risk Management of Financial Institutions Related to Lending*, Special Paper No. 205, Research and Statistics Dept., Bank of Japan.

Barro, R. J. (1974), 'Are Government Bonds Net Wealth?' *Journal of Political Economy*, 82: 1095–117.

Batchelor, R. C. (1986), 'The Avoidance of Catastrophe: Two Nineteenth Century Banking Crises', in F. Capie and G. E. Wood, eds., *Financial Crises and the World Banking System*, Macmillan, London.

Baumol, W. J. (1982), 'Contestable Markets, an Uprising in the Theory of Industrial Structure', *American Economic Review*, 72: 1–15.

Baxter, N. D. (1967), 'Leverage, Risk of Ruin and the Cost of Capital', *Journal of Finance*, 22: 395–404.

Bellanger, S. (1989), 'Looking Beyond the Thrifts Crisis', *The Bankers Magazine*, July–Aug. 1989.

Benink, H. A. (1991), 'Financial Fragility and Financial Disorder', mimeo, Univ. of Limburg.

Benveniste, L. M., and Berger, A. N. (1987), 'Securitisation with Recourse', *Journal of Banking and Finance*, 11: 403–24.

Berger, A. N., and Udell, G. F. (1990*a*), 'Some Evidence on the Empirical Significance of Credit Rationing', Finance and Economics Discussion Series, No. 105; Federal Reserve Board, Washington, DC.

—— and —— (1990*b*), 'Collateral, Loan Quality and Banks Risk', *Journal of Monetary Economics*, 25: 21–42.

—— and —— (1992), *Securitization, Risk and the Liquidity Problem in Banking*, Working Paper No. S-92-2, Salomon Center, New York Univ.

Bernanke, B. S. (1983), 'Non-Monetary Effects of the Financial Crisis in the Propagation of the Great Depression', *American Economic Review*, 73: 257–76.

—— Campbell, J. Y. and Whited, T. (1990), 'US Corporate Leverage; Developments in 1987 and 1988', *Brookings Papers in Economic Activity*, 1990/1: 255–86.

—— and Campbell, J. Y. (1988), 'Is There a Corporate Debt Crisis?' *Brookings Papers on Economic Activity*, 1988/1: 83–125.

—— and Gertler, M. (1989), 'Agency Costs, Net Worth and Business Fluctuations', *American Economic Review*, 79: 14–31.

—— and —— (1990), 'Financial Fragility and Economic Performance', *Quarterly Journal of Economics*, 105: 87–114.

—— and James, C. (1991), 'The Gold Standard, Deflation and Financial Crisis in the Great Depression: An International Comparison', in R. G. Hubbard, ed., *Financial Markets and Financial Crises*, National Bureau of Economic Research, Univ. of Chicago Press.

—— and Lown, C. S. (1991), 'The Credit Crunch', *Brookings Papers on Economic Activity*, 1992/1: 205–79.

Bester, H. (1985), 'Screenings vs Rationing in Credit Markets with Imperfect Information', *American Economic Review*, 75: 850–5.

Bhattacharya, S. (1979), 'Imperfect Information, Dividend Policy and the Bird in Hand Fallacy', *Bell Journal of Economics*, 10: 259–70.

Bingham, T. R. G. (1991*a*), *Securities Markets, Systemic Stability and Regulation*, Special Paper No. 26, Financial Markets Group, London School of Economics.

—— (1991*b*), 'The Changing Face of the Global Financial Marketplace', *Journal of International Securities Markets*, Autumn 191–3.

Bisignano, J. (1991), 'European Financial Deregulation: The Pressures for Change and the Cost of Achievement', in *The Deregulation of Financial Intermediaries: Proceedings of a Conference*, Research Dept., Reserve Bank of Australia.

Bispham, J. A. (1986), 'Rising Public-Sector Indebtedness: Some More Unpleasant Arithmetic', in M. J. Boskin, J. S. Flemming, and S. Gorini, eds., *Private Saving and Public Debt*, Blackwell, Oxford.

Blair, M. M., and Litan, R. E. (1990), 'Corporate Leverage and Leverage Buyouts in the eighties', in J. B. Shoven and J. Waldyogel, eds., *Debt, Taxes and Corporate Restructuring*, Brookings Institution, Washington, DC.

Blanchard, O. J., and Watson, M. W. (1982), 'Bubbles, Rational Expectations and Financial Markets', in P. Watchel, ed., *Crises in the Economic and Financial Structure*, Salomon Bros. series on Financial Institutions and Markets, Lexington Books, Lexington, Mass.

Blinder, A. S., and Stiglitz, J. E. (1983), 'Money, Credit Constraints, and Economic Activity', *American Economic Review*, 73: 297–302.

Blundell-Wignall, A., and Browne, F. X. (1991), *Macroeconomic Consequences of Financial Liberalisation: A Summary Report*, Working Paper No. 98; Dept. of Economics and Statistics, OECD, Paris.

——, ——, and Cavaglia, S. (1990), *Financial Liberalisation and Consumption Smoothing*, Working Paper No. 81; Dept. of Economics and Statistics, OECD, Paris.

Bolton, P. (1990), 'A Theory of Secured Debt: Contracting with Multiple Creditors', mimeo.

Bond, I. D. (1985), *The Syndicated Credits Market*, Discussion Paper No. 22; Bank of England, London.

—— and Briault, C. B. (1983*a*), 'Commercial Banks and International Debt: A Problem of Control?', mimeo, Bank of England, London.

—— and —— (1983*b*), 'Commercial and International Debt: The Experience of the 1970s', mimeo, Bank of England, London.

Bordes, C., and Melitz, J. (1989), *Business Debt and Default in France*, Discussion Paper, No. 333; Centre for Economic Policy Research, London.

Bordo, M. D. (1989), 'The Impact and International Transmission of Financial Crises: Some Historical Evidence 1870–1933', *Rivista di storia economica*, 2nd ser. 2: 41–78.

Borio, C. E. V. (1990*a*), *Leverage and Financing of Non-Financial Companies: An International Perspective*, BIS Economic Paper No. 27; Basle.

—— (1990*b*), *Banks' Involvement in Highly Leveraged Transactions*, BIS Economic Paper No. 28; Basle.

Brady, N. (1988), *Report of the Presidential Task Force on Market Mechanisms*, US Government Publications Office, Washington, DC.

Brealey, R., and Myers, S. (1988), *Principles of Corporate Finance*, 3rd edn., McGraw-Hill, New York.

Breusch, T. S., and Pagan, A. R. (1980), 'The Lagrange-Multiplier Test and its Applications to Model Specification in Econometrics', *Review of Economic Studies*, 47: 239–53.

Brimmer, A. F., and Dahl, F. R. (1975), 'Growth International Banking: Implications for Public Policy', *Journal of Finance*, 30: 341–63.

Broker, G. (1989), *Competition in Banking*, OECD, Paris.

Brumbaugh, L. R. D., *et al* (1989), 'Cleaning Up the Depositary Institutions Mess', *Brookings Papers of Economic Activity*, 1989/1: 243–84.

Budd, A. (1990), 'The Credit Crunch: Causes and Consequences', *Barclays Bank Economic Commentary*, Nov. 1990.

Bulow, J., and Shoven, J. (1979), 'The Bankruptcy Decision', *Bell Journal of Economics*, 9: 437–56.

Bush, J., and Kaletsky, A. (1990), 'When the Junk Pile Topples', *Financial Times*, 14 Feb.

Cable, J. R. (1985), 'Capital Market Information and Industrial Performance: The Role of West German Banks', *Economic Journal*, 95: 118–32.

—— and Turner, P. (1985), 'Asymmetric Information and Credit Rationing: Another View of Industrial Bank Lending and Britain's Economic Problem', in D. Currie, ed., *Advances in Monetary Economics*, Croom Helm, London.

Cagan, P. (1965), *Determinants and Effects of Changes in the Stock of Money 1875–1960*, Studies in Business Cycles, 13; NBER, Columbia Univ. Press, New York.

Callen, T., and Lomax, J. (1990), 'The Developments of the Building Societies Sector in the 1980s', *Bank of England Quarterly Bulletin*, 30: 503–10.

Calomiris, C. W., and Gorton, G. (1991), 'The Origins of Banking Panics, Models, Facts and Bank Regulation', in R. G. Hubbard, ed., *Financial Markets and Financial Crises*, NBER, Univ. of Chicago Press, Chicago.

Cantor, R. (1990), 'Effects of Leverage on Corporate Investment and Hiring Decisions', *Federal Reserve Bank of New York Quarterly Review*, Summer, 31–41.

Chan, Y. (1983), 'On the Positive Role of Financial Intermediation in Allocation of Venture Capital in a Market with Imperfect Information', *Journal of Finance*, 38: 1543–68.

Chant, J. (1987), 'Regulation of Financial Institutions: A Functional Analysis', *Bank of Canada Technical Report*, 45, Jan.

Christelow, D. B. (1987), 'Converging Household Debt Ratios for Four Industrial Countries', *Federal Reserve Bank of New York, Quarterly Bulletin*, Winter 1987–8: 35–47.

Colwell, R. J., and Davis, E. P. (1992), 'Output, Productivity and Externalities: The Case of Banking', forthcoming, *Scandinavian Journal of Economics*.

Cooper, R., and John, A. (1988), 'Coordinating Coordination Failures in Keynesian Models', *Quarterly Journal of Economics*, 103: 441–64.

Corbett, J., and Mayer, C. P. (1991), *Financial Reform in Eastern Europe: Progress with the Wrong Model*, Discussion Paper No. 603; Centre for Economic Policy Research, London.

Corrigan, E. G. (1987), 'Financial Structure: A Long View', in *Annual Report, Federal Reserve Bank of New York*.

—— (1990), 'Response of Four Central Banks to Institutions in Distress', *International Currency Review*.

Crabbe, L. E., Pickering, M. H., and Prowse, S. D. (1990), 'Recent Developments in Corporate Finance', *Federal Reserve Bulletin*, 76: 593–603.

Cukierman, A. (1978), 'A Horizontal Integration of the Banking Firm, Credit Rationing and Monetary Policy', *Review of Economic Studies*, 45: 165–78.

Cumming, C. (1987), 'The Economics of Securitisation', *Federal Reserve Bank of New York, Quarterly Review*, Autumn, 11–23.

Cuthbertson, K., and Hudson, J. (1990), 'The Determination of Compulsory Liquidations in the UK, 1972–88', mimeo, Bank of England, London.

Cutler, D. M., Poterba, J. M., and Summers, L. H. (1989), 'Speculative Dynamics', paper presented at London School of Economics Financial Markets Group Conference, June.

Davies, G., and Davies, J. (1984), 'The Revolution in Monopoly Theory', *Lloyds Bank Review*, July 1984, 38–52.

Davis, E. P. (1984*a*), 'The Consumption Function in Macroeconomic Models: A Comparative Study', *Applied Economics*, 16: 799–838.

—— (1984*b*), *A Recursive Model of Personal Sector Expenditure and Accumulation*, Discussion Paper, Technical Ser. No. 6; Bank of England, London.

—— (1986), *Portfolio Behaviour of the Non-Financial Private Sector in the Major Economies*, BIS Economic Paper No. 17; Basle.

—— (1987), *Rising Sectoral Debt–Income Ratios: A Cause for Concern?* BIS Economic Paper No. 20; Basle.

—— (1988*a*), *Financial Market Activity of Life Insurance Companies and Pension Funds*, BIS Economic Paper No. 21; Basle.

—— (1988*b*), *Industrial Structure and Dynamics of Financial Markets: The Primary Eurobond Market*, Discussion Paper No. 35; Bank of England, London.

—— (1989), *Instability in the Euromarkets and the Economic Theory of Financial Crisis*, Discussion Paper No. 43; Bank of England, London.

—— (1990*a*), *An Industrial Approach to Financial Instability*, Discussion Paper No. 50; Bank of England, London.

—— (1990*b*), 'International Investment of Life Insurance Companies', *European Affairs, Special Issue on the European Finance Symposium*, 240–59.

—— (1990*c*), *International Financial Centres: An Industrial Analysis*, Discussion Paper No. 51; Bank of England, London.

—— (1991*a*), 'International Diversification of Institutional Investors', *Journal of International Securities Markets*, Summer, 143–65.

—— (1991*b*), 'The Development of Pension Funds: An International Comparison', *Bank of England Quarterly Bulletin*, 31: 380–90.

—— (1992*a*), 'Credit Quality Spreads, Bond Market Efficiency and Financial Fragility', forthcoming, *Manchester School*.

—— (1992*b*) 'Euromarkets', *New Palgrave Dictionary of Money and Finance*, Macmillan, London.

—— (1992*c*), 'Pension Funds', *New Palgrave Dictionary of Money and Finance*, Macmillan, London.

—— (1992*d*), 'The Eurobond Market', in D. Cobham, ed., *The London Financial Markets*, Longman.

—— and Mayer, C. P. (1991), *Corporate Finance in the Euromarkets and the Economics of Intermediation*, Discussion Paper, Technical Ser. No. 45; Bank of England, London.

Deaton, A. S., and Muellbauer, J. (1980), *Economics and Consumer Behaviour*, Cambridge Univ. Press.

Diamond, D. (1984), 'Financial Intermediation and Delegated Monitoring', *Review of Economic Studies*, 51: 393–414.

—— (1989), 'Reputation Acquisition in Debt Markets', *Journal of Political Economy*, 97: 828–762.

—— (1991), 'Monitoring and Reputation: The Choice Between Bank Loans and Directly Placed Debt', *Journal of Political Economy*, 99: 689–721.

—— and Dybvig, P. (1983), 'Bank Runs, Deposit Insurance and Liquidity', *Journal of Political Economy*, 91: 401–19.

Dicks, M. J. (1991), 'The Ldc Debt Crisis', *Bank of England Quarterly Bulletin*, 31: 498–507.

Dixit, A. (1987), *Entry and Exit Decisions of a Firm under Fluctuating Exchange Rates*, Financial Research Centre, Memorandum No. 91; Princeton Univ., NJ.

Dornbusch, R. (1986), 'International Debt and Economic Instability', in *Debt, Financial Stability, and Public Policy*, Federal Reserve Bank of Kansas City, Kan.

—— (1991), 'International Financial Crises', in M. Feldstein, ed., *The Risk of Economic Crisis*, Univ. of Chicago Press.

Driscoll, M. (1991), 'Credit Rationing, Financial Fragility and Economic Performance', Working Paper No. 97, Department of Economics and Statistics, OECD, Paris.

Easterbrook, F. H. (1990), 'Is Corporate Bankruptcy Efficient?', *Journal of Financial Economics*, 27: 411–18.

Easton, W. (1990), 'The Monetary Transmission Mechanism', *Bank of England Quarterly Bulletin*, 30: 198–214.

Edwards, J., and Fischer, K. (1991*a*), *Banks, Finance and Investment in Germany since 1970*, Discussion Paper No. 497; Centre for Economic Policy Research, London.

—— and —— (1991*b*), 'An Overview of the German Financial System', mimeo, Univ. of Cambridge and Univ. of Bonn.

Eichengreen, B., and Portes, R. (1985), *Debt and Default in the 1930s: Causes and Consequences*, Discussion Paper No. 75; Centre for Policy Research, London.

Eisenbeis, R. A. (1986), 'Regulatory Policies and Financial Stability', in *Debt, Financial Stability and Public Policy*, Federal Reserve Bank of Kansas City, Kan.

Eisner, R. (1986), *How Real is the Federal Deficit?*, Free Press, New York.

Ellis, J. G. (1981), 'Euro-banks and the Interbank Market', *Bank of England Quarterly Bulletin*, 21: 351–64.

Englund, P. (1990), 'Financial Deregulation in Sweden', *European Economic Review*, 34: 385–93.

Estey, W. Z. (1986), *Report of the Inquiry into the Collapse of the CCB and Northland Bank*, Ministry of Supply and Services, Ottawa.

Fama, E. (1980), 'Banking in the Theory of Finance', *Journal of Monetary Economics*, 6: 39–57.

—— (1985), 'What's Different about Banks?' *Journal of Monetary Economics*, 15: 29–39.

—— and Miller, M. (1972), *The Theory of Finance*, Holt, Rinehart & Winston, New York.

Federal Reserve Bank of New York (1987), 'Recent Trends and Innovations in International Capital Markets', mimeo, FRBNY.

Federal Reserve Board (1974), *Minutes of the Federal Open Markets Committee*, FRB, Washington, DC.

Feldstein, M. (1991), *The Risk of Economic Crisis* (Introduction), Univ. of Chicago Press.

Fisher, F. G. (1988), *Eurobonds*, Euromoney Publications, London.

Fisher, I. (1932), *Booms and Depressions*, Adelphi, New York.

—— (1933), 'The Debt Deflation Theory of Great Depressions', *Econometrica*, 1: 337–57.

Fisher, L. (1959), 'Determinants of the Risk Premia on Corporate Bonds', *Journal of Political Economy*, 67: 217–37.

Flemming, J. S. (1973), 'The Consumption Function when Capital Markets are Imperfect: The Permanent Income Hypothesis Reconsidered', *Oxford Economic Papers*, 25: 160–72.

—— (1982), 'Comments on Minsky', in C. P. Kindleberger and J.-P. Laffargue, eds., *Financial Crises*, Cambridge Univ. Press.

Flood, R. P., and Garber, P. M. (1982), 'Bubbles, Rational Expectations and Gold Monetisation', in P. Wachtel, ed., *Crises in the Economic and Financial Structure*, Salomon Bros. series on Financial Institutions and Markets, Lexington Books, Lexington, Mass.

—— and—— (1984), 'Collapsing Exchange Rate Regimes: Some Linear Examples', *Journal of International Economics*, 17: 1–13.

Folkerts-Landau, D. J. (1985), 'The Changing Role of International Bank Lending in Development Finance', *IMF Staff Papers*, 32.

—— (1991), 'Systemic Financial Risk in Payments Systems', in *Determinants and Systemic Consequences of International Capital Flows*, IMF Occasional Paper.

Fons, J. S. (1986), *The Default Premium and Corporate Bond Experience*, Working Paper 8604, Federal Reserve Bank of Cleveland, Ohio.

Fossli, K. and Peston, R. (1991), 'The Troubles of Norway's Bankers', *Financial Times*, 25 Oct.

Frankel, A. B., and Montgomery, J. D. (1991), 'Financial Structure: An International Perspective', *Brookings Papers on Economic Activity*, 1991/1: 257–311.

Franks, J., and Mayer, C. P. (1989), *Risk, Regulation and Investor Protection: The Case of Investment Management*, Oxford Univ. Press.

—— —— (1990), 'Capital Requirements and Investor Protection: An International Perspective', *National Westminster Bank Quarterly Review*, Aug. 1990, 69–86.

Fried, J., and Howitt, P. (1980), 'Credit Rationing and Implicit Contract Theory', *Journal of Money, Credit and Banking*, 12: 477–87.

Friedman, B. M., (1984), 'Managing the US Government Deficit in the 1980s', in M. L. Wachter and S. M. Wachter, eds., *Removing Obstacles to Economic Growth*, Univ. of Pa., Press, Philadelphia.

—— (1990), *Implications of Corporate Indebtedness for Monetary Policy*, Working Paper No. 3266, National Bureau of Economic Research.

Friedman, M., and Schwartz, A. J. (1963), *A Monetary History of the US 1867–1960*, NBER, New York.

Fudenberg, D, and Tirole, J. (1984), 'The Fat Cat Effect, the Puppy Dog Ploy and the Lean and Hungry Look', *American Economic Review*, 74: 361–8.

Galbraith, J. K. (1954), *The Great Crash 1929*, Houghton Mifflin, Boston, Mass.

Gale, D., and Hellwig, M. (1985), 'Incentive-Compatible Debt Contracts: the One Period Problem', *Review of Economic Studies*, 52: 647–63.

Gardener, E. P. M. (1986), *UK Banking Supervision: Evolution, Practices and Issues*, Allen & Unwin, London.

Gennotte, G., and Leland, H. (1990), 'Market Liquidity, Hedging and Crashes', *American Economic Review*, 80: 999–1021.

Gertler, M. (1988), 'Financial Structure and Aggregate Economic Activity, an Overview', *Journal of Money, Credit and Banking*, 20: 559–96.

—— and Hubbard, R. G. (1989), *Taxation, Corporate Capital Structure and Financial Distress*, Working Paper No. 3202, National Bureau of Economic Research.

—— and —— (1991), 'Corporate Overindebtedness and Macroeconomic Risk', mimeo, New York Univ. and Colombia Univ.

Gilbert, R. A., and Wood, G. E. (1986), 'Coping with Bank Failures: Some Lessons from the US and UK', *Federal Reserve Bank of St Louis, Review*, 68: 5–14.

Gilson, S. C. (1990), 'Bankruptcy, Boards, Banks and Blockholders: Evidence on Changes in Corporate Ownership and Control when Firms Default', *Journal of Financial Economics*, 27: 355–88.

—— Kose, J., and Lang, I. H. P. (1990), 'Troubled Debt Restructurings: An Empirical Study of Private Reorganisation of Firms in Default', *Journal of Financial Economics*, 27: 315–54.

Glosten, L. R., and Milgrom, P. R. (1985), 'Bid, Ask and Transactions Prices in a Specialist Market with Heterogeneously Informed Traders', *Journals of Financial Economics*, 14: 71–100.

Goldsmith, R. W. (1985), *Comparative National Balance Sheets*, Univ. of Chicago Press.

Goldstein, M., Mathieson, D. J., and Lane, T. (1991), *Determinants and Systemic Consequences of International Capital Flows*, IMF Occasional Paper.

Goodhart, C. A. E. (1987), 'Why Do Banks Need a Central Bank?', *Oxford Economic Papers*, 39: 75–89.

—— (1989), *Money, Information and Uncertainty*, 2nd edn., Macmillan, London.

—— and King, M. A. (1987), 'Financial Stability and the Lender of Last Resort Function', mimeo, Financial Markets Group, London School of Economics.

Goodman, J. L. (1991), *The Characteristics of Home Mortgage Debt 1970–89: Trends and Implications*, Finance and Economics Discussion Series No. 149; Federal Reserve Board, Washington, DC.

Gordon, R. H., and Malkiel, B. G. (1981), 'Corporation Finance', in H. A. Aaron and J. A. Pechman, eds., *How Taxes Affect Economic Behaviour*, Brookings Institution, Washington, DC.

Gorton, G. (1989), 'Self-Regulating Bank Coalitions', mimeo, Wharton School, Univ. of Pa., Philadelphia.

Greenwald, B., and Stiglitz, J. E. (1986*a*), 'Information, Finance Constraints and Business Fluctuations', mimeo, Bell Laboratories and Princeton Univ. NJ.

—— and —— (1986*b*), *Imperfect Information, Credit Markets and Unemployment*, Working Paper No. 2093, National Bureau of Economic Research.

—— and —— (1987), *Money, Imperfect Information and Economic Fluctuations*, Working Paper No. 2188, National Bureau of Economic Research.

—— and —— (1991), *Information, Finance and Markets: The Architecture of Allocative Mechanisms*, Working Paper No. 3652, National Bureau of Economic Research.

Grundfest, J. A. (1991), 'When Markets Crash: The Consequences of Informa tion Failure in the Market for Liquidity', in M. Feldstein, ed., *The Risk of Economic Crisis*, Univ. of Chicago Press.

Grunewald, A. E., and Pollock, A. J. (1985), 'Money Managers and Bank Liquidity', in *Proceedings from a Conference on Bank Structure and Competition*, Federal Reserve Bank of Chicago.

Gurley, J., and Shaw, E. (1960), *Money in a Theory of Finance*, Brookings Institute, Washington, DC.

Guttentag, J. M. (1989), *Financial Crises, What Are They? Why Do They Happen? Are They Inevitable?*, Money and Finance Group, Discussion Paper No. 5; Victoria Univ., NZ.

—— and Herring, R. J. (1984*a*), 'Credit Rationing and Financial Disorder', *Journal of Finance*, 39: 1359–82.

—— and —— (1984*b*), 'Strategic Planning by International Banks to Cope with Uncertainty', *Brookings Discussion Papers in International Economics*, 23.

—— and —— (1987) 'Emergency Liquidity Assistance for International Banks', in R. Portes and A. Swoboda, eds., *Threats to International Financial Stability*, Cambridge Univ. Press.

—— and —— (1988), 'Prudential Supervision to Manage Systemic Vulnerability', mimeo, Wharton School, Univ. of Pa., Philadelphia.

Hall, M. J. B. (1988), 'Ths BIS Capital Adequacy Rules: A Critique', mimeo, Loughborough Univ.

Hamilton, J. D. (1987), 'Monetary Factors in the Great Depression', *Journal of Monetary Economics*, 19: 145–69.

Hart, O. (1986), 'Comment on Credit Rationing and Collateral', in J. Edwards *et al*, eds., *Recent Developments in Corporate Finance*, Cambridge Univ. Press.

—— and Moore, J. (1989), 'Default and Renegotiation, a Dynamic Model of Debt', mimeo, MIT, Cambridge, Mass.

Haubruch, J. A. (1990), 'Non-Monetary Effects of Financial Crises, Lessons from the Great Depression in Canada', *Journal of Monetary Economics*, 25: 223–52.

Hay, D. A., and Morris, D. J. (1979), *Industrial Economics, Theory and Evidence*, Oxford Univ. Press.

Hayashi, F. (1985), *Tests for Liquidity Constraints: A Critical Survey*, Working Paper No. 1720, National Bureau of Economic Research.

Hellwig, M. (1977), 'A Model of Borrowing and Lending with Bankruptcy', *Econometrica*, 45: 1879–1906.

—— (1991*a*), 'Banking, Financial Intermediation and Corporate Finance', in A. Giovannini and C. P. Mayer, eds., *European Financial Integration*, Cambridge Univ. Press.

—— (1991*b*), 'The Regulation of Banking: A Theoretical Appraisal', mimeo, Univ. of Basle.

Hendry, D. F. (1984), 'Econometric Modelling of House Prices in the UK', in D. F. Hendry and K. F. Wallis, eds., *Econometrics and Quantitative Economics*, Blackwell, Oxford.

—— Pagan, A. R., and Sargan, J. D. (1983), 'Dynamic Specification', in Z. Griliches, and M. D. Intriligator, eds., *Handbook for Econometrics*, ii, North Holland, Amsterdam.

Hepp, S. (1991), 'Asset Management in a Liberalised Capital Market', paper presented to conference on 'Planning for Retirement in Europe', Centre for European Policy Studies, Brussels.

Ho, T., and Saunders, A. (1981), 'The Determinants of Bank Interest Margins: Theory and Empirical Evidence', *Journal of Financial and Quantitative Economics*, 16.

Hoshi, T., Kashyap, A., and Scharfstein, D. (1989), *Bank Monitoring and Investment: Evidence from the Changing Structure of Japanese Corporate Banking Relations*, Finance and Economics Discussion Series, No. 86; Federal Reserve Board, Washington, DC.

—— —— and —— (1990), 'The Role of Banks in Reducing in Costs of Financial Distress in Japan', *Journal of Financial Economics*, 27: 67–88.

Hudson, J., and Cuthbertson, K. (1990), 'The Determination of Bankruptcies in the UK, 1971–88', paper presented at the Money Study Group Conference, London Business School.

Humphrey, D. B. (1986), 'Payments Finality and the Risk of Settlement Failure', in A. Saunders and L. J. White, eds., *Technology and the Regulation of Financial Markets*, D. C. Heath, Lexington, Mass.

Hutchinson, M., and Pyle, D. H. (1984), 'The Real Interest Rate/Budget Deficit Link, 1973–82', *Economic Review,* Federal Reserve Bank of San Francisco, Fall.

Jaffee, D. M., and Modigliani, F. (1979), 'A Theory and Test of Credit Rationing', *American Economic Review*, 59: 850–72.

—— and Russell, T. (1976), 'Imperfect Information, Uncertainty and Credit Rationing', *Quarterly Journal of Economics*, 91: 651–66.

James, C. (1987), 'Some Evidence on the Uniqueness of Bank Loans', *Journal of Financial Economics*, 16: 217–36.

Jappelli, T. (1991), 'Housing Finance Arrangements, Integenerational Transfers and Consumption: The Italian Experience', paper presented to International Conference on the Economics of Housing Markets, London Business School, Sept. 1991.

Jeanneau, J. G. S. (1989), *Structural Changes in World Capital Markets and Eurocommercial Paper*, Discussion Paper, No. 37; Bank of England, London.

Jensen, M. C. (1986), 'Agency Costs of Free Cash Flow, Corporate Finance and Takeovers', *American Economic Review*, 76: 323–9,

—— (1988), 'The Takeover Controversy: Analysis and Evidence', Managerial Economics Research Center, Working Paper No. 86–01, Univ. of Rochester, NY, Mar. 1986, in J. C. Coffee, L. Lowenstein, and S. Rose-Ackermann, eds., *Knights, Raiders, and Targets: The Impact of the Hostile Takeover*, Oxford Univ. Press.

—— and Meckling, W. (1976), 'Theory of the Firm: Managerial Behaviour, Agency Costs and Ownership Structure', Journal of Financial Economics, 3: 305–60.

Johnson, C. (1991), 'The Capital Ratio Model of Banks' Behaviour', mimeo, Lloyds Bank, London.

Johnson, R. (1991), 'The Bank Credit "Crumble" ', *Federal Reserve Bank of New York, Quarterly Review*, Summer, 40–51.

Johnston, R. B. (1980), *Banks' International Lending Decisions and the Determination of Spreads on Syndicated Medium-Term Eurocredits*, Discussion Paper No. 12; Bank of England, London.

—— (1983), *The Economics of the Euro-Market*, Macmillan, London.

Joyce, M., and Lomax, J. (1991), 'Patterns of Default in the Non-Financial Private Sectors', *Bank of England Quarterly Bulletin*, 31: 534–7.

Kamata, S. (1991), 'Measuring Herstatt Risk', *Bank of Japan Monetary and Economic Studies*, 8/2: 59–74.

Kane, E. J. (1984), 'Technological and Regulator Forces in the Developing Fusion of Financial Services Competition', *Journal of Finance*, 39: 759–72.

—— (1985), *The Gathering Crisis in Federal Deposit Insurance*, MIT Press, Cambridge, Mass.

—— (1986), 'Appearance and Reality in Deposit Insurance: The Case for Reform', *Journal of Banking and Finance*, 10: 175–88.

—— (1990), *Incentive Conflict in the International Regulatory Agreement on Risk-Based Capital*, Working Paper No. 3308, National Bureau of Economic Research.

—— (1991), 'Financial Regulation and Market Forces', *Swiss Journal of Economics and Statistics*, July.

Kaplan, S. N., and Reishus, D. (1990), 'Outside Directorships and Corporate Performance', *Journal of Financial Economics*, 27: 389–410.

Kaufman, H. (1986*a*), *Interest Rates, the Markets, and the New Financial World*, Times Books, New York.

—— (1986*b*), 'Debt: The Threat to Economic and Financial Stability', in *Debt, Financial Stability and Public Policy*, Federal Reserve Bank of Kansas City, Kan.

Keeley, M. C. (1990), 'Deposit Insurance, Risk and Market Power in Banking', *American Economic Review*, 80: 1138–99.

Keeton, W. R. (1979), *Equilibrium Credit Rationing*, Garland Publishing, New York.

Keynes, J. M. (1931), 'The Consequences to the Banks of the Collapse in Money Values', in *Essays in Persuasion*, *Collected Writings of J. M. Keynes*, xi, Macmillan, London.

Kindleberger, C. P. (1978), *Manias, Panics and Crashes, A History of Financial Crises*, Basic Books, New York.

—— (1988), 'The Financial Crises of the 1930s and the 1980s: Similarities and Differences', *Kyklos*, 4: 171–86.

—— (1991), 'International and Interregional Aspects of Financial Crises', in M. Feldstein, ed., *The Risk of Economic Crisis*, Univ. of Chicago Press.

King, M. A. (1988), 'Takeover Activity in the UK', in J. A. Fairburn and J. A. Kay, eds., *Mergers and Merger Policy*, Oxford Univ. Press.

—— and Fullerton, D. (1984), *The Taxation of Income from Capital*, Univ. of Chicago Press.

Knight, F. H. (1921), *Risk, Uncertainty and Profit*, Boston; No. 16 in series of reprints of scarce texts in economics, LSE, London.

KPMG (1988), *International Insolvency Procedures*, Klynveld Peat Marwick Goer deler, London.

Krugman, P. (1991), 'Financial Crises in the International Economy', in M. Feldstein, ed., *The Risk of Economic Crisis*. Univ. of Chicago Press.

Lamfalussy, A. (1992), 'The Restructuring of the Financial Industry: A Central Banking Perspective', SUERF lecture at City Univ., London, 5 Mar.

Lancaster, K. (1966), 'A New Approach to Consumer Theory', *Journal of Political Economy*, 74: 132–57.

—— (1971), *Consumer Demand: A New Approach*, Columbia Univ., New York.

Leigh-Pemberton, R. (1990), 'Corporate Finance, Banking Relationships and the London Rules', *Bank of England Quarterly Bulletin*, 31: 511–13.

Leland, H., and Pyle, D. (1977), 'Information Asymmetries, Financial Structures and Financial Intermediaries', *Journal of Finance*, 32: 371–87.

Lepetit, J. F. (1982), 'Comment on the Lender of Last Resort', in C. P. Kindleberger and J.-P. Laffargue, eds., *Financial Crises, Theory, History and Policy*, Cambridge Univ. Press.

Lewis, M. K. (1991), 'Theory and Practice of the Banking Firm', in C. J. Green and D. T. Llewellyn, eds., *Surveys in Monetary Economics*, ii, Blackwell, Oxford.

Llewellyn, D. T. (1988), 'The Strategic Dilemma of World Banking: Implications of Basle Capital Convergence', paper presented at the Prince Bertil Lecture, Gothenburg, 24 Nov.

—— and Holmes, M. (1991), *Competition or Credit Controls?* Hobart Paper No. 117; Institute of Economic Affairs, London.

Lomax, J. W. (1991), 'Housing Finance: An International Perspective', *Bank of England Quarterly Bulletin*, 31: 56–66.

Luckett, C. A. (1988), 'Personal Bankruptcies', *Federal Reserve Bulletin*, Sep. 589–603.

McFarlane, I. J. (1990), 'Credit and Debt: Part II', *Reserve Bank of Australia Bulletin*, May.

McKenzie, G., and Thomas, S. (1988). *The Economics of the BIS Capital Adequacy Proposals*, Discussion Papers in Economics and Econometrics, No. 8813, Univ. of Southampton.

Maddala, G. S., (1977), *Econometrics*, McGraw-Hill, New York.

Madhaven, A. N. (1990), *Trading Mechanisms in Securities Markets*, Working Paper 16-90, Rodney, L. White Center for Financial Research, Wharton School, Univ. of Pa., Philadelphia.

Malkiel, B. G. (1985), *A Random Walk down Wall Street*, edn., W. W. Norton, New York.

Mankiw, N. G. (1986), 'The Allocation of Credit and Financial Collapse', *Quarterly Journal of Economics*, 101: 455–70.

Martin, C. (1988), *Corporate Borrowing and Credit Constraints*, Working Paper No. 172, Queen Mary College, Univ. of London.

Mason, M. (1986), *Innovations in the Structures of International Securities*, Credit Suisse First Boston Ltd., London.

Mayer, C. P. (1985), 'The Assessment: Recent Developments in Industrial Economics and Their Implications for Policy', *Oxford Review of Economic Policy*, 1/3: 1–24.

—— (1988), 'New Issues in Corporate Finance', *European Economic Review*, 32: 1167–88.

—— (1990), 'Financial Systems, Corporate Finance and Economic Development', in G. Hubbard, ed., *Asymmetric Information, Corporate Finance and Investment*, Univ. of Chicago Press.

—— and Franks, J. (1991), 'European Capital Markets and Corporate Control', mimeo, London Business School and City Univ. Business School, London.

Mayer, T. (1982), 'Federal Reserve Policy in the 1973–75 Recession', in P. Wachtel, ed., *Crises in the Economic and Financial Structure*, Salomon Bros. series on Financial Institutions and Markets, Lexington Books, Lexington, Mass.

Melitz, I. (1990), 'Financial Deregulation in France', *European Economic Review*, 34: 394–402

—— and Bordes, C. (1991), 'The Macroeconomic Implications of Financial Deregulation', *European Economic Review* 35: 155–78.

Meltzer, A. H. (1982), 'Rational Expectations, Risk, Uncertainty, and Market Responses', in P. Watchel, ed., *Crisis in the Economic and Financial Structure*, Salomon Bros. series on Financial Institutions and Markets, Lexington Books, Lexington, Mass.

Merton, R. (1977), 'An Analytic Derivation of the Cost of Deposit Insurance and Loan Guarantees', *Journal of Banking and Finance*, 1: 3–11.

Miles, D. K. (1988), *Some Economic Issues in the Regulation of Financial Markets*, Special Paper, Financial Markets Group, London School of Economics.

—— (1992), 'Housing Markets, Consumption and Financial Liberalisation in the Major Economies', forthcoming, *European Economic Review*.

—— and Wilcox, J. B. (1989), 'The Money Transmission Mechanism', mimeo, Bank of England, London.

Miller, M. H. (1977), 'Debt and Taxes', Presidential address, *Journal of Finance*, 32: 261–97.

—— (1991), 'Leverage', *Journal of Finance*, 46: 479–88.

Minsky, H. P. (1977), 'A Theory of Systemic Fragility', in E. I. Altman and A. W. Sametz, eds., *Financial Crises*, Wiley, New York.

—— (1982), 'The Financial Instability Hypothesis, Capitalist Processes and the Behaviour of the Economy', in C. P. Kindleberger and J.-P, Laffargue, eds., *Financial Crises, Theory, History and Policy*, Cambridge Univ. Press.

Mishkin, F. S. (1991) 'Asymmetric Information and Financial Crises: A Historical Perspective', in R. G. Hubbard, ed., *Financial Markets and Financial Crises*, Univ. of Chicago Press.

Mitchell, B. R. (1981), *European Historical Statistics 1750–1975*, Butler & Tanner, Frome.

Modigliani, F., and Miller, M. H. (1958), 'The Cost of Capital, Corporation Finance and the Theory of Investment', *American Economic Review*, 48: 261–97.

Moffett, M. H. (1986), 'The International Interbank Market: A Behavioural Model of Credit Rationing and Bank Tiering', *Brookings Discussion Papers in International Economics*, 48.

Moody's (1991*a*), *Commercial Paper in Europe: Defaults and Developments in the Swedish Commercial Paper Market*, Moody's special report, Sep., Moody's Investors Service, New York.

—— (1991*b*), *Corporate Bond Defaults and Default Rates 1970–90*, Moody's special report, Moody's Investors Service, New York.

Muehring K. (1987), 'Turmoil in the FRN Market', *Institutional Investor*, Jan. 79–82.

Muellbauer, J. (1991), 'Anglo-German Differences in Housing Market Dynamics: The Role of Institutions and Macroeconomic Policy', mimeo, Nufffield College, Oxford.

—— and Murphy, A. (1991), 'Modelling UK Second-Hand House Prices 1956–90', mimeo, Nuffield College, Oxford.

Muth, R. (1961), 'Rational Expectations and the Theory of Price Movements', reprinted in M. Ricketts, ed., *Neoclassical Microeconomics*, i, Schools of Thought in Economics Series; Gower, Aldershot, 1988.

Myers, S. (1977), 'Determinants of Corporate Borrowing', *Journal of Financial Economics*, 5: 147–75.

—— and Majluf, N. (1984), 'Corporate Financing and Investment when Firms Have Information that Investors Do Not Have', *Journal of Financial Economics*. 12: 187–221.

Obstfeld, M. (1986), 'Rational and Self-Fulfilling Balance of Payments Crises', *American Economic Review*, 76: 72–81.

OECD (1987), *Bank Profitability*, Paris.

—— (1991), *Systemic Risks in Securities Markets*, Paris.

Osterberg, W. P. (1990), 'Bank Capital Requirements and Leverage: a Review of the Literature', *Federal Reserve Bank of Cleveland, Economic Review*, Quarter 4, 2–12.

Pagano, M., and Japelli, T. (1991), *Information Sharing in Credit Markets*, Discussion Paper No. 579; Centre for Economic Policy Research, London.

Pantalone, C. C., and Platt, M. B. (1987), 'Predicting Commercial Bank Failure Since Deregulation', *New England Economic Review*, 49, July/Aug., 37–46.

Pauley, B. (1989), *The Thrift Reform Programme; Summary and Implications*, Salomon Bros., New York.

Peltzman, S. (1976), 'Towards a More General Theory of Regulation', *Journal of Law and Economics*, 19/2: 211–40.

Pissarides, C. A. (1978), 'Liquidity Considerations in the Theory of Consumption', *Quarterly Journal of Economics*, 82: 279–96.

Price, L. D. D. (1987), 'Discussion of Contagion Effects in the Interbank Market', in R. Portes and A. Swoboda, eds., *Threats to International Financial Stability*, Cambridge Univ. Press.

Radner, R. (1986), 'The Internal Economy of Large Firms', *Economic Journal, Conference Papers*, 96: 1–22.

Reid, M. I. (1982), *The Secondary Banking Crisis 1973–5*, Macmillan, London.

Reserve Bank of Australia (1991), *The Deregulation of Financial Intermediaries: Proceedings of a Conference*, Research Dept., Reserve Bank of Australia.

Revell, J. (1980), *Costs and Margins in Banking: An International Study*, OECD, Paris.

Robinson, R. I., and Wrightsman, D. (1980), *Financial Markets*, 2nd edn., McGraw-Hill, New York.

Roley, V. V. (1983), *Asset Substitutability and the Impact of Federal Deficits*, Research Working Paper, Federal Reserve Bank of Kansas City, Kan.

Ross, S. (1990), 'Finance', *New Palgrave: Finance,* Macmillan, London.

Ryding, J. (1990*a*), 'Housing Finance and the Transmission Mechanism of Monetary Policy', *Federal Reserve Bank of New York, Quarterly Review*, Summer, 42–55.

—— (1990*b*), 'The Rise in US Corporate Leveraging in the 1980s', mimeo, Federal Reserve Bank of New York.

Salop, S. (1979), 'Strategic Entry Deterrence', *American Economic Review*, *Papers and Proceedings*, 69: 335–8.

Sargent, J. R. (1990), 'Deregulation, Debt and Downturn in the UK Economy', *National Institute Economic Review*, Aug., 75–87.

Saunders, A. (1987), 'Contagion Effects in the Interbank Market' in R. Portes and A. Swoboda, eds., *Threats to International Financial Stability*, Cambridge Univ. Press.

Schaefer, S. (1987), 'The Design of Banking Regulation and Supervision: Some Lessons from the Theory of Finance', in R. Portes and A. Swoboda, eds., *Threats to International Financial Stability*, Cambridge Univ. Press.

Schleifer, A., and Vishny, R. W. (1991), 'Takeovers in the 60s and 80s: Evidence and Implications', mimeo, Harvard Univ. and Univ. of Chicago.

Schumpeter, J. E. (1934), *The Theory of Economic Development*, Harvard Univ. Press, Cambridge, Mass.

—— (1942), *Capitalism, Socialism and Democracy*: republ. by Unwin Paperbacks, London, 1974.

Schwartz, A. J. (1986), 'Real and Pseudo-Financial Crises', in F. Capie and G. E. Wood, eds., *Financial Crises and the World Banking System*, Macmillan, London.

—— (1987), 'The Lender of Last Resort and the Federal Safety Net', *Journal of Financial Services Research*, 1: 77–111.

Shafer, J. R. (1986), 'Managing Crises in the Emerging Financial Landscape', *OECD Economic Studies*, 8: 56–77.

Sharpe, S. A. (1990), 'Asymmetric Information, Bank Lending and Implicit Contracts: A Stylised Model of Customer Relationships', *Journal of Finance*, 45: 1069–87.

Shepherd, W. (1984), 'Contestability vs Competition', *American Economic Review*, 74: 572–87.

Shigehara, K. (1990), 'Some Reflections on Monetary Policy Issues in Japan', *Bank of Japan Monetary and Economic Studies*, 8/2: 1–8.

—— (1991), 'Japan's Experience with Use of Monetary Policy and the Process of Liberalisation', *Bank of Japan Monetary and Economic Studies*, 9/1: 1–22.

Simon, H. A. (1978), 'Rationality as Process and as Product of Thought', *American Economic Review*, 68: 1–16.

Smith, A. (1776), *The Wealth of Nations*: repr. 1937, Canaan edn., Modern Library, New York.

Smith, R. C. and Walter, I. (1990), 'Economic Restructuring in Europe and the Market for Corporate Control', *Journal of International Securities Markets*, Winter, 291–313.

Solheim, J. A. (1990), 'The Norwegian Experience with Financial Liberalisation and Banking Problems', *Norges Bank Economic Bulletin*, 56: 185–98.

Spence, M. (1983), 'Contestable Markets and the Theory of Industrial Structure: A Review Article', *Journal of Economic Literature*, 21: 981–90.

Steinherr, A. (1990), 'Financial Innovation, Internationalisation, Deregulation and Market Innovation in Europe: Why Does it All Happen Now?' in D. Fair and C. De Boissieu, eds., *Financial Institutions in Europe Under New Competitive Conditions*, Kluwer, Dordrecht.

Stigler, G. J. (1971), 'The Theory of Economic Regulation', *Bell Journal of Economics*, 2/1.

Stiglitz, J. E. (1985), 'Credit Markets and the Control of Capital', *Journal of Money Credit and Banking*, 17: 133–52.

—— (1991), *Government, Financial Markets and Economic Development*, Working Paper No. 3669, National Bureau of Economic Research.

—— and Weiss, A. (1981), 'Credit Rationing in Markets with Imperfect Information', *American Economic Review*, 71: 393–410.

—— and —— (1983), 'Incentive Effects of Termination: Application to the Credit and Labour Markets,' *American Economic Review*, 72: 912–27.

—— and —— (1986), 'Credit Rationing and Collateral', in J. Edwards *et al*, eds., *Recent Developments in Corporate Finance*, Camridge Univ. Press.

Stigum, M. (1990), *The Money Market*, Dow-Jones Irwin, Homewood, Ill.

Stoll, H. (1985), 'Alternative Views of Market Making', in I. Amihud *et al*, eds., *Market Making and the Changing Structure of the Securities Industry*, Lexington Books, Lexington, Mass.

Summers, L. H. (1986), 'Debt Problems and Macroeconomic Policies', in *Debt, Financial Stability and Public Policy*, Federal Reserve Bank of Kansas City.

—— (1991), 'Planning for the Next Financial Crises', in M. Feldstein, ed., *The Risk of Economic Crisis*, Univ. of Chicago Press.

Suzuki, Y. (1987), *The Japanese Financial System*, Clarendon Press, Oxford.

Taggart, R. A. (1985), 'Secular Patterns in the Financing of US Corporations', in B. M. Friedman, ed., *Corporate Capital Structures in the United States*, Univ. of Chicago Press.

Tannenwald, R. (1991), 'Cyclical Swing or Secular Slide? Why have New England's Banks been Losing Money?', *New England Economic Review*, Nov./Dec., 29–46.

Tanzi, V. (1984), *Taxation, Inflation and Interest Rates*, IMF, Washington, DC.

Taylor, C. T., and Threadgold, A. R. (1979), *Real National Saving and its Sectoral Composition*, Discussion Paper No. 6; Bank of England, London.

Temin, P. (1976), *Did Monetary Forces Cause the Great Depression?* W. W. Norton, New York.

Tetlow, R. (1986), 'Some Developments in Financing and Capitalisation of Financial Business in Canada', *Bank of Canada Review*, Dec. 3–23.

Timlen, T. M. (1977), 'Commercial Paper—Penn Central and Others', in E. I. Altman and A. W. Sametz, eds., *Financial Crises*, John Wiley, New York.

Tirole, J. (1989), *The Theory of Industrial Organisation*, MIT Press, Cambridge, Mass.

Tobin, J. (1958), 'Liquidity Preference as Behaviour Towards Risk', reprinted in his *Essays in Economics. I, Microeconomics*, MIT Press, Cambridge, Mass., 1987.

—— (1972), 'Wealth, Liquidity and the Propensity to Consume', in B. Strumpel *et al*, eds. *Human Behaviour in Economic Affairs*, Elsevier, Amsterdam.

Tversky, A., and Kahnemann, D. (1982), 'Availability: A Heuristic for Judging Frequency and Probability', in D. Kahnemann, P. Slovc, and A Tversky, eds., *Judgement Under Uncertainty: Heuristics and Biases*, Harvard Univ. Press, Cambridge, Mass.

US Comptroller of the Currency (1988), *Bank Failure: An Evaluation of the Factors Contributing to the Failure of National Banks*, Washington, DC.

Wachter, M. L., and Williamson, O. (1978), 'Obligational Markets and the Mechanics of Inflation', *Bell Journal of Economics*, 9: 549–71.

Wadhwani, S. B. (1986), 'Inflation, Bankruptcy, Default Premia and the Stock Market', *Economic Journal*, 96: 120–38.

Wallace, N. (1981), 'A Modigliani-Miller Theorem for Open-Market Operations', *American Economic Review*, 71: 267–74.

Warner, J. B. (1977), 'Bankruptcy Costs: Some Evidence', *Journal of Finance*, 32: 337–48.

Warschawsky, M. (1991), 'Is There a Corporate Debt Crisis: Another Look', in G. Hubbard, ed., *Financial Markets and Financial Crises*, Univ. of Chicago Press.

Webb, D. C. (1989), *An Economic Evaluation of Insolvency Procedures in the UK*, Financial Markets Group Discussion Paper No. 55; London School of Economics.

Weiss, L. A. (1990), 'Bankruptcy Resolution: Direct Costs and Violation of Priority of Claims', *Journal of Financial Economics*, 27: 285–314.

White, A. P. (1989), *The Evolution of the Thrift Industry Crisis*, Finance and Economics Discussion Paper No. 101, Federal Reserve Board, Washington, DC.

White, L. J. (1989), 'The Reform of Federal Deposit Insurance', *Journal of Economic Perspectives*, 3: 11–29.

—— (1992), *A Cautionary Tale of Deregulation Gone Awry: The S & L Debacle*, Working Paper S–92–34, Salomon Center, New York Univ.

White, M. J. (1989), 'The Corporate Bankruptcy Decision', *Journal of Economic Perspectives*, 3: 129–51.

Williamson, O. E. (1970), *Corporate Control and Business Behaviour*, Prentice-Hall, Englewood Cliffs, NJ.

Wilson, S. A. (1991), 'Industrial and Commercial Companies' Gearing', *Bank of England Quarterly Bulletin*, 31: 228–33.

Wojnilower, A. M. (1980), 'The Central Role of Credit Crunches in Recent Financial History', *Brookings Papers on Economic Activity*, 1975/2: 277–326.

—— (1985), 'Private Credit Demand, Supply and Crunches. How Different are the 1980s?', *American Economic Review, Papers and Proceedings* 75: 351–6.

—— (1991), 'Some Principles of Financial Deregulation: Lessons from the United States', in *The Deregulation of Financial Intermediaries*, Research Dep., Reserve Bank of Australia.

Wolfson, M. H. (1989), *The Causes of Financial Instability*, Finance and Economics Discussion Series No. 78; Federal Reserve Board, Washington, DC.

Wruck, K. H. (1990), 'Financial Distress, Reorganisation and Organisational Efficiency', *Journal of Financial Economics*, 27: 419–44.

Young, G. (1992), 'Corporate Debt', *National Institute Economic Review*, 1/92: 88–94.

Index

Index of names